OLD ENGLISH GLOSSES
IN THE
ÉPINAL-ERFURT
GLOSSARY

OLD ENGLISH GLOSSES
IN THE
ÉPINAL-ERFURT
GLOSSARY

EDITED BY

J. D. PHEIFER

OXFORD

AT THE CLARENDON PRESS

1974

Oxford University Press, Ely House, London W. 1

GLASGOW NEW YORK TORONTO MELBOURNE WELLINGTON
CAPE TOWN IBADAN NAIROBI DAR ES SALAAM LUSAKA ADDIS ABABA
DELHI BOMBAY CALCUTTA MADRAS KARACHI LAHORE DACCA
KUALA LUMPUR SINGAPORE HONG KONG TOKYO

ISBN 0 19 811164 9

© *Oxford University Press 1974*

PA
2888
P48
1974

7-26-74 L16767

*Printed in Great Britain
at the University Press, Oxford
by Vivian Ridler
Printer to the University*

PREFACE

> To deal fully and successfully with these glossaries
> would require a combination of qualities that has never
> yet been achieved, together with several lifetimes.
>
> HENRY SWEET, *The Student's Dictionary of*
> *Anglo-Saxon* (Oxford, 1896), vi–vii.

IN view of Sweet's pessimism it is perhaps not surprising that
this is the first critical edition of the earliest OE. glosses, but
much has been done since he wrote, especially by Schlutter,
in his many articles and notes on individual glosses, and by
Lindsay, whose monograph on the Corpus, Épinal, Erfurt, and
Leiden glossaries demonstrated the existence of coherent
batches of source-material in Épinal–Erfurt. Lindsay was
sometimes led astray by preconceived ideas and by his ignorance
of Old English,[1] but his method is sound and stands up to
rigorous reassessment. More recently interest in the Old
English glossaries has been revived by Professor Meritt, and
the time would now seem ripe for a comprehensive treatment
of Épinal–Erfurt. The present one attempts no radical innova-
tions, but tries to make the glosses more intelligible by placing
them in the context of their sources and related material in
other glossaries, in the light of which some new interpretations
are offered.[2]

---

[1] Cf. Introduction, §§ 28, 35 and notes to 183, 220, 230, 348, 496, 709, 989.

[2] Cf. *sceabas* 30, *scirde* 86, *gitiungi* 97, *r(a)edisnae* 123, *clatae* 144, *duolma*
181, *palester* 225, *gybyrdid* 228, *g(e)leod* 229, *leactrogas* 247, *grundsuopa* 312,
uuituma 324, *roactun* 342, *tedridtid* 344, *grimrodr* 345a, *ascrefan (-þan)*, *-paeni*
354, 375, *ans(c)eot* 377, *candelthuist* 382, *hold* 415, *(a)raepsid*, *-fsed* 511, 523,
526, *algiuueorc* 556, *geradnodae* 618, *thebscib* 630, *scytil* 632, *handful* 645, *mengio*
659, *frangat* 685a, *suicae* 692, *gigiscdae* 693, *lithircadae* 722, *uuicing-* 736,
paad 779, *fahamae* 780a, *haca* 803, *ridusaendi* 816, *sadulfelgae* 818, *st(a)efad*
837, *del* 838a, *forae uuallum* 873, *thuerhfyri* 881, *gifoegnissae* 889, *satul* 926,
halbclungni 931, *faet(h)maendi* 939, *uueard* 950, *staeg* 962, *cearruccae* 968,
uuellyrgae 969, *leuuis* 977a, *(a)suollaen* 1018, *scofl* 1022, *edwalla* 1068, *hool*
1072, *quicae* 1088, *unþyctgi* 1093.

Even this modest object could hardly have been achieved, however, without much generous help, which I gratefully acknowledge. In the fifteen years since I began my Oxford B.Litt. thesis, 'The Anglo-Saxon Glosses of the Épinal Glossary', on which this book is based, I have been repeatedly indebted to members of the Oxford English School: first to the late Professor C. L. Wrenn, who accepted me for research and followed its progress sympathetically, and to my supervisor, Professor A. Campbell, whose lectures on the Old English dialects introduced me to these texts and who extended his supervision to include reading two drafts and the final typescript of my book; then to my examiners, Miss Pamela Gradon and Miss Celia Sisam, for their advice on questions of dialect and textual criticism; and latterly to Professor Norman Davis, who read the typescript twice and suggested numerous improvements. Special thanks are also due to Mrs. (Joan) Turville-Petre, who lent me her unpublished study of the Cleopatra Glossaries; to Dr. A. K. Brown, of Ohio State University, who gave me copies of his Stanford University dissertation on Épinal–Erfurt and the infra-red photographs of the Épinal manuscript prepared for him at the Bibliothèque nationale, Paris; to Mr. T. F. Hoad, of Queen Mary College, London, who collated my text with his forthcoming revision of Sweet's *Second Anglo-Saxon Reader*; to Dr. J. B. Wynn, of the University of Wales Institute of Science and Technology, Cardiff, who allowed me to use his Oxford D.Phil. thesis on the Corpus Glossary; to Mr. N. R. Ker, who lent me proofs of his then unpublished *Catalogue of Manuscripts containing Anglo-Saxon*; to Herr Walther Strobel, Bibliotheksdirektor of the Staatsbibliothek, Erfurt, for photographs and a detailed collation of the Erfurt manuscript; to Mr. W. O'Sullivan, Keeper of Manuscripts in the Library, Trinity College, Dublin, for his expert guidance in describing the handwriting of the Épinal manuscript; to my pupil and colleague, Miss Paula Simmonds, for Xeroxes of inaccessible books and articles; to the Provost, Fellows, and Scholars of Trinity College, Dublin, for a research grant to

visit Épinal and Erfurt; to the staff of the Clarendon Press
for many valuable suggestions; to the Delegates of the Oxford
University Press for undertaking this expensive publication;
and finally to my wife and children, who cheerfully sustained
me throughout my long task—'A ful lethy þinge it were, ȝif
þat loue nere.'

J. D. PHEIFER

Ard-na-Fairrge
Dalkey, Co. Dublin
June 1972

CONTENTS

ABBREVIATIONS AND SHORT TITLES   xi

INTRODUCTION   xxi

§§ 1–13. MANUSCRIPTS   xxi
1–7. The Épinal manuscript; 8–13. The Erfurt manuscript

§§ 14–24. RELATED GLOSSARIES   xxviii
14. The Corpus Glossary; 15–18. The Cleopatra
Glossaries; 19. The Harley Glossary; 20. The Brussels
Glossary; 21. The Junius Glossary; 22. The Bodley and
Durham Plant-Name Glossaries; 23. Continental
glossaries; 24. Relationship of Épinal, Erfurt, and the
other glossaries

§§ 25–35. SOURCES   xli
25–6. Erfurt II; 27. The Leiden Glossary; 28. The
Hermeneumata Glossary; 29. Phocas glosses;
30. Orosius glosses; 31. Rufinus glosses; 32. Bible
glosses; 33. The Abstrusa and Abolita Glossaries;
34–5. Other sources

§§ 36–90. LANGUAGE AND ORTHOGRAPHY   lvii
37–62. Stressed vowels and diphthongs: Gmc. *a* (37–8);
Gmc. *ǣ* (39); Gmc. *au* (40), Gmc. *eu* (41); Gmc. *iu*
(42); breaking or retraction of Prim. OE. front
vowels before consonants (43–5); Prim. OE. *æ* before
back vowels (46); influence of initial palatal
consonants (47); *i*-mutation (48–55); back mutation
(56); smoothing (57–8); contraction (59); lengthening
and shortening (60–1); influence of labial consonants
(62)

63–8. Unstressed vowels: Prim. OE. *æ* and *i* (63); Prim.
OE. *u* (64); *i*-mutation (65); syncope (66); secondary
vowels (67); suffix-ablaut (68)

69–76. Consonants: Prim. OE. *f* and *ƀ* (69); Prim.
OE. *þ* (70); palatalization of back consonants (71);
loss of Prim. OE. *h* and *w* (72–3); unvoicing of final
consonants (74); secondary consonants (75);
metathesis (76)

77–86. Inflexions: nouns (77–82); verbs (83–6)

LANGUAGE AND ORTHOGRAPHY (*cont.*)
    87. Syntax
    88–90. Date and dialect

THE TEXTS   1

NOTES   59

INDEX OF LEMMATA   136

INDEX OF INTERPRETATIONS   153

ABBREVIATIONS AND SHORT TITLES

AA	The AA Glossary (§ 33 fn. 2).
AB	*Beiblatt zur Anglia.*
Ab Absens	The Ab Absens Glossary (§ 33 fn. 2).
Abavus	The Abavus Glossary (§ 33).
Abba	The Abba Glossary (§ 33 fn. 2).
Abol.	The Abolita Glossary (§ 33).
Abstr.	The Abstrusa Glossary (§ 33).
Ælfric, *Coll.*	*Ælfric's Colloquy.* ed. G. N. Garmonsway. London, 1939.
Ælfric, *Gloss.*	Ælfric's Glossary (§ 21).
Aen.	Virgil's *Aeneid.*
Aenig.	see Aldhelm, *Aenig.*
AEW	F. Holthausen, *Altenglisches etymologisches Wörterbuch.* Heidelberg, 1934.
Affatim	The Affatim Glossary (§ 26).
AJP	*American Journal of Philology.*
Aldhelm, *Aenig.*	*Aldhelmi (a)enigmata* (R. Ehwald, *Aldhelmi opera* (Berlin, 1919), 97–149).
Aldhelm, *Epist.*	*Aldhelmi et ad Aldhelmum epistulae* (*Aldhelmi opera*, 475–503).
Aldhelm, *Metr.*	*Aldhelmus de metris et enigmatibus ac pedum regulis* (*Aldhelmi opera*, 61–204).
Aldhelm, *VC*	*Aldhelmus de uirginitate (carmen)* (*Aldhelmi opera*, 350–471).
Aldhelm, *VP*	*Aldhelmus de uirginitate (prosa)* (*Aldhelmi opera*, 228–323).
Altus	Columba's *Altus prosator* (F. J. E. Raby, *The Oxford Book of Medieval Latin Verse* (Oxford, 2nd edn. 1959), 59–68).
Angl.	Anglian.
Angl.	*Anglia.*
Anzeiger	*Anzeiger für Kunde der teutschen Vorzeit.*
Apoc.	Apocalypse (AV Revelation).
Archiv	*Archiv für das Studium der neueren Sprachen und Literaturen.*
ASPR	*The Anglo-Saxon Poetical Records.* Ed. G. P. Krapp and E. V. K. Dobbie, 6 vols. New York, 1931–53.

AV	The Authorized (King James) Version of the Bible.
Baesecke	G. Baesecke, *Der Vocabularius Sti Galli in der angelsächsischen Mission.* Halle, 1933.
Bd.	The Bodleian Plant-Name Glossary (§ 22).
BH	*Venerabilis Baedae historia ecclesiastica gentis Anglorum* (C. Plummer, *Baedae opera historica* (Oxford, 1896), i. 5–360).
Blickl. Hom.	*The Blickling Homilies.* ed. R. Morris. EETS, os, 58, 63, 73, 1874–80 (repr. in one vol. 1967).
B.M.	British Museum.
Bodl.	Bodleian Library.
Bond	E. A. Bond, *Facsimiles of Ancient Charters in the British Museum.* 4 vols. London, 1873–8.
Br.	The Brussels Glossary (§ 20).
Brown	A. K. Brown, 'The Épinal Glossary edited with Critical Commentary of the Vocabulary'. 2 vols. Stanford dissertation, 1969. (Dissertation Abstracts, 1970, 5428-A.)
BT	T. N. Toller, *An Anglo-Saxon Dictionary, based on the Manuscript Collections of the late Joseph Bosworth.* Oxford, 1898.
Bülbring	K. D. Bülbring, *Altenglisches Elementarbuch*, i. Heidelberg, 1902.
Campbell	A. Campbell, *Old English Grammar.* Oxford, 1959 (corrected repr., 1961).
Cant.	Canticles (AV Song of Solomon).
Carm. Rhythm.	*Carmina rhythmica* (R. Ehwald, *Aldhelmi opera* (Berlin, 1919), 524–37).
Cassian	*Johannis Cassiani de institutis coenobiorum.* Ed. M. Petschenig. Vienna, 1888.
Celt.	Celtic.
CGL	*Corpus glossariorum latinorum.* Ed. G. Goetz. 7 vols. Leipzig, 1888–1923.
CH	Cædmon's Hymn (*OET* 149).
Charisius	*Charisii artis grammaticae libri v* (Keil, i. 1–296).
Chron.	C. Plummer, *Two of the Saxon Chronicles Parallel.* 2 vols. Oxford, 1892–9 (repr. 1952).
Cl.	The Cleopatra Glossaries (§§ 15–18).
Cl.I	The First Cleopatra Glossary.
Cl.II	The Second Cleopatra Glossary.
Cl.III	The Third Cleopatra Glossary.

Cosijn	P. J. Cosijn, *Altwestsächsiche Grammatik*. 2 vols. The Hague, 1883–6.
Cp.	The Corpus Glossary (§ 14).
CP	*Classical Philology*.
CQ	*Classical Quarterly*.
CR	*Classical Review*.
Ct(s).	The early Old English charters (*OET* 426–60).
Cyrillus	The Cyrillus Glossary (*CGL* ii. 215–483).
Dahl	I. Dahl, *Substantival Inflexion in Early Old English*. Lund, 1938.
Dan.	The Book of Daniel.
Deut.	Deuteronomy.
Donatus	*Donati ars grammatica* (Keil, iv. 355–402).
DuCange	C. du Cange du Fresne, *Glossarium mediae et infimae latinitatis*. Ed. L. Favre. 10 vols. Paris, 1937–8.
Dur.	The Durham Plant-Name Glossary (§ 22).
Ecl.	Virgil's *Eclogues*.
Eccles.	Ecclesiastes.
Ecclus.	Ecclesiasticus.
EDD	J. Wright, *English Dialect Dictionary*. 6 vols. London, 1898–1905 (repr. 1961).
ÉE	The Épinal and Erfurt Glossaries.
EETS	Early English Text Society.
eNh.	early Northumbrian.
Ép.	The Épinal Glossary.
Erf.	The (First) Erfurt Glossary.
Erf.II	The Second Erfurt Glossary.
Erf.III	The Third Erfurt Glossary.
ESt.	*Englische Studien*.
Ety.	see Isidore, *Ety*.
Eucherius	*S. Eucherii Lugdunensis instructionum libri duo*. Ed. C. Wotke. Vienna, 1891.
eWS.	early West-Saxon.
Exod.	The Book of Exodus.
Ez.	Ezekiel.
FC	The Franks Casket inscription (*OET* 127).
Festus	*Festi de uerborum significatione* (*GL* iv. 93–467).
Flasdieck	H. Flasdieck, *Zinn und Zink: Studien zur abendländischen Wortgeschichte*. Tübingen, 1952.

Förster	M. Förster, 'Keltisches Wortgut im Englischen', *Texte und Forschungen zur englischen Kulturgeschichte* (Halle, 1921), 118–242.
Fris.	Frisian.
Gallée	J. H. Gallée, *Altsaechsische Sprachdenkmaeler.* Leiden, 1894.
Geldner	J. Geldner, *Untersuchungen einiger altenglischen Krankheitsnamen.* 3 pts. Brunswick, 1906–8.
Gen.	The Book of Genesis.
Geo.	Virgil's *Georgics.*
Ger.	German.
Gildas	*Gildae Sapientis de excidio Britanniae* (T. Mommsen, *Chronica minora,* iii (*MGH Auctores antiquissimi,* xiii.), 25–85).
GL	*Glossaria latina.* Ed. W. M. Lindsay and others. 5 vols. Paris, 1926–31.
Glogger	P. Glogger, *Das Leidener Glossar.* 3 pts. Augsburg, 1901–8.
Gloss.	*see* Lindsay, *Gloss.*
Gmc.	Germanic.
Go.	Gothic.
Gr.	Greek.
Gregory, *Dial.*	*S. Gregorii Magni dialogorum libri iv.* (*PL* lxxvii. 149–430; lxvi. 126–204).
Gregory, *Reg. Past.*	*S. Gregorii Magni regulae pastoralis liber* (*PL* lxxvii. 13–128).
Grimm	J. Grimm, *Teutonic Mythology.* Tr. J. S. Stallybrass. 4 vols. London, 1880–8.
Herm.	The Hermeneumata Glossary (§ 28).
Hessels, *Corpus*	J. H. Hessels, *An Eighth-Century Latin–Anglo-Saxon Glossary preserved in the Library of Corpus Christi College, Cambridge.* Cambridge, 1890.
Hessels, *Leiden*	J. H. Hessels, *A Late Eighth-Century Latin–Anglo-Saxon Glossary preserved in the Library of the Leiden University.* Cambridge, 1906.
HF	*The Hisperica Famina.* Ed. F. J. H. Jenkinson. Cambridge, 1908.
Hl.	The Harley Glossary (§ 19).
Hoops	J. Hoops, *Kommentar zum Beowulf.* Heidelberg, 1932.
IE.	Indo-European.

IEW	J. Pokorny, *Indogermanisches etymologisches Wörterbuch*, i. Berne, 1959.
IF	*Indogermanische Forschungen.*
Ir.	Irish.
Is.	Isaiah.
Isidore, *Diff.*	*S. Isidori differentiarum siue de proprietate sermonum libri ii* (*PL* lxxxiii. 9–98).
Isidore, *Ety.*	*Isidori Hispalensis etymologiarum siue originum libri xx.* Ed. W. M. Lindsay. Oxford, 1911.
Isidore, *Nat. Rer.*	*S. Isidori de natura rerum ad Sisebutum regem liber* (*PL* lxxxiii. 963–1018).
It.	Italian.
J(E)GP	*Journal of (English and) Germanic Philology.*
Jer.	Jeremiah.
Jn.	St. John's Gospel.
Jos.	The Book of Joshua.
Jud.	The Book of Judges.
Jun.	The Junius Glossary (§ 21).
Keil	H. Keil, *Grammatici latini.* 7 vols. Leipzig, 1856–80.
Ker	N. R. Ker, *Catalogue of Manuscripts containing Anglo-Saxon.* Oxford, 1957.
KG	The Kentish Glosses (Sweet, *Second Reader*, 152–75).
Kluge	F. Kluge, *Nominale Stammbildungslehre der altgermanischen Dialekte.* Halle, 1926.
Köhler	J. J. Köhler, *Die altenglischen Fischnamen.* Heidelberg, 1906. (Anglistische Forschungen, xxi.)
Kt.	Kentish.
L.	Latin.
Ld.	The Leiden Glossary (§ 27).
Leechdoms	O. Cockayne, *Leechdoms, Wortcunning, and Starcraft of early England.* 3 vols. London, 1864–6.
Lev.	Leviticus.
Li.	The Lindisfarne Gospels (W. W. Skeat, *The Four Gospels in Anglo-Saxon, Northumbrian, and Old Mercian Versions.* Cambridge, 1871–87).
Lib. Gloss.	The Liber Glossarum (§ 33).
von Lindheim	B. von Lindheim, *Das Durhamer Pflanzenglossar.* Bochum-Langendreer, 1941. (Beiträge zur englischen Philologie, xxxv.)

Lindsay, *Corpus*	W. M. Lindsay, *The Corpus Glossary*. Cambridge, 1921.
Lindsay, *Gloss.*	W. M. Lindsay, *The Corpus, Épinal, Erfurt and Leiden Glossaries*. London, 1921. (Publications of the Philological Society, viii.)
Literaturblatt	*Litteraturblatt für germanische und romanische Philologie.*
LG.	The Lorica Glosses (*OET* 172–4).
lL.	late Latin.
Lk.	St. Luke's Gospel.
lNh.	late Northumbrian.
Loewe	G. Loewe, *Prodromos corporis glossariorum latinorum*. Leipzig, 1876.
Lorica	The Lorica Hymn (F. J. H. Jenkinson, *The Hisperica Famina* (Cambridge, 1908), 51–4).
Lowe	E. A. Lowe, *Codices latini antiquiories*. 7 pts. Oxford, 1935–56.
LR	The Leiden Riddle (*OET* 150–1).
Luick	K. Luick, *Historische Grammatik der englischen Sprache*. 3 vols. Leipzig, 1921–40 (repr. in two vols., Oxford, 1964).
lWS.	late West-Saxon.
Mac.	Maccabees.
Mal.	Malachi.
ME.	Middle English.
MED	H. Kurath, S. M. Kuhn, *Middle English Dictionary*. Ann Arbor, 1956.
Meritt, *FL*	H. D. Meritt, *Fact and Lore about Old English Words*. Stanford, 1954.
Meritt, *HG*	H. D. Meritt, *Some of the Hardest Glosses in Old English*. Stanford, 1968.
Meritt, *OEG*	H. D. Meritt, *Old English Glosses, a collection*. New York, 1945.
Meritt, *PG*	H. D. Meritt, *The Old English Prudentius Glosses at Boulogne-sur-Mer*. Stanford, 1959.
Metr.	see Aldhelm, *Metr.*
MGH.	*Monumenta Germaniae historica.*
MHG.	Middle High German.
Michiels	H. Michiels, *Altenglisches im altdeutschen Glossar*. Bonn, 1911.
Mk.	St. Mark's Gospel.
ML.	Medieval Latin.
MLN	*Modern language notes.*
ModE.	Modern English.

Mt.	St. Matthew's Gospel.
Napier	A. S. Napier, *Old English Glosses chiefly unpublished*. Oxford, 1900.
NF.	Norman-French.
Nh.	Northumbrian.
Nonius	*Nonii Marcelli compendiosa doctrina*. Ed. L. Mueller. Leipzig, 1888.
Num.	Numbers.
OE.	Old English.
OE. Bede	*The Old English Version of Bede's Ecclesiastical History*. Ed. T. Miller, 2 vols. EETS, os, 96, 110, 1890, 1898.
OED	*The Oxford English Dictionary.*
OEG	see Meritt, *OEG.*
OE. Orosius	H. Sweet, *King Alfred's Orosius*. EETS, os, 79, 1883.
OET	see Sweet, *OET.*
OF.	Old French.
OFris.	Old Frisian.
OHG.	Old High German.
OIr.	Old Irish.
ON.	Old Norse.
Orosius	*Pauli Orosii historiarum aduersus paganos libri vii*. Ed. C. Zangmeister. Vienna, 1882.
OS.	Old Saxon.
OW.	Old Welsh.
Par.	Paralipomenon (AV Chronicles).
PBB	*Beiträge zur Geschichte der deutschen Sprache und Literatur.*
Pet.	Epistles of Peter.
PG	*Patrologia graeca.*
Philox.	The Philoxenus Glossary (*GL* ii. 138–291).
Phocas	*Ars Phocae* (§ 29).
PL	*Patrologia latina.*
Placidus	The Placidus Glossary (*GL* iv. 12–70).
Pliny	*C. Plini Secundi naturalis historiae libri xxxvii*. Ed. L. Janus. 6 vols. Leipzig, 1870–98.
PMLA	*Publications of the Modern Language Association of America.*
Pogatscher	A. Pogatscher, *Zum Lautlehre der griechischen, lateinischen, und romanischen Lehnworte im Altenglischen*. Strasbourg, 1888. (Quellen und Forschungen, lxiv.)

Polemius	*Polemii Siluii laterculi* (§ 28).
PP	*Promptorium paruulorum siue clericorum.* Ed. A. Way. 3 pts. London, 1843–65.
Prim. OE.	Primitive Old English.
Prov.	Proverbs.
Ps.	The Psalms.
RC	The Ruthwell Cross inscription (*OET* 125–6).
Reg.	Kings (I–II Reg. = AV Samuel).
RES	*The Review of English Studies.*
Revue	*Revue de dialectologie romaine.*
REW	W. Meyer-Lübke, *Romanisches etymologisches Wörterbuch.* Heidelberg, 1935.
Ritter	O. Ritter, *Vermischte Beiträge zur englischen Sprachgeschichte.* Halle, 1922.
Robert	U. Robert, *Pentateuchi uersio latina antiquissima e codice Lugdunensi.* Paris, 1881; *Heptateuchi partis posterioris uersio latina antiquissima e codice Lugdunensi.* Lyons, 1900.
Rufinus	*Tyrannii Rufini ecclesiasticae historiae libri xi.* Ed. T. Mommsen. 2 vols. Leipzig, 1903–8. (*Eusebius Werke*, ii. 1–2.)
Rushworth	The Rushworth Gospels (W. W. Skeat, *The Four Gospels in Anglo-Saxon, Northumbrian, and Old Mercian Versions.* Cambridge, 1871–87).
Sabatier	P. Sabatier, *Bibliorum sacrorum latinae uersiones antiquae seu uetus Italica.* 3 vols. Paris, 1751.
Sap.	Wisdom (Vulg. Sapientia).
SB	K. Brunner, *Altenglische Grammatik nach der angelsächsischen Grammatik von Eduard Sievers neubearbeitet.* Halle, 2nd edn., 1951.
Sc.	Scottish.
Schlutter, *Facs.*	O. B. Schlutter, *Das Epinaler und Erfurter Glossar.* I. Teil: *Faksimile und Transliteration des Epinaler Glossars.* Hamburg, 1912. (Bibliothek der angelsächsischen Prosa, viii. 1.)
Sedulius, *Carm. Pasch.*	*Caelii Sedulii carmen paschale.* (*Opera*, ed. J. Huemer (Vienna, 1885), 14–146.)
Sept.	The Greek Septuagint.
Servius	G. Thilo, H. Hagen, *Seruii grammatici in Vergilii carmina commentarii.* 3 vols. Leipzig, 1881–7.

Souter	A. Souter, *A Glossary of Later Latin to 600 A.D* Oxford, 1949.
Sp.	Spanish.
SS	E. Steinmeyer, E. Sievers, *Die althochdeutschen Glossen.* 5 vols. Berlin, 1879–1922.
Suolahti	H. Suolahti, *Die deutschen Vogelnamen.* Strasbourg, 1909.
Sweet, *Facs.*	H. Sweet, *The Épinal Glossary, Latin and Old English, of the Eighth Century.* EETS, os, 79b, 1883.
Sweet, *OET*	H. Sweet, *The Oldest English Texts.* EETS, os, 83, 1885.
Sweet, *Second Reader*	H. Sweet, *A Second Anglo-Saxon Reader, archaic and dialectal.* Oxford, 1887.
TCPS	*Transactions of the Cambridge Philological Society.*
Thurneysen	R. Thurneysen, *A Grammar of Old Irish.* Tr. D. A. Binchy, O. Bergin. Dublin, 1947.
Tim.	Epistles to Timothy.
TLL	*Thesaurus linguae latinae.*
Tob.	Tobit.
TPS	*Transactions of the Philological Society.*
Trier	The Trier Glossaries (§ 23. 2).
TS	T. N. Toller, *An Anglo-Saxon Dictionary, based on the Manuscript Collections of the late Joseph Bosworth. Supplement.* Oxford, 1921.
VC	see Aldhelm, *VC.*
VH	The Vespasian Hymns (*OET* 401–20).
Vit. Ant.	*Vita beati Antonii abbatis* (*PL* lxxiii. 127–70).
Vit. Eug.	*Vita Sanctae Eugeniae* (*PL* lxxiii. 605–20).
VL	Vetus Latina (§ 32).
Voss.	The Leiden Abavus Glossary (§ 23. 1).
VP	The Vespasian Psalter (*OET* 188–401).
VP	see Aldhelm, *VP.*
Vulg.	The Latin Vulgate (H. Quenlin and others, *Biblia sacra iuxta latinam uulgatam uersionem ad codicum fidem.* Rome, 1926– ; A. Collunga, L. Turrado, *Biblia sacra iuxta uulgatam Clementinam.* Madrid, 1946).
Werden	The Werden Fragments (§ 8).
WGmc.	West Germanic.
WS.	West-Saxon.

WS	*Wiener Studien.*
WW	T. Wright, R. P. Wülker, *Anglo-Saxon and Old English Vocabularies.* 2 vols. London, 1884.
ZfdA	*Zeitschrift für deutsches Altertum.*
ZfdW	*Zeitschrift für deutsche Wortforschung.*

INTRODUCTION

MANUSCRIPTS

The Épinal manuscript

§ 1. Épinal (Vosges), Bibliothèque municipale MS. 72 (2),[1] described in detail by Ker, No. 114, and Lowe, No. 760, consisting of 14 vellum[2] leaves bound up with a tenth-century Continental manuscript of St. Augustine's sermons, foliated 94–107 consecutively with the latter and also independently 1–14; it contains one alphabetical Latin glossary with some 3,200 (once about 3,800) entries, between $\frac{1}{4}$ and $\frac{1}{3}$ of which are glossed in Old English. There are two quires, the first originally of ten leaves now lacking its centre fold, and the second of six leaves; a single leaf, now lost, presumably followed, containing the remainder of the text. There are no quire signatures. The sheets are so arranged that the outside of both gatherings is a hair side, and flesh faces flesh, and hair hair, in the openings. The sheets were ruled after folding, with single bounding lines and pricks in both margins; pricking and ruling are visible on ff. 2, 7, 9ᵛ, and 13ᵛ. All these features are typical of early Insular manuscripts except for the arrangement of flesh and hair sides, which is exceptional in English manuscripts before the eleventh century.[3]

---

[1] Formerly 66, earlier 7; Sweet, *Facs.* v, *OET* 1, gives the number incorrectly as 17, which frustrated Schlutter's attempt to have the MS. sent to Leiden (*Angl.* xxxiv (1911), 266). The error was originally Mone's; cf. *Anzeiger*, vii (1838), col. 133.

[2] For the distinction between vellum and parchment cf. Lowe, i, p. xi. 'In Irish and Anglo-Saxon centres vellum seems to be the rule, so that membranes described as being of Insular type or rough to the touch may be taken as vellum (calfskin). The membranes used in Italian manuscripts of our period are smooth to the touch and somewhat glossy: these are parchment, made, it seems, from sheepskin or goatskin'; and again ii, p. viii. 'It may be discovered that what I have called vellum is in reality an insular variety of sheepskin, the difference in feel and look between Insular and Continental membranes being due to differences in the breed of sheep and in the manner of preparing the skins.' This roughness may be what led Schlutter, *Facs.* iv, to describe the manuscript as a palimpsest.

[3] Lowe, ii, p. vi; Ker, p. xxv.

§ 2. The leaves now measure 32·9×23·5–24·5 cm. (written
space *c.* 30×21 cm.), most of the upper margins having been
cut away by the binder, including part of an inscription in a
modern hand at the top of f. 1, *Lexicon Anglo-Saxonicum
Vetus. Vi⟨de⟩* . . . . *Hickesij Thesaurum.* The text is
written in six columns, three (cited as *a*, *c*, and *e* in this edition)
consisting of headwords or lemmata, and three (cited as *b*, *d*,
and *f*) of interpretations. There are normally 38 lines to the
page in the first quire (37 on f. 4ʳᵛ, 39 on f. 7ᵛ, 41 on f. 8ᵛ) and
39 in the second (40 on ff. 11ᵛ, 14ᵛ), with occasional interlineations and additions in the lower margins (cf. 9, 172,
666a); longer items are sometimes written continuously across
the lemma and interpretation columns. The writing is bold
and easily read except where the manuscript has been damaged.
Ff. 1 and 14ᵛ are faded and rubbed, and ff. 13 and 14 are wrinkled
by damp, which has also affected the upper margins of the
other leaves and damaged the text at the top of f. 1ʳᵛ and in col.
a on ff. 13ᵛ and 14. F. 14ᵛ and the tops of ff. 7ᵛ–14 have been
stained blue by the reagents applied by Mone when he trans-
scribed the glossary in 1835,[1] and at the Bibliothèque royale,
Paris, before it was transcribed by Quicherat in February 1837,
as noted on the front flyleaf of the volume.

§ 3. The manuscript was written by a single scribe in a
script which might be described as an Anglo-Saxon majuscule
heavily contaminated with minuscule forms. The scribe apparently intended to write in majuscule, but constantly lapses
into minuscule owing to haste or some other reason; the writing
becomes cursive in the interlineations and additions below the
text, and sometimes also in the main text itself (e.g. f. 9ᶜᵈ).
On the other hand, there are some calligraphic flourishes. *g* and
t at the beginning of a word sometimes commence with a down-
stroke joined by a hair-line to the horizontal, and final *a*, *c*, *e*,
f, *g*, *l*, and *t* often end in ornamental tags (occasionally also *n*
and *u*) which are difficult to distinguish from the full stop used
in punctuation. Lowe may have had these features in mind when
he described the script as recalling Northumbrian calligraphy.[2]

---

[1] *Anzeiger*, vii. 134.

[2] Cf. the examples from the Echternach Gospels in T. D. Kendrick and
others, *Codex Lindisfarnensis* (Oltun and Lausanne, 1960), ii, pl. 13.

§ 4. As usual in Old English manuscripts word-division is affected by stress, so that compounds are often divided and proclitics attached to the following word: cf. *haegu thorn* 19, *bio uuyrt* 20, *fulae trea* 36, *ear uuigga* 44, *alter holt* 46, *anbahalbae* 51, *huit fot* 55, *hynni laec* 62, *anuuegaferidae* 91, *tonyttum* 93, etc. Abbreviations are used sparingly, and mostly in the Latin. A horizontal stroke over a vowel normally stands for a following *m* in both Latin and Old English, but apparently represents an OE. *n* in *raedgaesrā* 493, *neuū seada* 505, and *brū* 837.[1] Insular 7 for *et* and *and* does not appear, and *&* is rare; it stands for *-et* in a word in *solet* 1059, and combines with OE. *æ* to represent *æt-* in *æthm* 89. A point, or rarely a comma, is frequently placed after interpretations, less often after lemmata, except where lemma and interpretation are written continuously. Continuations above the line are indicated by a slanting line with a tag or hook at the upper end. An accent is used once only, in 700. Plain capitals begin the alphabetical sections, sometimes followed by two or more letters larger than usual; initial *M* (f. 7^{vc} 10) has been filled in with a pigment, now pale pink.

§ 5. The Épinal manuscript is dated to the eighth century by Ker and Lowe, the latter assigning it to the first half of the century, which is the period suggested by the language of the Old English glosses (§ 88).[2] It was dated to the first quarter of the ninth century by Sir Edward Maunde Thompson[3] and W. Keller,[4] by a comparison with the B.M. Charter Cotton Augustus ii 79,[5] recording a transaction made between 805 and 832. This opinion has been widely accepted,[6] but the resemblance on which it was based is not really very close, and the consistently archaic character of the Old English favours the earlier date.

[1] Wrongly expanded as *-m* in *gihiodum* 76. r̃ = *rm* in *thuearm* 891.

[2] It was also dated to the early eighth century by Sweet, *Facs.* xi–xii, W. M. Lindsay, *Notae Latinae* (Cambridge, 1915), 456, and K. Brunner, SB, § 2. a. 3.

[3] Cf. Sweet, *Facs.* xi.

[4] *Angelsächsische Palaeographie* (Berlin, 1906), ii. 17–18.

[5] Bond, i. 15.

[6] Cf. Hessels, *Corpus*, ix; Goetz, *CGL* v, p. xxvi; Schlutter, *Facs.* i, p. vii; R. Girvan, *Angelsaksisch Handboek* (Haarlem, 1931), 7; Dahl, 29–30; H. M. Flasdieck, *Angl.* lxix (1950), 164; Campbell, § 12.

§ 6. The manuscript is first mentioned in the 1727 catalogue of the library of Moyen Moutier (*Medianum Monasterium*), a Benedictine abbey near Senon, in which it is entered under X. I. (*manuscriti in folio*) 19 as *Sermones xlviii. S. Augustini. ibidem; lexicon quoddam Anglo-Saxon.* (ii, f. 571^v). The present binding was therefore presumably executed between 1705, when Hickes's *Thesaurus linguarum ueterum septentrionalium*, referred to in the note on f. 1 (§ 2), was published, and 1727. It may be assumed that the glossary was at Moyen Moutier during the Middle Ages, but its origin and early history are otherwise unknown. The script and the treatment of the Old English show that it was written by an Englishman, not a Continental as was Erfurt (§ 11), and the writing material suggests that it was written in England rather than at an Anglo-Saxon centre on the Continent (§ 1 fn. 2), as Lowe pointed out. When the abbey was suppressed in 1790, its library was removed to Épinal, where it formed the nucleus of the municipal library.

§ 7. The importance of the Épinal manuscript was first recognized by F.-J. Mone, the pioneer German Anglicist and discoverer of the Vercelli Book, who was informed of its existence by Professor Huguenin of Metz[1] and examined it *en route* to visit the libraries of northern and western France in September 1835, as noted on the front flyleaf. The Old English glosses were transcribed by Mone,[2] and the entire glossary by Quicherat a year and a half later.[3] Mone's work is hasty and inaccurate, with many omissions, especially on f. 14^{rv}, and of no textual value; Quicherat's, on the other hand, is a careful apograph, and his readings are cited in the apparatus when they record letters no longer visible in the manuscript. Transcriptions of the full glossary are also included in the facsimiles of Sweet and Schlutter, and the Old English glosses are printed in [B. Thorpe,] *Appendix B to Mr. Cooper's Report on Rymer's Foedera* (London, 1836; published 1869), 153–64, *Anzeiger*, vii. 134–53 (both from Mone's transcription), Sweet, *OET* 36–106, *Second Reader*, 2–84, and F. Kluge, *Angelsächsisches*

---

[1] *Anzeiger*, vii. 132.
[2] Charles Purton Cooper MS. B2–7 in the Lincoln's Inn Library, London.
[3] MS. Bibliothèque nationale, suppl. français 2717.

Lesebuch (Halle, 1888), 1–8. A collation of Épinal is included in Goetz's edition of Erfurt (§ 13).

The Erfurt manuscript

§ 8. Erfurt, Codex Amplonianus f. 42, briefly described by Ker, Appendix No. 10, consisting of 37 parchment leaves foliated 1–37, preceded by two unfoliated parchment leaves (formerly the binding) which contain a legal document from Cologne dated 17 June 1323. The manuscript proper contains three alphabetical glossaries, the first of which (ff. 1–14ᵛ) is a complete but slightly shorter copy of the Épinal Glossary, omitting 8, 115a, 222, 238, 429, 452, 489, 620, 639, 649, 651–2, 654–9, 661–2, 713, 720, 739, 784, 804, 833, 936, 1083–4. The second (ff. 14ᵛ–34ᵛ), headed *incipit U* (i.e. *II*) *conscriptio glosarum in unam quibus uerba quoque uel nomenalia mixtim uel latina uel saxoniae inseruntur*, and the third (ff. 34ᵛ–37ᵛ), headed *nunc alia xui exiguae secuntur*,[1] are *ab*-order[2] Latin glossaries with some Old English interpretations, also preserved in part in the Werden Fragments (Ker, App. 39), Glossaries II and III.[3]

§ 9. The leaves are arranged in six quires: the first three regular quires of eight; the fourth a quire of four, the second and third of which are half-sheets; the fifth a regular quire of four; the sixth was originally a quire of eight but now lacks its second, sixth, and seventh leaves, which were presumably half-sheets like the third. At least one quire (comprising the letters L–Z of the third glossary) is missing at the end. Flesh normally faces flesh, and hair hair, in the openings, except in the second and fifth quires, where flesh faces hair. The sheets were ruled before folding, with double bounding lines and pricks in the outer margins, and the columns were also ruled; pricking and ruling are visible on the outside sheet of each quire. The quire

---

[1] *CGL* v. 259–337; ii. 563–74, 581–6. The OE. glosses are also found in Sweet, *OET* 108–10.

[2] i.e. glossaries with their lemmata arranged alphabetically according to the first two letters, not just the first letter ('*a* order'); cf. Lindsay, *CQ* xi (1917), 194.

[3] Gallée, 346–64; there is no direct connection between Werden I (*CGL* i. 156–7 + Gallée, 336–46) and Épinal-Erfurt. Goetz, *CGL* ii. 587 ff., prints further material (Latin only) corresponding to gaps in Erfurt III from the twelfth-century Peterhouse, Cambridge MS. 2. 4. 6.

signatures are small roman numerals in the centre of the lower margin on the last versos.

§ 10. The leaves measure 35–36·3 × 25·5–26·3 cm. (written space 28–29 × 21 cm.). The text is written in six columns, three of lemmata and three of interpretations as in Épinal, forty-six lines to a page. There are few interlineations or additions below the text, but two items are often squeezed on to the same line, and interpretations are occasionally continued vertically on the right-hand side of the column in the second glossary. The scribe also has a habit of adding left-over words or letters after neighbouring items, often without indicating where they belong. The manuscript is well preserved on the whole, but about 6 cm. has been lost from the bottom of f. 1, including the last 4–5 lines in coll. *ab* on the recto and coll. *ef* on the verso, and smaller amounts from the bottoms of ff. 2–5; the leaves have been repaired with paper, which covers a few letters on f. 1 (cf. 7, 9, 22, 24, 31–2). F. 1 is darkened by exposure, and f. 9 has been stained by some liquid, which soaked through the adjacent leaves. Several glosses on f. 27^{rv} have been obliterated by a reagent ('Swefelammonium') applied at Jena in August 1881 by G. Gundermann, whose readings are recorded on two foolscap sheets attached to the back flyleaf.

§ 11. The text was written by a single scribe in the neat, pointed minuscule in use at the Cathedral School of Cologne in the late eighth and early ninth centuries; Ker compares Cologne MS. Domsbibliothek 74, written between 785 and 819.[1] The German scribe often misinterprets Anglo-Saxon letter-forms, writing *a* for *cc* (presumably mistaking the latter for majuscule 'horned' *a*) in 162a, and for *oc* in 1008; *f* for *þ* in 33, 354, 390, for *w*(*p*) in 53; *p* for *f* in 342, 648, 1089, for *s* in 434, 1100, for *þ* in 601, for *w* in 173, 388, 444, 564; *r* for *p* in 861, for *s* in 166, 191, 370, 589, 643, 644, etc. (cf. *ł* (*ter*) for *tes* in 537); *s* for *f* in 379, 459, 807, for *p* in 32, 131, for *r* in 103, 155, 619, for *y* in 169, 379, 694.[2] Word-division is similar to that in Épinal, but abbreviations are more common in both Latin and Old English,

---

[1] Cf. the facsimile in L. W. Jones, *The Script of Cologne* (Cambridge, Mass., 1932), pl. lx.

[2] Possibly also in 701, where the *y* resembles English deep *s*, but the Erfurt scribe does not employ the latter.

and they are sometimes used inaccurately. $\bar{g}$ for OE. *gi-* was apparently mistaken for *g(raece)* in 693 (see apparatus), and *unt* is misrepresented by $\overset{\scriptscriptstyle 2}{t}$ *(tur)* in 673 and $\bar{t}$ *(ter)* in 724; t^t *(tur)* was apparently misinterpreted in *spatiareti* 932.[1] A horizontal stroke above a vowel stands for OE. *n* in 214, 342, 716, 1018.[2]

§ 12. The Erfurt manuscript is punctuated more heavily than Épinal, the point and comma, and occasionally also the semicolon, being used. Additions on the line above are marked with a curved or wavy line or a row of dots; marginal additions are indicated by the Insular symbols *ħ* and *ð* (cf. 425). Large initials, some with slight ornamentation, begin the alphabetical sections; the lemmata begin with small capitals. Large initial *A* and *B* are filled in with red, and the capital *A*'s on ff. 1–2^v are touched with red or silver; the headings on ff. 14^v and 34^v (§ 8) are also in silver. There are four small pencil drawings in the lower margins, a dog (traced in ink on the recto) and a bird on f. 17^v, a round face on f. 22^r, and an interlaced design on f. 32^v. In the outer margin of f. 2^r is a curious sequence of letters, one above the other, apparently in the same hand as the main text, which run as follows: *Al, Enḡ, Eng, T, A, A, H, f, D, T, V, E, H, A, B, E, H, G, Gü, V, L, G, F.* The letters are carefully written and arranged, and do not appear to be ordinary pen-trials or practice work; they might conceivably be sigla like those of Cleopatra I (§ 15), referring to the sources of Épinal–Erfurt or some other glossary on which the copyist was working.[3]

§ 13. The Erfurt manuscript is first mentioned in the autograph catalogue of books given by Magister Amplonius Ratinck de Berka (?1360–1434/5), former rector of Erfurt University and court physician to the Archbishop of Cologne, to the Collegium Amplonianum which he founded in 1412. The entry reads as follows:

8^m¶ Item antiquum uocabularium secundum ordinem alphabeti et

---

[1] t^t is written correctly in *territantur* 218.

[2] Wrongly expanded as *-m* in 159, 249, 313, 341, 342, 368, 493 (?), 797, 837, 1058.

[3] Suggested by Mrs. Turville-Petre in a private communication; she compares Cleopatra *eal* 'ex aliis libris' and *nig*, denoting Aldhelm's *Aenigmata*.

de conpositione uocabulorum latinorum grecorum et quorundam barbaricorum et est in se triplex ualde bonum

❡ Quedam eciam excerpta de diriuacionibus et expositionibus huguicio(nis).

No trace remains in the Amplonian collection of the excerpts from Huguicio's *Deriuationes*[1] which were presumably bound up with Erfurt; they can hardly have been more than a few leaves if they were included with the last quire of Erfurt III in the medieval binding referred to in § 8. Master Amplonius unfortunately failed to record where he obtained this manuscript; it may have been Cologne, where he collected many others, or perhaps Werden, where fragments of another copy were preserved (§ 8), as Schum and Gallée suggest.[2] Transcriptions of all the three glossaries were published by F. Oehler, *Neue Jahrbücher für Philologie*, xiii (1847), 256–97, 325–87, who records the letters now covered on f. 1 (§ 10), and by Goetz, *CGL* v. 259–401, ii. 563–74, 581–6; the OE. and OHG. glosses (those of the first glossary fused with Épinal) are printed by Sweet in *OET*, 36–110, and again in *Second Reader*, 2–84 (first glossary only). The manuscript was repaired and rebound in January 1925 according to a slip attached to the rear flyleaf.

RELATED GLOSSARIES

The Corpus Glossary

§ 14. Cambridge, Corpus Christi College MS. 144 (Ker 36, Lowe 122), of the late eighth or early ninth century according to Ker, formerly the property of St. Augustine's, Canterbury; it contains two alphabetical Latin glossaries with some OE. interpretations,[3] the second of which incorporates most of Épinal–Erfurt[4] combined with an approximately equal amount

---

[1] A glossarial compilation of *c.* 1200, described by P. Wessner, *CGL* i. 191 ff. See also J. E. Sandys, *A History of Classical Scholarship* (Cambridge, 1921), i. 557 and *passim*.

[2] Cf. G. Schum, *Bescreibendes Verzeichniss der Amplonianischen Handschriftensammlung zu Erfurt* (Berlin, 1887), xv ff., 35; Gallée, 333.

[3] Both glossaries are printed in full in Hessels, *Corpus*, the second only in Lindsay, *Corpus*; the OE. glosses from both are printed in Sweet, *OET* 35–107, *Second Reader*, 1–85, and also in WW 1–54.

[4] It omits 74, 100, 115a, 176, 216, 234, 240, 296, 407, 429, 443, 639, 662, 674, 713, 720, 833, 838a, 935, 981, 1089, 1094, excluding duplications.

of new material and rearranged in *ab* order (§ 8 fn. 2). The
Épinal–Erfurt material forms continuous batches in the alphabetical subsections, in which the original order of the items
is maintained; cf. Cp. 33 ff.:

       abelena haeselhnutu = ÉE 15
       abies etspe = ÉE 37
35   absinthium wermod = ÉE 66
35a   abdicauit negauit uel discerede = ÉE 73
       abortus misbyrd = ÉE 80
       ablata binumine = ÉE 104

Corpus thus provides what is virtually a third text of the
Épinal–Erfurt Glossary, and one which derives from the archetype independently of the common exemplar of Épinal and
Erfurt since it gives a more correct reading, not likely to be
the result of scribal correction, in a significant number of cases
where the latter share a common error:

       ÉE 97 apparatione : Cp. 185 apparitione
       ÉE 116a alapiosa : Cp. 132 alapiciosa
       ÉE 143 bucina : Cp. 266 baccinia
       ÉE 479 aedilra : Cp. 993 unaeðilsa (-ra)
       ÉE 1009a tabula : Cp. T32 tubolo (-ulo)

Cf. also the following all-Latin items:

Ép. 4 ab 29 adsertator, Erf. 344/13 adserator : Cp. A258 adsentator
Ép. 4 ef 31, Erf. 345/34 antestatus : Cp. A631 antefatus
Ép. 11 ab 8, Erf. 364/5 glaucum : Cp. G108 glaucoma
Ép. 12 ab 38, Erf. 366/34 inuitiandi : Cp. I189 infitiandi (infic-)
Ép. 13 cd 10 calonum, Erf. 368/44 coclonum : Cp. L167 consulum
Ép. 19 ab 5, Erf. 380/16 pudorem : Cp. P499 podorem (-erem)
Ép. 25 cd 39, Erf. 393/49 strabgulat : Cp. 1926 (S558) st(r)angulat
Ép. 25 ef 39, Erf. 394/29 sacrifolis : Cp. S97 sacrificolis
Ép. 27 cd 12, Erf. 397/25 tegrum : Cp. T98 tetrum

The OE. gloss in Corpus differs from that in Épinal–Erfurt
in 15, 126, 269, 352, 355, 406, 461, 482, 486, 505, 511, 524,
602, 680, 749, 840, 907, 933, and there are a number of cases
in which an OE. gloss occupies the same position in the

alphabetical sequence in Corpus as the identical lemma with a Latin interpretation in Épinal–Erfurt:

Cp. 195 armonia suinsung : Ép. 1 ab 23 consonantia
Cp. 231 ascopa kylle : Ép. 3 ef 3 in similitudinem utri
Cp. 248 auena atæ : Ép. 5 cd 29 agrestis harundo
Cp. 270 basterna scrid : Erf. 348/5 (cf. 137 note)
Cp. 354 cabillatio glio : Ép. 7 cd 4 iocus cum uicio
Cp. 378 cauanni ulae : Erf. 353/39 ulule aues
Cp. C148 caradrion laurice : Erf. 354/66 caradrion *only*
Cp. C887 crepundia maenoe : Ép. 8 cd 30 -ium monile guttoris
Cp. 924 fretus bald : Ép. 9 ef 12 confidens
Cp. 1044 inergumenos wodan : Ép. 11 ef 7 -is tempestate iectus
Cp. 1239 luscus anege : Ép. 13 ab 21 unum oculum habens
Cp. 1385 naualia faelging : Ép. 16 ab 16 noualia agri primum proscissi
Cp. 1432 offendit moette : Ép. 17 ab 14 inuenit
Cp. 1549 per hironiam ðorh hosp : Ép. 18 ef 7 per mendacem iocum
Cp. 1606 polenta smeoduma : Ép. 19 ab 8 farina subtilis
Cp. 1802 scotomaticus staerblind : Ép. 23 cd 23 qui tenebras ante oculos habet
Cp. 1818 scena uuebung : Ép. 24 cd 7 ubi scenici ludunt
Cp. 1820 scalmus thol : Ép. 24 cd 23 nauis
Cp. 1858 sicomoros heopan : Ép. 23 ef 4 deserti fici fructus
Cp. 1926 st(r)angulat wyrgeð uel smorað : Ép. 25 cd 39 strabgulat suggillat
Cp. 1997 tentorium geteld : Ép. 26 cd 11 papilionem
Cp. 2027 tipo draca uel inflatio : ÉE 1048 droco, draco *only*
Cp. 2066 tubera clate : Ép. 26 cd 4 genus cibi quod sub terra inuenitur
Cp. 2154 unguentum smeoru : Erf. 399/36 umguentum *only*[1]

Some of these differences may be due to the scribe of Corpus itself, but those confirmed by Cleopatra I (§ 15) must go back at least to their common original. Corpus is therefore an important witness to the archetype from which Épinal–Erfurt and the *ab*-order exemplar derive, but its value should not be

---

[1] Lindsay, *Gloss.* 88 ff. gives a number of similar items unconfirmed by position, the most probable of which are Cp. 1737 *retiunculas resunge* (Ép. 22 cd 5 *rationis partes diminutiuae*), 1848 *sensim softe* (Ép. 25 ef 8 *molliter*). Cf. also Cp. 1813 *scara scaed*, Ép. 24 cd 22 *sacra orborum (ar-) densitas* and Bradley, *CQ* xiii (1919), 107, Lindsay, *Corpus*, 208.

exaggerated, as it was by Hessels, who ranked it above Épinal–Erfurt.[1] The text it offers is on the whole more corrupt than that of Épinal, as might be expected from its later date and more complex transmission, and its compiler 'edited' his material, combining items which were originally distinct, sometimes clumsily (cf. ÉE 480, Erf. 487 : Cp. 961), and often truncating the longer interpretations.[2]

The Cleopatra Glossaries

§ 15. B.M. MS. Cotton Cleopatra A III (Ker 143), of the mid tenth century, containing three Old English glossaries, the first two of which incorporate a variety of material derived ultimately from Épinal–Erfurt; their relationship with the latter and the Old English glossaries in Wright–Wülcker is studied in detail by Lübke.[3] The first is an alphabetical glossary, mainly in *a* order, extending to the letter P.[4] The components of the alphabetical sections are indicated by marginal sigla, one of which, designated *eal* ('ex aliis libris', i.e. other glossaries), includes long batches[5] corresponding to roughly half the Old English glosses of Corpus in almost identical *ab* order, with some additions from other sources; cf. Cl. 344/11 ff.

> abilina hnutu = Cp. 33
> abies æspe = Cp. 34
> absintium wermod = Cp. 35
> (ancilla þinen)
> 15 abortus misbyrd = Cp. 36
> abunde gerihtlice = Cp. 38

[1] Cf. Hessels, *Corpus*, ix: 'The organic changes and scribal corruptions, observable in the spelling of Latin words, are already more advanced (in Épinal), and in some cases show greater slovenliness, than in Corpus.'

[2] Cf. 5, 17, 103, 171, 177, 180, 210, 278, 370, 379, 391, 400, 444, 487, 509, 515, 550, 558, 568, 571, 579, 583, 623–4, 667, 673, 718, 734, 766, 793, 835, 878, 887, 890–1, 894, 906, 928, 953, 962, 967, 978, 982–3, 988, 994, 997–8, 1001, 1017, 1042, 1044, 1054, 1059.

[3] H. Lübke, 'Über verwandschaftliche Beziehungen einiger altenglischer Glossare', *Archiv*, lxxxv (1890), 383–410.

[4] WW 338–473. Fragments of another copy are found in B.M. MS. Cotton Otho E 1, of the late tenth or early eleventh century (Ker 184).

[5] WW 344/11–345/15, 349/1–351/11, 357/17–359/5, 362/1–366/30, 384/25–385/42, 391/16–393/29, 401/45–404/35, 412/35–413/26, 416/35–417/22, 421/40–423/1, 431/35–433/28, 442/20–444/3, 452/15–453/2, 458/30–460/7, 468/6–470/16.

ab affrica suðanwestan = Cp. 43
ab borea eastannorðan = Cp. 44
abditis gehyddum = Cp. 42
20 ab euronothum eastsuð = Cp. 41

These *ab*-order batches normally agree with Corpus where the latter differs from Épinal–Erfurt,[1] and include three of the Old English glosses which correspond to all-Latin items in Épinal–Erfurt (§ 14):

Cl. 363/3 caradrion læwerce = Cp. C148
404/16 fretus confidens presumptus bald = Ép. 9 ef 12+Cp.
924
459/17 offendit mette = Cp. 1432

On the other hand they agree with Épinal–Erfurt in 15 (where the Corpus item is added at the end of the *ad* batch), 214, 269, 328, 486, 507, 781, 815, and they include Épinal–Erfurt material lacking in Corpus (cf. 17, 176, 278, 443–4, 583, 793), indicating that they derive independently from the *ab*-order exemplar rather than from Corpus itself. They sometimes preserve archaic forms, in contrast to the normal late West-Saxon orthography of Cleopatra, even where Corpus has 'modernized' ones (cf. 14, 569, 634 (*lim* for *liin*, as in Erf.), 645, 654, 733, and § 65. 4 fn. 4), suggesting that the copy of the *ab*-order exemplar from which they derive was at least as old as Corpus.

§ 16. In addition to the *ab*-order batches, the First Cleopatra Glossary contains smaller batches of Épinal–Erfurt material. A distinctive feature of this glossary are the additions to the main text,[2] which form a second column on the right-hand side of the page (printed after the corresponding word in the first column in Wright–Wülker). For the most part they consist of different inflexions or alternative forms of the lemmata in the first column (e.g. 365/21–2 *cox hwetestan, cotem hwetestan*, 366/24–5 *culcites bed, culcitatum bed*), but those opposite the second half of the *ab*-order batch under A are Épinal–Erfurt items in their original order:

349/35 armilausia serce = ÉE 18
350/5 æsculos bece = ÉE 22

[1] Cf. 11, 21, 37, 46, 87, 93, 103, 116a, 143, 180, 238, 247, 300, 340–3, 352, 355, 360, 366, 369–70, 379, 388, 391, 402, 408, 446, 460–1, 479, 531, 602, 630, 711. [2] Designated *marg.* in the critical apparatus.

```
 7 alchior isen = ÉE 25
 9 arpago awel uel clawu = ÉE 29
12 areoli sceafas = ÉE 30
14 asses corteas liþerene trymsas = ÉE 31
16 anguens bremel; cf. ÉE 68 breer
18 ægit fræc = ÉE 90
26 ad expensas to nyttum = ÉE 93
30 adsessore fultemendum = ÉE 95
```
351/11 arcister strælbora = ÉE 114

The *eal* components also include batches of material from the Second Cleopatra Glossary (*Archiv*, lxxxv. 397), some of it ultimately from Épinal–Erfurt, e.g. 367/29 ff.:

```
29 cucu hleapewince = Cl.II 260/2, Erf. 264
31 cornix crawe = Cl.II 260/9, Erf. 308
32 cornicula cio = Cl.II 260/11, ÉE. 240
35 cuculus geac = Cl.II 261/1, Erf. 265
37 crabro hyrnetu = Cl. II 261/11, Erf. 275
38 curculio emel = Cl. II 261/17, Erf. 257
39 cicada hama = Cl. II 261/18, Erf. 256
41 coclea weoloc = Cl. II 261/22, Erf. 267
42 cancer hæfern = Cl. II 261/35, Erf. 258
43 cladica wefl = Cl.II 262/11, Erf. 300
44 colus wulmod = Cl. II 262/15, Erf. 306
```

Finally, there are small Épinal–Erfurt batches in original order, marked with the siglum *frs/fri*, at the end of the alphabetical sections under A, F–M, and O,[1] e.g. 409/31 ff.:

```
fuscus tægl uel feax = ÉE 430a (403a)+Cp. 934
finicia baso = ÉE 411 (409)
fusarius wananbeam = ÉE 418
foederatus getrewde = ÉE 436
faonius westsuþwind = Ep. 452
```

The shared error in 659 suggests that these batches derive from an exemplar which was closely related to the common original of Épinal and Erfurt, yet they contain matter peculiar to Corpus (cf. 430a and Cl. 449/19 *madefactum gehweted*, Cp.

---

[1] WW 357/13–15, 409/31–5, 415/35–7, 419/19, 428/18–37, 439/2–6, 449/18–19, 463/15–21; the *frs* sections under B and N (WW 361/29–35, 456 34–457/3) come from Isidore's *Etymologies*.

C

1298 *-ta geuueted*), like the alphabetical section of Cleopatra II
(§ 17). They also contain a high proportion of items not found
in the *ab*-order batches,[1] suggesting that the compiler was
selecting from a longer list so as to avoid duplication.

§ 17. The Second Cleopatra Glossary[2] is a class glossary with an
alphabetical section,[3] *incipit nomina secundum ordinem litterarum*,
which consists largely of rather corrupt Épinal–Erfurt batches
in original order, interspersed with Corpus items, e.g. under
B (275/12 ff.):

        balus embrin = ÉE 121+121a
        bona stoppa = ÉE 121a bothona+122
        bodonicula amber = ÉE 122+?
15   urcius handwyrm = ?+ÉE 126 handwyrp, Cp. 320
          handwyrm
        briensis teter = ÉE 126+128
        balsis isenfeter = ÉE 128+121
        bulla sigil = ÉE 134
        balsus wlips = Cp. 271
20   blessus stamor = Cp. 308
        batuitum gebeaten = ÉE 140
        broel ensc = ÉE 147 edisc
        broelarius ediscweard = ÉE 148
        buculus randbeah = ÉE 153
25   byrseus lypenwyrhta = ÉE 155 ledir-

Here the dislocation of items 12–17 was caused by the misplace-
ment of *isenfeter* in the exemplar; *urcius amber* (?Isidore, *Ety.*
xx. 6/5), which breaks the alphabetical order, is an addition
on the same subject as the preceding items, *bo(tho)na* and
bodonicula,[4] made before the dislocation occurred. Its exemplar
agreed with Corpus against Épinal–Erfurt in 325, 883, 887,
1009a, and vice versa in 83, 274.

§ 18. Material identical with Épinal–Erfurt and Corpus is
also found in the class sections of Cleopatra II, especially *de
auibus, de piscibus, de textrinalibus, de igne, de alea, de plaustribus,*

---

[1] i.e. 357/13, 409/31, 33, 415/35–7, 418/19, 428/18–34, 36–7, 439/2–4, 6,
449/18–19, 463/15–18, 20; 37 out of 45.
[2] WW 258–83 and 474–477/27.
[3] 274/33–279/30, 282/15–283/22, 474/1–477/27.
[4] Cf. 276/11 *lenes hwer*, after *cacabum citel* under C, etc., and 452 n. for
a similar dislocation.

de lignis, de herbis terræ, de suibus, and *de mensa,*[1] and sometimes forms alphabetical clusters in Épinal–Erfurt order, e.g. 271/4 ff.:

> acitula hramse = ÉE 59
> acitelum hramsancrop = ÉE 60
> accitulium iacessure = ÉE 63
> arniglosa wegbræde = ÉE 65

The relationship of this material to Épinal–Erfurt is uncertain, since the sources of the latter certainly included class lists (§ 28), but it seems more likely that the class sections of Cleopatra II derived it from a source intermediate between Épinal–Erfurt and Corpus which already contained at least some of the items peculiar to Corpus but was not yet reduced to *ab* order, like the alphabetical section just described and the *frs* batches of Cleopatra I, rather than from a hypothetical source of Épinal–Erfurt in which the class-glossary material was already alphabetized, as Lübke rather tentatively argues (*Archiv*, lxxxv. 390 ff.). This explanation would account for the presence of items apparently of literary origin in the class lists, such as 390, 764a, 972, 1082, 1088, but cf. § 28.

The Harley Glossary

§ 19. B.M. MS. Harley 3376 (Ker 240), of the late tenth or early eleventh century, a fragmentary Latin glossary in *abc* order extending from the latter part of A to the end of F, about a third of which is glossed in Old English;[2] another leaf, containing part of I, is in Bodl. MS. Lat. Misc. a 3, f. 49.[3] Harley incorporates about two-fifths of the OE. glosses in the corresponding portion of Corpus, sometimes in their original sequence, as in the *bal* section:

> B32 balus isernfeotor = Cp. 272
> B37 balatio crop = Cp. 276 ballationes cnop
> B47 balbus qui uult loqui et non potest wlips uel swetwyrde
>   = Cp. 271 balbus uulisp *only*

---

[1] 258/3 ff., 261/21 ff., 262/7 ff., 266/29 ff., 267/5 ff., 267/23 ff., 268/37 ff., 270/23 ff., 271/28 ff., 280/20 ff.

[2] Printed in full in R. T. Oliphant, *The Harley Latin–Old English Glossary* (The Hague, 1966); OE. only in WW 192–247. Citations from Oliphant.

[3] Cf. H. D. Meritt, *JEGP* lx (1961), 447; it contains no glosses corresponding to Épinal–Erfurt.

B48 balbutus stomer = Cp. 277 balbutus stom wlips
B53 balsis teter = Cp. 262

Like the Cleopatra *ab*-order batches, it contains Épinal–Erfurt material not found in Corpus (cf. 216, 234, 278, 296, 370, 406, 443). Its *ab*-order source seems to have been closer to that of Cleopatra than to Corpus (Lübke, *Archiv*, lxxxv. 407–8), but distinct from it, since it agreed with Épinal, Erfurt, and Corpus against Cleopatra in 214, 232, with Erfurt and Corpus against Cleopatra in 336, and with Erfurt against Corpus and Cleopatra in 370. A peculiar feature is the compiler's habit of translating Old English interpretations into Latin, which then precedes or replaces them.[1] Harley is the fullest and most elaborate of the Old English glossaries, and the only one that treats its material at all intelligently, but its textual value is limited by the lack of coherent batches and the practice of combining material from different sources in a single interpretation (cf. 323, 357, 405–6).

The Brussels Glossary

§ 20. Brussels, Bibliothèque royale MS. 1828–30 (Ker 9); a composite manuscript, the second half of which is an early-eleventh-century collection of Latin glossaries with five Old English class lists in the margins.[2] The first three, *nomina uolucrum* (followed by the parts of a ship),[3] *de membris hominum*,[4] *nomina piscium* (followed by terms of weaving, dicing, and coach-building),[5] are closely related to the corresponding sections of Cleopatra II;[6] cf. Br. 286/4 ff., Cl. II 260/9 ff.:

cornix crawe	cornix crawe
5 cornicula cyo uel graula	10 grallus hroc
gralus hroc	cornicula cio
beacita tearn	beacita stearn
marsopicus fina uel ficus	mursopicus fina
picus higera uel gagia	picus higere
10 noctua ule uel strix uel cauanna	15 noctua ule
	ulula ule

[1] Cf. 126, 131, 134–6, 147, 216, 223 (n.), 269, 273, 281, 307, 317, 321, 326, 329, 332, 336–7, 351, 360, 365, 404, 418 (n.), 431, 437, 445, 454.
[2] WW 284–303.   [3] 284/3 ff., 287/23 ff.
[4] 289/26 ff.   [5] 293/11 ff., 38 ff. 295/6 ff., 11 ff.
[6] Two more lists, of bird and fish names, obviously closely related but in somewhat different order, are found in B.M. MS. Harley 107 (Ker 229), pr. Zupitza, *ZfdA* xxxiii (1889), 239–41.

The fourth list, *nomina herbarum grece et latine*,[1] is a roughly alphabetical glossary of plant-names, about a third of which occur in Épinal–Erfurt, occasionally in the same order, e.g. 295/21–3, 297/26–9:

(a)scolonia ynnleac = ÉE 62
anbila leac = ÉE 64
acimus hyndberige = ÉE 69

gladiolum secgg = ÉE 463
(malba mealewe)
gramina cwice = ÉE 464
genista brom = ÉE 465

Since this list also contains a few items peculiar to Corpus,[2] it presumably drew its Épinal–Erfurt material from a source like that of the Cleopatra I *frs* batches and the alphabetical section of Cleopatra II (§§ 16–17).

The Junius Glossary

§ 21. Antwerp, Plantin–Moretus Museum MS. 47+B.M. MS. Add. 32246 (Ker 2); an eleventh-century Continental manuscript of the *Excerptiones de Prisciano*, the margins of which contain four glossaries in contemporary English hands. Two of these contain Old English material,[3] some of which comes from Épinal–Erfurt and Corpus:

(1) An alphabetical Latin glossary extending from A to E with some Old English interpretations,[4] including Corpus batches in approximately original order, e.g. 109/3 ff.:

actionator folcgerefa = Cp. 48 actionaris folcgeroebum
acisculum pic = Cp. 49
5 asscopa flaxe uel cylle = Cp. 231 ascopa kylle
agapem ælmesse; cf. Cp. 108 agapem suoesendo

[1] 295/21 ff.
[2] 296/22 co(li)antrum cellendre, 297/15 *innulor eolone*, 19 *cinnamomum cymen*, 301/16 *scolonia cipe* (Cp. 569 *coliandrum*, 1057 *inola*, 475, 1791).
[3] WW 104–91 from Junius's transcript (Bodl. MS. Junius 71); M. Förster, *Angl.* xli (1917), 104–46 (Plantin–Moretus only); citations from WW. For the history of this manuscript see C. A. Ladd, *RES* xi (1960), 353–64.
[4] Mixed with (2) in Junius's transcript; the alphabetical glosses are 108/27–109/11, 116/41–117/6, 139/37–140/36, 149/36–150/5, 165/27–33.

altanus þeoden = Cp. 136
anastasis dygelnyssum = Cp. 163
9–10 angiportus i. refrigerium nauium hyð = Cp. A621, Ép. 33
ab 33 (Latin only)

(2) An extensive Latin–OE. class glossary related in part to Cleopatra II and Brussels (Lübke, *Archiv*, lxxxv. 383–4), which combines Épinal–Erfurt items with material from other sources, especially Isidore's *Etymologies*: cf. 469, 686, 787, 880, 954, 987. There may be some connection between these items and the *frs* batches of Cleopatra I, which also stand in close proximity to Isidore material, as Lübke pointed out (*Archiv*, lxxxv. 402), but here, as in the similarly constituted glossary of Ælfric,[1] the lack of coherent batches makes it impossible to trace the provenance of individual glosses.

The Bodley and Durham Plant-Name Glossaries

§ 22. Bodl. MS. Laud Misc. 567 (Ker 345)[2] and Durham Cathedral MS. Hunter 100 (Ker 110),[3] two twelfth-century versions of an alphabetical plant-name glossary partly in *ab* order related to the *nomina herbarum* section of the Brussels Glossary;[4] they appear to have drawn material independently from Épinal–Erfurt and Corpus, occasionally in continuous batches like the following:

Bodl. 68ᵃ   cartamo i. lybcorn = Erf. 279, Cp. 435
           calta i. clefre riede = Erf. 250, Cp. 375
           calesta i. hwite clefre = Erf 254, Cp. 377
           camella i. wulues camb = ÉE 183, Cp. 355
           canis lingua i. ribbe = ÉE 184, Cp. 356
           carex i. seg. cardus i. þistil = Erf. 251, 271,
             Cp. 371, 384

Dur. 301–4   scasa uel scapa uel sisca eofor-throte = ÉE 927, 973,
             Cp. 1816, 1868
           scalonia cype-leac = Cp. 1791
           senecio grunde-svilge = ÉE 976, Cp. 1850
           serpillus organe uel brade lec = ÉE 895, Cp. 1835

---

[1] WW 304–37; J. Zupitza, *Ælfrics Grammatik und Glossar* (Berlin, 1880), 297–322. Citations from Zupitza.

[2] Ff. 67–73; cited by folio and column.

[3] Printed in *Leechdoms*, iii. 299–305, and von Lindheim, 8–19; citations from von Lindheim.   [4] Cf. von Lindheim, 6.

As these examples indicate, the *ab*-order arrangement in both glossaries is independent of that in Corpus.

Continental glossaries

§ 23. In addition to the Old English glossaries already described, significant extracts from Épinal–Erfurt are found in the following Continental glossaries:

(1) Leiden MS. Vossianus Lat. Fol. 24 (Ker, App. 17), a ninth-century collection of glossaries; one, a copy of the Abavus Glossary with interpolations, includes forty-seven Old English glosses,[1] all but three of which occur in Épinal–Erfurt or Corpus. Their source, like that of the Cleopatra *ab*-order batches and that of Harley, was presumably a copy of the *ab*-order exemplar which was independent of Corpus, since it contained Épinal–Erfurt material not found in the latter (cf. 161, 171, 180, 550, 994).

(2) Trier, Stadtbibliothek MS. 40 (Ker, App. 35), a tenth-century collection of glossaries including an expanded copy of the Abactus Glossary[2] with fifteen Old English items corresponding to Épinal–Erfurt or Corpus (some with different interpretations), all except two in the A section. This glossary contains a much larger number of all-Latin items corresponding to Old English glosses in Épinal–Erfurt,[3] which sometimes appear to be re-translations of the Old English like those in Harley (§ 19), but often seem to preserve an original Latin interpretation.[4] The Trier manuscript also contains a short marginal glossary[5] with thirty-two OE. or OHG. items corresponding to Épinal–Erfurt or Corpus, including two short batches in Épinal–Erfurt order (47/31–3, 48/22–4).

---

[1] Printed in Meritt, *OEG* 59–60.

[2] OE. and OHG. glosses in SS v. 46/1–13, 19–31.

[3] A selection of this all-Latin material is given by Schlutter, 'Altenglisches-althochdeutsches aus dem Codex Trevirensis No. 40', *Angl.* xxxv (1911), 152–4. It has been fully collated by Brown, whence the citations in this edition. The same manuscript contains a set of all-Latin Bible glosses, also collated by Dr. Brown, which often shed light on corresponding items in Épinal–Erfurt: cf. the notes on 115, 227, 382, 453, 602, 613, 693, 889.

[4] Cf. the notes on 34, 45, 130–1, 152, 178, 218, 269, 405, 461, 477, 486, 554, 562, 567, 624, 626, 644, 667, 672, 941, 970.

[5] SS v. 47/7–17, 23–33, 48/1–41; cf. notes on 30, 45.

(3) Bodl. MS. Auct. F. 1. 16, of the tenth century, containing Virgil's *Georgics* and *Aeneid*, Virgil scholia, and 'uaria glosemata'[1] which include thirty-five OE. or OHG. items from Épinal–Erfurt, often in their original order, with affinities to both the Trier glossaries; cf. the following:

245/21 axedones id est humeruli lunisas = Trier 47/24 axedones lunisos (ÉE 1)

    26 andela brandereda = Trier 46/19 andeda brandridæ, 47/16 brantreide (ÉE 4)

    30 aestuaria flod uel bitalassum ubi duo maria conueniunt = Trier 46/1 aestuaria bithalassum uel flod (Ép. 4 cd 1, 6 ab 16 (Latin only))

    42 bracium malt (ÉE 130); cf. Trier 60va 3 bratum unde conficitur ceruesia

    43 bracinarium brouhus; cf. Trier 60va 9 brationarium ubi brationatur (sc. ceruisia)

    45 bradigabo feldhoppo (ÉE 131); cf. Trier 60va 4 bratigapo herba quae admiscetur

There may also be some connection with the Old English class glossaries: cf. Cl.II 266/26 *ardeda brandrida*, Jun. 185/25 *brationarium mealthus*.

Relationship of Épinal, Erfurt, and the other glossaries

§ 24. From the nature of the evidence it is impossible to establish the precise relationship of all the glossaries containing Épinal–Erfurt material to each other or to the archetype, but it is clear that Épinal and Erfurt represent a branch of the tradition distinct from the *ab*-order recension found in Corpus and Cleopatra I (§§ 14–15) and from the intermediate stage of the text in which the original *a* order was retained but some at least of the Corpus additions were present, represented by the alphabetical section of Cleopatra II (§ 17), and that this branch is closer to the archetype than the other two, although the latter sometimes give a better reading in individual cases. Épinal is in general fuller and more accurate, but Erfurt sometimes preserves the original order where it was disrupted in Épinal (cf. 120, 430a, 486), and contains material found in

[1] SS iv. 245/1–50, 246/1–6, 24–7.

other manuscripts but not in Épinal (cf. 487, 721); it also agrees
with other manuscripts in a number of cases where Épinal
is in error (cf. 15, 46, 67, 72, 73, 84, 100, etc.) or substitutes
a different interpretation (77, 613, 676, 709, 1078). Erfurt
therefore cannot be a copy of Épinal, but derives independently from their common exemplar, and there must have been at
least one intermediate copy by an English scribe, since the
German scribe of Erfurt could not have introduced OE. ð in
456, 542, 583, and 997 and other 'modern' features in the
orthography of the Old English glosses, as Dieter pointed out;[1]
an Englishman must also have been responsible for the Old
English variants in 108, 195, 618, 929, 1059, 1082, and for the
correction in 1051. Similarly, a comparison between Corpus and
the material derived from the *ab*-order exemplar in Cleopatra I,
Harley, and MS. Vossianus Lat. Fol. 24 (§ 23. 1) shows that at
least one copy, and very possibly more, intervened between
the *ab*-order exemplar and Corpus. Hence the relationship of
the common exemplar of Épinal and Erfurt to that of Corpus
is not so simple as Chadwick's two-branched stemma implies,[2]
and the undoubtedly close correspondence of the three texts,
even in obvious errors,[3] is an indication of the mechanical way
in which the early glossaries were transcribed.

SOURCES

Erfurt II

§ 25. The early Latin glossaries were first studied systematic-
ally by Loewe, who pointed out[4] that Épinal–Erfurt is a
combination of two glossaries, one in *a* order which takes up
the bulk of the alphabetical sections and contains most of the

---

[1] F. Dieter, 'Zum Verhältniss der ältesten Glossen-Hss.', *ESt.* xi (1888),
491–2.

[2] H. M. Chadwick, 'Studies in Old English', *TCPS* iv (1899), 85–265;
see p. 189. Chadwick's very full and careful analysis of the language of
Épinal, Erfurt, and Corpus is still valuable, however.

[3] Cf. 105, 186, 232, 539, 733, 772, 827, 969, and Ép. 1 e 16, Erf. 339/21, Cp.
A757 *artum* for *astum*; Ép. 3 e 26, Erf. 343/29, Cp. A52 *abduxit* for *abdixit*;
Ép. 5 a 33, Erf. 346/19, Cp. A786 *arguere* for *augere*; Ép. 15 c 33, Erf. 373/3,
Cp. M346 *mutilat* for *mussitat*; Ép. 19 a 28, Erf. 380/39, Cp. P691 *proculum*
for *piaculum*; Ép. 20 d 32, Erf. 383/21, Cp. P796 *oratorum* for *hortorum*;
Ép. 22 f 24, Erf. 387/64, Cp. R98 *castra* for *claustra*.

[4] *Prodromos*, 114 ff.; cf. Lindsay, *CQ* xi. 194.

Old English material, and the other in *ab* order which follows it under every letter except D, E, H, and X, Y, Z, consisting of extracts from a glossary closely related to Erfurt II; cf. the AB section (Ép. 3 ef 14 ff.):

14 aberuncat abstirpat = Erf.II 259/36
17 abrisit longe est; cf. Erf.II 259/47-8 absistit recessit, aborret longe est
18 abactus ab actu remotus = Erf.II 259/21
19 abaro infirma domus = Erf.II 259/24
20 abigelus qui tollit seruum aut pecus alienum = Erf.II 259/31 qui seruum seducit uel qui tollit aut pecus alienum
23 abstenus sobrius = Erf.II 259/20 sobris uel uigil, strenuus
24 abusitatus minus instructus in scientia = Erf. II 259/28
25 abdicat exheredat; cf. Cp. A51 abdicat refutat uel exheredat uel abieecit uel alienat, Erf.II 259/5 abdicat abiecit repellit
28 absonus sine sono homo = Erf.II 259/46
29 abiudices negas = Erf.II 259/50
33 absedas aedificu latiores conculas = Erf.II 259/9 absidias aedificii lautioris
35 abacta inuolata = Erf.II 259/14 inuiolata
36 ab latere longe = Erf.II 259/15

The normal arrangement is broken under A by a small batch of *a*-order material (including 117-19) which follows the *ab*-order section in both manuscripts; under B the second half of the *ab*-order section (including 120) stands before the *a*-order section in Épinal; and isolated stragglers from the *a*-order sections follow the *ab*-order sections under I (562) and T in Épinal, and under E (397), G, O, and U (1099a) in Erfurt.

§ 26. There is little connection between the Old English elements in the *ab*-order sections and in Erfurt II. Out of twenty-eight Old English glosses in the former (116a-b, 120, 312, 453-5, 486-7, 666a, 717-20, 832-8a, 979a-82, 1048, 1099), several of which are doubtful Old English, only six (116a, 312, 455, 719, 979a, and 1048), mostly doubtful, occur in Erfurt II or in the related Affatim Glossary[1] and Werden Fragments (§ 8). Ten others correspond to all-Latin items in Erfurt II (487, 666a, 832, 834-7, 980-2). Of the remainder, 486, 717, 720, 838,

---

[1] *CGL* iv. 471-581; for its relationship with Erfurt II see Lindsay, *Gloss.* 48-9.

and 1099 are either stragglers or repetitions from the *a*-order sections, and 453–4, 833, and 838a, all of which break the *ab* order, are probably stragglers as well, while 116b, 120, and 718 can be traced to the sources of Erfurt II (§ 33).

The Leiden Glossary

§ 27. Unlike the *ab*-order sections, which are taken from a single glossary, the *a*-order sections combine material from a variety of sources, several of which are represented among the *glossae collectae* of the Leiden Glossary.[1] The latter, one of a late-ninth-century Continental collection of glossaries in Leiden MS. Vossianus Lat. 4° 69 (Ker, App. 18),[2] consists of forty-eight chapters or sections containing lists of glosses from sources indicated (not always accurately) by their headings. These include some 260 OE. (or occasionally OHG.) glosses, about half of which are also found in Épinal–Erfurt, in addition to some all-Latin items which are common to both glossaries or correspond to Old English items in Épinal–Erfurt. More than a third of this Old English material is concentrated in Section xlvii 'Item alia' (sc. 'uerba'), almost the whole of which appears in Épinal–Erfurt, forming well-defined batches, often in similar order, in the alphabetical sections, e.g. 33 ff.:

33 acerabulus mapuldur = Ld. 47/97 -fulus mapaldurt
34 acrifolus holegn = Ld. 47/96 -lium holera
35 alnus alaer = Ld. 47/99
39 auriculum dros = Ld. 47/50
40 arpa earngeat = Ld. 47/57 arngeus
41 acega holthana = Ld. 47/59 holthona
42 ardea et dieperdulum hragra; cf. Ld. 47/64 perdulum hragra
43 aquilium anga = Ld. 47/85 -lius onga
44 auriculum earuuiga = Ld. 47/86 -la æruigga
46 almeta alterholt = Ld. 47/101 almenta alerholt
47 alga uaar = Ld. 47/23 uuac
48 argella laam = Ld. 47/37
49 accearium steeli = Ld. 47/38 stel
50 auellanus aesil = Ld. 47/1 abellana hel

[1] Printed in full in Hessels, *Leiden*; OE. only in Sweet, *OET* 111–17. Citations from Hessels.
[2] Another copy (Latin only) is in the twelfth-century Milan Codex Ambrosianus M. 79 (*CGL* v. 425–31); cf. 953 n.

The Hermeneumata Glossary

§ 28. The close relationship between Épinal–Erfurt and
Leiden xlvii was demonstrated by Sweet,[1] who also observed
that this section of Leiden was drawn from class glossaries
rather than literary texts,[2] and that Épinal–Erfurt contains
more material of the same type, e.g. plant-names, not found in
Leiden. This additional material is often closely associated
with the Leiden batches in Épinal–Erfurt (e.g. 35–6, 58–60,
62–4, 68–9), and the natural inference is that the compiler of
the latter drew more extensively from the same class lists, or
more probably *glossae collectae* derived from class lists, used in
Leiden xlvii. Furthermore, Lindsay pointed out that the class-
glossary items form more extended batches in Épinal–Erfurt[3]
(so arranged that the Leiden material is concentrated in one
batch, generally the largest, in each alphabetical section) and
traced their source to the Hermeneumata Glossary,[4] a Graeco-
Latin compilation of the second century A.D. which consisted
mainly of 'capitula' or classified vocabularies such as *deorum
nomina* (cf. 558), *de elementis* (cf. 954), *tempora et anni* (cf. 782),
de membris humanis (cf. 154, 644), *de moribus humanis* (cf. 654),
de natura humana (cf. 589), *de escis* (cf. 261, 804), *de mensa
secunda* (cf. 15), *de piscibus* (cf. 47, 146, 270, 592), *de auibus* (cf.
41–2, 240, 259, 275, 277, etc.), *de quadrupedibus* (cf. 649, 1014),
de porcis (cf. 151, 652, 811, 912), *de habitatione* (cf. 1009a), *de
ueste* (cf. 244, 557), *de suppellectile* (cf. 56, 243, 260, 955, 1029),
de aereis (cf. 153), *de ferreis* (cf. 49), *de laneis* (cf. 472), *de coloribus*
(cf. 61), *de scorteis* (cf. 926, 1067), *de artificibus* (cf. 155), *de
arboribus* (cf. 35, 50, 237, 249, 416, etc.), *de oleribus* cf. 16, 20–1,
65–6, 253, 271, etc.), *de ciuilitate* (cf. 859), *de militia* (cf.
1031), *de nauigatione* (cf. 855), and *de medicina* (cf. 635, 958).
The capitula were preceded by an alphabetical 'glossarium'

---

[1] *Facs.* vii–viii, *OET* 13–14.

[2] *Facs.* vii, *OET* 10.

[3] *Gloss.* 17–20; Lindsay's batches include 15–25, 33–69, 121–34, 146–56,
234–72, 275–85, 319–22, 393–6, 414–26, 464–77a, 554–9, 586–92, 602–6,
635–9, 643–57, 672–6, 692–4, 700–5, 779–82, 792–4, 801–11, 827–31,
848–9, 853–61, 879–80, 893–5, 905–14, 924–7, 954–76, 1004–17, 1020–32,
1067–72, 1074–88.

[4] *Gloss.* 7 ff. The surviving copies of Hermeneumata are printed in *CGL*
iii; for its composition see *CGL* i. 17–23.

composed largely of verb paradigms (cf. 785) and followed by
'conuersationes' or colloquia (cf. 261, 910, 1057). The *Hermeneumata Medico-botanica*,[1] alphabetical plant-name glossaries
like Bodley and Durham (§ 22), also contributed (cf. 24,246,253,
272, 279–80, etc.). Lindsay's identification of Hermeneumata
as the primary source of Leiden xlvii and the corresponding
Épinal–Erfurt batches marks an important advance in the
study of these glossaries, but his attributions require careful
checking. The earliest (ninth-century) copies of Hermeneumata
already vary considerably in their arrangement and composition, and it is not unlikely that the version from which the
glossae collectae used in Épinal–Erfurt and Leiden were taken
contained items not found in any existing copy, but hardly
as many as Lindsay assumes. Leiden xlvii itself appears to
contain material from other sources (cf. 43, 50a, 558, 673, 693,
1067, 1085) and the Épinal–Erfurt batches offer a much wider
selection, including probable borrowings from Isidore's *Etymologies* (17–18, 39, 235, 905, 907), Virgil scholia (21–6, 247, 421,
801a, 828–9, 895, 1082, 1088), *Hisperica Famina* (129, 972), the
Vulgate, especially Leviticus 11 (319, 461, 557–8, 673–4, 807,
819, 1026, 1071–2, 1085), Gregory's *Dialogues* (322, 394, 1087),
Phocas, *Ars Grammatica* (251, 470), Aldhelm (462, 468, 925),
Rufinus (701), the *Lorica Hymn* (702), and Orosius (913a).
The *Laterculus* of Polemius Silvius[2] also contains class material
common to Épinal–Erfurt and Leiden (cf. 675, 911, 1015 nn.),
not found in Hermeneumata. Under the circumstances it is
perhaps misleading to speak of 'Hermeneumata batches', as
Lindsay does, without some qualification.

Phocas glosses

§ 29. There is a rather looser connection between Épinal–
Erfurt and Leiden xlv *uerba de multis* and xlvi *item alia*, traced
by Glogger[3] to the *Ars Phocae*,[4] a short grammatical treatise
concerned with the inflexion of nouns and verbs. Leiden xlv
and xlvi contain twenty-four Old English items, nine of which
appear in Épinal–Erfurt (251, 346a, 456, 470, 594, 778, 823,

[1] *CGL* i. 47 ff., iii. 535–633.
[2] Ed. T. Mommsen, *MGH Auctores Antiquissimi*, ix. 543–4.
[3] ii. 74–7.   [4] Keil, v. 410–39.

977a, 1073),[1] six in batches with other material from the same source.[2] Several other Old English items in these batches duplicate all-Latin ones in Leiden, but their interpretations seem in most cases unrelated:

ÉE 597 lacunar flodae : Ld. 46/12 lucunar camera
ÉE 607 lanx helor : Ld. 45/7 lanx unde lancis
Ép. 659 margo mengio : Ld. 45/30 mango comitator equorum
Ép. 661 matrix quiða : Ld. 46/28 matrix radix uel uterus
ÉE 778 pedo uel paturum fetor : Ld. 45/18 pedum fustis quem
    pastores habent in modum /\
ÉE 860 rien lændino : Ld. 46/5 rien lumbis
ÉE 1046 tuber ofr : Ld. 46/13 tuber in dorso cameli

Since this is also true of the all-Latin items common to the Épinal–Erfurt batches and Leiden,[3] it would appear that the connection between the two glossaries at this point is confined to the Old English element common to both. Leiden xlv and xlvi also contain four Old English items found only in Corpus:

45/4   fors uyrd = Cp. 904
46/32 libertabus friulactum = Cp. 1218 frioletan
   33 cune cildtrog unde cunabula; cf. Cp. 623 cildclaðas
   37 magalia byrae = Cp. 1294

These items stand outside the Épinal–Erfurt batches in Corpus, suggesting that the compiler of Corpus drew independently on the Phocas material used in Épinal–Erfurt.

Orosius glosses

§ 30. There is no apparent connection between the large and well-defined batches of lemmata from Orosius' *Historia ad-*

---

[1] Ld. 45/25 *alea tebl*, 46/4 *cos ueostun* also correspond to ÉE 7, 294, but the latter are probably from other sources (see notes).

[2] Lindsay, *Gloss.* 3 ff., 16–17; the batches include 304–6, 346a, 397, 456, 484–5, 594–600, 607–9, 657a–64, 687, 776–8, 820–6, 921–2, 977–9, 1045–7.

[3] Cf. Ép. 5 cd 19 *astus calliditas* : Ld. 46/23 *astutus uel callidus*; 5 cd 20 *ador genus uarris uel frumenti* : Ld. 45/15 *genus frumenti*; 5 cd 21 *antes extrime ordines uinearum* : Ld. 45/16 *dicitur ordo uinearum*; 10 cd 12 *gyt olus* : Ld. 45/10 *git genus seminis herbis minuta bona in panes mittere*; 12 ef 30 *inferiale sacra mortuorum* : Ld. 46/34 *inferie hostie mortuorum*; 13 ef 34 *las laris id est ignis* : Ld. 45/3 *las ignis*; 14 ab 4 *lucar negotiatio* : Ld. 46/11 *uectigal*; 14 ab 5 *liciter qui cum lituo canit* : Ld. 46/10 *liricen qui lira cantat*; 15 cd 7 *mango negotiator* : Ld. 45/30 *comitator equorum*; 19 cd 9 *pugil gladiator* : Ld. 46/2 *milis*; 27 cd 24 *tibicen qui cum tibia canit* : Ld. 46/7 *qui tibia cantat*.

uersum Paganos in Épinal–Erfurt,[1] the majority of which are glossed in Old English, and the short Section xxxvi 'De Orosio', mostly all-Latin, in Leiden. Only three of the twenty-two items in the latter are found in Épinal–Erfurt or Corpus (913a, 1069–70), and these fall outside the Orosius batches. The Orosius glosses of Épinal–Erfurt are exceptionally full and thorough (few of the difficult words in their source are left unexplained), and there is ample evidence to show that their Old English interpretations were part of a running gloss on the text,[2] and not merely substituted for Latin ones at the *glossae collectae* stage, indicating that Latin texts were being construed in the vernacular when the *a*-order sections of Épinal–Erfurt were compiled, probably before 700 (§ 89). The presence of an Irish interpretation (342) also reflects an early stage in Anglo-Saxon learning. The lemmata do not follow the order of the original text except for short sequences (e.g. 84–6 from Book v, 92–6 from Book vii), which led Lindsay to suspect 'that more than one collection of Orosius glosses was used by the compiler and that he dipped his hand now into one of them, now into another',[3] as he apparently did with the Rufinus glosses in Leiden xxxv (§ 31), but the order may have been disturbed when the glosses were extracted or alphabetized (see notes to 109, 187, 370), and similarly with the duplications mentioned by Lindsay (cf. 754:838, 769:944): once the glosses were separated from the text to which they referred, the original order no longer mattered. Intruders from other sources, often different forms or meanings of lemmata found in Orosius (cf. 87, 99, 137, 206, 213, 340, 479, 580–1, 873, 1092), may have begun as marginalia like the second-column glosses in Cleopatra I (§ 16) and then replaced the corresponding Orosius items. Like the Phocas glosses, these Orosius *glossae collectae* seem to have been used independently

---

[1] Lindsay, *Gloss.* 12–13, 23–31; they include 72–113, 135–7, 186–214, 329–45, 354–74, 434–7, 478–81, 488–92, 527–52, 574–80, 616–22, 678–83, 710–12, 721–61, 864–73, 928–47, 1033–47, 1033–44, 1089–96. The F and I batches should be extended to include 438–9, 442–3, and 521–6, and there is a second batch under I (510–14). Many of these items had already been traced to Orosius by Schlutter (cf. *CGL* i. 154–5) and K. W. Gruber, *Romanische Forschungen*, xx (1907), 393–494.

[2] Cf. 72, 86, 91, 94, 102, 207, 210, 334, 479, 490, 543, 616, 733, 743, 865, 941, 947, 1036, 1042, 1044.

[3] *Gloss.* 12.

by the compiler of Corpus, which contains numerous Orosius glosses outside its Épinal–Erfurt batches, e.g. 40–4:

> ab euro eastsudan = Orosius i. 2/57
> ad euronothum eastsuth = Orosius i. 2/99
> abditis gehyddum = Orosius vii. 9/39
> ab affrico suðanwestan = Orosius i. 2/49
> ab borea eastannorþan = Orosius i. 2/57

Their title may be preserved in Cl.I 393/28 *ex ormista*[1] *middangeardes metend*, at the end of the *ab*-order batch.

Rufinus glosses

§ 31. Leiden iv, v, and xxxv contain three collections of material from Rufinus' translation of Eusebius' *Historia Ecclesiastica*, possibly from a single source, since there are few duplications. The last, consisting of three lengthy sequences of *glossae collectae* in roughly their original order, is the only one related to Épinal–Erfurt, the brief Rufinus batches of which[2] consist mainly of identical items, e.g. under A:

Ép. 1 ab 18 apparitorium adiutorium = Ld. 35/10
> 19 adstipulatio adfirmatio = Ld. 35/129
> 20 ariopagitica archisinagogus = Ld. 35/130 amopaga
2 cd 22 angiportus angustus locus = Ld. 35/240
> 23 anulum fidei libertatem fidei = Ld. 35/218 libertatem
> *only*
> 24 arcet depulit = Ld. 35/105
3 cd 16 adyta templa; cf. Ld. 35/224 delubra templa deorum,
> 227 aduta occulta
> 18 aeditui ostiarii = Ld. 35/99

There is little connection, however, between the slight Old English elements in the two texts: only one Old English item appears in both (502), in addition to one with the same Latin interpretation and different Old English interpretations added in each text (177), and two with the same Latin interpretations to which Old English interpretations are added in Épinal–Erfurt

---

[1] i.e. *Hormesta Mundi*, the medieval title of Orosius' history; (*h*)*ormista* here is presumably taken as Gr. ἁρμοστής 'governor', i.e. God or Providence, but cf. I. Williams. *Armes Prydein*, tr. R. Bromwich (Dublin, 1972), xlv–xlviii.
[2] Cf. Lindsay, *Gloss.* 11–12, 21–3; they include 168, 175–7, 402–3a, 499–502, 563–6, 788–90, 850–2, 992–4.

but not in Leiden (992, 995).[1] In any case the majority of the Old English items in Lindsay's batches are intruders from other sources—especially the Bible (cf. 168, 176, 403–4, 501–2, 565, 789–90, 993–4,), which seems to have penetrated Leiden xxxv as well (cf. notes to 381, 502).

Bible glosses

§ 32. Leiden vii–xxv contain Bible scholia extending from I–II Paralipomenon (AV Chronicles) to the gospels of Mark, Luke, and John, also found in Karlsruhe MS. Aug. 99 (Ker, App. 14) and elsewhere,[2] which have been associated with Theodore of Tarsus and the Abbot Hadrian,[3] as have the Old English Leviticus glosses in St. Gall MS. 913 (Ker, App. 29).[4] Old English glosses from both these sources appear in Épinal–Erfurt, five of them in Lindsay's Bible batches[5] (290, 293, 497, 610, 613), which also include the following all-Latin items common to Leiden vii–xxv:

Ép. 2 cd 19 agiographa sancta scriptura = Ld. 16/23
      21 abra ancella = Ld. 21/6
      9 cd 25 flaccentia contracta = Ld. 13/27

[1] Some of the OE. glosses in Leiden xxxv appear in Corpus, however: cf. Cp. 274 *baratrum dael* (Ld. 35/176 *loh l dal*), 400 *callos weorras l ill* (Ld. 35/122 *tensam cutem idest uarras*), 1039 *igni sacrum oman* (Ld. 35/66 *ignis acer oma*), 1182 *lacerta aðexe* (Ld. 35/55 *adexa*), 2093 *uexilla seign* (Ld. 35/69 *uixilla et labrum idem sunt idest segin*).

[2] Extracts in A. Holtzmann, *Germania*, viii (1863), 399–401, SS v. 278 ff.; cf. C. T. Onions, *CR* xxxvii (1923), 86–8.

[3] Baesecke, 10–11. Cf. the Karlsruhe glosses on IV Reg. 18: 16 (SS v. 276/16–17) *ualuas muros templi in circuitu adrianus dicit*, VL Ecclus. 39: 20 (SS v. 327/21–2) *cynaris nablis idest citharis longioribus quam psalterium, nam psalterium triangulum fit theodorus dixit* (= Ld. 12/40 *longiores*).

[4] SS iv. 460; Meritt, *OEG* xxxvi. Baesecke, 80–1, argues that a copy of Hermeneumata was brought to England by Theodore and Hadrian and used to gloss Leviticus; cf. notes to 469, 610, 674.

[5] Lindsay, *Gloss.* 14–15, 32–5; these batches (some rather tenuous) include 10–13, 70, 169–71, 288–98, 348–51, 497–8, 517–20, 610–13, 625, 685–5a, 698–9, 767, 770–1, 795–9, 862–4, 882–9, 984–5, 987–90, 1065. Some of the OE. items in Leiden are found in Corpus but not Épinal–Erfurt: cf. Cp. 894 *flauescit glitinat albescit* (Ld. 8/15 *color olei glitinot*), 1072 *incuda onfilti* (Ld. 19/41 *incus osifelti*), 1234 *lima fiil* (Ld. 13/52 *qua limatur ferrum fiil*), 1401 *obrizum smaete gold* (Ld. 19/54), 1497 *paxillum palum naegl* (Ld. 15/5 *-lis festicellus qui in stantem mittitur negil*), 1553 *perpendiculum pundur* (Ld. 13/40 *modica petra de plumbo qua licant in filo quando edificant parietes pundar*), 2152 *umecta gibrec* (Ld. 24/3).

11 ef 10 idioma proprietas = Ld. 19/7
12 ab 25 in triuiis in tribus uiis = Ld. 13/30
19 ab 8 polenta farina subtilis = Ld. 21/15 subtilissima
19 ab 11 praetoriala domuncula in naue = Ld. 15/11 pretoriola
    domuncula micina in naue unius cubiti in quibus
    abscondunt cibos suos
22 ab 35 rithmus dulcis sermo = Ld. 19/10 ridhmus dulcis
    sermo sine pedibus
    39 repticius demoniosus = Ld. 14/17 arrepticium demon-
    iosum
24 cd 34 saraballa apud caldeos crura hominum dicuntur = Ld.
    16/11 crura hominum uocant apud caldeos
    35 sandalia calciamenta quae non habent desuper corium
    = Ld. 21/10
28 ef 15 uiri cordati bona corde = Ld. 19/62 bono corde

In the majority of cases, however, the same lemmata are interpreted differently, e.g. under C:

Erf. 354/26 conplori iubilati : Ld. 15/8 conplosi plausum feci
    27 conpluta plumis repleta : Ld. 15/7 non conpluta sine
    pluuiis
    28 culinia c(l)oacas : Ld. 15/42 culine fornacula
    32 cementum lim l(ap)idum : Ld. 12/15 -ta petre molliores
    34 commisuras cimbing : Ld. 7/3 ligaturas uel conposituras
    40 cassidele pung : Ld. 20/9 de cassidie pera pastorum
    41 carpassini græsgroeni : Ld. 22/7 carbasini color gemme
    idest uiridis

A similar relationship exists between the items from Genesis to
Kings and the corresponding scholia in Karlsruhe MS. Aug. 99,
St. Gall MS. 295, etc.[1] (cf. 433, 984, 1065), and the glosses on
III–IV Kings in Karlsruhe MS. Aug. 135, etc.[2] (cf. 625). Here
too the majority of the Épinal–Erfurt glosses are different, and
the same is true of the Bible glosses in the Cleopatra glossaries.
There is only one item (292) common to Lindsay's Bible batches
and the Old Testament batches of Cleopatra I,[3] which also cover
Genesis–Kings, and one other (170) common to them and the
New Testament glosses (mostly Old English with some all-Latin
items) in Cleopatra III,[4] from which the New Testament

---

[1] SS v. 135–225; *Germania* viii. 397–9.   [2] Meritt, *OEG* xliii–iv.
[3] Cf. Lübke, *Archiv*, lxxxv. 402–3.
[4] WW i. 478–85; cf. 483/19 *cados amphora i. amber.* The Cleopatra III

batches of Cleopatra I are derived,[1] although a few common items appear elsewhere in Épinal–Erfurt (cf. 181, 222). The Épinal–Erfurt batches only rarely show any recognizable sequence, as in 770–1.[2] Épinal–Erfurt glosses can also be traced to the Vetus Latina or pre-Vulgate Latin versions of the Bible (cf. 1, 29, 53–4, 223, 287, 321, 383–4, 582, 714, 995), but only one, Ép. 19 ab 15 (p. lvi fn. 3), is in Lindsay's batches.[3]

The Abstrusa and Abolita Glossaries

§ 33. An important source not represented in Leiden is the combined Abstrusa and Abolita Glossaries,[4] which were the principal components of Erfurt II,[5] and hence of the *ab*-order sections (§§ 25–6); they also contribute batches to the *a*-order sections,[6] e.g. Ép. 1 cd 12 ff.:

12 assellum spolium = Abstr. AS 10 as(y)lum
15 artefta genus uassis = Abstr. AR 45 artepta . . . ut pigella
16 aquilium fuscum uel subnigrum = Abol. AQ 1 -leum fuscum subnigrum

glosses are also unrelated to the New Testament glosses in Leiden xxiv–v: cf. Cl.III 481/12 *staterem genus nummi* : Ld. 24/7 *stater .iii. solidos*; 481/31 *nomisma denarius* : 24/11 *solidus*; 484/17 *institis in swapum* : 25/12 *suithelon* (cf. ÉE 506); 485/3 *decurio consiliarius* : 25/9 *principes super x homines*.

[1] Lübke, *Archiv*, lxxxv. 398.

[2] Also Ép. 2 cd 29 *anfora iiii. modos tenet* (Dan. 14: 2), following 70; 19 ab 14 *panis colyri(dam) panis quadrangulus* (II Reg. 6: 19), following 767.

[3] A comprehensive edition of the Vetus Latina is now in progress, edited by B. Fischer and others (Freiburg, 1949–); meanwhile the basic collection is still Sabatier (54), supplemented by Robert (11, 29, 287, 582, 714) and quotations from ancient writers (1, 53, 321, 384, Ép. 19 ab 15). A good account of its character and relationship to the Vulgate is given by A. V. Billen, *The Old Latin Texts of the Heptateuch* (Cambridge, 1927).

[4] *CGL* iv. 3–198, *GL* iii. 1–90 and 97–183; cited from *GL*. Abolita survives only as batches interpolated into the *ab*-order sections of Abstrusa.

[5] Cf. Lindsay, *Gloss.* 53–67, 68–75.

[6] Lindsay, *Gloss.* 37–43; they include 6–9, 14, 31–2, 115, 138–9, 172–4, 178–8a, 217–19, 345a–6, 383–4, 405–11, 494–6, 667, 686, 764a, 768, 840, 872–3, 878, 881, 983, 997–1003. Some of Lindsay's attributions are doubtful, especially the all-Latin items with different interpretations: cf. Ép. 1 ab 33 *agonitheta princeps artis illius* (Abol. AG 9 *praemii indultor*), 35 *agonista qui discit illam artem* (Abstr. AG 10 *certator*), 1 ef 13 *agasso minister officialis* (Abstr. AG 7 *agaso domesticus*), 22 *aerarium ubi errari inclusi sunt* (Abstr. AE 16 *thesaurum publicum*), 23 *a(g)natus cognatus* (Abol. AG 3 *-tos propinquos*), 26 *alliciat alligat* (Abstr. AL 9 *allectat spectat*), etc. On this principle almost any two glossaries could be identified.

17 aplustra giroedro; cf. Abol. AP 5 -tria ornamenta (v.l. armamenta) nauis
20 aneatores tubicines = Abstr. AE 25 aenatores
21 alogia conuiuium = Abstr. AL 45
23 archia initium = Abstr. AR 46
24 apolitarium ubi ponitur res labentium = Abstr. AP 14
apoliterium . . . lauantium

These batches also contain items not found in existing copies
of Abstrusa and Abolita but in other glossaries incorporating
Abstrusa–Abolita material such as Erfurt II (218, 768), Abavus[1]
(878), and the 'de glossis' items of the Liber Glossarum[2]
(667), and they contain other items which can be traced
to particular sources of Abstrusa or Abolita such as Festus and
Eucherius (cf. 686 and 1001). Both types can reasonably be
attributed to the original Abstrusa–Abolita; but material from
common sources like Bible glosses (115, 174, 383–4, 410, 1003)
and Virgil scholia (9, 997, 999a, 1002), the latter of which are also
found in conjunction with Abstrusa–Abolita material in Erfurt
II and Affatim,[3] may be derived independently from the original
source, and there are other intruders, notably from the Graeco-
Latin Philoxenus Glossary,[4] which was likewise a component
of Erfurt II[5] (cf. 6–7, 178, 998). All this suggests that the im-
mediate source of these batches was one in which the Abstrusa–
Abolita element was already mixed with material from other
sources, like that of the Hermeneumata batches (§ 28), and the
order of the Abstrusa–Abolita glosses would seem to indicate
derivation from an earlier stage in the history of those glossaries,
before they were reduced to *ab* order.[6] If so, the relationship of
the Abstrusa–Abolita batches in Épinal–Erfurt with Erfurt II

[1] *CGL* iv. 301–403, *GL* ii. 29–121; cited from *GL*.
[2] *GL* i (referred to as 'Ansileubius' by Lindsay). Other glossaries containing Abstrusa–Abolita material are Ab Absens (*CGL* iv. 404–27), Abba
(*GL* v. 15–143), and AA (*GL* v. 159–388).
[3] Cf. N. F. D. Dall, *CQ* xii (1918), 171–8; Lindsay, *Gloss.* 75 ff. Dall
argues convincingly that Corpus drew independently on the same Virgil
scholia used for Erfurt II and Affatim, but this does not prove that their
common source was an English manuscript.
[4] *CGL* ii. 3–212, *GL* ii. 138–291; cited from *GL*.
[5] Cf. Lindsay, *Gloss.* 79–83; it is also the source of Erfurt III.
[6] The Arma glossary (*GL* ii. 1–22), otherwise unrelated to Épinal–Erfurt,
also contains batches of Abstrusa–Abolita material in *a* order.

and the Continental *ab*-order glossaries, in which the Abstrusa–
Abolita material appears in its final order, could only be a
collateral one.

Other sources

§ 34. Lindsay's source-batches include more than two-thirds
of the Old English glosses in the *a*-order sections, and many of
the remainder can be traced with reasonable probability to the
same sources, especially when they occur in pairs or clusters:
cf. 117–18, 183–5, 294–5, 308–9, 310–11, 427–9, 446–7, 451–2,
503–5, 633–4, 665–6, 772–5, 812–13, 917–18, 923–4, 1056–7
from Hermeneumata;[1] 1018–19 from Phocas;[2] 438–9, 442–3,
510–14, 521–6, 706–8, 814–16, 862–4, 1069–70 from Orosius;[3]
765–6 from Rufinus;[4] 1–2, 29–30, 133–4, 222–3, 319–21, 432–3,
762–3, 915–16, 995–6, 1053, 1071–2 from the Bible;[5] 165–6,
172–3, 273–5, 614–15, 668–70, 694–5 from Abstrusa–Abolita.[6]
In view of the many intruders from these sources within
the batches themselves, it would seem that the same method
of composition was followed inside as well as outside the
batches, and that Épinal–Erfurt is consequently what Lindsay
termed an extract-glossary, in which the compiler selects an
item now from one source, now from the other,[7] the batches
being simply extra-long runs from one particular source. In
any case, in speaking of sources, a distinction must be made
between the sources immediately before the compiler, which
occur frequently and form batches or at least clusters, and
the ultimate sources of particular glosses, which may have
reached him through other glossaries, marginalia, etc. The
former category includes Lindsay's batches and two other

[1] Ép. 5 cd 24–5; 7 cd 6–8; Erf. 354/37–8; 354/65–6; 354/71–2; Ép. 9 cd
14–16; 9 ef 16–17; 9 ef 37–8; 11 ef 28–30; 14 ef 30–1; 15 cd 13–14; 19 cd
2–5; 20 ab 22–3; 24 ab 6–7; 24 ab 14–15; 28 ab 16–17.
[2] Ép. 27 ab 19–20.
[3] Ép. 9 ef 1–2; 9 ef 7, 11; 12 ab 12–16; 12 ab 33–cd 1; 17 ab 6–8; 20 ab
24–6; 22 cd 1–3; 28 ab 34–5.
[4] Ép. 19 ab 2–4.
[5] Ép. 1 ab 4–5; 1 ef 9–10; 6 ab 5–6; 8 cd 25–6; Erf. 356/3–5; Ép. 9 cd
32–3; 18 cd 12, 14; 24 ab 3, 5; 26 ef 26–7; 28 ab 38–9.
[6] Ép. 6 ef 20–1; 6 ef 38–7 ab 1; Erf. 353/67–9; Ép. 14 ab 13–14; 16 ab
7–9; 16 ef 23–4.
[7] *CQ* xi. 184; he uses the term differently in *Gloss.* 52.

important sources, Virgil scholia (cf. 21–4, 25–7, 163, 221, 247, 441, 493, 571, 716, 800–1, 801a, 899–903, 985–6, 997, 1050–1, 1060–1) and Isidore's *Etymologies* (cf. 17–18, 167, 388, 391, 430, 445, 449, 458, 786, 839, 873, 875–6, 891, 905, 907, 1064,). The material from these two sources is sufficient to prove independent derivation, although the absence of extended batches suggests that the compiler used short lists of *glossae collectae* rather than the full text of a Virgil commentary or of the *Etymologies*. The same is apparently the case with the Old English glosses from the *Vita Antonii* (347, 390, 953), Jerome, *In Mattheum* (584, 624), and Pope Gregory's *Dialogues* and *Regula Pastoralis* (322, 394, 890, 1087), some of which occur in the relevant chapters of Leiden in conjunction with all-Latin items also found in Épinal–Erfurt.[1] Here the material involved is too slight to afford much in the way of batches, but cf. 953 n. On the other hand, the Old English glosses from Donatus' *Ars Grammatica* (378, 768) and Sedulius' *Carmen Paschale* (340, 576, 578) probably came through some intermediate source, since there is no further evidence to suggest that collections of Donatus or Sedulius glosses were used directly by the compiler of the *a*-order sections.[2] Similarly, the occasional items in the *a*-order sections which can be traced to the Philoxenus Glossary (6–7, 140, 159, 178, 830, 843–4, 998) may have been marginal additions to the archetype, or transmitted

---

[1] Cf. Ld. 28/1 *deficiet fatiget* (Erf. 356/15 *defiget*), 5 *infitiandi negandi* (Ép. 12 ab 38 *inuitiandi*), 6 *frugali larga uel lata* (9 cd 19 *frugalis largus?*), 8 *sputacum sputum* (24 ef 29), 10 *luridam luto sordidam* (13 ef 21 *luto pollutum*), 14 *explosi extincti* (Erf. 357/18), 16 *argula acuta* (Ép. 2 cd 25 *argute acute?*), 22 *sophismatum questionum* (24 ef 28 *quaestionem*), 29/8 *elucubratrum euigilantem* (Erf. 357/72 *euigilatum*), 16 *friuolis frugalis* (Ép. 9 ab 21 *fribolum fragile?*), 17 *emulumentum mercis laborum* (Erf. 357/74 *emolo-, laboris*), 25 *exuuia spolia* (359/57 *excubiae*), 34 *nardum arbor* (Ép. 16 ab 37 *nardus*); 39/16 *modernos nouos* (15 ab 23), 19 *freniticus insanus ob dolorem capitis*, etc. (9 cd 7 *ex dolore capitis*), 32 *dalmatica tonica lata habens manicas misalis* (Erf. 356/72 *tunica latas manicas habens*), 40 *paralisin desolutio omnium membrorum* (Ép. 20 ab 12), 44 *glebum ascensus singularis uia* (8 ab 18 *clibum . . . uiae*), 48 *calculum dicitur infirmitas eius qui non potest mingere quasi lapis obdurat uirilia* (Erf. 353/58 *infirmitas quae . . . mitigare*, etc.).

[2] The only other item common to Épinal–Erfurt and the Donatus glosses of Leiden xliii is Ép. 4 cd 19 *agrippa qui in pedes nascitur* (= Ld. 43/13), which belongs to an Abolita batch in the *ab*-order section (Lindsay, *Gloss*. 68). For the relationship between the Leiden Donatus glosses and Abstrusa–Abolita see 768 n.

through some other glossary of which Philoxenus was a source, such as Erfurt II.[1]

§ 35. A special problem is raised by the 'Hisperic' vocabulary used in Insular writings such as the works of Aldhelm, Gildas' *De Excidio Britanniae* (220, 1063), Columba's *Altus Prosator*[2] (316), the *Vita Sancti Maedoc* (596), the *Lorica Hymn*[3] (702), Adamnan's *Vita Sancti Columbae* (779), Felix of Crowland's *Vita Sancti Guthlaci* (971), and the *Hisperica Famina* themselves (129, 972), since the writers of the Hisperic school drew their peculiar language at least in part from glossaries.[4] Aldhelm's works in particular were regarded as a major source of Épinal–Erfurt by Napier and Bradley,[5] and their claim is supported by a substantial number of common items in the Aldhelm lists of Cleopatra III[6] and the three series of Aldhelm batches in Cleopatra I,[7] the first of which is cognate with Cleopatra III; cf. under A:

Ép. 1 ab 17 astrologia ratio siderum = Cl.III 500/26
ÉE 28 antiae loccas = Cl.III 514/4, Cl.I 343/33
ÉE 51 altrinsecus an ba halbae = Cl.I 338/8 twa

---

[1] Cf. 312 n. and Lindsay, *Gloss.* 79–80. Philoxenus also appears to have been a major source of Erfurt III (Lindsay, *Gloss.* 80–1) and the all-Latin glossaries Ab Absens, Abavus, Abba, and AA (Lindsay, *CQ* xi (1917), 196 ff.; *GL* v. 5, 11, 149–50).

[2] For the all-Latin items from this source see Lindsay, *Gloss.* 85–6 and add Ép. 28 ef 37 *uernans laetans* (*Altus*, 257–8 *tripudiis . . . angelorum uernantibus*?).

[3] In Jenkinson, *Hisperica Famina*, 51–4.

[4] Cf. Lindsay, *Gloss.* 97 ff. Jenkinson, *Hisperica Famina*, xiii–iv, regards the Hisperic writings as the source of common items, but his examples can be traced elsewhere: Ép. 4 ef 16 *amites fustis aucupalis* (*HF* 275 *perculam amite amiclios*) to Abol. AM 4; 7 cd 33 *competis terminis* (*HF* 9 *remota uasti . . . competa*) to Orosius i, prol. 9; 7 ef 32 *chorus coeuorum cantus et saltatio* (*HF* 26 *robustos multaui coeuos*) to Servius, *Geo.* i. 346; 8 ab 30 *cripta spelunca peruia* (*Rubisca* 71 *cantus in cripta cane*) to Ld. 16/3; 9 ab 10 *fastes libri* (*HF* 20 *quos edocetis fastos*) to Abstr. FA 79 *fastos libri consolatus*; 13 ef 34 *las laris id est ignis* (*HF* 93 *rosea æstiui laris . . . pira*) to Phocas 411/33.

[5] *Old English Glosses*, xii; *CQ* xiii. 97 ff.

[6] WW i. 485–535.

[7] Lübke, *Archiv*, lxxxv. 398–401. These batches also contain intruders and marginalia (*) from Épinal–Erfurt: cf. 343/22 *actionabatur scirde* (ÉE 86), 419/8* *inhians grædig* (ÉE 500), 10* *intestinum þearm* (ÉE 503), 430/17 *lenta toh* (ÉE 581 *tarda uel toch*), 440/21* *malus apuldor* (ÉE 636), 442/9* *mastigium swipan* (ÉE 641 -*ia*), 454/7* *nodus ost* (ÉE 688), 466/21 *penitus longe* (ÉE 801a).

ÉE 83 astu facni = Cl.I 354/22
ÉE 84 amiculo hraecli = Cl.I 346/18
Ép. 2 ef 33 ammodum ualde = Cl.III 487/27
ÉE 108 alumne fosturbearn = Cl.III 516/6, Cl.I 347/5
Ép. 5 cd 21 antes extrime ordines uinearum = Cl.III 505/4
ordines *only*

The interlinear Aldhelm glosses printed by Napier and Bouterwek[1] are less closely related to Épinal–Erfurt, but cf. 52, 227, 325, 716, 873. Much of this material stands in Épinal–Erfurt batches which can be traced to other sources,[2] in which cases Aldhelm is probably the debtor, since he undoubtedly borrowed heavily from the glossaries (cf. 6–7, 114, 181, 345a, 447, 568, 611–12, 716, 760, 874, 881, 947, 997),[3] and there is evidence suggesting that Épinal–Erfurt itself was used to gloss his writings (see notes to 495, 576, 615, 626). On the other hand, inflexional forms found in Aldhelm but not in a putative source (cf. 206, 232, 1092) may be intruders from the former which displaced the original items, a process illustrated by the marginalia of Cleopatra I (§ 16), and it is not unreasonable to suppose that Aldhelm was also the source of unusual words or senses first recorded in his works (218, 224, 313, 462, 569, 713, 716).[4] For the most part such items occur singly, but cf. 225–7, 232,

[1] *Old English Glosses*, 1 (Bodl. MS. Digby 146), 2 (B.M. MS. Royal 6 b vii), etc.; *ZfdA* ix (1853), 403–530 (Brussels, Bibliothèque royale MS. 1650). For their relationship with one another and Cleopatra see Napier, xxiii–vi; Ker, 320.

[2] Of the twenty-three Épinal–Erfurt items in Napier's list, nine (108, 211, 374, 681, 737, 744, 873, 943, 1092) fall within Lindsay's Orosius batches. Bradley withdrew his proposed Aldhelm batches (164–72, 180–2, 209–11, 220–33) at Lindsay's instance in a postscript (*CQ* xiii. 108), while affirming his belief that a few such glosses existed in Épinal–Erfurt; his fourth batch does in fact contain some likely Aldhelm items.

[3] Cf. Lindsay, *Gloss.* 97–8. The most cogent example is *Aenig.* 11 title *poalum* 'bellows', apparently from Ép. 19 ab 15 *poala uentium folles fabrorum*, explained by Lindsay as a misinterpretation of *poa lauantium* (Gildas, 75/31, quoting VL (?) Mal. 3: 2, where Sept. has ποία πλυνόντων, Vulg. *herba fullonum*).

[4] Other probable Aldhelm glosses are Ép. 8 ef 9 *crustu ornato* (*VP* 317/25 *crustu interdicto*), 10 cd 23 *gabulum patibulum* (*VP* 276/20 *gabuli patibulo*), 11 cd 33 *hiulcas leones fauces* (*VP* 284/10 *hiulcas faucium gurguliones*), 19 ab 29 *portisculo malleo* (*VP* 230/23 *crepitante naucleri portisculo*), 19 ef 34 *pipant resonant* (*Metr.* 180/13 *pulli et pueri pipant*), 26 ef 11 *thoraciclas sculptae imagines* (*VP* 287/5 *omnes simulacrorum toracidas*, v.l. *toraciclas*), and Erf. 353/62 *cirris crinibus* (*VP* 305/15 *cirris crispantibus*).

313–14, 407–8, 568–9. It seems reasonable to accept that material of this type comes from the works of Aldhelm and other Insular writers rather than to multiply hypotheses in attempting to trace it to other sources as Lindsay does, especially in view of the unquestioned Aldhelm and Gildas material in Corpus.[1] Insular influence is also seen in the Irish interpretation of 342,[2] and in the glosses derived from the *Compendiosa Doctrina* of Nonius Marcellus (cf. 509 n.), which was apparently unknown on the Continent before the time of Alcuin.[3] Épinal–Erfurt, like the works of Aldhelm himself, if on a more pedestrian level, thus expresses 'the new Christian culture of England, which arose between 650 and 680 after the conversion of the Anglo-Saxons . . . in which not only Irish and Roman but also Graeco-Oriental (Theodore of Tarsus and the African Hadrian) influences mingled with British and Anglo-Saxon native culture',[4] and the study of its sources offers a unique insight into the beginnings of Anglo-Latin scholarship (cf. § 30). Where and when it was compiled is a matter of conjecture, but Bradley's suggestion 'that the archetype of Épinal and Erfurt was compiled in the school of Aldhelm at Malmesbury, and perhaps under his personal superintendence'[5] is an attractive possibility which is not at variance with the linguistic evidence (§ 90).

LANGUAGE AND ORTHOGRAPHY

§ 36. In considering the language of an early text, the question naturally arises how far the manuscript forms represent the actual speech of the time and place in which they were written. It is generally accepted that Old English spelling down to the eleventh century was roughly phonetic, but the degree of

---

[1] Cf. Lindsay, *Gloss.* 98–9; Hessels, *Leiden* 240–1.

[2] Cf. 493 n. and the Irish lemma in Ép. 17 ab 28 *orge occide* (OIr. *org(a)id* 'slays'), pointed out by Schlutter, *AJP* xxi (1900), 188.

[3] Lindsay, *Gloss.* 85.

[4] E. R. Curtius, *European Literature and the Latin Middle Ages*, tr. W. R. Trask (London, 1953), 457. For the connection between Épinal–Erfurt and the 'new learning' introduced by Theodore and Hadrian see § 33.

[5] *CQ* xiii. 101; cf. p. 102: 'The general correctness of the Aldhelm renderings in Epinal, as compared with the frequent blundering of later glossators, seems to suggest that the information may have been derived from the fountain head.' Aldhelm's apparent borrowings from Épinal–Erfurt or closely related glossaries would point in the same direction.

approximation obviously varied in particular cases, and the problem is especially acute in dealing with archaic texts of uncertain date and provenance, and incorporating material from a variety of sources, like these glossaries. Sisam has pointed out the hazard of applying criteria deduced from later dialects to the early poetry,[1] and the glossaries suffer from the added complication that the compiler of the archetype may have copied the orthography of his sources. Intellectually and culturally England was already one nation in the later seventh century, after the Synod of Whitby, as Bede's *History* makes clear,[2] and spellings appropriate to the pronunciation of one dialect might find their way into others; cf. the Mercian 'colouring' in early West-Saxon and Kentish texts.[3] Moreover, the dating of texts prior to 800 depends on the early copies of Cædmon's Hymn and Bede's Death Song (both in Northumbrian dialects) and a handful of names in early manuscripts of Bede's *History* and Latin charters,[4] the evidence of which has often been overstretched, e.g. in dating the loss of medial *h*.[5] Still, the general orthographical pattern exhibited by both manuscripts and also by Corpus is reasonably consistent, suggesting that the three texts reflect, in varying degrees, a settled spelling-system, the implications of which can be assessed in the light of other evidence. The following account aims to present its salient features in the order of Luick's *Historische Grammatik*, which remains the most consistent and satisfactory exposition of the Old English sound-changes (cf. Campbell, §§ 246–50).

Stressed vowels and diphthongs

§ 37. Gmc. *a* before nasal consonants always appears as *a* in Épinal, except in *onettae* 712 (**anhǣtidæ*), where lengthening

---

[1] K. Sisam, *Studies in the History of Old English Literature* (Oxford, 1953), 119 ff.

[2] Cf. esp. his preface to Ceolwulf and iv. 2, 16 (18).

[3] Cf. A. Campbell, *Medium Ævum*, xxiv (1955), 54: 'It is possible that the influence of the well-established Mercian spelling-system is enough to explain the apparent impurity of most *nicht-strengwestsächsische* texts, and that the 'Saxon Patois' can disappear from OE. grammars.' The same applies to Wildhagen's so-called Mercio-Kentish *Kirchensprache* (*Studien zur Englischen Philologie*, 1 (1913), 436–7); cf. H. Flasdieck, *PBB* xlviii (1924), 387.   [4] *OET*, Cts. 1–19.

[5] Cf. H. M. Chadwick, *The Heroic Age* (Cambridge, 1912), 66 ff.

may have taken place (§ 60); Erfurt has *a* and *o* about equally (31 *o* : 29 *a*).[1] Cf. Ép. *brandrad* 4 (Erf. *brond-*), *fyrpannae* 5 (Erf. *-ponne*), *holthana* 41, *anga* 43, *an* 51 (Erf. *on*), *hramsa* 59, 60 (Erf. *hromsa* 60), *fraam* 71 (Erf. *from*),[2] *an* 91, etc. Corpus has *a* and *o* spellings like Erfurt, but their distribution is different,[3] suggesting that the *o* spellings in both texts may be due to independent scribal alteration. In any case, the uniform *a* spellings of Épinal are a distinctive feature of its orthography, the significance of which is uncertain. Assuming that Prim. OE. *a* in this position was already rounded to some extent, as suggested by *onettae* (Luick, §110 a. 2) and prevalent *o* in the early Northumbrian texts, it might be a conservative spelling, or a dialect feature which is no longer identifiable,[4] or simply a matter of individual scribal preference. *æ* in *hraen* 400 (**hraʒn-*), *uuinaern* 1040 (**raʒn-*), and Erf. *hafaern* 258 (§ 38) is due to fronting of Gmc. *a* before assimilation of *ʒn* to *nn*.[5]

§ 38. Gmc. *a* developed independently is normally *ae* (*æ*, *e*) in both manuscripts: cf. (*h)aesil* 50, *hraecli* 84, *uuraec* 87, 90, *scaet* 157, *naesgristlae* 174, etc. Both texts have *e* for Gmc. *a* in *sceptloum* 106 (also Cp. 156), *mera(e)* 558, Épinal only in *redisnae* 123 (n.), *huet* 604 (n.), *cebærtuun* 1058 (? a mistake for Erf. *caeber-*), Erfurt only in *hebrebletae* 124, *steblidrae* 136, *uuydumer* 347 (also Cp. 715), *medlæ* 549, *nebæ* 625, *uuelreab* 642, *hegtis* 913, *espæ* 1006, *best* 1017.[6] The *e* spellings peculiar to Erfurt may

---

[1] Not counting *scoma* 732, which may be an error for **scamo*.

[2] For double *a* in *fraam* cf. *haam* 244 and double *o* for *ð* in *sooc* 951, *hool* 1072, *broord* Erf. 782. Except for ME. *weel* there is no other evidence for the lengthening before a single final consonant in monosyllables postulated by Bülbring (§ 284), and doubling here may therefore be an indication of stress rather than length, like the accent on short monosyllables according to Luick (§ 54).

[3] Cf. Cp. *brandrod* 157, *fyrponne* 208, *holthana* 54, *onga* 192, *on* 121, *hromsa* 56, *hromsan* 57, *from* 60, *on* 246.

[4] Possibly southern, since *a* prevails in late West-Saxon and in the Kentish Glosses, and the *o* spellings which predominate in eWS. and the Kentish charters might have been due to Mercian spelling influence. The Suffolk Charter (Bond, iii. 35) has *a* exclusively, but this may be just lWS. spelling.

[5] Sievers, *PBB* ix (1884), 211. *e* in *habern* 684 may be due to weak stress.

[6] *e* may be otherwise explained in *teblae* 6, *teblere* 7, *tebel-* 172 (§ 68 fn. 2), *cefr* 150 (cf. OHG. *chevaro* < **kebr-*), *lerb* (*-br*) 894 (cf. OHG. *leber*), *thuerae* 1029 (n.), and Erf. *esc* 772 (Gmc. **askiz IEW* 729). For Erf. *-gela(e)* 26, 673 see § 46 fn. 6.

be due to scribal confusion of *æ* and *e* by the foreign scribe;
the few examples common to Épinal and Corpus may be due
to scribal misinterpretation of 'hooked' *e*, the loop of which is
much attenuated in these manuscripts, or reflect the dialectal
'second fronting' (Campbell, §§ 164 ff.) which also affected Prim.
OE. *a* before back vowels (§ 46). *habern* 684 and Erf. *hafaern*
258 beside *hæfer* 'crab' (Hl. C199), by popular analogy with *hæf*
'sea' and *ærn* 'house' (*AEW* 144), may have *a* after pl. *hafu.*
a in *quatern* 847 (lL. *quaternio* Pogatscher, § 186) is due to
late borrowing.

§ 39. Prim. OE. *æ* from Gmc. *æ* or WGmc. *ā*[1] is predominantly
e(e)[2] in both texts: cf. *meeli* 56, *breer* 68, *setungae* 72, *gerlicae* 94,
megsibbi 109, etc. (Ép. 35, Erf. 41). Both texts have *ae* (*æ*, *ę*)
for Gmc. *æ*/WGmc. *ā* in *obaerstaelendi* 192, *obaerstaelid* 194,
Épinal only in *æthm* 89, *raedinnae* 212, 1035, *blae[e]d* 445, *naep*
687, *naeðlae* 796, *suae* 843, 844, 865, *felospraeci* 1009, *o(e)ghuuaer*
1061, and perhaps also in *raed(gaesran)* 493 (n.), Erfurt only
in *snaedil* 381, *coldraed* 763, *biraednae* 800. Since Corpus has
ae, *æ* in several of these forms,[3] *æ* spellings were presumably
a feature of the archetype as well. They have been regarded
as archaic rather than dialectal in these texts, reflecting early
uncertainty in the representation of non-WS. [e:] (Campbell,
§ 128 fn. 2), the development of which was certainly pre-literary
(cf. Luick, §§ 142 a., 163 a. 2); but occasional West-Saxon forms
cannot be precluded (§ 90). *ei* in Erf. *breitibannæ* 885, *felu-
spreici* 1009 could be an archaic spelling representing the
hypothetical *i*-mutation of Prim. OE. *e* (cf. Campbell, § 42), or
due to a false equation by the German scribe of an *æ* spelling

---

[1] Cf. Campbell, §§ 127 ff. The development to *ō* before nasal consonants
would be easier to understand if its starting-point were WGmc. *ā* (presumably front [a:]).

[2] For *ee* cf. *aa* in *faag* 61, etc., *oo* in *boog* 67, etc., *uu* in *uuf* 142, etc., *ii* in
sciir 941. Doubling to indicate length is occasional in later Old English,
especially in Northumbrian; A. C. S. Ross, *Studies in the Accidence of the
Lindisfarne Gospels* (Leeds, 1957), 157 ff., attributes it to Irish influence.
It is found mostly in monosyllables (44 times in Épinal, 32 times in Erfurt),
in open syllables in *meeli* 56, Ép. *steeli* 49, *naamun* 113, Erf. *ungiseem* (-*ni*)
333, and in *ciisnis* 406 after adj. *cīs* (BT 156).

[3] Cf. Cp. *aethm* 130, *raedinne* 260, *oberstaelende* 506, *oberstaeled* 515,
raedenne 529, *snaedilþearm* 794, *blæd* 892, *raedgasram* 1035, *naeþ* 1363, *suae*
1691, 1692, 1722, *raedinne* 1980.

in his exemplar with the *i*-mutation of Prim. OE. *ā* from Gmc.
ai (= OHG. *ei*).[1]

§ 40. Gmc. *au* developed independently is uniformly *ea* in
Épinal (cf. *sceabas* 30, *earngeat* 40, *earuuiga* 44, *geacaes* 63,
streamrad 88, etc.), except before Gmc. *w*, where it is spelt *e(u)*
in *screuua* 649, *mundleu(u)* 1055 (n.), *eo* in *snidstreo* (Erf. *-streu*)
973.[2] Before consonants other than *w* Erf. normally has *ea* also
(cf. *gebeatten* 140, *cysirbeam* 237, *leactrogas* 247, *cistimbeam* 249,
etc.), but *eu* appears in *aerngeup* 40, *streumrad* 88, *eustnorduind*
162, *uuslucreud* 169, *deudlicustan* 439; it has *eo* in *reod* 404. In
later Old English *eo* for Gmc. *au* except before *w* is peculiar
to the Northumbrian dialect of Rushworth Mark, Luke, and
John (Campbell, § 278 (a)), but here *eo* and *eu* are probably to
be regarded as archaic rather than dialectal (Campbell, § 275
and fn. 2). Erf. *iaces* 263 for *gēaces* (also Cl.I 362/26) may be
an isolated early example of the shift of stress by which *gēa-*
became [ja:] (cf. Campbell, § 303 fn. 2). *ae* in Erf. *aeruuica* 44,
(h)laepaeuincæ 264 (n.), and *laesung* 426 could be simply graphic
transposition of *ea*, like *oe* for *eo* in *oerendil* 554, or an abbreviation of archaic *aeu/aeo* (Campbell, § 275 fn. 3).[3] *e* in Erf. *scebas*
30 could be due to palatal *sċ*,[4] or a scribal error for *ea* or *æ*
(cf. § 38).

§ 41. Gmc. *eu* developed independently is normally *eo* in both
texts: cf. *ceol* 230, *hleor* 438, 482, *leoma* 554, *steor* 596, 780, etc.
(Ép. 16, Erf. 15).[5] It appears as *eu* in *treulesnis* 726 (§ 73), Ép.
steupfaedaer 1070, Erf. *ansueus* (*-p*) 32, *falatreu* 36 (pl. *-trewō*),
fleutas 107, *spreutum* 211, *cleuuue* 472, *leuma* 478, *steur* 780. The
first element is written as *i* in *briosa* 27, 1016, *buturfliogae* 817,
cnioholaen 879, Ép. *gihiodum* 76, *criopungae* 696 (Erf. *criupungae*),[6]
the second as *a* in *uueadhoc* 887, Ép. *fulaetrea* 36, *neuunseada* 505
(n.), Erf. *gaeadun* 76. *e* in *sceld(h)reda* 997 (*-hrēoða*) may be
due to reduced stress.

[1] Cf. *ei* for OE. *ā* in Erf. *meinfol* 512 (Ép. *maanful*).
[2] Gmc. **strawa-* with vocalization of *w* after loss of unstressed *a* (Campbell,
§ 120. 3 (b)); but *snidstreo* (also Cp. *-streo* 13, 1868) may have been influenced
by *trēo(w)* (Campbell, § 275 fn. 4). *eu* may also = *eaw* in Erf. *-heui* 262 (n.).
[3] *aeu* is preserved in *gaeuo* (*-c*) 'cuckoo' Ld. 47/65.
[4] So M. Kolkwitz, *Angl.* xvii (1895), 458; cf. § 47.
[5] Not counting Ép. *hlaeodrindi* 508 (§ 86).
[6] Also Cp. *briosa* 225, 1976, *cnioholen* 1759, *criopunge* 1405. A form with
io may also lie behind Ép. *hlaeodrindi* 508 (§ 86).

§ 42. Gmc. *iu* developed independently appears as *io* in Ép. *anhriosith* 520 (Erf. *onhrisit*), as *eo* in Ép. *burgleod* 620.[1] *ie* in Ép. *hunhieri* 983 could be taken as a non-WS. form with sporadic unrounding of the second element of the diphthong (Campbell, § 281), but *ie* for Prim. OE. *iu* from breaking in *georuuierdid*, etc. (§ 45) is specifically West-Saxon, so *ie* here might reasonably be taken as West-Saxon also. *y* in Erf. *unhyri* may be due to scribal confusion of *iu* and *ui*, the archaic graph for [y(:)] (Campbell, § 42). WGmc. *iu* by contraction with vocalized *w* (Campbell, § 120) appears as *iu* in *gliuuae* 550 (**gliuwj-*), *bisiuuidi* 699, *asiuuid* 796, *gisiuuid* 886 (**-siuwid-*);[2] *eu* in *gitre[e]udae* 436 (**-triuw(i)d-*) may show the influence of *trēowian* (cf. Cp. *getreuuade* 900). For *flio*, *gitiungi* see §§ 57. 3, 59. 3.

§ 43. The treatment of Prim. OE. *æ* where it was subject to breaking or retraction before consonants conforms in general to the Anglian pattern:

(1) Before *r* plus consonant it normally appears as *ea* in both texts: cf. *pearroc* 224, *fearn* (Erf. †*feran*) 420, *mearth* 425, *spearuua* 435, *thearm* 503, etc. It also appears as *ea* before *r* plus a back consonant in Ép. *mear(c)isern* 227, *uueargrod* 409, *fristmearc* 547 besides forms with smoothing (§ 57. 1). *isærn* 25, *baers* 592 and Erf. *aerngeup* 40, *stærn* 125, *uaertae* 154 (also Ld. 47/36), *duæram* 891 (for *duæarm*?) may be taken as archaic spellings in which breaking was not expressed (Campbell, § 140).[3] Retraction instead of breaking in the neighbourhood of labial consonants as in eNh. texts[4] is indicated in *sparuua* 897, Erf. *foe(s)tribarn* 108, *ediscuard* 148, *u(u)ard* 333, 737.

---

[1] *leod* is usually taken as an *i*-stem (cf. pl. *leode*), but mixed declension is possible (*leode* has *eo* consistently in early West-Saxon, Cosijn, i. § 103), in which case the diphthong would be Gmc. *eu*. The same stem may be found in Erf. *geleod* 229 (n.).

[2] Cf. Cp. *gliowe* 1112, *bisiudi* 1450, *asiowid* 1591, *gesiouuid* 1763. *gliu* 398 (Cp. *glio* 825) is ambiguous, since *iu* here may represent a nom. sg. **gliw(i)* without WGmc. diphthongization (Campbell, § 579. 4).

[3] *æ* in *isærn* might also be due to confusion with *īsern* 'iron' (cf. Cl. *isen*). *baers* is taken as an example of metathesis as in *-aern*, *hraen* (§ 37) by SB, § 179. 1, Campbell, § 155 fn. 2, but its IE. base seems to have been **bhors-* (*IEW* 109); hence the forms with *æ* in later glossaries should be regarded as fossilized.

[4] Cf. CH *uard* 1, 7, *barnum* 5, Bede's Death Song *tharf* 2, LR *uarþ* 5.

(2) Before *l* plus consonant both texts have regular *a*: cf. *halbae* 51, *spaldr* 54, *aldot* 57 *scaldthyflas* 58, *tohald* 96, etc.; *ea* appears only once, in Ép. *fealga* 713. There may also have been retraction before intervocalic *l* (Luick, § 146 a. 3) in *n(e)ctigalae* 26, (Erf. †*-gela*), *alaer* 35, *al[t]erholt* 46, *falaed* 129, 959, *palester* 225 (n.), and Ép. *nectigalae* 673, 857. Most of these forms can, however, be explained differently (cf. §§ 46, 68).

(3) Before *h ea* appears only once, in Ép. *leax* 555 (*læhs), beside several forms with smoothing (§ 57. 1). Retraction appears to have taken place after *w* in Erf. *thuachl* 326.[1]

(4) Before *w* there is retraction in all the relevant forms: *auuel* 29, *clauuo* 29, *thrauu* 53.[2]

§ 44. Prim. OE. *e* before breaking consonants is normally *eo*:

(1) Before *r* plus consonant in *eordrestae* 219, *geornlice* 708, *eornæsti* 945, Ép. *feruuitgeornnis* 208, *feormat* (Erf. †*caeormad*) 402, *ge[e]ornissae* 527, *geormantlab* 656, *aqueorna* 911, Erf. *gine[h]ord* 276; before *r* plus a back consonant in Ép. *algiuueorc* 556 beside several forms with smoothing (§ 57. 2). *io* appears once, in Ép. *uuandaeuuiorpae* 1045.[3] *e* in *herth* 5 appears to be an archaic spelling in which breaking was not expressed, like *isærn*, etc. (§ 43. 1),[4] and likewise perhaps in Erf. *feruitgernis*, *uuondæuuerpe*; but *e* in *smeruui* 944 (also †*sperwi*, †*spreui* 769) may be after nom. sg. *smeru* (so Campbell, § 140 fn. 2), since similar forms occur in later texts (BT 888). Lack of breaking in Ép. *merze* 657a (L. *mercem*) is due to late borrowing (Luick, § 212 and a. 3). Retraction to *o* after *w* as in later Nh. texts (Luick, § 156) may be indicated in Erf. *aquorna* 911; cf. § 62.

(2) Before *lh* in *sceol(h)egi* 981, Erf. *eola* 346a (*elhō), beside forms with smoothing (§ 57. 2).[5]

§ 45. Prim. OE. *i* remains unbroken before *r* plus consonant under conditions of *i*-mutation as in later Anglian texts

---

[1] Possibly influenced by forms of *þwēan* with *a* after other Class VII verbs with retraction (Campbell, § 145 fn. 2). Erf. *nachtegelae* 673 may have been influenced by OHG. *nahtigala*.

[2] Beside later *clēa, *þrēa* with loss of *w* before *-u* and contraction (Campbell, § 598. 2); cf. *pauua* 826 (L. *pāuo*) beside *pēa*.

[3] Cf. Erf. *gyrnissæ*, where *i* may be due to confusion of *iu* and *ui* as in *unhyri* (§ 42).

[4] The equation of *-r* and *-ur* as in Erf. *grimrodr* (§ 66) may also be involved in these spellings.

[5] Breaking before Prim. OE. *h* is indicated in Erf. *(e)oritmon* 320 (**eoh-*).

(Campbell, § 154. 3) in *bismiridae* 534 (**-smirwi-*), *firgingaett* 560 (**firgunj-* § 65. 4), *birciae* 792,[1] Erf. *fir(s)t* 595 (also Cp. 1176) beside *georuuierdid* 990 and Ép. *fierst* 595, *orfiermae* 933 with *i*-mutation of the breaking diphthong (§ 55). *sifunsterri* 762 (also Cp. 1599)[2] and Erf. *orfermae* show lowering to *e* in the same surroundings, which was an occasional feature in Anglian texts (Campbell, § 154. 3). Retraction to *u* between *w* and *r* plus consonant has taken place in *sin(h)uurbul* 1047 (Cp. *-huurful* 2008) < **-hwirbil* with suffix interchange (§ 68).[3] Breaking of Prim. OE. *i* before *w* may be indicated by the spelling in Ép. *neuunseada* 505, if the first element represents **niwan-*.[4]

§ 46. Prim. OE. *æ* which was subject to retraction before a single consonant followed by a back vowel appears as *a* in the majority of cases in both texts: cf. *uuapul* 447, *aslacudae* 491, *ragu* 629, *apuld(u)r* 636, 638, etc. (Ép. 18, Erf. 18).[5] It appears as *ae, æ* in *gaebuli* 115, *slægu* 603, Ép. *haeguthorn* 19, 956, *claedur* 218, *baeso* 411, *scaedugeardas* 991, Erf. *maefuldur* 33, *uualhhaebuc* 497, *hæra* 608; as *e* in *bruunbesu* 716 and Ép. *uualhhebuc* 497, Erf. *cledur* 218, *hegudorn* 956, and also in *cesol* 457 (n.), 1054, if it represents L. *casula*, beside forms with back mutation (§ 56). *a* in Ép. *nabae* 625 (also Cp. 1322) may be from n. s. *nafu* or g. d. p. *nafa, -um*;[6] *cladærsticca* 116 and Erf. *gabelrend* 293, *uulating* 667 have suffix interchange (§ 68). OE. *a* in this position was certainly pre-literary, since it was affected by *i*-mutation (§ 51), and *ae, æ* are therefore to be taken as examples of the 'second fronting' which must have preceded back mutation to *ea* (§ 56) in dialects where the latter occurred

---

[1] *firgin-* and *birciae* could also be explained by Anglian smoothing (§ 57. 3), but if breaking failed before *r* followed by other consonants, it presumably failed here also (Luick, § 236. 1).

[2] Presumably a neut. *ja*-noun like OHG. *gistirri* (Kluge, § 66). These forms could also be regarded as examples of the 'Saxon Patois' *e* for WS. *ie* (Bülbring, § 186 a.), but such spellings in *nicht-strengwestsächsische* texts are probably due to Anglian influence in any case (§ 36 fn. 3).

[3] Cf. OHG. *sinawerbal* 'round' (BT 877) and ON. *hvirfill* 'circle'.

[4] Cf. *newe-, niweseoða* (BT 717) and *niwel, niowol* (*AEW* 237).

[5] Not counting *scalu* 462, *falu* 483, *stalu* 1067, where *a* may already have been retracted before intervocalic *l* (§ 43. 2).

[6] Cf. Campbell, § 160. 3. The same may be the case with nom. sg. *-galae* Ép. 26, 673, 857, unless *a* is due to intervocalic *l* (§ 43. 2). *e* in Erf. *-gela(e)* 26, 673 presumably represents unretracted *æ* with Kt. 'second fronting' (cf. Luick, § 179. a. 1).

(Luick, § 174 a. 3). Corpus shows a similar distribution of *a* and *ae*, *ea* suggesting that this variation them goes back[1] to the archetype. *e* in this context may be simply a scribal blunder for *ę*,[2] or a mixed spelling perpetrated by Kentish scribes, whose native dialect had *a* for Prim. OE. *æ* before back vowels and *e* in other positions. Before a back vowel preceded by a double consonant *a* appears only in the doubtful form *maffa* 719 (n.), *ae* in *librlaeppan* 405, Ép. *maettoc* 1003, Erf. *hræc(c)a* 715 (n.); *e* in Erf. *mettoc* 1003 and *mettocas* 565, 586, Ép. 878 (also Cp. 1709) might be due to *i*-mutation followed by suffix interchange (§ 68), as Erf. *metticas* 878 suggests, but all these forms could be derived from a single interpretation with *e* for *æ*.

§ 47. As in other non-West-Saxon texts, the influence of initial palatal consonants is limited. Prim. OE. *e* appears to have been raised to *i* after [j] in Ép. *gibaen* 525,[3] *biginan* 1041,[4] but remains unaffected after *ċ*, *sċ* in *cest* 231, *sceldreda* 997. Prim. OE. *æ* remains after [j] in *bigaet* 706, *ludgaet* 741, and *e* after *ċ*, *sċ* in *sceptloum* 106 beside *scaet* 157, *edscaept* 783, Ép. *scaeptloan* 489, and in Ép. *cebærtuun* 1058 may be due to 'second fronting' (§ 38). *ea* for Prim. OE. *æ* in *uuicingsceadan* 736, *sceaba* 853, *sceadu* 902, and Erf. *sceadugeardas* 991 may therefore be taken as the result of back mutation, which apparently operated more strongly after palatal consonants (Luick § 231 a. 3),[5] rather than diphthongization of the West-Saxon type

---

[1] Cf. Cp. *heago-*, *heaguðorn* 114, 1897, *cladersticca* 171, *cleadur* 599, *wapul* 835, *aslacadae* 1014, *slaegu* 1230, *ragu* 1324, *(-)apuldur* 1273, 1302, *sceadugeardas* 1998.

[2] This is Professor Campbell's opinion (private communication).

[3] For Angl. *gifan* see K. Luick, *Untersuchungen zur englischen Lautgeschichte* (Strasbourg, 1896), 302; E. Björkmann, *Scandinavian Loan-words in Middle English* (Halle, 1900), 154 ff. It is possible that the occasional *i*-forms in early Angl. texts (one in Épinal and seven in the Durham Ritual, according to Luick) were borrowed from dialects in which palatal influence operated, and their extension in Middle English was due to East Norse *gifa* (Björkmann, pp. 155–6). Campbell, § 300 fn. 1, assumes an alternative root-form *gif-* (after *niman*?) here and in lWS. *gifan*.

[4] Luick, § 196, and Campbell, § 177, equate *biginan* and Li. *bigienda* < **jan-* with *i*-mutation of the palatal diphthong, but cf. Erf., Cp. *-ge(o)nan* and Go. *jains*, etc. < **jen-* (SB, § 92 a. 5).

[5] This is phonetically probable, since [æ] would be pronounced higher after a front consonant, and the back glide would develop more rapidly and distinctly after it. The *e* might also be taken as a diacritic indicating the palatal quality of *sc* before *a*, but it occurs only in conditions of back mutation.

after *sċ*. The *e* for *e* for *ĕa* from breaking in *geruuae* 'yarrow'
623 beside Ép. *gearuue* 639,[1] and *i*(*i*) for the mutation of
Prim. OE. *ǣo* in *ciisnis* 406 (§ 55) may be early examples of
WS.-type smoothing after an initial palatal consonant (Luick,
§ 279); and likewise *e* in Erf. *scebas* 30 (§ 40), and *i* in Erf.
cistimbeam 249 (§ 49) if diphthongization preceded *i*-mutation.

§ 48. The *i*-mutation of Prim. OE. *a* before nasal consonants
is predominantly *ae*, *æ* in Épinal, *e* in Erfurt: cf. Ép. *aenid* 17,
aend 98, *gimaengiungiae* 203, *lændnum* 216, *caempan* 481, etc.
(23 examples) beside *embrin* 121a, *fremu* 135, *stegn* (*-ng*) 209,
menescillingas 570, *anhendi* 626, *mengio* 659, *gimengedlicæ* 750,
emer 909, *le*(*n*)*ctinadl* 999, and Erf. *end* 98, *embrin* 121a, *fremu*
135, *gemengiungae* 203, *cempan* 481, etc. (21 examples) beside
aenit 17, *stæng* 209, *lænd*(*n*)*um* 216, *æmil*, *aemil* 257, 484, *dopae-*
nid 419, *anhaendi* 626, *faengae* 727, *gemaengidlicæ* 750, *graemung*
(*graenn-*) 852, *hæn* 906, *fænucæ* 997. Corpus has *ae*, *æ* only three
times, in *laendino* 1740 (Ép. *lændino*, Erf. *lendino* 860), *gemængan*
547, *wodhae*(*n*) 583. Chadwick took the *æ* spellings as evidence
that the dialect of the archetype was East-Saxon,[2] but they have
generally been regarded as archaic rather than dialectal, and
taken to represent an intermediate stage in the development of
Prim. OE. *a* before a nasal consonant followed by *i*/*j* to *e*
(cf. Luick, § 186; Campbell, § 193. d).[3] Lack of mutation in Erf.
candelthuist 382 (L. *candēla*) is due to late borrowing (Pogatscher,
§ 262).

§ 49. The *i*-mutation of Prim. OE. *æ* before single consonants
and geminates except *l*, *ll* (§ 50. 2) is uniformly *e*: cf. *teblae* 6,
teblere 7 (§ 66), *merici* 24, *hindberiæ* 69, *aferidae* 91, etc., and
bed(*d*) 243, 971, (-)*uueb*(*b*) 441, 1026, 1030, (-)*segg* 463, 781,
966, *nettae* 702. *ae* in *saeppae* 37 (L. *sappīnus*) is presumably
due to late borrowing,[4] and likewise in Cp. *glaedine* 1815 (L.
gladiola with altered suffix) beside Ép. †*gladinae* 920, Erf.
gledinae. Before consonant groups (other than those causing

---

[1] Cf. Kt. *fulgere* 'readily' Ct. 41/65, *gerewe* 'parata' KG 721.

[2] *TCPS* iv. 251, comparing B.M. MS. Cotton Tiberius C ii of Bede's
History, written in southern England towards 800 (Lowe 191), which has
ae, *æ* regularly: cf. *haengest* i. 15, etc., *middelængli* iii. 21, *paente*, *raendles*,
raendili iii. 22.

[3] For *ae*, *æ* before nasals in unstressed syllables see § 65. 2.

[4] Pogatscher, § 184, derives it from OFr. *sap*, which leaves *-pp-* unexplained.

breaking or retraction) *ae* predominates in both texts, e.g. in *staefnændra* 75, *faestinnum* 110, *aesc*(-) 180, 416, 450, *naecht-hraebn* 673, 674, *edscaept* 783, *hraebnæs* 848 (Ép. 18, Erf. 14). Both texts have *e* in *reftras* 11, *restaendum* 443, Épinal only in *eordrestae* 219, Erfurt only in (*a*)*respit* 511, 523, *refset* 526, *esc* 772, *mestum* 930, *festin* 1042.[1] *i* in Erf. *cistimbeam* 249 (L. *castanea* with altered suffix) may be due to raising or diphthongization of Prim. OE. *æ* after palatal *ċ* (§ 47).[2]

§ 50. Where Prim. OE. *æ* stood before consonants causing breaking or retraction followed by *i*-mutation, *ae* and *e* alternate according to the developments described in § 43:

(1) Before *r* plus consonant *e*, the Anglian and Kentish mutation of the breaking diphthong, appears in *sercae* 18, *bisceredae* 73 (§ 73), *gegeruuednae* 196, *gerd* 614, Ép. *heruuendlicae* 186, *gigeruuid* 730,[3] Erf. *uuergendi* 318, *fertd* 373, *auuerdid* 1091. *ae* in Ép. *auuaerdid*, Erf. *haeruuendlicae* is presumably the mutation of Prim. OE. *a* by retraction in the neighbourhood of a labial consonant (§ 43. 1); in *segilgaerd* 111 (also Cp. *seglgærd* 165) it may represent the same development with retraction instead of breaking under reduced stress (cf. Campbell, § 338).

(2) Before *l* plus consonant *ae*, the mutation of Prim. OE. *a* by retraction, appears in *blestbaelg* 454, *aeldrum* 546, *aelbitu* 718, Ép. *unamaelti* 769, *ohaelði* 838; *e*, presumably the Kentish or 'Saxon Patois' mutation of the breaking diphthong,[4] appears in *sadulfelgae* 818, *uuellyrgae* 969, *gundaesuelgiae* 976, and perhaps *edwella* 1019,[5] Erf. *felge* 292, *giheldae* 371, †*cinamelti* 769, *oheldi* 838. *ae* appears for Prim. OE. *a* before intervocalic *l* in Ép. *aelifnae* 115a (n.), Erf. *cæle* 862 (n.), *e* in -*huuelci* 709, 842 (**-hwælik*- SB, § 342 a. 2) and *ellaen* 893 (? **ælirin*- *IEW* 302).

(3) Before *h*, where breaking was the normal development in all dialects, the mutated vowel appears as *e* in Ép. *nectigalae* 673, as *e*(*e*) with lengthening after loss of medial *h* (§ 72) in

---

[1] Cf. Cp. *reftras* 150, *gerested* 854, *eordreste* 360.

[2] Cf. Nh. *sci*(*e*)*ppend* (Campbell, § 189).

[3] Erf. *gigarauuit* is influenced by OHG. orthography.

[4] If the theory referred to in § 36 fn. 3 is correct, the 'Saxon Patois' forms in Bülbring, § 181 a., are presumably due to the equation of WS. *ie* with Angl. *e* in other positions.

[5] Cf. Cp. *sadulfelge* 1563, *wellyrgae* 1876. *edwella* beside Cp. *eduuaelle* 2034 may represent an ablaut variant with Gmc. *e* as in OHG. *uuella*; cf. VP *wellan* 113/8(1), VH *wellu*(*m*) 2/5 (Campbell, § 193 (a) fn. 1).

steeli 49 (**stæhlī*), *thuelan* 1060 (**þwæhil-*),[1] and perhaps in Erf. *ungiseem* (*-ni*) 333.[2] *ae* in *aehrian* (Erf. †*aegrihan*) 840 could be taken as the mutation of Prim. OE. *a* by retraction before *h* instead of breaking (§ 43. 3) in **æhurjō(n)*,[3] but the suffix may have been Gmc. **-azjō(n)* (cf. OS. *ahar*), in which case *ae* would result from the smoothing of the unmutated diphthong.

§ 51. Where Prim. OE. *a* by retraction before a back vowel became subject to *i*-mutation by 'double umlaut' (Campbell, § 203), inflexion, or suffix interchange (§ 68), the result is normally *ae*, *æ*: cf. *caelith* 561, *haecid* 587, Ép. *fæcilae* 407, *haecilae* 572, 740, *haecid* 660, Erf. *gedæbin* 336, *faerslaeginum* 744. Ép. *forsleginum* and Erf. *gebil* 336, *gebles* 394, *hecile* 572, *hecid* 660, *hecæli* (*-ilæ*) 740, if the *e* is original, may be suffix variants in which retraction did not occur (Campbell, § 204. 8), or forms in which Prim. OE. *æ* had been restored by second fronting (Campbell, § 193 (c)).

§ 52. The *i*-mutation of Prim. OE. *ā* < Gmc. *ai* is generally *ae*, *æ* in both texts: cf. (*raed*)*gaesran* 493 (n.), *uuraestendi* 499, *taecnaendi* 544, *firgingaett* 560, *saegesetu* 728, etc. (Ép. 27, Erf. 20). *e*, which might be the result of Kentish second fronting or of Anglian raising before palatal and dental consonants (Bülbring, § 167 a.), appears for the *i*-mutation of Prim. OE. *ā* in *blecthrustfel* 139, *fex* 430a (n.), and *blectha* 1069 (also Cp. 2123), and in Erf. *tenil* 403, *bedændræ* 539, *etrinani* 576, *unfecni* 679, *scinlecan* 681, *stegelræ* 747, *ureni* 835, *screc* 1013 (n.).[4] Erf. *urastum* 332 (also Cp. *wrastum* 645) is the historically correct form without *i*-mutation in the dat. pl. (§ 82); Erf. *aetgaru* 440 (also Cl.I *ætgare* 404/15) and *hau(u)i* 221, 473 (cf. Ld. *haue* 22/3) may be influenced by suffix variants.[5] *oe* in *oeghuuelci* 709, Erf. *oeghuuer* (Ép. †*og-*) 1061 (also Cp. 1442, 2173) beside normal *æg-*(**agi-*) is the mutation of Prim. OE. *o* in a weakly stressed form (Luick, § 121).

---

[1] Cf. OHG. *duuehila* beside Erf. *thuachl* 326 (Campbell, § 241. 1 fn. 2).

[2] If from **sæhnī* (SB, § 218. 2); but Kolkwitz, *Angl.* xvii. 406, derives it from Gmc. **sauniz*, in ablaut with Go. *siuns*.

[3] Schlutter, *Angl.* xxx (1907), 251. If so, retraction may have been caused by the following *u*, as it appears to have been by the preceding *w* in *thuachl*.

[4] Also before *w* in †*men*, *meu* 610 (**maiwiz*), but *eu* here may represent *eaw* as in *screuua*, *mundleu(u)* (§ 40): cf. Cp. *meau* 1183 and Campbell, § 273.

[5] Cf. *ætgar* Hl. F85, pl. *ategaras* Napier 2/502, and ME. *hawe* (< **hāwen* with Gmc. **-ainaz* for **-inaz*?).

§ 53. The *i*-mutation of Prim. OE. *ŏ* is uniformly *oe*: cf. *loerge* 1 (Celt. **lorgī*)[1] and Erf. †*coerim* 313, *coerin* 314 (L. *carēnum*)[2] with Prim. OE *ŏ*; *giroedru* 14, *boecae* 22, *giroefa(n)* 197, 223, *groetu* 210, etc. with Prim. OE. *ō*. *oæ* in Ép. *soærgændi* 97 shows scribal anticipation of *æ* in the following syllable. *e* appears as the mutation of Prim. OE. *ō* in Erf. *beccae* 391, *gefegnessi* 889.

§ 54. The *i*-mutation of Prim. OE. *ŭ* is uniformly *y*: cf. *biouuyrt* 20, [*h*]*ynnilaec* 62, *misbyrd* 80, *tyctendi* 85, *nyttum* 93, etc. with Prim. OE *ў*; *fyrpannae* 5, *scaldthyflas* 58, *lytisna* 200, *lytlae* 217, *thys* 494, etc. with Prim. OE. *ȳ*. It is spelt *uy* in Erf. *huymblicae* 185, *buygenas* (*-ras*) 760.[3] *e*, presumably the Kentish spelling which implies lowering and unrounding of [y] (Campbell, § 288), appears for Prim. OE. *ў* in *cendlic* 729 and for Prim. OE. *ȳ* in Erf. *aeohed* (*aet-*) 362 (n.).[4] *u* for Prim. OE. *ў* in *uurmillae* 691, Ép. *uppae* 553, Erf. *gedurstip* 81, *munit* 670 and for Prim. OE. *ȳ* in *ifaenucæ* 997, and *i* for Prim. OE. *ў* in Ép. *smigilas* 199, *cistigan* 621, *genicldae* 701, Erf. *risil* 2 (also Cp. 219), *hirnitu* 275 (cf. Cp. *hurnitu* 603), *mich* 277, *aritrid* (for *arydid*) 372, *libb* 711 may be scribal for archaic *ui* (Campbell, §§ 199, 315), which appears in Cp. *buiris* 11, *gruiit* 1619. Apparent failure of mutation in Ép. *binumini* 104, Erf. (*g*)*enumini* 100 is due to suffix interchange (§ 68), in *cunillae* 246 (L. *cunīla*), *buturfliogae* 817 (lL. *bŭtirum* with suffix interchange) to late borrowing (Pogatscher, § 262; Campbell, § 547 fn. 1).

§ 55. The *i*-mutation of Prim. OE. *æo* (Gmc. *au*) is *e* in *fleti* 605, 1075, *treulesnis* 726 (cf. Campbell, § 204. 2 fn. 3), *sceolhegi* 981, *gilebdae* 1089, Erf. *heardheui* 262, *ifeg* 392,[5] *streidæ* 899.[6]

---

[1] Cf. Schlutter, *AB* xxxv (1924), 254; *IEW* 691–2.
[2] Also Cp. 628, Cl. 384/25 beside Cp. *caerin* 709, Cl. *cyren* 385/41; Prim. OE. *o* may be due to a lL. form with pre-tonic rounding, like *popaeg* 824 < L. *papāver*.   [3] Cf. Nh. *suyndriga* Li. Mt. 9: 1, Lk. 3: 7 (twice).
[4] Also Cp. *a(e)thed* 768, *cenlic* 1534. Kt. *e* for *y* becomes common only in the tenth-century Kentish Glosses, but cf. *heregeðe* Ct. 28/9 (858) and the inverted spelling *yfter* Ct. 38/5, 13 (831); the preservation of *y* normally in ninth-century Kentish charters may be ascribed to Mercian spelling influence (cf. § 36 fn. 3). In this respect also it would seem that 'Kentish scribes advanced slowly towards the phonetic expression of their dialect' (Campbell, § 207).
[5] Cf. OHG. *ebahewi*, *ebahouwi*, re-formed on the analogy of WGmc. **hau(u)j-* 'hay', according to Kluge, *Etymologische Wörterbuch der deutschen Sprache* (Berlin, 1963), 152.   [6] If from *strēgan*, but cf. § 59. 2 fn.

i in *ciisnis* 406 (*kausi-) and Erf. *cistimbeam* 249 (§ 47) may be due to smoothing of eWS. *ĭe* after palatal *c̣* (cf. Cosijn, i. § 94). *ie* appears for Prim. OE. *īu* in Ép. *hunhieri* 983, for Prim. OE. *ĭu* from breaking in *georuuierdid* 990, Ép. *fierst* 595, *orfiermae* 933 beside alternate developments (§§ 42, 45).

§ 56. Evidence of back mutation is rare in Épinal–Erfurt. Prim. OE. *æ* appears several times as *ea*, especially after *sc̣* (§ 47 fn. 5), in *uuicingsceadan* 736, *sceaba* 853, *sceadu* 902, Ép. *bearug* 652 (Campbell, § 361 fn. 2), *hreacca* (*hn*-) 715, Erf. *sceadugeardas* 991 beside forms with *ae*, *æ*, or *a* (§ 47); *eo* in Erf. *beoso* 409 (also Cp. *beosu* 877) is presumably an archaic spelling of Prim. OE. *ǣo* (Campbell, § 276). Prim. OE. *e* appears as *eo* in *geolu* 1064 and perhaps (*he*)*olor* 573a (n.), †*oe* in Erf. *t(h)rifoedur* 1039 (cf. Cp. -*feoðor* 2052), Prim. OE. *i* as *iu* in Erf. *unliuduuac* 521 (Cp. *unliopuwac* 1079), but *e* and *i* normally remain in this position: cf. *fetor* 121, 778, *stela* 215, *gelu* 242, 432, 458, *staebplegan* 577, *helor* 607, 988, etc. (Ép. 30. Erf. 34); *earuuigga* 44, *stigu* 45, *tilgendum* 78, *bitulin* 145, *ginath* 149, etc. (Ép. 33, Erf. 30). Combinative back mutation of Prim. OE. *i* before *u* after *w* (Campbell, § 218) appears only once, in Ép. *uudubil* 430, beside *uuidubil* 449, *suicudae* 932, Ép. *uuilocread* 169, *uuilucscel* 182, *uuidubindlae* 559, *huuitquidu* 655, *wi*(*ð*)*uwindae* 1059, *uuiduuuindae* 1082, Erf. *uuituma* 324, *uuidouuindae* 348, *uuidubil* 430, *uuidubindae* 1059, 1082. Both ordinary and combinative back mutation are common in Corpus,[1] and the forms without them in Épinal–Erfurt are presumably conservative spellings in which the change is not yet expressed (Campbell, § 247).[2]

§ 57. Unlike back mutation, smoothing—the monophthongization of Prim. OE. long and short diphthongs before back consonants which was a distinguishing feature of the Anglian

---

[1] Cf. Cp. *geonath* 269, *isernfeotor* 272, *steola* 358, *wiolocread* 496, *uuduwinde* 717, *wudubil* 834, 836, *geolu* 890, 966, *uudubinde* 1116, *heolor* 1177, 2041, *huitcudu* 1287, *uuduuuinde* 2129, 2158 beside *earwicga* 240, *stigu* 242 without back mutation before *g*(*g*).

[2] The early Northumbrian texts have back mutation only in *geolu* LR 10 (MS. *goelu*). Luick, § 221 a. 1, regards *uuidu*-, *uuiloc*- as due to inflected *wida and *wilic with suffix interchange; the same principle might be applied to other forms with *wi*- (cf. Cp. *wetma* 704, *suicade* 1893), but the scarcity of ordinary back mutation in Épinal–Erfurt supports the explanation offered above.

dialects (Campbell, § 263)—is well attested in both texts, especially Erfurt:

(1) Prim. OE. *ǣo* (Gmc. *au*) appears as *ae*, *æ* in *laec* 64, *aec* 846, Ép. *garlæc* 16, *hynnilaec* 62, *herebaecon* 919, Erf. *rondbaeg* 153, *gæc* 265, *aegur* 316, *læg* 591, *ægan* 1093; as *e* in *lelodrae* 606 (n.), *lelothrae* 861, Ép. *egan* 1093, Erf. *garlec* 16, *ynnilec* 62, *gecaes* 63, *leccressae* 676, *bradelec* 895, *herebecon* 919 beside *leactrogas* 247 (also Cp. 540), *andleac* 872, *teac* (-*g*) 964, *sigbeacn* 992, Ép. *geacaes* 63, *randbeag* 153, *leag* 591, *fleah* 813, *bradaeleac* 895. Prim. OE. *ǣo* from breaking appears as *ae*, *æ* in *aex* 13, *maerh* 588, *faerh* 811, *aectath* 836, *aehrian* 840 (§ 50. 3), Ép. *naechthraebn* 673, 674, Erf. *næctægela* 26, *uaergrod* 410, *fri(s)tmaerc* 547; as *e* in *arectae* 204, *nectaegalae* 857, *brectme* 928, Erf. *mer(c)isaen* 227, *lex* 555 beside Ép. *mear(c)isern* 227, *uueargrod* 409, *fristmearc* 547, *leax* 555, *fealga* 713.

(2) Prim. OE. *ĕu* from breaking appears as *e* in *berc* 132, *elch* 233, 1001, *duerg*(-) 686, 831, *uuerci* 699, *þor(h)gifect* 738, *ferth* (-*ht*) 748, *thuerhfyri* 881, Ép. *suehoras* 1062,[1] Erf. *ceapcnext* 349, *algiuerc* 556 beside *sceol(h)egi* 981, Ép. *algiuueorc* 556, Erf. (*e*)*oritmon* 320 (§ 44. 2 fn. 5), *eola* 346a (§ 60). Prim. OE. *ēu* appears as *io* in *buturfliogae* 817, as *eo* in Erf. *theoh* 295.

(3) Prim. OE. *ĭu* by breaking before *h* is uniformly *i(i)*: cf. *bituic(h)n* 546, *dislum* 1043 (**þiuhsl-* § 72 (c)), Erf. *siid* 384 (*siuhiþ) with Prim. OE. *ĭu*; *frictrung* 10, *nihol* 799[1] with Prim. OE. *ĭu*. Prim. OE. *ĭu* in *flio*, *gitiungi* (§ 59. 3) may therefore be assumed to have been smoothed before contraction.[2]

§ 58. This medley of smoothed and unsmoothed forms might be regarded as a mixture of spellings belonging to different dialects, like those expressing retraction and second fronting of Prim. OE. *æ* before back vowels (§ 46), but the fact that the numerous unsmoothed forms in Épinal are mostly ones containing Prim. OE. *ǣo* and Prim. OE. *ǣo* and *ĕu* by breaking before *r* plus a back consonant suggests that the pattern is chronological rather than dialectal, i.e. that Anglian smoothing

---

[1] Intervocalic *h* may be only a diacritic indicating hiatus (cf. § 72 fn. 6), but a form with smoothing would still underlie it.

[2] Breaking is assumed not to have taken place before *r* plus back consonant followed by *i* or *j* in *firgingaett*, *birciae* (§ 45 fn. 3).

first affected short diphthongs immediately before *h*, which is inherently reasonable and borne out by the evidence, as far as it goes, of other early texts (cf. Campbell, §§ 223 ff.). If so, Ép. *leax* may be taken as a stray Kentish or West-Saxon form, like *fealga* with breaking before *l* plus consonant instead of retraction (§ 43. 2). Since the smoothing of Prim. OE. *ǽo* immediately before *h* is still *æ* in the Vespasian Psalter and later Anglian texts (Campbell, §§ 223–4), *arectae* may have *e* after pres. *areccan* as in the Vespasian Psalter and West-Saxon texts (Campbell, § 753. 9 (b 1)), and *nectaegalae* may have been influenced by *necti-* with *i*-mutation (§ 50. 3); *brectme* and Erf. *lex* beside Cp. *braechtme* 1916, *laex* 1155 are presumably scribal errors (cf. § 46).

§ 59. Contraction, like Anglian smoothing, is a normal feature of Épinal–Erfurt, but both texts preserve uncontracted forms and there are some ambiguous spellings:

(1) Prim. OE. *ǽ+i* is contracted to *ae* in *faedun* 797 (**fǽhidun*) beside *faehit* 785. Prim. OE. *ǽ+u* becomes *eo* in *eorisc* 795, 960 (**æohu-* with smoothing), presumably the archaic spelling of Prim. OE. *ǽo* with the second element still rounded (Campbell, § 238. 2 (a)).

(2) Prim. OE. *ě+i* is contracted to *e* in *thuelan* 1060 (§ 50. 3) beside Erf. *streidæ* 899.[1] Prim. OE. *ě+u* appears as *eo* in *huueolrad* 710 (**hweuhul-* with smoothing), Erf. *sueoras* 1062 (Ép. *suehoras*) and *sueor* 1099.

(3) Prim. OE. *ī+u* appears as *iu* in Ép. *gitiungi* 97 (**-tīuhung-* with smoothing), as *io* in Erf. *getiong*. Prim. OE. *ī+a/o* appears as *io* in *flio* 12 (**flīuhjō* with smoothing),[2] Ép. *biouuyrt* 20 (**bī-ō IEW* 116); as *ia* in *cian* 158 (**kijan IEW* 355), *friat* 666a (? **frījaþ* Campbell, § 761. 4), Erf. *scia* 299 (**skī-ō IEW* 920).

---

[1] Also Cp. *streide* 1910 beside Ép. †*stridae*. If this is the pret. of *strēgan* (**strau(u)jan* Campbell, § 120. 2), the spelling may indicate hiatus, which is also assumed on metrical grounds in *Beowulf* 2436 *morðǫrbed stred* (Sievers, *Altgermanische Metrik* (Strasbourg, 1893), § 84. 8 a. 5); but a weak pret. of *stregdan* (Campbell, § 741) is also possible, in which case *ei* would represent Prim. OE. *e*+vocalized *ġ* (§ 59. 6).

[2] An old *iz/uz*-stem according to Sievers, *PBB* ix. 232, with both strong and weak forms (TS 223–4); this is presumably the weak form, since Prim. OE. *-iz* would have been dropped after a long stressed syllable before the loss of medial *h*.

Erf. *siid* 384 (also Cp. 800) is ambiguous, since *ii* could represent *ī* (§ 39 fn. 2) or *ī-i* with hiatus after loss of medial *h* (cf. § 57. 3).

(4) Prim. OE. *ō* and a following vowel remain uncontracted in *sceptloum* 106 (d.p. of **-lōhan IEW* 676), *adoenre* 870, Ép. *scaeptloan* 489, Erf. *thoæ* 3 (Ép. *thohae*); cf. Erf. *crous* 773 (also Cp. 1486 beside Ép. *cros*), for **croas* (?).

(5) Prim. OE. *ȳ+æ* becomes *iæ*, presumably a diphthong similar to WS. *īe*, in Erf. *ciae* 240 (**kūhjæ*) beside Ép. *chyae*;[1] they remain uncontracted in Ép. *ryae* 1020 beside Erf. *[h]ryhae* and *ryhae* 1080, 1081. The apparent preference for uncontracted forms with Prim. OE. *ō* and *ȳ* suggests that hiatus persisted longer where the first vowel was rounded.

(6) Blending of Prim. OE. front vowels and vocalized *ġ* and *w* (Campbell, §§ 266–71) is indicated by the spelling in *grei* 473 (also Cp. 981), Ép. *strel* 9 (Cp. *stregl* 249 beside *strel* 1907), *bridils* 127 (also Cp. *bridels* 261 beside Erf. *brigdils*), *snel* 611, Erf. *meu* 610 (Ép. †*men*).[2] Cf. *cnioholaen* 879, *bodæi* 947 with the same development in an unstressed syllable, and the inverted spelling *i(i)g* for *ī* in *tiig* 663, *brüig* 767, and Erf. *tuigin* 138 (for **tuiign*?).

§ 60. Compensatory lengthening of a short vowel due to loss of a following *h* may be indicated by the spelling in *onettae* 712 (**anhǣtidæ*), since Épinal otherwise has only *a* in this position (§ 37), and in Ép. *steeli* 49, Erf. *ungiseem* (*-ni*) 333 (§ 50. 3 fn. 2). Other forms in which such lengthening might be assumed are *fala* 1009a (**falha*), Erf. (*e*)*oritmon* 320 (§ 44 fn. 5), *eola* 346a (**eolha*), *ifeg* 392 (§ 55 fn. 5), *sceolegi* 981 (Ép. *sceolh-*); but the vowel must have remained short in *thuerhfyri* 881 if it represents the original consonant-stem pl. **furhiz*,[3] and presumably also in *uualhmorae* 794 (cf. OS. *morha*), since there is also a strong form *moru* (BT 697) like *lufu* (Campbell, § 619. 4). The only evidence of lengthening in words where *h* followed *r* or *l* is metrical, as Campbell points out (§ 240 fn. 1), and these

---

[1] Presumably for **cyhae*; cf. Ld. *chyun* 20/3 beside *cian* 158. The etymology of *cēo* 'chough' is fully discussed by Ritter, 5–6.

[2] Perhaps also in *bred* 1023 (n.), *tin* 1024 (n.), and Erf. *streidæ* 899 (§ 59. 2 fn. 1). *gliu* 398 is ambiguous (§ 42 fn. 2), and similarly *iuu* 1005 (**iwa-*), which may represent *iow* or *iw* (cf. Campbell, § 411).

[3] Presumably with *-i* retained after original short-stem pls. like *styde* (Campbell, § 624); for other possibilities see §§ 67, 80.

words may simply have retained their traditional quantity in poetry after the root syllable was shortened by loss of *h*. Lengthening is confirmed by the spelling, however, in *steeli* and *-seeni*, where the *h* came immediately after the vowel, and by the Modern English pronunciation in *ifeg*, where *h* began the second element of a compound, as it did in *onettae*.

§ 61. Shortening of the preceding long vowel is indicated by the doubled consonant in Ép. *linnin* 1081 (Campbell, § 287),[1] and the same development might be inferred in *suggit* 455, if it is really a form of OE. *sūgan*, and perhaps in Ép. *scinneras* 952 (n.). The more extensive doubling peculiar to Erfurt in *b(o)ecc(a)e* 22, 391, 415, *gebeatten* 140, *hattendae* 206, *huitti* 254, *hydde* 329, *unbrycci* 522, *bisuiccend* 545, *atte* 599, unsupported by other evidence, may be merely a graphic peculiarity of its English exemplar (§ 24) without phonetic significance, like the similar spellings in Northumbrian texts (Campbell, § 65).[2]

§ 62. Finally, there are occasional spellings in both texts which appear to anticipate later developments in the neighbourhood of labial consonants. Prim. OE. *e* is apparently rounded after *w* in *huuananhuuoega* 1095, Erf. *uuoeg* 91 as in later Northumbrian (Campbell, § 319), and, alternatively, lowered as in the dialect of Rushworth Matthew (Campbell, § 328) in Ép. *uuaeg-* 793, *uuaega* 842, Erf. *horuaeg* 340, *uuæb* 1030. Rounding of Prim. OE. *ĭ* in the neighbourhood of *r*, *s*, and/or labial consonants as in late West-Saxon (Campbell, § 318) is indicated in *uuyr* 637, Erf. *trynsas* (*trym-*) 31, *uuylucscel* 182,[3] *cysirbeam* 237, *uuryd* 252 (also Cp. *wyrð* 612), *uuylocas* 267, *uuydumer* 347, *ry(s)cthyfil* 517, *uuydublindæ* 559, *baanryft* 1031, and perhaps Ép. *multi* 594, where *u* may represent archaic *ui* (§ 54). On the other hand, unrounding of Prim. OE. *o* in similar surroundings is indicated in Erf. *dualma* 181, *suarnadun* 198.[4] This development has not been explained; it always occurs in the neighbour-

---

[1] Cf. Cp. *fiffalde* 1484 beside Ép. *fifaldae* 768. *hynni-* 62 < L. *ūniōnem* shows a similar development after a pretonic long vowel which was shortened in late Latin (Campbell, § 542).

[2] Cf. RC *gistoddun*, etc. and the later Northumbrian doubling of intervocalic stops after short vowels (Luick, § 670). *ll* is etymological in Ép. *gillistrae* 833, however; see note. [3] Cf. Erf. *uuslucreud* 169 (§ 11).

[4] Cf. Cp. *gewarht* 567 and similar forms in later Anglian texts (Campbell, § 156).

hood of *r*, *l*, and/or labial consonants, and may therefore involve dissimilation.

Unstressed vowels

§ 63. As in other very early texts, Prim. OE. unstressed *æ* and *i* are well preserved, especially in Épinal. In unstressed prefixes Prim. OE. *i* appears uniformly in *bi-* (11 examples in each text), and Épinal has it predominantly in *gi-* (40 *i* : 13 *e*), where Erfurt has *e* slightly more often than *i* (34 *e* : 31 *i*). In *ti-* Épinal has *i* once (195), Erfurt *e* twice (343, 344). The high proportion of *e* to *i* in *gi-* compared with *bi-* may be due to stressed *bi-* (e.g. 357), or to the ablaut variant of *gi-* corresponding to OHG. *ga-* which is apparently preserved in Erf. *-gaesetu* 728.[1] Medially and finally Prim. OE. *i* resists weakening to *e* more firmly medially, Prim. OE. *æ* more firmly finally. In medial syllables and finally before consonants Épinal has *i* (excluding *i* before *n* plus consonant) 134 times against 11 *e*, and *ae*, *æ* 30 times against 16 *e*;[2] Erfurt has *i* 149 times against 14 *e*,[3] and *ae*, *æ* 16 times against 35 *e*.[4] In absolute finality (including the first elements of compounds) Épinal has *i* 82 times against 8 *e*, and *ae*, *e* 192 times against 8 *e*;[5] Erfurt has *i* 86 times against 8 *e*, and *ae*, *æ* 182 times against 40 *e*.[6] Both texts have *e* in the same forms for Prim. OE. *æ* 10 times medially, 4 times finally, and for Prim. OE. *i* 5 times medially, 6 times finally, suggesting that there were occasional *e* forms for both vowels in their common exemplar. Except in the instr. sg., where the endings of the *ō-* and *a-*declensions appear to have been used interchangeably (§ 79),

---

[1] And perhaps in Erf. *gaeadun* 76 (? OHG. *ga-*). Stressed **gæ-* underlies *geatwe* 'armour' beside *getawe* (Campbell, § 74 fn. 5).

[2] Not counting *beouua(e)s* 645, *cebær-* 1058 (§ 38), or forms with *i*-mutation (§ 65).

[3] Not counting *tuigin* 138 (§ 59. 6), (*e*)*orit-* 320 (n.), *hecæli* 740, with *æ* and *i* transposed, or *gefegnessi* 889, with *e* and *i* transposed (?).

[4] Not counting *papoeg* 824, with *o* and *a* transposed, *gesnida(e)n* 315, *assuolla(e)n* 1018, *omba(e)r* 1076, or forms with *i*-mutation (§ 65).

[5] Not counting *mera(e)* 558, *suualua(e)* 828, *cneorissa(e)* 903, *sura(e)* 1077a, or *brectme*, *cliderme* 928 (§ 79, fn. 1).

[6] Not counting *-gela(e)* 26, *lidrinna(e)* 31, *fala(e)-* 36, *sura(e)* 263, 1077a, *bismirida(e)* 534, *uiualdra(e)* 768, *bre(c)tme* 928 or *hecæli* 740, *pefegnessi* 889 (fn. 3).

there is little evidence of spelling confusion. *ae*, *æ* appears for etymological *i* medially in *sibaed* 70 beside *siuida* 428 (Gmc. **-iþo* Kluge, § 121) and Ép. *eornæsti* 945 beside Cp. *eornisti* 1845 (**-usti*);[1] *i* appears for etymological *æ* finally in Erf. *huitti* 254, *uuidirhlinienti* 537, *eduelli* 1019. *ae* also appears for Prim. OE. unstressed *e* before *r* (Campbell, § 331. 2) in *faer-* 52, Erf. 744 beside *fer-* 467, 548, 739, Ép. *obare-* 192, 194, *-ofaer-* 536 beside *ober-* 538, and Ép. *-faedaer* 1071 beside *uuaeter-* 232.[2]

§ 64. Lowering of Prim. OE. unstressed *u* to *o* is not infrequent in Épinal, while Erfurt prefers *u*. In medial syllables and finally before consonants (except *m* and *ng*) Épinal has 40 *u* against 41 *o*, Erfurt 49 *u* against 30 *o*;[3] in absolute finality (including the first elements of compounds) Épinal has 37 *u* and 12 *o*, Erfurt 40 *u* and 10 *o*.[4] Both texts have *o* in the same forms 26 times medially, 6 times finally. In the wk. acc. pl. *gisuirgion* Ép. 214 *o* could be taken to represent Prim. OE. *u* < IE. *o* before the ending **-uns* (Campbell, § 331. 6),[5] but *o* for unstressed *a* before *n* is not uncommon, especially after stressed *o* as in Erf. *sadulbogo* 283, *geboronae* 359 (also Cp. *geborone* 781), where Luick believed that rounding survived in early texts.[6]

§ 65. As in the stressed vowels, the most extensive of the Prim. OE. sound-changes is *i*-mutation:

(1) The mutation of Prim. OE. unstressed *æ* is *e* in *ambechtae* 187 (cf. Go. *andbahti*), *byrgeras* 760, *flitere* 854, *scinneras* 952, Ép. *teblere* 7, Erf. *egderi* 396 (L. *-arius* Kluge, § 60), *boret(t)it* 1092, *agnet(t)æ* 1096 (Gmc. **-atjan* Campbell, § 339). *ae*, *æ* in *brocdaettendi* 735 and Ép. *borættit, agnaettae* could be taken as an inverted spelling due to the raising of Prim. OE. unstressed *æ* (§ 63), but these forms might also be influenced by Prim. OE.

---

[1] Cf. Sievers, *Ags. Vokalismus* (Leipzig, 1900), 20: a mistake for adv. **eornistæ*, with *æ* and *i* transposed?

[2] Cf. LR *ofær* 11, RC *bismærædu* 8, FC *gibroþæra* 1. Campbell, § 369, regards *-ær* as an inverted spelling due to the change of Prim. OE. *æ* to *e*; lowering of *e* before *r* as in Go. *fadar*, etc. would be another possibility. *faer-* could be an ablaut variant with IE. *o*, like OHG. *far-* (?).

[3] Not counting *apuldro* (*-or*) 636.

[4] Not counting *scoma* 732, with *a* and *o* transposed (?).

[5] Cf. acc. pl. *spaedun* Ld. 39/12; acc. sg. *galgu* RC 2, *foldu* CH 9, *eorŏu* LR 11 (**-ŏnum*).

[6] § 323 a. 1; Campbell, § 735 (k) fn. 1, regards these spellings as scribal errors.

-hǣtan (-haitjan) as in onettae 712, which appears to have been assimilated to -ettan.[1] The diminutive suffix -icli failed to cause i-mutation in fornaeticli Ép. 178a (cf. Campbell, § 204. 6).

(2) The mutation of Prim. OE. unstressed a before nasals appears as ae, æ in Ép. staefnændra 75, soærgændi 79, risaendi 434, restaendum 443, etc. (14 examples); as e in fultemendi 74, tilgendum 78, tyctendi 85, fultemendum 95, heruuendlicae 186, etc. (20 examples).[2] Erfurt has æ only once, in bedændræ 539 (? for bædendræ). Prim. OE. ā < Gmc. ai appears as ae in Ép. sparaen 460 (Erf. -en), (a)suollaen 1018 (Erf. †-an).

(3) The mutation of Prim. OE. o is e in clibecti 166 (cf. OHG. -ohti Luick, § 302. 2).

(4) The mutation of Prim. OE. u is i in innifli 504 (cf. ON. innyfli), firgingaett 560 (cf. Go. fairguni), haegtis 913 (cf. OHG. hagazussa), Erf. hirnitu 275 (cf. OS. hornut)[3] beside uuellyrgae 969 with y apparently preserved by the following r.[4]

§ 66. Syncope of Prim. OE. i and u before l and r after a short accented syllable (Campbell, § 388) has already taken place after certain consonants.[5] Prim. OE. i is lost after b in teblere 7, teblith 178, scybla 627 (cf. OHG. scubil), Ép. teblae 6 (cf. Erf. tebil), Erf. gebles 394 (cf. gebil 336), lebrae 894 (cf. OHG. leber), after g in sneglas 217 (cf. OS. snegil), Ép. eglae 470 (cf. OHG. ahil) beside smigilas 199 (Cp. smyglas 608), sigiras 568 (Cp. si(g)ras 1241), Erf. egilae 470; it remains uniformly after c in fæcilae 407, haecilae 572, 740, gecilae 954, stricilum 994, after ð in suedilas 506. Prim. OE. u is lost after g in higrae 156, 808, but remains after other consonants in fibulae 3a, gaebuli 115, bitulin (-um) 145, sceroro 401, uuesulae 650, Ép. suehoras 1062. Syncope is extended to uninflected forms (where the l or r becomes syllabic) in sne(g)l 611 (§ 59. 6), Ép. lerb 894 (Cp. lebr

---

[1] Campbell, § 455, explains tt in onettan, etc. as a repetition of WGmc. gemination after Prim. OE. shortening, which seems unnecessary.

[2] Including uu(e)send 160 (also Cp. weosend 337) beside Erf. uuesand (cf. Go. Visandus AEW 391), where -end may be after nouns of agency like bisuicend.

[3] And perhaps in byris 891, 907 (*burusjō Ritter, 121), cneorissa 903 (*-rȳsi < *runsiz Kluge, PBB viii (1882), 528), but comparative evidence is lacking.

[4] Cf. suchtyrga Cl.I 404/8 (Cp. suhterga 915).

[5] For the chronology of this process see H. Weyhe, PBB xxx (1905), 87 ff. It may also have occurred between l hnd r in ellaen 893 (§ 50. 2).

1804), Erf. *g[r]imrodr* 345a (also Cp. D364), and perhaps in Ép. *spaldr* 54 (n.).[1] Before other consonants after a short accented syllable there is syncope of Prim. OE. *i* in *trimsas* 31 (L. *tremissis*) beside Ép. *lynisas* 8 (also Cp. 257), *suilcae* 98 (**swilīk*-SB, § 342 a. 3), *sigdi* 430 (cf. MLG. *segede*), *-huu(u)elci* 709, 842 (**-hwalīk*- SB, § 342 a. 2), *lectha* 890 (Gmc. **-ipō(n)* Kluge, § 118), *blegnae* 1094 (**blajinō(n) IEW* 156), Erf. *egdae* 395, *egderi* 396 (cf. OHG. *egida, -are*),[2] extended to uninflected forms in *milsc* 638 (**-iska-* Kluge, § 210), Erf. *regn-* 612 (Ép. *regen-*); Prim. OE. *u* remains undisturbed, e.g. in *obust* 757, *helustras* 867, *helostr* 901 beside Cp. *obst* 1546, *heolstras* 1723, *heolstr* 1838. Prim. OE. *ī* in final position is lost in composition after a long accented syllable in *blecthrustfel* 139 (cf. Cp. *bleci* 2117), Prim. OE. *ī* after a short accented syllable in Ép. *sigbeacn* 992 (Cp. *sigebecn* 2043).

§ 67. Besides original Prim. OE. medial *i* and *u* there are a number of secondary vowels developed before syllabic consonants (Campbell, § 363). Secondary *i* appears after an accented syllable containing a front vowel in *segil-* 111 (cf. ON. *segl*), *ledir-* 155 (cf. ON. *leðr*), *uuidir-* 537 (cf. Go. *wiþra*), *-þistil* 601 (cf. OS. *thisla*), Ép. *(h)aesil* 50, 236 (cf. ON. *hasl*), *hrisil* 851 (cf. ON. *hrīsla*), Erf. *bebir* 272 (Gmc. **beƀru- IEW* 136), *thistil* 266, 271, *fingir-* 346 (cf. Go. *figgrs*), and in Erf. *genyccilde* 701, where *l* became syllabic after loss of medial *i* (cf. Campbell, § 364); *e* in *teter* 128 (Gmc. **tetru- IEW* 209), *palester* 225 (n.), Erf. *caeber-* 1058 (n.). Secondary *u* appears after an accented syllable containing a back vowel in *mapuldur* 33 (Gmc. **-ulðr-* Kluge, § 94(b)), Ép. *fostur-* 108 (cf. ON. *fōstr*), *apuldur* 636 (Gmc. **-ulðr-* Kluge, § 94 (b)), *sculdur* 963 (Gmc. **skulðrō IEW* 925), Erf. *o[c]tur* 585 (cf. ON. *otr*), and perhaps *spaldur* 54 (n.); *o* in *-b(a)econ* 919 (Gmc. **baukna- IEW* 105), Ép. *clustor-* 220 (L. *claustrum*), *thothor* 787, *otor* 914, *rothor* 986 (Gmc. **-þra-* Kluge, § 93), and Erf. *logdor* 268 (n.).[3] More often the syllabic consonant remains, especially in Erfurt: cf. *thegn* 101, *atr* 141,

---

[1] Such forms appear to have given rise to an inverted spelling with *r* for a medial vowel plus *r* in *aehrian* 840 (§ 50. 3). Cf. *lauuercae* 1012 and Erf. *clusterlocae* 220 with *er* for syllabic *r* medially before a consonant (§ 67 fn. 3).

[2] Probably also in Erf. †*plaster* 225, Cp. *palstr* 534, 622 beside Ép. *palester*, but its etymology is uncertain; see note.

[3] *er* after a back vowel in *lauuercae* 1012 (**laiw(a)rikōn*, whence Cp.

cefr 150, *bebr* 399, *libr*(-) 405, 1057, *riftr* 430 (*h*)*ofr* 459, 1046, *apuldr* 638, *scalfr* 647, *tetr* 765, 791, -*aepl* 830, *helostr* 901, -*beacn* 992, -*adl* 999, (-)*scofl* 1022, 1065, *cort*(*h*)*r* 1074, Ép. *tetr* 502, *otr* 585, *scalfr* 662, *genicldae* 701, Erf. *haesl* 50, 236, *hrægl* 84, *hraebn* 285, *uuefl* 300, *thuachl* 326, *fothr* 378, *elothr* 386, *segn* (Ép. *seng*) 567, †*thorr* 787 (Cp. *thothr* 1584), *hrisl* 851, *otr* 914, *ro*(*t*)*hr* 986. Luick, § 318, explains the forms without secondary vowels as analogical, due to inflected cases in which the consonant was not syllabic (e.g. Ép. *hraecli*), but they might also be regarded as archaic spellings in an early text; in any case, the distribution of forms with and without secondary vowels in later OE. suggests that their development was not a uniform one. The secondary vowel which developed occasionally between *r* and *h* in accented syllables (Campbell, § 360) appears in Erf. -[*h*]*uyrihta* 996 and perhaps in -*fyri* 881 (*-*fyrih* Campbell, § 628. 1). A similar development appears to have taken place in *cocunung* 841 (cf. *cōcnian*) and perhaps in Erf. -*doccuna* 346 (§ 81). *ae*, *e* appear as the secondary connecting vowel of a compound (Campbell, § 367) in *hraebrebletae* 124, (*h*)*laepaeuincæ* 264, *duergaedost*(*l*)*ae* 831, *gundaesuelgiae* 976, *uuandaeuuiorpae* 1045, and Ép. *hreadaemus* 1098.[1]

§ 68. Interchange of Prim. OE. *æ*, *i*, and *u* medially ('suffix ablaut') is indicated by etymological or phonological considerations in *teblae* 6, *tebel*- 172,[2] *alaer* 35, *al*[*t*]*er*- 46 (but cf. § 67 fn. 3), *cladær*- 116 (§ 46), *falaed* 129, 959 (cf. Cp. *falud* 310), *fæcilae* 407 (§ 51), *afigaen* 414 (n.), *cesol* 457 (n.), 1054, *aedilra*

lauricae 2026, etc., with syncope of medial *i*?) and Erf. *cluster*- 220 may be an inverted spelling for syllabic *r*. *e* must also be a secondary vowel in Ép. *alterholt* 46 if *t* represents a genuine phonetic development between *l* and *r* (§ 75) after syncope of the original vowel of Gmc. **aluz*- (*IEW* 302).

[1] Medial *a* in Erf. *hreadamus* and *hreathamus* 978 (both texts beside Cp. *hraede*- 1924) is presumably a mistake, since later OE. forms of the word have *e* (BT 557). The medial vowels of *n*(*e*)*ctigalae*, *næctægela*(*e*) 26, *fulaetrea* Ép. 36 (Erf. †*fala*-), *uuodaeuuiostlae*, *uuodeuuisle* 248, †*poedibergæ* Erf. 388, *egisigrima* 569, *nectigalae*, *na*(*e*)*cthegelae* 673, *nectae*-, *nec*(*t*)*eg*(*a*)*le* 857, *bredipannae*, *breitibannæ* 885, *bradaeleac*, *bradelec* 895 may represent old inflexional endings (§§ 77, 78, 87 fn. 1).

[2] Hence *teblere* 7, *teblith* 178. Consistent *e* in Épinal–Erfurt and Cp. *tebl*(-) 110, 349, *teblere* 111, *tebleth* 497, Ld. *tebl* 45/25, *teblheri* 45/24 suggests that their source was a form of L. *tabula* with suffix interchange, while later OE. *tæfl*, *tæflere*, *tæfl*(*i*)*an* represent lL. **tav'la* (Pogatcher, § 261); but cf. § 38. *tabule* 'tablet, board' (BT 966) is a still later, literary borrowing.

479 (cf. OS. *aðali*), *anslegaengrae* 535 (*-slægin-*), *haecid* 587 (§ 51), *butur-* 817 (§ 54), *tasol* 998 (n.), *sin(h)uurbul* 1047 (§ 45), Ép. *binumini* 104 (§ 54), *uu(e)send* 160 (§ 65. 2 fn. 2), *haecilae* 572, 740 (§ 51), *haecid* 660, *ambaer* 923, 1076 (L. *amphora*),[1] Erf. (*g*)*enumini* 100, *cistimbeam* 249 (n.), *gabelrend* 293 (OIr. *gabol-*), *gedæbin* 336 (§ 51), *elothr* 386 (n.), *uulating* 667 (§ 46), *faerslaeginum* 744 (§ 51).[2] Suffix interchange of the type common in the Vespasian Psalter and later texts, by which *e* was substituted for a back vowel in medial syllables before another back vowel (Campbell, § 385), is found only in *fultemendi* 74, *fultemendum* 95 < **fultum-* with *e* for *u* extended from forms like *fultemode*, the tendency presumably being stronger before a medial syllable with secondary stress (so Bülbring, § 417 a.).

Consonants

§ 69. The Prim. OE. labial spirants *f* and *b̄*, which fell together when the former was voiced medially between voiced sounds and the latter was unvoiced in final position (Campbell, §§ 444, 446), are still normally distinguished as *f* and *b* in both texts, as Sievers pointed out:[3] cf. *uuf* 142, 161 (OHG. *uvo*), *cefr* 150 (OHG. *kevar*), *uulfes-* 183 (OHG. *wolf*), *giroefa(n)* 197, 223 (cf. OHG. *grāvo*), *unnifli* 504 (OHG. *innuovili*), *raefsed* 526 (OHG. *refsan*), (*h*)*ofr* 1046 (OHG. *hovar*), Ép. *hofr* 459 (Erf. †*hosr*), *fifaldae* 768 (OHG. *fifaltra*), *waeffsas* 1071 (OHG. *wafsa*) with Prim. OE. *f*[4] beside *fibulae* 3a (L. *fibula*), *teblere* 7 (cf. L. *tabula*), *sceabas* 30, 468 (OHG. *skoub*), *halbae* 51 (OHG. *halb*), *sibaed* 70 (cf. OHG. *sib*), *gaebuli* 115 (lL. *gabulum*), *h[r]aebre-* 124 (cf. Ger. dial. *Haberling*), *staeb-* 136, 577 (OHG. *stab*), etc. with Prim. OE. *b̄*.[5] *f* represents Prim. OE. *b̄* in *-thyfil* 517 (cf. L. *tūber*), *-ofaer-* 536 (OHG. *obar*), *clofae* 653 (cf. OHG. *klobo*), *sifun-* 762 (OHG. *sibun*), *stefad* 837 (OHG. *stabēn*), Ép. *-thyflas* 58, *nafo-* 1010 (OHG. *nabu-*), Erf. *tefil* 6, *faerscrifen* 52 (L.

---

[1] Associated by 'popular etymology' with OE. *beran*? Erf. *ember* 923 might represent a Prim. OE. **ambir-* with suffix interchange, but cf. *embrin*.

[2] And perhaps *mettocas* 565, 586, Ép. 878 (§ 46), *ellaen* 893 (§ 50. 2). For interchange of *a* and *u/o* in the preterite of Class II weak verbs see § 86.

[3] *PBB* xi (1885), 542 ff. Gmc. *f* and *b̄* are distinguished as *v* (medial)/*f* (final) and *b* in OHG., as *f* and *b* (medially) in Gothic.

[4] Also *hrof-* 609, 996 if < IE. **krăpo-* (*IEW* 616).

[5] *u* represents Prim. OE. *b̄* in *siuida* 428, Prim. OE. *f* in Erf. *uiualdra* 768.

tabula, scribere), *haf(a)ern* 258, 684 (cf. OHG. *hab*), *ifeg* 392 (OHG. *ebah*), *clife* 613 (OHG. *klībe*), *sinuulfur* (*-uurful*) 1047 (OHG. *sinawerbal*).[1] *b* represents Prim. OE. *f* in *gloob* 631,[2] Ép. *raebsid* 523. Unvoicing of Prim. OE. *b* before *n* may be indicated by *f* in *staefnændra* 75 (cf. OHG. *stab*), Ép. *hraefnaes-* 1084, Erf. *hræfnæs-* 848 (OHG. *hraban*),[3] and similarly before *l* in (*-*)*scofl* 1022, 1065, Erf. *uuefl* 300.[4] It is unlikely that this distinction between Prim. OE. *f* and *b* was still one between a voiceless and voiced spirant, as Sievers originally assumed (*PBB* ix. 545), since Prim. OE. *f* appears to have been voiced medially in forms like *getwǣfde, oferhrēfde* before the loss of medial *i* (Luick, § 639 a. 4); Sievers's later view, that the distinction was between a bilabial (*b*) and a labio-dental (*f*), which was overcome when Prim. OE. *b* also became a labio-dental early in the literary period (SB, § 192 a. 5), is phonetically reasonable, though incapable of positive proof. Prim. OE. *f* becomes *p* before *s* by dissimilation in *araepsid* 511, Erf. *repsit* 523, *u(u)aeps* 255, 1071.

§ 70. The Prim. OE. dental spirant *þ*, which was voiced medially between voiced sounds and then became *d* before *l* after a long vowel by dissimilation in West-Saxon (Campbell, § 422) appears as *d* in *-adl* 999 (Cp. *-ald* 2001), Erf. *nedlæ* 796, as *ð* in Ép. *naeðlae*. Prim. OE. *þ* is lost after a short vowel before *l* in *obaerstaelendi* 192, *-staelid* 194 beside *maethlae, medlæ* 549; the alternate developments to *tl* and *ld* (Campbell, §§ 419, 425) are not found in Épinal–Erfurt.[5] Prim. OE. *þ* is preserved finally after *l* in *spilth* 755, Erf. *-halth* 694 beside *tohald* 96, *feld-* 131 after the inflected forms where *lð* became *ld* (Campbell,

---

[1] And in *scalfr* 647, Ép. 662 if from Gmc. **skarbar-* (cf. OHG. *scarba*) by dissimilation (Suolahti, 394).

[2] If <**gilōf-*; cf. Go. *lōfa* 'palm' (Holthausen, *AB* xxxii (1921), 61).

[3] Sievers, *PBB* ix. 544. If so, it was presumably an alternative to the change of *bn* to *mn* in *hremn*, etc., which also took place before bilabial *b* became labio-dental (H. Flasdieck, *Angl.* lxix (1950), 165 ff.). But *f* may represent Gmc. *b* here as in *riscthyfil*, etc.

[4] Cf. OHG. *skūfla* beside *skūbla* < IE. **skeubh-* (Weyhe, *PBB* xxx. 109 fn. 1), OHG. *weval* beside *weban* < IE. **webh-*. This development presumably took place when *b* was pronounced final in its own syllable: **skub-lō, *web-lō*.

[5] Erf. *meldadum* (*-n*) 342 beside *maethlae, mæðelian* is an apparent exception, but here *ld* for *þl* (by metathesis?) is common-WGmc.: cf. OFris. *meldia*, OS./OHG. *meldōn*. If *spald(u)r* 54 is from IL. *aspaltrus* (see note), *ld* may be an analogical development.

§ 414). Conversely, *þ* is apparently extended to the medial position in Ép. *halði* 754 (n.), *ohaelði* 838 after **halð*, but Campbell regards these as mixed spellings due to alternate forms with -*lþ* and -*ld*. The distinction between *d* and *ð/th* may be merely graphic, at least in some cases, however, since *d* is often written for Prim. OE. *ð* (medially) and *þ* (finally) in both texts, e.g. *giroedro* 14, *lidrinae* 31, *sibaed* 70, *staeblidrae* 136. *t* for Prim. OE. *ð* medially in Ép. *faetmaendi* 939 (Erf. *faed-*, Cp. *faeðmendi* 1862) and *cortr* 1074 (Erf. *cordr*, Cp. *corthr* 2009), and for Prim. OE. *þ* finally in *aldot* 57, Ép. *þoot* (w-) 444, -*halt* 694, *earbet-* 619 (also Cp. 1320) may be a graph for *th* borrowed from Irish, where *t*, *þ*, and *c* were also used for the corresponding spirants (Thurneysen, § 28); but *t* for -*þ* in the 3rd sg. pres. indic. in *faehit* 785, *scripit* 906, *stridit* 1086, *boraettit* 1092, Ép. *siftit* 213, *feormat* 402, *suggit* 455, *friat* 666a, *tychtit* 936, Erf. *onhrisit* 520, *gifremit* 725[1] is found often enough in later texts to be considered a genuine phonological variant.[2]

§ 71. Palatalization of Prim. OE. back consonants before and after front vowels and before *j* (Campbell, §§ 427–9) is indicated by *i* for Prim. OE. *g* initially in *iesca* 958, Erf. *iaces* 263 (§ 40) and finally in *grei* 473, *bodæi* 947;[3] by *ci*, *gi* medially in *gimaengiung[i]ae* 203, *birciae* 792, Ép. *hringiae* 410, *cistigian* 621, *mengio* 659,[4] *gundaesuelgiae* 976, Erf. *arectio* (-*ccio*) 396a; by *ce*, *ge* medially in *leceas* 746, *byrgea* 776, 921, Ép. *scinlaecean* 681. Assibilation of IL. *c* before *e* (Pogatcher, § 347) is indicated by *z* (phonetically [ts] Campbell, § 53) in Ép. *merze* 657a (L. *mercem*), by *d(i)s* (?) in *r(a)edisnae* 123 (n.). Palatal *ġ* was lost before *d*, *l*, *n* in -*holaen* 879 (also Cp. -*holen* 1759), Ép. *strel* 9 (L. *strāgulum*), *bridils* 127, *snel* 611,[5] with lengthening of the preceding vowel if short (Campbell, §§ 243–5).

§ 72. Prim. OE. *h* is lost initially in *risaendi* 434 (also Cp. *risende* 879), *ofr* 1046, -*uurbul* 1047, Ép. *aesil* 50, Erf. *raen* 400.[6]

---

[1] Also Cp. *suggit* 862, *feormat* 899, *friat* M350, *faehit* 1582, *stridit* 2078, etc. (22 examples). Cf. pl. (?) *frangat* 685a (n.), Cp. N34.

[2] Possibly by assimilation to a preceding *i* under reduced stress; cf. lNh. -*s* for -*þ* in the 3rd sg. and pl., regarded as a sound-change by A. C. S. Ross, *JEGP* xxxiii (1934), 68–73.

[3] Also perhaps medially in Erf. *streidæ* 899 (§ 59. 2 fn. 1).

[4] Unless -*i*- represents the Class II wk. suffix; see note.

[5] And in *bred* 1023, *tin* 1024, if from **bræ(g)d* and L. *tignum*; see notes.

[6] Initial *h* was added in the margin in Ép. *hleor* 438, *hrooc* 469, *haecid* 587,

and initially in the second elements of compounds in *feld(h)uuop*
131 (n.), *uuodae(h)uistlae* 248 (also Cp. *wodewistle* 463), Ép.
sceld(h)reda 997, Erf. *holt(h)ana* 41, *ifeg* 392 (§ 55 fn. 5).
Medially, where it was normally lost between voiced sounds
(Campbell, § 461), Prim. OE. *h* is preserved: (*a*) between vowels
in *crocha* 171, *scocha* 579, *faehit* 785, *nihol* 799, *aehrian* 840
(§ 66 fn. 1), *uulohum* 1066, *ryhae* 1080, 1081, Ép. *thohae* 3,
scyhend 654, *suehoras* 1062, Erf. [*h*]*ryhae* 1020;[1] (*b*) between a
vowel and a syllabic consonant in *bituic(h)n* 546, Erf. *thuachl*
326;[2] (*c*) between a voiced consonant and a vowel in *ebhatis*
(-*um*) 854, *furhum* 884, Ép. *sceolhegi* 981. *hs* becomes *ks* in *leax*
555 and perhaps *fex* 430a (n.), and in Erf. *dixlum* 1043 (so Cp.
2007) after uninflected *pīhsl with vocalic *l*[3] beside Ép. *dislum*
with WGmc. loss of *h* before *sl*- (Campbell, § 417).

§ 73. Prim. OE. *w* is lost medially before *i* (Campbell, § 406)
in the preterites *bisceredae* 73 (§ 45),[4] *bismiridae* 534 (§ 50),
and perhaps Erf. *streidæ* 899 (§ 59. 2 fn. 1), and in *sae*- 728
(*saiwiz) beside Erf. *meu* 610 (*maiwiz); also finally after *ī*
(Campbell, § 411) in *tiig* 663, *briig* 767, *sli* 1015 beside *iuu* 1005
(§ 59. 6 fn. 2) with *w* restored from the inflected forms. The *w*
lost medially before *u* in WGmc. (Campbell, § 405) is restored
in *clauuo* 29, *thrauu* 53, *asuundnan* 1044, Erf. *searuum* 278,
mun(d)leuu 1055 beside *trea*-, *treu*- 36 (§ 41), *resung* 190 (*ræsw-),
treu- 726 (*trēowu), Erf. *asundum* (-*n*) 341 (also Cp. 683).

§ 74. Unvoicing of final consonants, including those final in
the first elements of compounds, is indicated in the following:
(with Prim. OE. *b*) Erf. *lypbcorn* 279; (with Prim. OE. *d*) Ép.
deatlicostan 439, Erf. *aenit* 17, *gefetatnae* 105, (*e*)*oritmon* 320 (n.),
gisalbot 325, *fertd* 373, (*a*)*repsit* 511, 523, *refset* 526 (also Cp.

hrof 609, *hraed* 742. Weakening of Prim. OE. *h* is also indicated by the
'inorganic' *h* in Ép. *hynnilaec* 62, *haam* 177, *hsniuuith* 669, *hunhieri* 983, Erf.
horuaeg 340 (also Cp. *horweg* 651, etc.), and perhaps in *hu(a)et* 604 (n.); in
Ép. *gihiodum* 76 it is apparently a diacritic to show hiatus, used incorrectly in
Erf. *ginehord* 276 (n.), *geholu* 1064.

[1] Also Cp. *croha* 461, *faehit* 1582, *nihold* 1659, Ld. *rihum* 42/2, *scyhend*
47/35. For Ép. *chyae* 240 (*cyhae?) see § 59. 5 fn. 1.
[2] Cf. Cp. *ðuehl* 641 beside *þweal* Cl.I 384/33, Hl. D128, and *ðuahles* Li.
Jn. 12: 3. Campbell, § 242, supposes doubling before *l* to account for these
forms.   [3] Sievers, *PBB* ix. 227.
[4] Cf. *bescerwe* Kentish Psalm 98 and *ealu*-, *meoduscerwen*; for the etymology see Hoops, 97–8, and C. L. Wrenn, *Beowulf* (London, 1953), 243–4.

raefsit 1084, 1087), *gigremit* 515, *hueolraat* 710, *gigarauuit* 730, *ensuebitum* 942, *assuant* 1036, *afulat* 1044;[1] (with Prim. OE. *g*, *gg*) *teac(h)* 964,[2] Erf. *sech* 251, *mich* 277. Unvoicing of final *g* is also attested by the 'inverted' spelling of Prim. OE. *h* as *g* in (-)*faag* 61, 798, 924, 984 and *gh* in Ép. *slaghthorn* 957.[3] Failure to un-voice medial *d* after *sċ* in *gigiscdae* 693 (also Ld. 47/26 beside Cp. *gigiscte* 1447) is presumably due to analogy with other weak preterites.[4]

§ 75. Secondary *b* and *d*, *t*, which developed between a hom-organic consonant and *l* (cf. Campbell, § 478) appear in *hymblicae* 185 (Cp. *hymlice* 462), *cendlic* 729 (Cp. *cenlic* 1534), Ép. *uuodae-uistlae* 248 (also Cp. -*wistle* 463 beside Erf. -*uuislae*), *geormantl(e)ab* 656 (Br. *geormenleaf* 301/27), Erf. *morgendlic* 729; *t* also appears to have developed after *h* in Erf. *tochtlicae* 1063. Ép. *alterholt* 46 may show the same development before *r* (cf. ModE. *alder*), but *d* outside the stress in Erf. *adoændrae* 870 is probably due to confusion with the present participle.

§ 76. Full metathesis, by which a consonant or consonants change position in relation to an adjacent vowel (Campbell, § 459), appears in *cisir-* 237 (also Cp. 445 beside Cl.II *ciris-* 269/18), -(*a*)*ern* 684, 1040 (§ 43. 1 fn. 3), *elonae* 697 (L. *inula*), Ép. *spyrng* 175, Erf. -*aern* 258, *ŏroþ* 307 (cf. OS. *thorp*), -*blindæ* 559, -*thron* 880, *brod-* 997 (Cp. *bord-* 1999), -*frech(t)* 1027, -*uulfur* 1047 beside *hraen* 400 (later OE. *hærn*). Pairs of consonants are reversed in *bridils* 127 (Gmc. *-*isla*- Kluge, § 98), -*thrustfel* 139 (cf. Go. *þrutsfill*), *gyrdils* 573, Ép. *stegn* 207, *seng* 567,[5]

---

[1] Some of the Erf. examples may be influenced by OHG., e.g. *gigarauuit*, *gisalbot*, but the wk. pret. part. in -*t* is also a feature of Li. (Campbell, § 450); cf. *geendat* Lk. 22: 22, etc., *gemoetet* Lk. 17: 18, etc., *geset(t)et* Mk. 15: 47, Lk. 13: 6, etc.

[2] For the spelling cf. § 70. The same development appears to have taken place medially in Ép. *brocdaettendi* 735, where Prim. OE. *g* was final in its own syllable (so Campbell, § 446 fn. 2), and hence *c* for *g* in Ép. *hraecli* 84; but *c* in some of these forms may be a mistake for majuscule *G* as in Erf. *leactrocas* 247 (Ép. -*troGas*).

[3] Cf. Erf. *ægrihan* 840 (? *ǣghr-). The 'compromise' spellings *þb*, *td*, *gh* may arise from corrections like that in Ép. 1010 (MS. *nabfogar*), which were misunderstood by the copyist: cf. MS. *feṙtd*.

[4] Cf. Cp. *ræfsde* 1082 and lWS. *adwescdon*, *hyspdun* (Sievers, *PBB* ix. 291). In all these cases, however, the analogy may be only a matter of spelling.

[5] For the phonological significance of *ng* for *gn* and *nc* for *cn* in *beanc* see Campbell, § 400 fn. 4; *stegn* apparently reverses the process.

lerb 894, Erf. *merix* 302 (Cp. *mersc* 394), *moleng* 477b (also Cp. *moling* 953),[1] *frots* 485, *gyrdils-* 582, *beanc* 992,[1] *scolf* 1022 beside *innifli* 504 (also Cp. 1059 beside Cl.II *inilfe* 476/12, etc.),*uuorsm* 777 (later OE. *worms*), Ép. *gyrdisl-* 582.

Inflexions

§ 77. The etymological nom. sg. of the masc./neut. *ja*-stems in which *-i* was preceded by a single consonant (Campbell, § 579. 3) is preserved in *sigdi* 430 (**sigiŏi*, § 68), *durhere* 925, *-heri* 1053, and Ép. *merici* 24. Similarly, the original nom. sg. of the fem. *jō*-nouns may be preserved in the composition form *egisi-* 569 if it represents a *jō*-stem like *byris* 891, 907 (cf. OHG. *bursa*); *aelbitu* 718 and Erf. *hirnitu* 275 already show analogical *-u* from the pure *ō*-stems, which has also been extended to the short-stemmed fem. *i*-nouns in *fremu* 135, and to the short-stemmed fem. consonant nouns in *hrutu* (*hn-*) 15, *hnitu* 590, *eo-* 795, 960 (**æhu*, § 59. 1) beside the composition form *hnut-* 671. *aetgaeru* 440 (n.) may represent an alternative development of the long-stemmed nom. sg. fem. **-ijō* (Dahl, 148), also seen in the adj. *-laestu* Erf. 321. *dil* 21 may represent an original *ja*-decl. nom. sg. (cf. OS. *dilli*) beside Cp. *dili* 159, Cl.I *dile* 349/25 with *-i* after the short *i*-stems (Dahl, 85), and similarly Erf. *ryg* 918 beside Ep. *rygi*, Cp. *ryge* 1861. The single consonant of the nom. sg. is extended analogically to the oblique cases of the fem. *jō*-decl. in acc. pl. *cebisae* Ép. 745 (also Cp. *cebise* 1540).[2]

§ 78. The original gen. sg. of the masc./neut. *i*-nouns < IE. **-isō* (Dahl, 161) survives in the compound *lytisna* 200.[3] G. s. f. *-i* after a long consonant-stem in Ép. *n(e)cti-* 26, 673 is presumably borrowed from the *i*-decl., and *-ae*, *-æ* in Ép. *nectae-* 857, Erf. *næctæ-* 26 from the *ō*-decl. (Campbell, § 628. 3 fn. 2). The gen. sg. suffix of the *es/os*-nouns is preserved in Ép. *aeger-* 429 (Campbell, § 635).

§ 79. The instr. sg. of the fem. *ō*-decl. is *-i* in *-sibbi* 109, Ép.

---

[1] See note 5, p. lxxxiv.
[2] Perhaps also in instr. sg. *cliderme* (*-ine*?) Ép. 928 beside Erf. *clidrinnae*; Dahl, 152–3, regards **-innjō* (Kluge, § 150) here as a secondary development from Gmc. **-iniz* (cf. § 61), but his evidence is weak. Later OE. *cefes* has the single cons. regularly in inflected forms (TS 123), due to the loss of secondary stress (Campbell, § 457).
[3] Cf. *folcuuinis OET*, Ct. 8/5 (dated 770), *Eadwinis* OE. Bede 144/12, etc.

gitiungi 97 beside historical *-ae, -æ* in 72, 203, 524, 527, 532, 539(n.), 696, 796, 864, 871, 1035, and conversely the instr. sg. of the masc./neut. *a*-decl. is *-ae* in *ambechtae* 187, *-locae* 220, and the adjectives *geregnodae, -radnodae* 618, *berændae* 790, Erf. *geboronae* 359, *sumae* 731 (Ép. *-e*) beside historical *-i* in 83, 84, 85, 100, 102, 104, 115, 374, 375, 575, 699, 709, 769, 842, 845, 869, 931, 944, 1093.[1] Since final *-ae, -æ,* and *-i* are carefully distinguished elsewhere in both texts (§ 63), the fem. *-i* endings are presumably borrowed from the *a*-decl. (so Dahl, 139–40), where the instr. apears to have fallen together with loc. *-æ* < IE. **-oi*:[2] cf. loc. *geri* 494 beside *maethlae* 549, *gliuuae* 550, *threatae* Erf. 369. Similarly, the *i*-decl. dat./instr. sg. masc. is *-ae*, presumably after the *a*-decl., in *suicae* 692 (n.), *faengae* 727 beside *daeli* 731.

§ 80. There is also confusion between the historically correct forms of the nom. and acc. pl. of the fem. *ō*-decl., *-a* (Gmc. **-ōʒ* as in early West-Saxon (Campbell, § 586)) and *-ae, -e* (Gmc. **-ōns*): cf. acc. *-ae, -e* in *halbae, -e* 51, *sandae* 188, *haetendae* 206 (?), *raedinnae* 212, *gitreeudae* 436, *tyctinnae* 516, *burgrunae* 761, Ép. *cebisae* 745 beside nom. *-ae, -e* in *eordrestae* 219, *nabae* 625, Erf. *felge* 292 (Cp. *faelge* 390), acc. *-a* in Ép. *fealga* 713 (also Cl.I 463/20), Erf. *anstiga* 1042 (n.); acc. pl. *-ae* also appears in *orfiermae* 933, originally of the *īn*-decl. (Campbell, § 589. 7 fn. 3). The casus indefinitus is *-a* in *siuida* 428,[3] *-ae, -e* in *redisnae* 123, *githuornae, -e* 605, *quicae, -e* 1088, Ép. *gifoegnissae* 884 (Erf. †*-essi*), Erf. *lebrae* 894 (n.). The original nom./acc. pl. of the fem. *i*-decl. survives in *fleti* 605 (n.), Ép. 1075 beside *-ae* from the *ō*-decl. in nom. *uuyrdae* 764 and casus indefinitus *loergae* Erf. 1 (also Cp. *laergae* 143), and it may have been transferred to the long consonant-stem sin *thuerhfyri* 881 (cf. g. s. *necti-*, etc., § 78). Ép. *gesuirgion* 214 may preserve the original suffix of the *ōn*-stem acc. pl. (WGmc. **-ununs*), but cf. § 64.

---

[1] Instr. *-e* is ambiguous in *brechtme* 928 (also Cp. *braechtme* 1916), Ép. *cliderme* 928 (n.). For *eornæsti* 945 see §63 and fn. 1 (p. lxxvi).

[2] H. Hirt, *Handbuch des Urgermanischen* (Heidelberg, 1932), ii. 36. The instr. sg. fem. also appears as *-i* in *rodi* RC 11, *romæcæstri* FC 2; the instr. sg. masc./neut. as *-æ* in *blodæ* RC 8, *plægsceldæ* LG 11.

[3] Campbell, § 589. 6 fn. 1, regards *siuida* (also Voss. 38) as an error for Cp. *sifiðan* 940, but cf. *ða siofoþa* BT 871; it is presumably a heteroclitic formation with Gmc. **-iþō* (Kluge, § 122) the sg. of which is represented by *sibaed* (§ 63).

§ 81. The gen. pl. *-una* in Erf. *fingirdoccuna* 346 may represent the original null-grade of the inflexional suffix (Campbell, § 617) preceded by a secondary vowel (§ 67), unless medial *u* is a scribal error for the *a* which appears in Cp. *-doccana* 687, Voss. *-toc(c)ana* 22.

§ 82. The dat. pl. of the *i*-decl. adj. *urastum* Erf. 332 without *i*-mutation (also Cp. *wrastum* 645) can be explained by early substitution of the *a/ō*-decl. ending *-um* for original **-im* (cf. Dahl, 167),[1] but nom. sg. *wrast* Cp. 630 and the compound *wrāstlīc* (BT 1270) suggest an *a/ō*-stem variant.

§ 83. The 1st sg. pres. indic. of verbs is *-u*, *-o*: cf. *groetu* 210, Ép. *mengio* 659 (n.), Erf. *gifyrdro* 327, *arectio* (*-ccio*) 396a. The 3rd sg. pres. indic. of strong verbs shows mutation in *caelith* 561, *milciþ* 628, *scripit* 906[2] beside *suggit* 455 (n.). For the 3rd sg. ending in *-t* see § 70.

§ 84. The ending of the pret. sg. subj. is *-ae*, *-æ* in *arectae* 204, *oberuuaenidae* 538, *lithircadae* 722, *str(e)idae* 899, *suicudae* 932, *gilebdae* 1089, Erf. *auægdæ* 356, presumably after the pret. indic. or pres. subj., instead of historical **-i* (Campbell, § 731 (d)), which never appears in Old English. *-un* in the pret. pl. subj. *suornodun* 198, however, may be due to a difference between Latin and Old English syntax (cf. § 87), since *-en* survives in much later texts (Campbell, § 735 (g)).

§ 85. The strong pret. part. suffix is *-in* in *forsleginum, faerslaeginum* 744, Ép. *binumini* 104, Erf. (*g)enumini* 100, *gedæbin* 336, *agnidin[n]e* 345 (n.); *-aen*, *-æn* in *asolcaen* 531, *forslaegæn* 814, Ép. *faerscribaen* 52, *gibeataen* 140, *utathrungaen* 176, *afigaen* 414, *gibaen* 525, *anslegaen[g]rae* 535, Erf. *gesnida(e)n* 315, *ascrepaeni* 375. The phonology of *-numini*, *-slegaen[g]rae*, and *-slaeginum* indicates suffix interchange (§ 68). For *o* in *geboronae* Erf. 359 see § 64.

§ 86. The pres. part. suffix of Class II wk. verbs is *-(a)end-* after long or disyllabic stems in *fultemendi* 74, *fultemendum* 95, *torctendi* 544, *ganaendae* 690, *ridusaendi* 816 (n.), Erf. *sorgendi* 79, *hat[t]ende* 206, *hleodendri* (*-rendi*) 508 beside

---

[1] That **wrǣst(e)* was originally an *i*-stem is indicated by nom. sg. *unwrest* without *-e* in *Chron.* 1086E and several times in Middle English.

[2] And probably *anhriosith* Ép. 520 (Erf. *onhrisit*), but Prim. OE. *io* and *eo* are sometimes confused in these texts (cf. §§ 41–2).

tilgendum 78, *uuidirhliniendae* 537 with Prim. OE. *j* retained after a short stem-syllable (SB, § 412 a. 10). (*h*)*risaendi* 434 (also Cp. *risende* 879) and Erf. *dobendi* 322 (cf. Ld. *dobend* 39/30) with loss of Prim. OE. *j* beside Hl. *hrysiende* F318, Cp. *dobgendi* 638 may show extension of the long-stem type as in Rushworth Matthew and Northumbrian (Campbell, § 757), but there is evidence suggesting that both verbs belonged originally to Class III.[1] Ép. *hlaeodrindi* has been taken as an isolated form preserving the suffix grade found in ON. *hyggindi*,[2] but transposition of *ae* and *i* seems more likely. The pret. suffix shows interchange of *a* < Prim. OE. *-ōdæ* and *u*/*o* < Prim. OE. *-ūdun* (Campbell, § 331. 6): cf. *gesuidrad*[*r*]*ae* 207, *lithircadae* 722, *stefad* 837, Erf. *fettad* 103, *gefetatnae* 105, *suarnadun* 198, *unsibbadae* 323, *meldadum* (*-n*) 342, *achlocadum* (*-n*) 364, *throuadae* 365, *gesuedradum* (*-n*) 368, *afulat* 1044 beside *aslacudae* 491, *geregnodae*, *-radnodae* 618, *suicudae* 932, Ép. *fetod* 103, *gefetodnae* 105, *suornodun* 198, *afulodan* 1044, Erf. *gisalbot* 325. Original Class III conjugation is indicated by the presence or absence of *i*-mutation (Campbell, § 763. 3) in *fetod* 103, *gefetodnae* 105, *stefad*/*staefad* 837 (cf. ON. *stefja*, *stafaðr*), *anhaebd* 915 (cf. OHG. *enthabēn*), Ép. *soærgændi* 79,[3] *haetendae* 206 (cf. OHG. *heizēn*), *gesuidradrae* 207.

Syntax

§ 87. Syntactical evidence is naturally limited in a glossary, but it conforms to later Old English usage as far as it goes. An Old English present renders a Latin future in 396a and a Latin future perfect in 520, and the present participle is accordingly used for the Latin future participle in 318. The preterite renders the Latin historical present in 76, 342, 507, 749, 1002, and a Latin present participle is rendered paratactically by the preterite indicative in 701. A finite verb regularly translates the Latin infinitive of indirect discourse (207, 353, 365, 756), and the indicative is used for the Latin subjunctive in a temporal clause introduced by *cum* (198) and a final clause (490). The

---

[1] Cf. Cl. I *hrissende* 403/19 beside pres. subj. *ahrisige* (Cosijn, ii. § 128), OHG *tobēn* beside *tobōn*.

[2] So H. Paul, *PBB* vi (1879), 236–7, followed by SB, § 363. 3.

[3] Cf. ME. *serrghenn*, *Ormulum* 8950 (Campbell, § 764).

preterite participle with *uuaes* translates a Latin imperfect passive in 525, and preterite participles translate other Latin passives in 526, 543, 800, with forms of *wesan* or *weorðan* presumably understood; the present participle apparently represents a Latin relative clause in 334 (n.). An Old English adverb stands for a Latin adjective in 94, 205, 733, and 743. The weak declension of the adjective is used after *þa* in 439, 542, 576, 707, and without a preceding demonstrative or possessive, as in the early poetry, in 250, 621, 1044.[1]

Date and dialect

§ 88. The common ancestor of Épinal and Erfurt (§ 24) clearly belonged to the earliest period of written English, since they alone among early texts preserve the distinction between Prim. OE. *f* and *ƀ* (§ 69), and Flasdieck accordingly dates it about 675.[2] Chadwick likewise dated it between 670 and 680 because it already showed loss of medial *h*, which he placed between 650 and 680, in the majority of cases,[3] and Dahl dates the exemplar of Épinal (which he regards as a later copy) 'hardly later than the end of the seventh century' because of its high proportion of forms preserving final -*ae*, -*æ*, and -*i* compared with other non-Northumbrian texts.[4] The date of Épinal itself has been much disputed on palaeographic grounds (§ 5), but it is hard to believe, in view of its consistently archaic orthography, that it was written more than a generation or two after its exemplar, perhaps about 725. If it were as late as the early ninth century, as Maunde Thompson and Keller held, one would expect either a mixture of early and late forms or a thoroughgoing modernization like that in Corpus, as Sweet pointed out.[5] Keller's comparison with Leiden is not a valid one, since Leiden is a mechanical copy by a continental scribe like Erfurt,[6] and

---

[1] Probably also in †*huitti* 254 (cf. Cp. *huite* 977, Cl. *hwite* 362/24) and the compounds *fulaetrea* 36, *uuodaeuistlae* 248, *bradaeleac* 895 (§ 67 fn. 1).
[2] Flasdieck, 102: cf. *Angl.* lxix. 163 ff.
[3] *TCPS* iv. 246; cf. 12, 49, 97, 106, 131, 248, 333, 346a, 384, 489, 606, 648 (? **fihna- AEW* 105), 710, 712, 717, 773, 794, 795, 797, 881, 960, 997, 1009a, 1069, 1099 beside the forms with *h* retained in § 72.
[4] Dahl, 191.　　　　　　　　　　　　　　　[5] *OET* 3, *Facs.* xiv.
[6] Cf. the scribe's colophon, *sicut inueni scripsi: ne reputes scriptori* (Hessels, *Leiden* 50).

the twelfth-century copies of Bede's Death Song in Simeon
of Durham cited by Dahl are only a few lines of great anti-
quarian and religious interest, which are even so subject to
orthographic variations.[1] The Old English exemplar of Erfurt
was presumably somewhat later than Épinal, since it modifies
many of the latter's archaic features, but still substantially
earlier than Corpus; Chadwick dated it about 750.[2]

§ 89. With regard to dialect, within the limits of present know-
ledge (§ 36) the general character of the language may be taken as
Anglian in view of the almost universal retraction of Prim. OE.
æ before *l* (§ 43. 2) and the number and distribution of forms
with smoothing (§ 58),[3] and as Mercian rather than Northumbrian in the virtual absence of specifically Northumbrian features
such as the distinction between *e* and *i* in the first elements of
diphthongs and the levelling-out of *a* or *o* in the second (Campbell, § 278), and the loss of final *n* in inflexions.[4] It agrees for
the most part with the early Mercian characters (*OET* 9–16,
46–8) against the dialect of the Vespasian Psalter in retaining
Prim. OE. æ without second fronting (§ 38) beside some forms
showing the parallel development of Prim. OE. *a* before back
vowels to æ and *ea* (§§ 46, 56),[5] which is also a feature of the
Old English poetic dialect. More precise localization is difficult
without external evidence, but the lowering of Prim. OE. *e* to
æ after *w* (§ 62) is characteristic of Rushworth Matthew
(Campbell, § 328), usually regarded as East Mercian (SB, § 2).

§ 90. In contrast to this generally Anglian colouring, both

---

[1] Dahl, 30. Cf. ME. *e* for OE. *ǽ* in *neodfere, nenig* 1 and ME. *-en* for *-an*
in *heonen* 5 (*ASPR* vi, p. cvi).

[2] *TCPS* iv. 249. He dated Corpus 'about 770–800'.

[3] Words exclusively or predominantly Anglian in later OE. are *fraam* 71,
aend 98, *begir* 143, *ambechtae* 187, *resung* 190, *lytisna* 200, *foernissae* 530,
þor(h)- 738, *þor(c)h* 741, 757, 760, *ambect* 866, *uulohum* 1066, Ép. *scyhend*
654, *miŏ* 796, Erf. *araebndae* 353, *achlocadum* 364 (R. Jordan, *Eigentümlich-
keiten des anglischen Wortschatzes* (Heidelberg, 1906), *passim*; J. J. Campbell,
JEGP l (1951), 356–8, 363).

[4] *hramsa, hromsa* 60 for gen. sg. *hromsan* Cp. 57, etc. beside frequent *-an*
(35 Ép., 25 Erf.) may be due to nom. sg. *hramsa* 59, while *-a* in Erf. *-plega*
577 is probably nom. sg. or casus indefinitus like fem. *-ae, -æ* in 655a, 736,
826a. Retraction before single *l* in *alaer*, etc. (§ 43. 2) might also be a Mercian
feature.

[5] Cf. Ct. 12/4 *haŏoberht*, 5 *heaŏoberht*, 15/2 *aben*, 4 *haŏoredi*, 9 *eafing*, 16/4
haŏoredi, 8 *eafing*, 47/11 *haeccaham*.

texts contain occasional forms of a West-Saxon or Kentish type: cf. Ep. *fealga* 713 with WS./Kt. *ea* before *l* plus consonant (§ 43. 2); *georuuierdid* 990, Ép. *fierst* 595, *orfiermae* 933, [*h*]*unhieri* 983 with WS. *ĭe* (§§ 42. 45, 55); *sadulfelgae* 818, etc. with Kt. *e* for the *i*-mutation of *ea* before *l* plus consonant (§ 50. 2); *cendlic* 739 and Erf. *ae*(*t*)*hed* 362 with Kt. *e* for the *i*-mutation of *ŭ* (§ 54); and the forms with *ae*, *æ* for Gmc. *ǣ* (§ 39) and *e* for the *i*-mutation of Prim. OE. *ā* < Gmc. *ai* (§ 52). The significance one attaches to these forms depends on whether one regards them as isolated survivals of source material in other dialects, like the archaisms in Cleopatra (§ 15), or as the slips of a West-Saxon or Kentish scribe writing the Mercian *Schriftsprache* which appears in the early Saxon and Kentish charters. Thus Wildhagen includes Épinal, Erfurt, and Corpus among the products of his Mercio-Kentish *Kirchensprache* (§ 36 fn. 3), and a similar case might be made for a Saxon origin, since the earliest West-Saxon texts show a Mercian influence which must have been stronger in the period of Mercian ascendancy between 657 and 825, and there appears to be a direct connection between these glossaries and the works of Aldhelm of Malmesbury (§ 35). Either of these theories by itself is attractive, but they are mutually exclusive: if the glossaries belong to the Mercio-Kentish *Kirchensprache*, the West-Saxon forms must be carried over from their sources, and *vice versa*. The origin of Épinal–Erfurt cannot therefore be determined by linguistic evidence.

THE TEXTS

THE glosses which follow are printed as they appear in the manuscripts except for capitalization, word-division, and punctuation. The division between the lemma and interpretation columns in the originals is shown by wide spacing, the absence of which indicates that the gloss was written continuously across both columns. Expanded abbreviations, ligatures, and subscribed letters are shown by italics; corrections, super-scriptions, line divisions, etc. are noted below the texts. The collations at the foot of the page are intended to show the relationship between Épinal, Erfurt, and the glossaries described in §§ 14–24; merely ortho-graphic or phonological differences in the Old English interpretations are not recorded. The following sigla, agreeing where possible with Lübke's (*Archiv*, lxxxv. 383), are used:

A   = Second Cleopatra Glossary, alphabetical section (§ 17)
A*   = Second Cleopatra Glossary, class section (§ 18)
A²   = The Brussels Glossary (§ 20)
Æ   = Ælfric's Glossary (§ 21)
B   = Bodl. MS. Laud 567 (§ 22)
B²   = Durham MS. Hunter 100 (§ 22)
C   = The Corpus Glossary (§ 14)
D   = First Cleopatra Glossary, *ab*-order batches (§ 15)
D*   = First Cleopatra Glossary, class-glossary batches (§ 16)
D** = First Cleopatra Glossary, *frs* batches (§ 16)
E²   = Second Erfurt Glossary (§ 25)
H   = The Harley Glossary (§ 19)
K   = Karlsruhe MS. Aug. 99 (§ 32)
L   = The Leiden Glossary (§ 27)
M   = Mone's transcript (§ 7)
Q   = Quicherat's transcript (§ 7)
R   = The Junius Glossary (§ 21)
S   = Sweet, *OET*
T   = Trier MS. 40, main glossary (§ 23. 2)
T*   = Trier MS. 40, marginal glossary (§ 23. 2)
T²   = Bodl. MS. Auct. F. 1. 16 (§ 23. 3)
V   = Leiden MS. Voss. Lat. Fol. 24 (§ 23. 1)
W²   = Second Werden Glossary (§ 8)

The glosses are numbered as in Sweet, *OET* and *Second Reader*; Erfurt glosses renumbered according to their position in the manu-script and glosses not in Sweet are marked *a*, *b*. All-Latin glosses referred to in the apparatus are cited from Sweet, *Facs.* and *CGL* v, Corpus glosses are cited from Sweet, *OET* and Hessels, *Corpus*.

	ÉPINAL	ERFURT	
f. 1^{ab}	Amites loerge	Amites loergae	f. 1^{ab}
	axungia rysil	axungia risil	
	argillus thohae	argillus thoæ	
	ansa fibulae	3a ansa fibulæ	
	andeda brandrad	andeda brondrad	
	arula fyrpannae *ue*l herth	anula fyrponne *ue*l herd	
	alea teblae	alea tefil	
	aleator teblere	a . . . . . tebl.re	
	axedones lynisas		
	aulea strel uel curtina ab aula	. . . . .b aula	
f. 1^{cd}	ariolatus frictrung	ariolatus frictung	f. 1^{cd}
	amites reftras	(30a)	
	albugo flio	albugo flio	
	axis aex	axis aex	
	aplustra giroedro	apulustra geroedra	

2 a^{x}ungia   8 axedones] o *indistinct*: *S*, *M* *read* e^{u} 9 alea *in lower margin*

3 th^{o}ę   5 herd] erd *after* brondrad *on line above*   7 a . . . . . tebl.re] a *and* t *now covered* (§ 10)   9 baula *partly covered* (§ 10)   12 axis] i *and part of* x *no longer visible*; aex] *preceded by* [quadra]tum from 338/33   14 geroedra] a *indistinct*

---

1 *cf.* A* 268/32, D* 352/34 amitis lorg   2 rysel C 256; *cf.* R 159/5 aruina . . . ł axungia . . . hrysel   3 argilla C 207; *cf.* Cl.I 348/13 argilla ðo   3a fibula C A559   4 andeda C 157, L 47/42 andena D 349/23; *cf.* A* 266/26 ardeda brandrida, A^2 294/28 andeda brondreda (§ 23. 3), Æ 316/4 andena brandisen, R 127/9 andena ł tripes brandisen   5 arula C 208, A^2 289/6, 294/29, T^2 245/27 arula ł batilla R 124/11 (*cf.* 1065); fiurpannæ ł herd T^2 fyrponne, -panne *only* CA^2 (2) R heorð *only* A^2 (1)   6 tebl C 110 *etc.* taflæ T 46/4   8 axredones C 257, D 351/7 axedones T* 47/24 axedones idest humeruli T^2 245/21; *cf.* A* 267/29 axedo lynis, C 258, D 351/8 axredo   9 stregl *only* C 249; *cf.* C A912 auleum curtina ab aula = (3 ab 28)   10 frihtrung C 196, D** 357/13   11 fugultreo ł reftras C 150, fugeltrio ræftras D 349/19 (*cf.* 4 ef 16 amites fustis aucupalis)   14 aplustra C 178, D 350/1, D** 357/15, A^2 288/34; geroeðro, -reþro, -reðru CD**A^2 geredro D

ÉPINAL		ERFURT	
abilina	hrutu	15 abilina	hnutu
alium	garlæc	alium	garlec
aneta	aenid a natando	aneta	aenit a natando
armilausia	sercae	armilausia	sercae
alba spina	haeguthorn	alba spina	hagudorn
apiastrum	biouuyrt	20 apiastrum	buuyrt
f. 1^ef anetum	dil	anetum	dil
aesculus	boecae	aesculus	boeccae
aconita	thungas	.... thungas	
apio	merici	a ..... meru ...	
alchior	isærn	25 alchior isaern	f. 1^ef
achalantis *uel* luscina *uel* ros-cina nctigalae		achalantis *uel* luscinia *uel* roscina næctægela	
asilo	briosa	asilo	briosa
antiae	loccas	antiae	loccas
arpago	auuel uel clauuo	arpago	auuel uel clauuo
areoli	sceabas	30 areoli	scebas
(11)		30a amites reftras	
f. 1^vab asses scorteas	lidrinae	asses corteas	lidrinna
trimsas		trynsas	
atflarat	ansueop	.dflarat	ansueus
acerabulus	mapuldur	acterabulus	maefuldur f. 1^vab

26 roscina] *lower half of* n *indistinct*   29 arpago] r *and* p *blotted*

17 natando] do *after* garlec *on line above*   22 aesculus] ae *and most of* sc *now covered* (§ 10)   24 *now covered* (§ 10)   25 isaern] s *faint*, rn *indistinct*   29 clauuo] o *incomplete*   31 lidrinna] a *and part of second* n *covered*   32 .dflarat] *loop of* d *covered*; ansueus] an *and part of* su *indistinct*, us *covered*

---

15 abelena C 33   abilina D 344/11   auilina A* 268/41   abellana D 345/15 *marg.*;   haesel-, haslhnutu CD *marg.* hnutu DA*;   *cf.* L 47/1 abellana hel (= 50), R 139/17 hæsl ł hæslhnutu   17 ened a natanda D 349/24   anud a natando dicta T 56vb   enid *only* C 158 *etc.*   20 biowyrt C 181   beowyrt A* 267/19, D* 352/2; *cf.* D 350/3 apiaster swines mearce 21 dili C 159, -e D 349/25 *etc.*   22 boece C 93   boc A* 268/39, R 137/20 25 alcion C 115, D 349/5   alchior D 350/7 *marg.*   26 luscinia ł roscinia nehtægale C 52   luscina ł roscinia nightegale D 344/26-7   30 aromatum horti (= 1 cd 6) ł scauos T* 47/23   sceabas, -fas *only* C 197, D 350/12 *marg.* 31 scorteas C 226   corteas D 350/14 *marg.*; liþrine, liþerene trymsas CD 32 atflarat onsueop C 235,   ansueop D 350/31   33 aerabulus C 51 acerabulos A* 269/9   acerabulus ioclis D 344/38;   mapuldur, -or CD

ÉPINAL		ERFURT	
acrifolus	holegn	acrifolus	holegn
alnus	alaer	35 alnus	aler
alneum	fulaetrea	alneum	falatreu
abies	saeppae	abies	sæpae
ascella	ocusta	ascella	ocusta
auriculum	dros	ariculum	dros
arpa	earngeat	40 arpa	aerngeup
acega	holthana	accega	holtana
ardea et dieperdulum hragra		ardea *et* dieperdulum hragra	
aquilium	anga	aquilium	anga
auriculum	earuuigga	auriculum	aeruuica
auriola	stigu	45 auriola	stigu
almeta	alterholt	almeta	alerholt
alga	uaar	alga	uar
argella	laam	argella	lam
accearium	steeli	accearium	steli
auellanus	aesil	50 auellanus	haesl
anconos	uncenos	50a anconos	uncenos
altrinsecus	an ba halbae	altrinsecus on ba halbe	
addictus	faerscribaen	addictus	faerscrifen
argutie	thrauu	argutiae	trafu
asfaltum	spaldr	asfaltum	spaldur
albipedius	huitfot	55 albipedius huitfot	
aluium	meeli	albiolum	aldot
f. 1ᵛᶜᵈ aluiolum	aldot	albium	meelu

mabuldor A*   34 acrifolus C 53, D 344/29, -uolus A* 269/11   acrifolius R 138/38   acrifolium L 47/96   36 fulaetreo C 117 fuletreow D 349/8 37 etspe C 34 æspe D 344/12 æps Æ 312/12 sæppe gyr A* 269/14 39 auriculum C 239, D 350/36, D* 353/20 *marg.*, L 47/50; earwicga ł dros D dros *only* D*L dorsos *only* C   40 earngeot C 212, -geat C 232, A² 284/4 eargeat A* 258/4, D* 351/14 ærengeat R 117/24 arngeus L 47/57 41 acega holthona C 54 *etc.*   42 hragra ł dieperdulum C 198 hragra *only* D* 351/25 *etc.*; *cf.* L 47/64 perdvlum hragra   44 earwicga C 240, D 350/36 æruigga L 47/86   45 *cf.* T* 47/13–14 ara stabulum porcorum inde areola stigu   46 alneta C 119, D 349/6 almenta L 47/101; alerholt CL alorholt D   50 auellanus C 243 abellanus D 350/38 abellanus ł colurnus A* 268/40 (*cf.* 236 n.); haesl C hæsl DA*   50a anconos C A575 ancones L 47/4; urcenos C untinos L   52 forscrifen C 69   53 thrauuo C 200 54 aspaltum spaldur C 228, L 12/18 56(7) aluuium C 123 albium A* 268/24, D* 352/23; meeli C mele A*D*   57(6) aluiolum aldaht C 124

alga	scaldthyflas	
actula	hramsa	
acitelum	hramsa crop	
arrius	faag	
ascolonium	hynnilaec	
accitulium	geacaes surae	
ambila	laec	
arniglosa	uuegbradae	
absintium	uuermod	
armos	boog	
anguens	breer	
acinum	hindberiæ	
arbatae	sibaed	
acris	fraam	
aucapatione	setungae	
addicauit	bisceredae	
adstipulatus	fultemendi	
alternantium	staefnændra	
adgrediuntur	gihiodum	

f. 1ᵛᵉᶠ alacris snel

adnitentib*us*	tilgendum	
anxius	soærgændi	
abortus	misbyrd	
ausus	gidyrstig	

alge	scaldthyblas	
accitula	hramsa	
60 accitulu*m*	hromsa crop	
arr*i*us	faag	
ascalon*ium*	ynnilec	
accitulu*m*	gecaes sarae	
ambila	laec	
65 arm*i*glossa	uegbradae	
absintiu*m*	uermodae	
armus	boog	
anguens	breer	
acinu*m*	hindbergen	
70 arbate	sibaed	f. 1ᵛᶜᵈ
acris	from	
aucupatione	setungae	
abdicauit	biscer*i*dae	
adstipulatus	fultemendi	
75 alternan*ti*um	staefnendra	
adgrediuntur	gaeadun	
alacris	blidi	
adnitentibus	tilgendun	
anxius	sorgendi	
80 abortus	misbyrd	
ausus	gedurstip	

76 adgrediuntur] g *erased after*
first d   79 anxius] nx *in-*
ᵍ   ᶜ
distinct; soeᵣendi   83 fani

58 scaldthyblas (*cf.* C)
          ᵒ
60 hracmsacrop

---

58 alga scaldhyflas ɫ sondhyllas C 125   59 acitula C 56 *etc.*   60 acitelum hromsan C 57 *etc.*   61 *sic* C 201, D 350/17; *cf.* C 841 farius faag, H B86 barius uarius fah, Æ 306/18 uarius fah, R 163/13 uarius ɫ discolor fah   62 ascalonium C 229 scolonia A² 295/21;   ynnelaec, -leac CA² 65 anaglossa C 213   arniglosa A* 271/7   arnaglosa D* 352/33 *marg.*, 353/9, -glosse A² 296/11   arnoglossa T² 246/4   66 absinthium wermod C 35   absintium wermod D 344/13 *etc.*   67 armus C 215   armum D 350/13   68 breer C 161   bremel D 350/16 *marg.*   69 hindberiae C 59, -berge A* 269/39 *etc.*   71 fortio ɫ from C 60 (*cf.* E² 260/51 acris fortis uelox) from *only* A 274/33, D* 353/19   72 aucupatione C 244, D 350/39, 73 abdicauit negauit ɫ discerede C A11 (*cf.* C A52 abduxit negauit (= 3 ef 26))   74 *om.* C *etc.*   76 geeodun, -on C 78, D 345/7   77 snel bliðe A 274/34   snel *only* C 127, D 349/11   78 tilgendum C 80 79 sorgendi C 169 *etc.*   81 gedyrstig C 245, D 350/40

ÉPINAL			ERFURT	
appetitus	gitsung		appetitus	gitsung
astu	facni		astu	facni
amiculo	hraecli		amiculo	hraegl
adridente	tyctendi	85	adridente	tyctendi
actionabatur	scirde		accionabatur	scirde
actuaris	uuraec		actuaris	uraec
alueus	streamrad		alueus	streumrad
adlitus	æthm		adlitus	
aegit	uuraec	90	aegit	uraec
auehit	an uueg aferidae		auehit	an uoeg aueridae
aquilae	segnas		aquila	segnas
ad expensas	to nyttum		ad expensas	to nytum
annua	gerlicae		annua	gernlicae
adsessore	fultemendum	95	adsessores	fultemendum
adclinis	tohald		adclinis	tohald
apparatione	gitiungi		apparatione	getiong
adqueue	aend suilcae		atqueue	end suilce
agrestes	uuildae		agrestes	uuildae
adepto	ginumni	100	adempto	.enumini
adsaeculam	thegn		adsexulam	degn	f. 1^{vef}
adepta	binumni		adempta	binumni
arcessitus	uel euocatus fetod		ascessitus	uel euocatus fettad

f
91 anuuega$\underset{\downarrow}{}$eridae
93 expensas] *first stroke of* e (?)
         i
before p   99 uuldae
100 adepto] i *erased before* o

         i   o
96 adclinas   97 giting
100 .enumini *now covered*
         t
103 fetad

82 gidsung C 184   gitsung A 274/36, D* 353/22   83 facni ł fraefeli
C 230   fæcne, facne *only* A 275/1, D* 353/23   84 hrægli, -le C 155,
D 349/21   86 actionabatur C 61   87 actuarius C 62, D 344/36
89 alitus aethm C 130 *etc.*   90 *cf.* H E158 egit . . . wræc   91 aferidae,
-ede C 62, D 351/1   fereþ A 275/4   92 aquilae C 194, -le A 275/5,
D* 353/24   93 ad pensas C 72, D 345/3   ad expensas D 350/26 *marg.*;
nyttum CD (*both places*)   94 gerlice C 170, D 349/28   95 adsen-
sore C 73, -sessore D 350/30   96 tohald ł incumbens C 74 (*cf.* C A152
acclinis resupinus et incumbens (= 4 ab 7))   toheald *only* D 345/4, A 275/6
97 apparitione getiunge C 185   98 adqueue C 75, D 345/5   atqueue
C 238, D 350/34   99 agretis C 104   agrestis R 109/18   agreste D 349/2
100 *om.* C *etc.*   101 adsaeculum *with first* u *erased* C 77   adseculam
D 345/6;   minister turpitudinis *corr.* C (*cf.* 4 ab 20 turpitudinis minister)
102 ademto gebinumini (*cf.* 100) C 76   103 arcessitus feotod *only* C 222
arcersitus fetod *only* D 350/27; *cf.* C E326 euocatus eductus

	ÉPINAL			ERFURT		

ablata   binumini   ablata   binoman
accetum   gefetodnae   105   accetum   gefetatnae
f. 2^ab amentis   sceptloum   amentis   sceptloum
aestuaria   fleotas   aestuaria   fleutas
alumne   fosturbearn   alumnae   foetri̇barn
affectui   megsibbi *uel*   affectui   megsibbi *uel*
dilectione   dilectione
arci*bus*   faestinnum   110   arcibus   fæstinnun
antempna   segilgaerd   antemna   segilgaerd
adrogantissime   uulanclicae   adrogantissimæ   gelplih
auserunt   naamun   auserunt   noumun
arcister   strelbora   arcister   strelbora
aere alieno   gaebuli   115   aere alieno   gaebuli
f. 2^cd alumnis   aelifnae   115a
f. 2^ef anate   cladærsticca   anate   claderstecca   f. 2^ab
f. 2^vcd alapiosa   calua   116a alapiosa calua   f. 2^vab
f. 2^vef alites   challes   116b alites challes
f. 3^cd anser   goos   anser   goos   f. 2^vef
affricus   westsuþwind   affric*us*   uestsuduui̇nd
atticus   dora   atticus   dora

f. 3^ef Buccula   bucc   120   (162a)
balus   isærn fetor   balus   isaern fetor
bothona   embrin   121a bothana   embrin
bothonicula   stappa   bothoni̇cula   stoppa

               ne   109 dilectione] ne *after* foetribarn
109 dilectio   121a bothona]   *on line above*   116 clader-
i *erased before* a   122 stappa]   stecca] d *from* t   116a *on same*
horns of first a *joined to form* o (?)   *line as following item,* 344/57
                                                    116b *on same line as preceding*
                                                    item, 345/8   118 affric;s

---

104 binumine C 37   105 accetum gefeotodne C 63   accitum gefetod-
ne D 344/37   107 *cf.* H E361 estuaria fleotas   108 fostorbearn C 131
111 antemna C 165, A² 288/10   112 wlonclī C 85   wlanclice D 351/9
113 hlodun *ad.* C 247   114 and scytta (? andscytta) *ad.* D 350/28
115a *om.* C *etc.; cf.* R 146/21 alumen efne, 134/38 alumen ɫ stipteria
(= Herm. 195/1 *etc.*) efne, B 67vb alium ɫ stipteria . . . ɫ ef   116 cladersticca C 171   sollicitudo ɫ clederstico T 46/22 (*cf.* Placidus III A60 anate solli-
citudine cura)   116a alapiciosa calwa C 132, D 349/15; *cf.* T 55va alopicia
calua   119 atticus C 236, R 121/16   attacus D 350/35   120 buuc
C 338   bucc D 358/41   buc H B391   121a bothonia C B146
(*altered from* bothoma), H B366   bothoma D 358/19   bothona V 12
122 stoppa C 307 *etc.*   stuppa V 13

ÉPINAL		ERFURT	
bacidones	redisnae	bacidones	rædisnae
bicoca	hraebrebletae	bicoca hebrebletae	
beacita	stearno	125 biacita	stærn
briensis	handuyrp	briensis	honduyrp
bagula	bridils	bagula	brigdils
basis	teter	balsis	teter
f. 3ᵛᵃᵇ bobellum	falaed	bobellum	falaed
bratium	malt	130 bratium	malt
bradigabo	felduuop	badrigabo	felduus
beta	berc arb *dicitu*r	beta	berc arbor dicit*ur*
bitumen	lim	bitum*en*	lim
bulla	sigil	bulla	sigil
beneficium	fremu	135 beneficium fremu	f. 3ᵃᵇ
ballista	staeblidrae	ballista	steblidrae
basterna	beer	basterna	beer
byssum	tuum	byssu*m*	tuigin
bitiligo	blecthrustfel	bitiligo	blecthrustfel
battuitum	gibeataen	140 batuitu*m* gebeatten	
bile	atr	bile	art
bubu	uuf	bubu	uuf
bucina	begir	bucina	begir
f. 3ᵛᶜᵈ blitum	clatae	blitum	clate

123 a *erased after* bacidones
      u   g
126 handyrp   127 baçula
131 felduuop] *first stroke of* d *erased*
after e   142 uuf *followed by*
delicata (6 ab 35)

127 brigdils] g *from* s   138 *on*
same line as preceding item, 347/24

123 raedinne C 260 rædenne D 357/18; *cf.* A* 269/17 uacedo redisn,
R 139/7 bacido botrus clyster   124 haebreblete C 294 *etc.* hæferblæta
H B197   125 beacita stearn C 284 *etc.*, sterno V 6   126 honduyrm C
320 *etc.*; *cf.* H B509 briensis uermis manus   127 bridels C 261, D 357/19
bridel i. frenum R 116/33 (*cf.* T 60ᵛᵃ bagula frenum)   128 balsis
C 262 *etc.*   129 bofellum C 310   bobellum D 358/21, R 106/5,
V 11 bouellum H B377, -ium T* 47/31, T² 245/44   131 bradigabo
C 323, D 359/1, T² 245/45 bradigatio ploratio campi H B488;   felduop
C, -wuop D, -wop H feldhoppo T²   132 arbor C 285; *cf.* A* 269/12,
D* 359/13 beta birce   134 gemma ... ł sigl H B411 sigl *only* C 331 *etc.*
135 *cf.* H B119 beneficium i. donum freme gife   136 ł searu i. machina
belli *ad.* D 357/21; *cf.* H B46 ballista catpulta ł machina bellii. searu, T²245/46
balista stafslengrie   138 tuin C 343 twin D 358/14   140 batuitum
gebeaten C 265 *etc.*   141 atr C 297 *etc.* attre H B223   142 bubo
C 334 *etc.*   143 baccinia C 266, D 357/24; *cf.* A² 296/26 bacinia berige

ÉPINAL	ERFURT
blattis bitulin	145 bla*tis* bitulum
ballena hran	broel edisc
broel edisc	ballena hron
broelarius ediscueard	broellear*ius* ediscuard
batat ginath	battat ginath
bruchus cefr	150 bruchus cefr
berrus baar	berrus baar
bruncus uurot	brunchus urot
(161)	152a bubu uuf
buculus randbeag	baculus rondbaeg
berruca uueartae	berruca uaertae
byrseus lediruuyrcta	155 byrreus lediruyrhta
berna higrae	berna higræ f. 3^cd
bona scaet	bona scaet
branciae cian	brancie cian
burrum bruun	burru*m* bruum
bubalis uusend	160 babalis uesand
bufo uuf	(152a)
boreus eastnorþwind	boreus eustnorduind
(120)	162a buccula bua f. 3^ef
f. 3^vef Colonus gibuur	Colonus uicinus
contribulus meeg	contri*b*ulus consanguinis
calculus calc	165 calculus calc
clibosum clibecti	cliborum clibec*tis*

145 bituli..n [*hole in MS.*]
148 eşdiscueard *with* ş *erased*
150 bruchus] *first stroke of* c (?)
                                          f
after r;   cer   154 uuertae
                                   a

149 gimath *with first stroke of* m
erased   156–7 *on same line*
164 consanguinis *over erasure; tail
of* g *visible below* n

---

145 blattis C 307 blatis H B467;   bitulum C, -elum H   146(7) horn
C 267   hron L 47/10 *etc.*   hran ł hwæl D 357/26   147(6) edisc deor-
tuun C 324   hortus ceruorum deortun ł edisc H B517   ensc *only* A 275/22
148 broellarius C 325, H B518   broelarius A 275/23, D* 359/20
149 battat C 269 *etc.*   152 bruncus C 327 *etc.*   153 buculus C 335 *etc.*
155 byrseus C 344 *etc.*   byrsarius ł byrseus H B548;   leðerwyrhta ł lypenwyrhta D (*cf.* A 275/25 byrseus lypenwyrhta)   leðeruyrhta *only* C H
159 bruun C 336, D 358/38   160 bubalis C 337, D 358/40   bubalus H
B381;   weosend C   wesend DH; *cf.* R 118/38–9 urus wesend, bubalus wilde
oxa *and* 1097   161 bufo V 14;   *om.* C *etc. but cf.* 142   163 gebuur C
493, -bur A 276/7, -byr D* 369/16   164 contribulius C 495   contribulus H
C1648; meig ł sanguiñ C   consanguineus mæg H   165 numestan *ad.* D 362/1
(? *cf.* 172)   166 clibosum C 478, D 364/19, V 21 cliuosum H C1116; clibecti CV, -fihte D   inclinatum cliftæhtig H; *cf.* R 111/36 cliuosus clifig tohyld

ÉPINAL		ERFURT	
colobium	ham	colobium	hom
caccabum	cetil	caccabum	cetil
coccum bis tinctum uuiloc-read		coccum bis tinctum uusluc-reud	
cados	ambras	170 cados	ambras
citropodes	crocha super .iiii. pedes	citropodes	chroca super iiij pedes
calculus ratio uel sententia uel tebelstan uel lapillus		calculus ratio uel sententia uel tebiltan uel labillus	
f. 4ab cartellus	windil	cartellus	pindil f. 3vab
cartilaga	naesgristlae	cartalago	naesgristlae
carbunculus	spyrng	175 carbunculus	spryng
celatum	utathrungaen	caelatum	utathrungen
cautere	ferrum idest haam	cautere	ferrum fam
cotizat	teblith	cotizat	teblith
cyprinus	fornaeticli	178a capprinus	forneticcli
conuexum	hualb	conuexum	halb
cercylus	aesc uel nauis	180 cerciclus aesc uel nauis	
f. 4cd chaos	duolma	chos dualma	
conquilium	uuilucscel	conquilium uuylucscel	
camellea	uulfes camb	camellea	uulfes camb

169 uuilocráed   172 łlapillus
in lower margin   176 uta-
  thrugaen

169 us lucreud   172 ł tebil
after 349/39 *two lines above*; tan ł
labillus *below* ł tebil
173 cartelus;   pindil *followed by*
& hispani (349/42)   180 *on
same line as following item,* 350/
20   181–2 *on same line*

167 *cf.* H C1582 colobium dictum quia longum est sine manicis (Isidore, *Ety.*
xix. 22/24)... hom łsmoc, R 151/35 colobium slefleas scrud   169 wiolocread
C 496 *etc.*   171 croa croha, croca *only* C 461, T* 48/3   crocha super
quattuor pedes V 19   172 ratio ł sententia ł numerus ł teblstan C 349
tæfl-, tæfelstan *only* A* 267/6, A² 295/7; *cf.* H C62 calculus ... lapis breuis ł
ratio sententia ł numerus   173 cartallus H C379   cartellus C 348, D
362/4; windil C, -el DH   174 cartilago C 350, D 362/5   175 ł
angseta ł pustula *ad.* R 112/15 (*cf.* 770, 791)   176 abracod utaþrungen
D 364/2 (*cf.* C 451 celatum abrectat); *om.* C   177 aam *only* C 352,
H C602; *cf.* L 35/201 cautere ferrum melius tindre   178 tebleth C 497
tæflaþ H C1723   178a cyprinus forneted cli C C974   179 hualf C 498
180 cercilus C 438, V 18   cercylus D 363/34;   aesc, æsc *only* CD aesc
ł inauis V   181 chaus C 457;   prima confusio omnium rerum *ad.* C
(*cf.* Abstr. CA 73 chaus confusio rerum)   182 wilocscel C 499   weoloces
scyll R 140/14   weoloc *only* A 283/16

ÉPINAL			ERFURT	
canis lingua	ribbae		canis lingua	ribbae
cicuta	hymblicae	185	cicuta	huymblicae
contemptum	heruuendlicae		contemptum	haeruendlicae
conlatio	ambechtae		conlato	ambechtae
commeatos	sandae		commeatus	sondae
contubernalis	gidopta		contubernalis	gidogta	f. 3ᵛᶜᵈ
coniectura	resung	190	coniectura	resung
condidit	gisettae		condidit	girette
conuincens	obaerstaelendi		conuincens	oberstælendi
corben	mand		corben	mondi
conuicta	obaerstaelid		conuicta	oberstaelid
concidit	tislog	195	concidit	gislog
conparantem	gegeruuednae		conparantem	gegeruednae
censores	giroefan		censores	geroefan
coaluissent	suornodun		coaluissent	suarnadun
cuniculos	smigilas recessus		cuniculos	smygilas recessus
concedam	lytisna	200	concedam lytisna	
coniurati	gimodae		coniurati gimode	
contumax	anmod		contumax onmod	
confussione	gimaengiungiae		confusione	gemengiungae
concesserim	arectae		concesserim	arectae
conpar	gihaeplice	205	conpar	gihaeplicae
f. 4ᵉᶠ calentes	haetendae		calentes	hattendae

188 sandae] ç *erased after* s
189 gidapta   192 obaertae-
lendi   199 recessus] *from
following item,* 7 cd 30: *see note*
204 arectae] e *erased after first* a

192 *on same line as following item,*
350/38   193 *on same line as
following item,* 350/40
194–5 *on same line*   199 smygilas *followed by* cereacas (350/48);
recessus *after* 200–1 *on line below*
    de
200–1 *on same line*   201 gimo
202 *on same line as preceding item,*
350/51   206 *on same line as
following item,* 350/57

184 hundestunge *ad.* D 362/8   186 contemtum C 500   187 con-
lato C 501, D 364/38;   oembecht C   ambehte D   188 commeatos
C 502 *etc.*   189 geþofta C 503 *etc.*   190 ł rædels *ad.* H C1479
191 gesette C 505   193 mand C 511   195 toslog C 516, -sloh H
C1889   196 gegaerwendne C 517   198 suornadun C 518
swornodon D 364/44   199 smyglas, -elas *only* C 608, D 366/23; *cf.* H
C2158 cuniculus snægl smygels   202 anmood C 521   anmode D
365/2 (? *after* 365/1 gemode) anmoda H C1687   203 confusione C 522,
D 365/3; gemengiunge C   gemengunge D   206 hatende C 357

ÉPINAL		ERFURT	
constipuisse	gesuidradrae	constipuissen	gisuderadae
curiositas	feruuitgeornnis	curiositas	feruitgernis
claua	stegn	claua	stæng
conuenio	groetu *uel* adiuro 210	conuenio	gloeto *uel* adiuro
contis	spreotum	con*tis*	spreutum
condiciones	raedinnae	condi*ti*ones	redinnae
crebrat	siftit	crefrat	siftid
consubrinus	gesuirgion	consubrinus	gisuirgia*n*
caulem	stela 215	caulem	stela
clunis	lændnum	clunis	laendum f. 3vef
f. 4vab cocleae	lytlae sneglas	cocleae	lytlae sneglas
crepacula	claedur id*est* tabula qua a segitib*us* territantur aues	crepacula	cledur id*est* tabula qua a segitib*us* terri-tant*ur* aues
caumeuniae	eordrestae	caumaeuni*æ*	eordraestae
f. 4vcd caustella	clustorlocae	clustella	clusterlocae 220 f. 4ab
cerula	haeuui	cerula	h*a*ui
cofinus	mand		
commentariensis	giroefa	commentari*ensis*	geroefa
clatrum	pearroc	cleatrum	pearroc
cospis	palester	cospis	plast*er* 225
calear	spora	calear	spora
cauterium	mearisern	cauter*ium*	merisaen
clabatum	gybyrdid	clabatum	gebyrdid

207 gesuidradrae] *first* e *from* i
218 (segi)tibus ... aues *above line* e
219 caumuniae 223 com- t mendariensis

207 gisuderadae] *second* d *from* t
209 *on same line as following item,* 351/3 218 cledŕ; qua ... aues *across both columns on line below*; ā

---

207 constipuisse C 525, D 365/6; gesuedrade C geswiðrade D   208 feor-witgeornis C 609 ferwetnes H C2215   209 steng C 480 *etc.*   210 ic groetu *only* C 526   212 condicione C 529; *cf.* A 276/19, D* 369/20 condicio redin   213 crebrat C 596 *etc.*   214 consobrinus C 530, D 365/9 consobrini H C1549; gesuigran C geswegran H geswiria ł swustursunu D   216 *om.* C *etc. but cf.* C C491 clunis coxae, H C1142 clunis renibus coxe gupan   219 caumeuniae, -e C 360, D 362/22, H C1147; clustorloc C clusterloc DH   223 *cf.* H C1237 commentariensis uilicus   224 clatrum C 486 *etc.*   225 palstr C 534, 622   226 calcar C 361 *etc.*; *cf.* H C51 calcis finis (= 6 ef 19) ... spura   227 mearciseren, -isen C 362, D 362/13   mearcisern ł tynder H C600 (*cf.* 177)   228 clabatum C 487   clauatum T² 246/3, H C1083; gebyrded C   giburdid T²   sutum ł gebyrd H

f. 4^vef

catasta	gloed		catasta geleod	
celox	ceol	230	caelox ceol	
capsis	cest		capsis cest	
caractis	uuaeterthruch		caractes uaeterthrouch	f. 4^cd
cerus	elch		cerus elch	
cyatus	bolla		cutus bollae	
color	aac	235	color aac	
corylus	haesil		corylus haesl	
cerasius	cisirbeam		caerassius cysirbeam	
cariscus	cuicbeam			
capitium	hood		capitium hood	
cornicula	chyae	240	cornicula ciae	
cornacula	crauuae		cornacula crauuae	
crocus	gelu		croccus gelo	
culcites	bedd		culcites bedd	
camisa	haam		camissa haam	
cappa	scicing	245	cappa scinccing	
cerefolium	cunillae		cerefolium cunillae	
corimbus	leactrogas		corimbus leactrocas	
cicuta	uuodaeuistlae		cicuta uuodeuuislae	

e
232 uuaterthruch   235 color]
very faint   236 corylus] *very*
                         a
faint   241 cornicula
244 ca:misa;   haam] *second* a
from first stroke of m (?)

229–30 *on same line*   231 *on*
same line as following item, 352/52
                                          c
232–3 *on same line*   233 elęh

---

229 geloed C 363   gæleþ A 275/35   genus supplicii (= Affatim 491/49) . . . ł
geled quadrupalium ł poene eculeo simile (*cf.* Abstr. CA 41 genus poenae est
eculeo similis) H C527   230 celox C 442 *etc.*   231 cestum H C280   cest
C 365   cyst D 362/14   cist A 276/6   232 caractis C 367, H C394   cataracte
þeotan D 362/10   234 cratus H C2009, T 48/10   gratus T² 245/50
ciatus A* 282/9;   bolla HT² A* bulla T;   *om.* CDA   237 cerasius C 445,
A* 269/18, R 138/3;   ciser-, cirisbeam CA* cyrstreow R   238 cuicbeam uuice C 368, cwicbeam wice D 362/16, wic ł cwicbeam H C407 (*cf.* A*
269/19 cariscus wice)   cwicbeam *only* R 138/2   quecbom *only* T* 48/7
240 cio A* 260/11, D* 367/32 cyo ł graula A² 286/5;   *om.* CDAH
242 crucus C 598   crocus A 276/22, H C2119, D* 369/23;   gelo, geolu
CD*   gæle geolo A   lutei coloris est geolu H   243 *cf.* R 124/19 culcites
feþerbed   244 camisa C 370, D 362/18, A 276/23;   cemes *ad.* D
245 scicging C 373   scicc ing D 362/19, A* 268/3   247 corimbos
leactrogas C 540, D 365/13; *cf.* H C1804 corimbus cacumen nauis (= C
C661 nauibus ł cacumen) leactroh, B 68^b corimbus i. leahtric   248 wodewistle C 463, A² 297/8

castania   cistimbea*m*
250 calta   rede clabre
carix   sech
culmus   uuryd
cucumis   popeg
calcesta   huitti clabre
255 cabro uaeps
cicade   h*a*ma*n*
cuculio   æm*i*l
cancer   hafaern
ciconia   storc
260 cupa   bydin
colobostru*m*   beost
ciscillus   heardheui
calciculiu*m*   iaces sura
cucuzata   laepaeuincæ
265 cuculus   gæc
cardella   thistil
cocleas   uuylocas   f. 4ef
cacom*i*camus   logd*o*r
calom*a*cus   haeth
270 cefalus   heardhara
carduus   th*i*stil

249–397 *lacuna in* Ép.

253 cucumis] *first* cu *after* uuryd
                           c
on line above   254 calesta
255 cabro *after* clabre (254);
uaeps *after* popeg (253) *on line
above*   256–7 *on same line*

---

249 castanea C 374, D 362/20, R 138/20   castaneus A* 269/20, D* 368/37;
cistenbeam CDA*D* cystel ł cystbeam R   250 reade C 375, D 362/21, A²
298/12 ræde A 276/24; ł genus floris *ad.* C (= Abstr. CA 116)   251 secg
C 371 *etc.* seic L 46/26   252 wyrð C 612   254 huite C 377 *etc.*
255 crabro waefs ł hurnitu C 603 (*cf.* 275)   256 secggescere ł haman C
464   257 curculio C 613 *etc.*   258 haebrn C 379 hæfern D 362/25
etc. hæfer H C199   261 colostrum C 541 *etc.*; ł obestum *ad.* H C1568
262 cisculus C 467   ciscillus D 364/14, L 47/49   circillus H C959;
heardheau, -heaw CD haerdheau L   nauicula ł heardheawa H (*cf.* 180)
263 surae C 380, -e D 362/26, A² 297/17   264 lepeuince C 619 laepi-
uincæ L 47/60 hleapewince A* 260/2, D* 367/29, A² 285/11   266 þistel-
tuige C 381 *etc.*   267 *cf.* H C1740 cocleae lytle snæglas ł weolacas *and*
217   268 cacomicanus C 382 *etc.*   269 calomachus C 383 calomacus
D 362/28 colomacus H C1581 calomaucus L 47/7 calamanca R 153/22;
haet, -æt CR het L hæð D genesta hæþ H

castorius bebir
ca*m*pos faegen
camos suol
275 crabro hirnitu
contentus ginehord
culix mich longas tibias
h*a*bens
comme*n*tis searuum *ue*l
ordoncu*m*
cartamo lypbcorn
280 cynoglossa ribbae
cors tuun*i*
cummi teru
carpella sadulbogo
cicer bean
285 corax hraebn
caepa cipae
culinia coacas   f. 4^vab
crustulla halstan
cemetum merisc
289a cementu*m* lim lipidium
290 carectum hreod
commissuras cimbing

         c
277 mihç   288 crustulla] *first*
curve of cursive u (?) *after* c
     li
289 pidium *with second* i *over* a

272 *cf.* H C482–3 castor befer, castorium testiculi beluorum uirilia castoris
273 conpos C 543; *cf.* H C1320 compos . . . facetus   274 chaumos C 458
camos A 276/16, D* 369/18; *cf. Æ* 306/15 cauma swoloð   275 hyrnetu A* 261/
11, D*367/37   hyrnettu H C2024; *om.* C (*cf.* 255)   276 geneorð C 544
277 mygg longas tibias habet C 617   mycg, -gc *only* D 366/27, A 261/6
278 seorwum *only* C 545   orðoncum searwum D 365/17; *cf.* H C1231
commenta . . . sarwa orþanc dicta   279 cartamo, chartamo C 435, 459
cartamo A* 271/3   cartomo D 363/32;   lybcorn C (*both places*) DA*
281 cors C 546   choors A 283/1, D* 370/4;   numerus militum (= Abstr.
CO 41) tuun C tun *only* AD*; *cf.* H C1838 cors uilla   283 sadulboga
C 388 *etc.*   286 ynnilaec cipe C 448 (*cf.* R 134/19 cepe ennelec) cipe *only*
V 17   287 culinia C 620, H C2190 culini D 366/28; cocas CD cloacas H;
cf. A 283/11–12 culinia coc, coquina cycene, Abavus CO 45 colina coquina
288 crustula C 604, H C2142;   similis haalstaan C helsta ł rinde H
289 *om.* C *etc.* (*cf.* 302)   289a liim lapidum C 449 limi lapidem V 15
cesura lapidis . . . ł lim H C793   291 commisura C 554, H C1196

canti   felge
circinno   gabelrend
cox   huetistan
295 coxa   theoh
ceruical   bol
cassidele   pung
carpassini   græsgroeni
crus   scia
300 caldica   uuefl
cappa   snod
calmetu*m*   merix
colicum   aebordrotae
carbo   gloed
305 coruis   couel
colus   uuilmod
conpetum tuun *uel* ðrop
cornix   crauua
carduelis   linaethuigae
310 cantarus   uuibil
circius   uuestnorduuid
cartilago *grece*   grundsuopa f.4ᵛᶜᵈ

e
298 grẹs groni   307 *preceded by*
fraus regalis (354/58)   309 *fol-*
lowed by caradrion [on *after* crauua
on line above]: *cf.* C C148 caradrion
laurice, D 363/3 læwerce (§ 14)

---

292 faelge C 390   felga D 362/32   ferrum circa rotas (= C C92)
felga H C221; *cf.* A* 267/28 canti felg, A² 295/16 felgan, R 106/26
cantus felga   293 ferrum duplex unde pictores faciunt circulos i.
gaborind L 13/53   gabulrond *only* C 469; *cf.* H C961 circinnus gafelrod
294 cox C 555, D 365/21   cos L 46/4 *etc.*   296 capitale bolster ł
wongere H C686 (*cf.* 8 ef 30 ceruical et capitale unum sunt, R 124/21-2
capitale heafdbolster, ceruical wangere, A* 267/41 ceruical heafodbolster);
om. CDA   298 carpasini græsgroeni C 394   carbasini gærsgrene H C334
carrassinum grene gærs D 362/35   300 cladica C 482, D 364/23, A*
262/11, D* 367/43   cladia A² 294/3 cadicla H C1091;   wefl ł owef CD,
łoweb H (*cf.* A* 262/20 subtemen aweb)   wefl *only* A*D*A²   302 mersc
C 394 *etc.*   303 colicus eoburthrote C 558 *etc.*   305 corbus C 513
coruis D 365/26; cauuel, -wel CD   306 wulfmod C 559 wulmod H
C1612 *etc.*   307 conpetum C 557, D 365/24   competum H C1283; tuun,
tun þrop CD   uilla . . . ł þrop H   308 crawe C 538 *etc.*   309 linetuige
C 397, -twige D 363/2, R 132/29   311 westnorðwind C 470, D 364/6
312 grundsopa C 402 *etc.*

Dulcis sapa coerim   f. 4ᵛᵉᶠ
defructu*m* coerin
315 dolatum   gesn*i*dan
dodrans   aegur
dumus   thyrnae
deuotaturus   uuergendi
drom*idus* afyrid obbenda
320 dromidari*us*   se oritmon
dalaturae   braedlaestu aesc
decrepita   dobendi
desidebat   unsibbadae
dos   uuituma
325 delibutus   gisalbot   f. 5ᵃᵇ
delum*en*tem   thuachl
ditor   gifyrdro
depoline   uueftan
de confugione   statione hydde
330 disceptant   flitad
deliberatio   ymbdritung
delicatis et   quaerulosis
urastum

313–14 *on same line*   319 *on*
same line as preceding item, 356/2;

                                   u
āfyrid   326 thachl
328 *followed by* de exitu animae
                                   t
(356/30)   330 flicad

---

313 dulcis sapa C 709, V 24   dulcisapa D 385/41;   caerin C   coerin
V   cyren ł awylled win D (*cf.* A* 281/21 dulcisapa awilled win)   314 defrutum C 628, D 384/25   315 gesniden C 701, D 385/36   317 þyrne C
710   þorn ł þyrne D 385/42   spina spineta þyrne H D831   319 olbenda
C 707   olfenda D 385/39   320 se eorodmon C 708   321 dolatura
C 703, H D765;   braadlastæcus C   lata securis bradæx H; *cf.* Cl.I 390/13
dolatura bradæx (? Isidore, *Ety.* xix. 19/11 dolabra), L 47/47 dolabella
bradacus   322 *cf.* L 39/30 decrepitam dobend   323 *cf.* H D283 desidet
i. discordat (= Abstr. DI 71) . . . unsibbaþ   324 ł uuetma *ad.* C 704
325 gesmirwid C 676   gesmired, -smyred A 474/6, D* 386/31   326 delumentum C 641, D 384/33, A* 282/10, R 191/2, H D128;   ðhuehl C
þweal DA*R   lauatio þweal H   328 deponile C 642, A* 262/12, A² 294/4,
R 187/32, H D210   depoline D 384/34;   wefta CDA*A²   wefta ł weft R
weftan H   329 hyðae C 643; *cf.* H C1476 confugium i. statium portus
hyþ   331 ymbðriodung C 644 *etc.*   332 end seobgendum *ad.* C
645; *cf.* H D103 delicatus i. tenerus querulus

disparuit   ungiseem uard
defectura   aspringendi
335 decidens   geuuitendi
debita pensio   gedæbin gebil
deditio   hondgong
difficile   uernuislicæ
detractauit   forsoc
340 deuia callis horuaeg stug
distabueret   asundum
deperuntur   meldadum *uel*
roactu*n*
dehisciat   tecin*i*d
defecit   tedridtid
345 detr*i*turigine   agnidinne
345a dracontia   grimrodr
digitalium munusculoru*m*   f. 5^{cd}
fingirdoccun*a*
346a damina   bestia id*est* eola

Echo   uuydumer
edera   uuidouuindae
empticius   ceapcnext
350 enunum   cetil
ebor   elpendes ban

339 *followed by* uendidit diuidit
(356/48)   340 *followed by*
                                    c
distraxit (356/48)   346 docuna
after 357/1 *on line above*

---

333 ungesene C 682   336 gedaebeni geabuli C 648   gedefum gafule D 384/37
digna tributa gedafene gabul H D385   337 handgand C 649   handgong
D 384/38   traditio handgang H D371   340 callus C 651, D 384/40, H D359;
horweg stig CD   orweg stig H   341 distabuerunt C 683, D 385/24;
asundun C   aswundon D; *cf.* H D680 distabuit aswand   342 defferuntur
C 652, D 384/41;   meldadun ł wroegdun C   meldedon ł wregdan D
343 dehiscat C 653, D 384/42;   tocinit C, -eþ D   344 desicit C 654,
H D285;   tetridit C tetreþ H   345 detriturigine C 655 detriturugine
H D339; agnidine, -ene CH   345a gimrodr̄ C D364, -rodor D 385/40
346 musculorum C 687   masculorum V 22   346a damma C D12, L45/20;
bestia idest *om.* L.   349 ceapcneht C 742, -cniht D 392/5; *cf.* H
E251 empticius i. emptor uenditor cepemon   350 enum C 749, D
392/12   351 ebor C 712, D 391/17 ebur H E6;   elpendbaan C
elpanban ł elpend D   os elefantis elepenban H

erimio   hindbrere
expendisse   araebndae
egerere   ascrefan
355 exundauit   uueol
eluderet   auægdæ
exercitus   bigongu*m*
extorti   athraestae
exposito   geboronae   f. 5ᵉᶠ
360 emolom*entum*   fulteam
exaltauit   stanc
euiscerata   aeohed
egre   erabedlicae
effossis   achlocadum
365 expendisse   throu*a*dae
expedier*unt*   aræddun
exito   stæb *uel* p*er*di*t*io
exoleuer*unt*   gesuedradum
ex falange   ob threatae
370 e uertigo   stati*m uel* an landae
exauctorauit   *gi*heldae
expilatam   aritrid

$$\overset{r}{358\ \text{athaestae}}\qquad\overset{l}{364\ \text{achocadum}}$$

352 erimio C 758   erimo D 392/16   erimigio A² 298/2   erimius H E327; hindberge C hynd-, hindberige DA² hindbrer H   354 ascrepan C 730 *etc.* 355 auueol C 777 *etc.*   357 exercitus D 392/35   exercitiis C 779   exercitiis laboribus studiis H E448 (*cf.* T 76ᵇ exercitus laboribus, exercitatus studiis) 360 emolumentum C 743, D 392/6;   lean fultum C   fultum ł lean D; *cf.* H E253 emolumentum ... auxilium ... ł lean   361 exalauit (*altered from* exaltauit) D 392/39   exaltauit C 782   362 athed C 768   æthyd D 392/27 363 earfedlice C 729 *etc.*   365 expedisset C 783   expendisset D 392/40; *cf.* H E612 expendisset ... patiebatur   366 expedierant C 784, D 392/41   expedierunt H E603;   araeddun C   arærdon D   aræfdon ł ræddon H (*cf.* 353) 367 perditio endistaeb C 785 (*cf.* H E505–6 exitus ... endestæf, exitium ... perdictio)   endestæf *only* D 393/1   368 gesweðradun C 786   gesweþredon H E694   369 phalange C 787   falange D 393/2, V 30;   of ðreote of foeðan C of feþan of þreate D   ob treate *only* V; *cf.* H F80 falanx...þreat...feþa (= C 840) 370 uestigio C 769, D 392/29   uestigio H E385;   on lande (*corr.*) on laste C on laste ł on luste D   statim ł of laste H; *cf.* C E345 euestigio statim (= Abstr. EV 11)   371 geheende C 788   gehiende D 393/3   deordinauit gehende H E410; *cf.* A 474/9 exactoratus gehened   372 aþryid arytrid C 789 ahrydred aþrid D 393/4   conquassatam aþrydł arydred H E547; *cf.* C 817 expilatam arydid

expeditio   fertd
elegio   geddi
375 egesta   ascrepaeni
echinus   piscis uel scel
extentera   anseot   f. 5ᵛᵃᵇ
emlemma   fothr
eptasyllon   vii folia idest
gilodusrt
380 exagium   handmitta
extale   snaedil uel thearm   f. 5ᵛᶜᵈ
emunctoria   candelthuist
ephilenticus uuoda
excolat   siid
385 exta   bæcdermi
electirum   elothr
eptafolium   sinfullae
elleborus   poedibergæ
epimemia   nest
390 efetidem   cop   f. 5ᵛᵉᶠ
esculus ob edendo beccae

373 feịtd [*punctuation intended
for* t ?]   379 gilodusrt] t *after*
fothr *on line above*
391 *followed by* enfatibus (? 359/34
cf. C E220 enfaticus) *circled,
presumably for deletion*

373 fird herenitig D 393/5, hergung ferd H E607 (*cf.* C 821 expeditio hergiung)
faerd *only* C 790   374 elogio C 733   eulogio (*altered from* elogio) D 391/39;
cf. A 474/10 eologium gedd, H E213 elogium . . . carmen fanum ł gyd
375 ascrepen C 731, D 391/36   377 exintera C 791   exentera D 393/7,
R 190/30;   ansceat, -sceot CD   unsceot ł geopena R   378 emblema C 744, L 43/30   emlemma D 392/7   379 eftafylon, eptafyllon C
725, 753   eptafylon D 391/30,   -filon A² 298/31, B 69ᵃ, B² 155;   gelodwyrt
only C (*both places*) DA²   gelowyrt vii. folia B   idest vii folia gelodvyrt B²
380 andmitta C 793   onmitta H E413   handmitta A 475/3   381 snaedil-,
snædelþearm C 794, D 393/10   snædelþearm . . . ł bacþearm H E584,
snædel ł bærcþearm R 159/39 (*cf.* 385)   snædel *only* A* 272/13   382 can-
deltuist C 745 *etc.*   383 epilenticus C 754   385 praecordia (Abol. EX
11) baecþearm C 801   386 electrum C 735, R 134/31, Æ 310/11–12
eleotrum B² 147;   elotr C   elehtre RÆ   eleotre B²; *cf.* B 69ᶜ electrum
i. lupinus   388 þung woedeberge C 736   wedeberge þung D 391/40
vedeberige ł thung B² 148   rediberge *only* B 69ᵛᶜ; *cf.* C 1017 helleborus
woidiberge   389 epimenia C 756   390 ependiten C 757, A* 268/5   eren-
diten D 392/20   ependeton R 188/14   391 boece, bece *only* C 766, D 392/26

	edera	ifeg
	ebulu*m*	uualhuyrt
	exactio	gebles monung
395	erpica	egdae
	erpicarius	egderi
396a	expediam	arectio
	erugo	rost

f 5^{ab}

ÉPINAL			ERFURT		
Facitiae	gliu		Facitiae	gliu	
fiber	bebr		fiber	bebr	
flustra	undae *uel* hraen	400	frustra	unde *uel* raen	
forfices	sceroro		forfices	sceroro	
fouit	feormat		fouit caeormad		
fiscilla	taenil		fiscella	tenil	
(430a)		403a	fucus	fex	
flauu*m*	*uel* fulfu*m* read		flauum *uel* fulfum	reod	f. 6^{ab}
fibrae	librlaeppan	405	fibrae	librlaeppan	
fastidiu*m*	ciisnis		fastidiu*m*	ciinis	
fax	fæcilae		fax	faecile	
fibula	sigil		fibula	sigil	

396 egderi *followed by* [pere]
grinorum (359/49)   396a ex-
pediam] a *from* u   402 *on
same line as preceding item*, 360/5;
caeormad] d *from* t

---

392 ifegn C 718   ifig D 391/22 *etc.*; *cf.* L 17/11 hederam ibaei   393 wal-
hwyrt C 714   wealwyrt D 391/19   walwyrt R 134/23   welwyrt siue
ellenþyrt B 69ᵃ   vealvyrt ł ellenvyrt B² 146; *cf.* L 42/4 elleus ualuyrt
394 *cf.* L 39/27 exactio monung gaebles   396a arecio C E523
397 rust C 763, D 392/23, H E332;   om ł tinea *ad.* H   398 facetia
(*altered from* facitia) C 825   facitiæ D 401/45; *cf.* R 191/1 facetiae wynsum
gliw   400 flustra C F212, D 403/27, H F543;   unda *only* C
undæ sigend D   unda yþ ædwella H; *cf.* Cl.I 399/14 flustra flod ł hærn
401 *cf.* A 475/6 fofex, D* 405/29 forfex scer, H F644 forfices ræglsceara
402 fouet C 899   fouit D 403/39;   feormat broedeth C   bredeþ feormaþ D
403 fiscilla C 868, D 403/1   404 fuluum read C 887, D 403/28
fuluum rubeum geoleread ł geolecrog H F420 (*cf.* 432)   405 lifre
læppan ł þearmas R 160/39   librlaeppan *only* C 873   þearmas *only* D 403/6
marg.; *cf.* C 870, D 403/4 fibra þearm, H F317 fibra i. uena iecoris (=
Abol. FI 13) . . . liferlappa þearm   406 odium (*corr.*) cymnis C 829
odium . . . ł nausia (= Abol. FA 31) . . . ł cisnes H F7   407 *om.* CDAH;
cf. A* 266/38 fax þæcile blysige, Cl.I 399/38 fecele blysige   408 hringe
sigl C 874, sigel ł hringe fifele D 403/7 (*cf.* 410)   sigl spennels H F319

	ÉPINAL			ERFURT	
	furca	uueargrod		finicia	beoso
	fibula	hringiae	410	furca	uaergrod
	fenicia	baeso		fibula	hringae
	flegmata	horh		flegmata	horh
	frugus	uncystig *uel* heamol		frugus uncystig *uel* healful	
	frixum	afigaen		fraxinus	aastc
	ferinum	hold	415	fagus	boecce
f. 5cd	fraximus	aesc		frixum	afigen
	fagus	boecae		ferinum	hold
	fusarius	uuananbeam		fagus	uuonanbeam
	fulix	ganot *uel* dopaenid		fulix ganot uel dopaenid	
	filix	fearn	420	filix	feran
	fraga	obtt		fraga	obea
	ficetula	sugga		ficetula	sucga
	fringella	finc		fringella	finc
	fasianus	uuorhana		fassianus	uuorhona
	furuncus	mearth	425	furuncus	meard
	famfaluca	leasung *uel* faam		famfaluca laesung *uel* faam	
	fungus	suamm		fungus	suamm
	furfures	siuida		furfures	siuida
	fitilium	aegergelu			

a
409 uuergrod   411 fenicia] e
                      g
very faint   413 uncysti
417 fagus] r *erased after* f
                 g
423 frincella

425 furuncus *followed by* ð (§ 12);
meard *preceded by* ħ (§ 12), *after*
uuorhona *on line above*
426 *after* furuncus (425)

409(10) furcimen furca H F976   furcimen *only* C 930   furca *only* A 476/3
410(11) *cf.* 408   411(409) finicia C 877, D** 409/32   finitia V 32
finicium H F324   fenicia D 403/11   412 flegmata C 888, D 403/29
flegma D 403/30 *marg.*, A 475/10, A* 264/5, A² 290/32, H F456; ł mældroppa
ad. H   413 uncystig heamul C 917   uncystig ł heamol D 404/9–10;
fercuþ *ad.* D *marg.* (= A 476/1 frugus fercuþ); *cf.* R 165/11 frugi ł parcus
(= Abol. FU 36 frugi parci an auari) uncystig   416(14) fraxinus aesc
C 920 *etc.*   417(15) boece C 828 *etc.*   418 fusarius C 935, D**
409/33; *cf.* H F925 fusarius trabs uinee winbeam   420 fearn C 871 *etc.*
421 obet C 919   ofet D 404/13 *etc.*   424 fasianus C 830, D 402/3
425 furunculus H F908, -as L 47/76   furuncus C 937, D 404/25   feruncus Æ
309/9   ferunca ł ferunculus R 118/44   426 faam (*corr.*) leasung C 832
leasung ł fam D 402/5; *cf.* L 47/19 famfelvcas laesungae   427 ł feld-
swam *ad.* D 404/26   428 sifiðan C 940   siuida V 38   sifeða A² 297/20;
cf. B² 178 furfur sifeþa   429 *om.* C *etc.*

falces uudubil sigdi riftr	430 falcis uuidubil sigdi riftr	f. 6^{cd}

falces   uudubil sigdi riftr

fucus   fex

flabanus   suan

flabum   gelu

furuum   bruun

fibrans risaendi

fenus   spearuua

foederatas   gitreeudae

funestauere   smitor

f. 5^{ef} frons   hleor

funestissima   tha deatlicostan

framea   aetgaeru

fasces   goduuebb

fornicem   bogan

feriatis quietis *ue*l securis *ue*l
restaendu*m*

facundia   eloquentia *ue*l
þoot

flamma   blaeed

430 falcis uuidubil sigdi riftr   f. 6^{cd}

430a   (403a)

flabanus   suan

flauum   gelu

furuum   bruun

fibrans   ripendi

435 fenus   spearua

foederatas   getreudæ

funestauere   smiton

fros   hleor

funestissim*a*   da deudlicustan

440 framea   aetgaru

faces   guoduueb

fornicem   bogan

feriatus   quietis   securis *ue*l
restendu*m*

facundia   eloquentia *ue*l
puood

445 flamm*a*   bled

---

434 *between the lines*
437 funestauere] *first curve of* e (?)
after first u   **438** hleor] h
added in margin   **439** funestis-
sima] *first curve of* e (?) *before* u

e
436 getrudæ   **442** bogant
d
444 puoo

---

430 falcis C 834, D 402/7, A 477/21; uudubil sigdi *om.* A; riftras C rifter, -tre DA; *cf.* H F63 falcis wingeardseax rifter ł sicul **430a** faex taelg C 934   tælg ł feax D** 409/31; *cf.* A 475/9 fucus telg deah, D* 405/30 telg deag, H F858 deah ł telg   **431** *cf.* H F432 flabanus custos porcorum   **432** flabum C 890, D 403/32   **433** furuum i. nigrum (= Abstr. FU 37) D 404/21   furbum *only* C 931   **434** risende C 879 hrissende D 403/19   hrysiende H F318   **436** getreuuade C 900 getrewde D** 409/34   getreowed getreude D 402/31   **437** smiton C 941   maculauere smittodan H F887   **438** fons C 923   frons H F771; andwlita *ad.* H   **439** deadlicustan C 942 *etc.*   **440** aetgaeru C 922   sweord ł ætgare D 404/15 (*cf.* Isidore, *Ety.* xviii. 6/3 framea uero gladius)   **441** fasces C 827, D 402/8, H F11;   libri (*corr.*) goduueb C (*cf.* 9 ab 10 fastes libri) godweb ł ealdordomas D (*cf.* R 155/19 fasces ealdordomas) honores (= Abstr. FA 78) . . . cynedomas ł ealdor[domas] . . . ł godweb H   **443** feriæs D 402/27   fereatis H F190; *om.* C *but cf.* 854 feriatus gerested   **444** eloquentia *only* C F36   eloquentia woþ D 402/9   **445** flamina D 403/33, A* 266/31   flamma C 892;   blæd CA* biscophadas ł blæd D (*cf.* H F406 flaminea i. episcopali gradu ł sacerdotali biscophadas ł sacerd[hadas])

ÉPINAL		ERFURT	
fragor	suoeg	fragor	suoeg
famfaluca	uuapul	fanfaluca	uuapul
floccus	loca	flocous	loca
falcastru*m*	uuidubil	falcastru*m*	uuidubil
ferula	aescthrotae	450 ferola	aescdrotae
finiculus	finugl	finiculus	finugl f. 6*ef*
faonius	uuestsuduuind		

f. 5*vab*

ÉPINAL		ERFURT	
fornix	boga sup*er* columnis	fornix	boga sup*er* columnis
follis	blestbaelg	follis	blestbaelg
fellitat	suggit	455 fellitat	suggid

f. 5*vcd*

ÉPINAL		ERFURT	
Gurgulio	throtbolla	Gurgulio	ðrotbolla f. 6*vab*
gurgustiu*m*	cesol	gurgustiu*m*	cesol
giluus	gelu	giluus	gelu
gibbus	hofr	gypb*us*	hosr
gipsus	sparaen	460 gypsus	sparen
glarea	cisil	glare	cisal
glumula	scalu	glamula	scalu
gladiolu*m*	segg	gladiolum	secg
gramen	quiquae	gram*en*	quicae
genistae	broom	465 geniste	broom
galla	galluc	galla	galluc

i
453 forn*a*x
461 *followed by* [re]rum gignenda/
rum (10 cd 22)   463 *followed*
by nubentibus (10 cd 28)
    q
464 cuiquae

451 *followed by* habent (361/50)
455 ꞅ *before* suggid;   suggid] d
from t   456 *on same line as*
following item, 362/46
461 *followed by* omnium rerum
(362/56)   463 *followed by*
nubentibus (363/6)
466 galluc] c *from* s

---

446 suoeg cirm C 925   cirm sweg gebrec (*corr.*) D 404/17   cirm ł sweg H
F653   447 famfaluca C 835, D 402/10   448 floccus C 893, D 403/36
449 wudubil ł siþe D 402/7 (*cf.* Cl.I 400/12 falcastrum siþe) ferramentum
curuum a similitudine falcis (= Isidore, *Ety.* xx. 14/5) wudubil ł foddur[bil]
H F66 wudubil *only* C 836   450 ferula C 861, H F203, A² 298/20 furula
D 402/35 *marg.*   451 finulae C 880   finul D 403/20   452 faonius C 837,
D** 409/35 fauonius D 402/12   454 *cf.* H F625 follis . . . mantica fabrilis
blædbylig   455 suggit C 862, H F271   457 *cf.* L 19/38 gurgustium
chelor   459 gippus hofr C 969; *cf.* Æ 322/1 gibbus ł struma hofer
460 gipsus C 968, D 413/8;   spaeren C spæren D; cf. Æ 319/6 gipsum
spærstan   461 glarea cisilstan C 975, D 413/10, ceosolstan A²288/36
462 glumula C 976   464 cuice C 989 *etc.* birecta cwice A² 301/5 (*cf.*
1088)   465 genista C 959 *etc.*

grassator ferhergænd	grassator ferhergend
garbas sceabas	garbas sceabas
f. 5^vef grallus hrooc	grallus hrooc f. 6^vcd
genisculas muscellas	469a geniscul*a*e muscellae
glis eglae	470 glis egilae
galmaria caluuaer	galmaria caluuer
glomer cleouuae	glomer cleuuue
glaucum hæuui *uel* grei	glaucum h*a*uui *uel* grei
gracilis smael	(477a)
glus frecnis	475 glus frecnis
galbalacru*m* caluuaer	galm*a*ria caluuer
galmum molegn	galmu*m* moleng
(474)	477a gracilis sm*a*l
(486)	477b gam*i*lla lim molegn
globus leoma	globus leuma
gregarioru*m* aedilra	gregarioru*m* aedilra
genuino gecyndilican	480 genuino gecyndilican
gladiatores caempan	gladiatores cempan
genas hleor	genus hleor
giluus falu	giluus falu
gurgulio aemil	gurgulio aemil
gelum frost	485 gelum frots

469 hrooc] h *added in margin*
472 cleouuae] *no stroke over* e *as read by Schlutter*

      c   u
476 galbalarū caluaer
480 gecyndilican] e *from* i

        ri
471 galmaa

469 grallus C 991, A* 260/10, D* 413/33   gralus A² 286/6   garallus L 47/51 grauculus D 412/20; *cf.* R 132/15 cracculus ł garrulus (? Isidore, *Ety.* xii. 7/45) hroc, Æ 307/11–12 graculus hroc   469a genisculas muscellas C G55; *cf.* A* 261/34 genicula muxle, D* 413/37, A² 293/21 mucxle 470 fonfyr ł egle D 413/12   egle *only* C 973, L 45/6   471 *cf.* A* 280/34 calmaria cealfre, D* 369/29 cealre   472 clouue C 979 cleowen D 413/13, R 187/31   cliwen A* 262/16, A² 294/8   474 smæl C 992 *etc.*   475 ł lim *ad.* D 413/15 (*cf.* Cl.III 526/26 glus lim) 476 gabalacrum C 956, D 413/3   477 moling C G20   molegn D 413/4; *cf.* A* 280/35, D* 369/30 calmum molegn, C 953(G21) galmulum molegn-stycci   479 unaeðilsa C 993 unæþelra D 413/25   480 *om.* C *etc. but cf.* 487   482 genas C 962, D** 415/36; heagaspen C (*cf.* A* 263/34 genæ heagoswind, D* 413/39 heagospind) hleor D**   484 *sic* C 1003; *cf.* 257   485 gelum C 964 gelu D** 415/37, R 175/13, Æ 306/3; forst CD**RÆ

galmilla liim molegn   (477b)
            genuinum intimum *uel* dens
            id*est* tusc

f. 6ab	Hebitatus astyntid		Hebetatus astyntid	f. 6vef
	Hastilia teloru*m* scaeptloan			
	hebesceret asuand	490	hebescer*et* ansuand	
	hebitauit aslacudae		habitauit aslacudae	
	habitudines geberu		habitudines geberu	
f. 6cd	hyadas raedgaesra*n*		hyadas redgaesram	
	horno thys geri		horno thys geri	f. 7ab
	hiulca cinaendi	495	hiulca cinendi	
	hibiscum biscopuuyrt		hibiscum biscopuuyrt	
	horodius uualhhebuc		horodius uualhhaebuc	
	hirundo sualuuae		hirundo sualuae	

f. 6ef	Indruticans uuraestendi		Indruticans uraesgendi	
	inhians gredig	500	inhians gredig	
	inluuies secundaru*m* hama in		inluuies secundaru*m*	f. 7cd
	quo fit paruulus	(501a)	hama in quo fit paruulus	
	inpetigo tetr		inpegit teg	
	intestinu*m* thearm		intestinum thearm	
	interamen innifli		interamen inifli	
	iliu*m* neuu*n*seada	505	ilium naensida	
f. 6vab	instites suedilas		instites suedilas	

488 astyn:::tid 490 hebesceret
    h
497 uualhebuc *with* uu *over an*
        e
erasure 499 uurastendi
    u
501 paruulis 502 t:etr

487 tuṅsc   498 sualṅuae
501a hama . . . paruulus *written as*
separate item on line below 501
    r
503 theam

---

486 galmilla C 954, D 413/5; liim caluuer C lim molegn D;
cf. A* 280/36 calmilla lim 487 genuino tusc naturale C 961 (*cf.* 480)
488 hebitatus C 1012, D 417/7 490 asuand C 1013 aswand D 417/9
491 hebitabit C 1014, -uit D** 418/19; *cf.* Cl.I 418/19 habitauit aslacude
492 habitudines C 1006 habitudo D 416/35 493 raedgasram (*altered*
from -an?) C 1035 496 merscmealwe *ad.* D 417/13 497 herodius C
1016 *etc.* 499 wraestendi C 1045 502 impetigo teter C 1047, D
422/1 504 innifli C 1059 inilfe A 476/12 inelue A* 272/14 505 *om.*
C *etc. but cf.* C 1041(I44) ilia midhridir nioðanweard hype, I45 ilium uiscera

intexunt	auundun		intexunt	auundun
increpitans	hlaeodrindi		increpitans	hleodendri
inlex	tyctaend anb inlici-		inlex	tychtend ab inlici-
endi			endo	
infestus	flach	510	infestus	flach
intercaeptum	araepsid		interceptum	arepsit
infandum	maanful		infandum	meinfol
inlecebris	tyctinnum		inlecebris	tyctinnum
ingratus	lath		ingratus	laad
inritatus	in rixam	515	inritatus	in rixam gigremit
gigræmid				
incitamenta	tyctinnae		incitamenta	tyctinnae
iota	soctha	516a	iota	soctha f. 7ef
iungetum	riscthyfil		iungetum	rycthyfil
intula	uualhuuyrt		intula	uualhuyrt
inprobus	gimach		inprobus	gemach
ingruerit	anhriosith	520	ingruerit	onhrisit
intractabilis	unlidouuac		intractabilis	unliuduuac
incomodum	unbryci		incommodum	unbrycci
interceptum est	raebsid		interceptum est	repsit uaes
uuaes				
insimulatione	uuroctae		insimulatione	uurochtae
inpendebatur	gibaen uuaes	525	inpendebatur	geben uaes
f. 6vcd interpellari	raefsed		interpellari	refset
industria	geeornnissae		industria	gyrnissæ

	ciendi
507 auundū̄	509 inli
n	ta
513 tyctinum	516 incimenta
g	a
520 inruerit	523 rebsid

525 uuaes] curve of a after first u
527 gereorḍnnissae with first r and
ḍ erased

516 tyctinnāe   518 uuahuyrt
526 de erased before refset
527 after habitat (365/48) from
column d and o from next item

507 wundun C 1062 awunden D 422/12   508 hleoþrendi C 1065
hleþrende D** 428/18   509 tyctendi only C 1063   511 interceptum arasad C 1067   512 manful C 1069   515 in rixam om. C
1073; gegremid C   516a sochtha C 1151 sohctha D 422/36; cf. A*
281/10 iuta awilled milc   517 riscŏyfel C 1159 etc.   518 uualhwyrt
C 1075 wealewyrt D** 428/23 walwyrt A² 299/8 welwyrt B 70ᵃ valvyrt
B² 207   520 onhrioseŏ C 1077   522 incommodum unbryce C 1050
523 raefsit C 1084   524 feringe C 1085   526 interpellare raefsit C
1087   527 geornis C 1088 geornnisse D** 428/25

ÉPINAL			ERFURT	
inpendebat	saldae		inpendebat saltae	
in dies	crudesceret a fordh		in dies crudesceret	a forthe
in transmigratione in foer- nissae		530	in transmigrationem	in fornissæ
iners	asolcaen		iners	asolcæn
interuentu	þingungae		interuentu	ingungae
inlectus	gitychtid		inlectus	getyctid
interlitam	bismiridae		interlitan	bismirida
inpactæ	anslegaengrae	535	inpactæ	aslegenræ
indigestae	unofaercumen- rae		indigestae	unofercumenræ
innitentes	uuidirhliniendae		innitenter	uuidirlinienti
insolesceret	oberuuaenidae		insolesceret	oberuenedæ
inpulsore	baedendrae		inpulsore	bedændræ
infractus	giuuaemmid	540	infractus	geuemmid
inopimum	unaseddae		inopimum	unasettæ
inditas	þa gisettan		inditas	þa gisettai
infici	gimaengdae		infici	gimengdæ
index	taecnaendi torctendi		index	taecnendi torchtendi f. 7ᵛᵃᵇ
inpostorem	bisuicend	545	inposterem	bisuiccend
inter primores bituicn ael- drum			inter primores bituichn æeldrum	
intercapido	fristmearc		intercapito	fritmaerc

ne
530 transmigratio

n
535 asle-
rae
gaengrae   536 unofaer cumen

e
538 insolescerįt   542 þagi:settan

di
544 torcten

c
546 bituin

528 *after* perfecti[o] (365/49) *from*
column d   544 torchtendi]
tendi *after* 367/5 *on line above*

---

528 salde C 1089   sealde D** 428/26   529 aforht C 1090   aforð D**
428/27   530 transmigrationem, foernisse C 1091   531 eswind
asolcen C 1092   æswind asolcen D 422/13   532 þingunge C 1093,
D** 428/28   534 interlitam C 1095, D 422/14;   bismiride C besmyred
D   535 onligenre C 1096   anslægenre D** 428/29   536 unober-
cumenre C 1097   unofercumene D 422/15   539 baedendre C 1100
bædendre D** 428/31   540 ungeuuemmid C 1101   gewemmed D**
428/32   541 unasaedde C 1102   unasedde D** 428/33   542 gesettan C 1103, D** 428/34   544 tacnendi C 1105   545 inposterem
C 1106 inpastorem D 422/17;   besuuicend C, -swicend D   546 bitun
C 1107   betweon D 422/17   betweoh D** 428/35   547 intercapido
firstmaerc C 1108

ÉPINAL		ERFURT	
insolens	feruuaenid	insolens	feruendid
in curia	in maethlae	in cur*ia*	in medlæ
in mimo	in gliuuae q*uod*	in mimo	in gliuuae q*uod*
tamen ad	mimarios *uel*	t*amen* ad	mimarios *uel*
mimografos	p*er*tinet	mimigraphos	p*er*tinet
iurisperiti	redboran	iurisperiti	redboran
inuisus	laath	inuissus	lath
in aestiuo	caenaculi uppae	in aestiuo	cænaculo yppe p*er*
ubi per	aestate*m* frigus	aestate*m* fr*i*gus capiatur	
captant			
iuuar	leoma *uel* earendil	iuuar leoma *uel* oerendil	
isic	leax	isic	lex
(562)		isca	tyndrin
ignariu*m*	algiuueorc	ignarium	algiuerc
inuolucus	uulluc	inuociucus	uulluc
incuba	mera *uel* satyrus	incuba	merae *uel* saturn*us*
inuoluco	uuidubindlae	inuolucu	uuydublindæ
ibices	firgingaett	ibices	firgingaett
infridat	caelith	infr*i*gidat	cælid
isca	tyndirm	(555a)	

f. 6^vef (left, at "in mimo" row) · 550 (Erfurt, at "in mimo") · 555 (Erfurt, at "isic") · 555a (Erfurt, at "isca") · 560 (Erfurt, at "ibices") · f. 7^vcd (right) · f. 7^ab (left, at "isca tyndirm")

Lebes	huuer	Leues	huuer
lepor	subtilitas *uel* uuoþ	lepor	subtilitas *uel* puod

550 mimografos pertinet *above line*
553 :: uppae;   [aes]tatem . . .
captant *above line*
      eo
556 algiuurc   557 inuolucus]
c *from* s   558 satyrus] u *erased*
after t *and* y *written over it*

550 [mi]marios . . . pertinet *on line*
below   553 aestatem . . .
capiatur *on line below*
563 huuer *followed by* ł porcos
(368/9)   564 ꝑuod

548 foruuened C 1109   550 in gliowe *only* C 1112   in gluuiæ quod
tamen ad minarios ł mimographus pertinet V 40; *cf.* A 476/14 mimum gliw
552 inuisus C 1113, D** 428/21   553 coenaculo yppe ubi . . . captant
C 1114   554 iubar earendel C 1161, iubar leoma C 1166   555 isic
C 1155, A* 261/32, D* 423/36   ysox A² 293/19   esocius ł salmo R 180/33
ysicius ł salmo Æ 308/4–5   557 inuolucus C 1115, D 422/19   inuo-
lucrus L 47/20   558 maere *only* C 1111   maerae ł saturus L 47/81
559 inuoluco C 1116, D** 428/36, L 47/98; uudubinde C uudubindlae L
wiþewinde D** (*cf.* 1059)   560 firgengaet C 1037, -gæt D** 428/37
561 infridat C 1119   562 isca C 1156, D 422/38   isica L 47/29, A*
266/39   sica A² 294/30;   tyndrin C tyndri L tyndre DA* tindre A²
563 lebes C 1197, D 432/15, R 123/39, Æ 316/5   lenes A 276/11; ł cytel
ad. R   564 wooð *only* C 1196

lagones	mettocas		565 lagonas	mettocas
liburnices	gerec		liburnices	gerec
labarum	seng		labarum	segn
lurcones	auidi *uel* sigiras		lurcones	sigiras *uel* auidi
larbula	egisigrima		larbula	egisigrima
lunules	menescillingas		570 lunules	meniscillingas

f. 7^{cd} lituus baculum augurale in   lituus baculum augurale in f. 7^{vef}
　　prima parte curuum idest   　　prima parte curuum idest
　　crycc   　　crycc

lacerna	haecilae *uel* lotha	lacerna hecile *uel* lotha	
lumbare	gyrdils *uel* broec	laxe olor	
laxhe olor		573a lumbare gyrdils broec	
luculentum	torchtnis	luculentum torhtnis	
lymphatico	uuoendendi	575 lymphatico uuodenti	
liuida toxica	tha uuannan	liuida toxica tha uuannan	
aetrinan		etrinani	
ludi litterari	staebplegan	ludi litterali scæbplega	
liquentes	hlutrae	linquentes hlutrae	
lenocium	thyctin *uel* scocha	lenotium tyctin *uel* scocha	
lacessit	graemid	580 lacessit gremid	
lenta	tarda *uel* toch	lenta tarda *uel* thoch	
legula	gyrdislrhingae	legu gyrdilshringe	

---

567 labarum] *tail of first* a *faint*
571 curuum . . . crycc *in upper*
margin;　curuum] *stroke over* u
partly cut away　　572 lotha]
th *from* d　　576 liuida] d
erased before u　　583 thres]
first curve of e *before* r

569 egisigriṁma　　　　571 in
prima . . . crycc *across both columns*
on line below　　　　　ni
　　　　　　　　576 etrina

---

565 *om.* C *etc.* (*cf.* 586)　　567 labrum segn C 1167; *cf.* L 35/69 uixilla
et labrum idem sunt idest segin, Cp. 2093 uexilla seign　　568 siras *only*
C 1241; *cf.* A 476/20 lurco sur　　569 egisgrima C 1168　　egesegrima
D 431/35　　grima A 476/21　　570 lunulus C 1242　　lunules A 476/22;
mene A　menescillingas C　　571 baculum idest *om.* C 1222　　572 *cf.*
R 187/14–15 lacerna hacele geflenod ł gecorded (? Isidore, *Ety.* xix. 24/14
lacerna pallium fimbriatum)　　573(3a) gyrdils broec C 1244　　gyrdel ł
brec D 433/12　　573a(3) laxhe holor C L16; *cf.* 607　　575 woedendi
C 1263　wedende D** 439/3　　576 aetrinan C 1215　ætrenan D 432/30
577 litterari C 1245, -re D 433/14;　　staefplegan C　stæfplegan D
578 liquentes C 1216　　579 lenocinium tyhten *only* C 1199　　580 *sic*
C 1170 laccesiens gremmende D 432/6　　581 lenta toh *only* C 1198
582 legula C 1202, D 432/17;　　gyrdilshringe C　gyrdelhringe D; *cf.*
C 1226 lingula gyrdilshringe, D 432/16 gyrdelhringe

ÉPINAL			ERFURT	
	lembum	listan uel thres	lembum	listan uel ðres
	lagoena	croog	lagoena	croog
f. 7ef	lutrus	otr	585 lutrus	octur
	ligones	mettocas	lagones	metocas
	lucius	haecid	lucius	haecid
	lucanica	maerh	lucanica	mærh
	lurdus	laempihalt	lurdur	lemphihalt
	lendina	hnitu	590 lendina	hnitu
	lexiua	leag	lexiua	læg
	lupus	baers	lupus	baers
	lacessitus	gigraemid	lacessitus	gigremid
	lien	multi	lien	milti
	laquear	fierst	595 laquear	firt
	ludaris	steor	ludaris	steor
	lacunar	flodae	lacunar	flodae
	leuir	tacor	leuir	tacor
	lolium	atae	lolium	atte
	lodix	lotha	600 lodix	lotha
	lactuca	þuþistil	lactuca	popistil
	liciatorium	hebild	licitorium	hebild
	lihargum	slægu	lihargum	slægu
	licidus	huet	lucidus	huaet
	lectidiclatum	githuornae	605 lectidicladum	githuorne
	fleti		fleti	

f. 8ab

587 haecid] h *added in margin*
590 lendina] *first* n *from* m   602
:::::: hebild   603 *between the lines*

584 lagon͡a   585 lotr͡us

583 listan *only* C 1201   liste ł þræs D 432/18; *cf.* C 1228 limbus ðres liste,
D 432/19 listum ł þræsum   585 otr C 1246 *etc.*   586 ligones C 1211,
D 432/27;   meottucas C mettocas D   589 lemphalt C 1250, -healt D
433/17, A 476/24, -hald L 47/45   591 laexiua C 1175   lexiua D 431/39
lixa A 476/26, D* 435/19   592 bres C 1251   bears D 433/18   bærs A*
261/37, A² 293/29, R 180/26; *cf.* L 47/72 lupus breuis   594 milte C 1217 *etc.*
595 first hrof C 1176 (*cf.* 609) fierst *only* D 432/3 *etc.*   596 ludarius C
1252, -res D 433/19   laudaris A* 274/26   597 flode hrof D 432/5 (*cf.* 609)
flode *only* C 1178, D** 439/5   598 frater mariti *ad.* R 174/38 (Isidore,
Ety. ix. 7/17)   599 ate C 1235 *etc.*   601 þuðistel C 1179, D 432/7;   leahtric
ad. D (*cf.* A² 297/18 lactuca leahtric)   602 liciatorium C 1219, D 432/33;
hebelgerd C   hefeldgyrd D; *cf.* C 1232 licium hebeld, D 433/10 hefeld
604 licidus C 1223 licidus, liquidus D 433/4–5;   huæt C huet D (*both places*)
605 lectidiclatum C 1205, D 432/22   lac tudiclum A* 280/29, D* 435/12;
geþuorne C geþroren D geþrofen A* geþrorene D*

ÉPINAL			ERFURT		
lapatiu*m*	lelodrae		lapatiu*m*	lelodrae	
lanx	helor		lanx	helor	
f. 7ᵛᵃᵇ lepus leporis	hara		lepus læporis hæra		
lacuna	hrof		lacun*a*	hrof	
laris	men	610	laris	meu	
limax	snel		lim*ax*	snegl	
lumbricus	regenuuyrm		lumbr*i*cus	regnuuyrm	f. 8ᶜᵈ
lappa	cliþae		lappa	clifae	
lentu*m* uimen	toch gerd		lentu*m*	uim*en* thoh gerd	
ligustru*m*	hunaegsugae	615	ligustru*m*	hunegsugae	

f. 7ᵛᶜᵈ Mordicos	bibitnae		Mordicos	bibitnae	
manipulatim	threatmelu*m*		manipulatim	theatmelu*m*	
mendacio conposito gereg-			mendacio	*con*psito gerad-	f. 8ᵉᶠ
nodae			nodae		
molestissimu*m*	earbet-		molestissimu*m*	easbed-	
licust			licust		
municeps burgleod a mucipio		620			
munifica	cistigian		munificit		
monarchia	anuuald		monarch*i*a	anuald	
mirifillon	millefoliu*m* ger-		mirifillon	millefoliu*m* ger-	
uuae			uæ		
murica gespan aureu*m* in tu-			murica	gespan *a*ureum in	
nica			tonica		
f. 7ᵛᵉᶠ modioli	nabae	625	modioli	nebæ	

609 hrof] h *added in margin*	608 *followed by* quæ cum intro
618 geregnodae] eg *from* e	canit [= 14 b 5 qui cum lituo canit]
619 earbetlicust] c *from* s	609 *followed by* lititen [= 14 a 5 lici-
620 *between the lines*; municeps]	ter, *for* liciten] 624 tonica] nica
curve of c (?) *before* u	*on line above*
623 millefolium] e *erased before*	
first i	

608 lepus leporis C 1206 lepus *only* D 432/23, Æ 309/15 lepus ł lagos R 119/11 609 *om.* C *etc. but cf.* C 1180 lacunar hebenhus, D 432/8 hushefen ł heofenhrof *and* 595 610 larus C 1183, D 432/9; meau C meu D 613 clibe C 1184, -ue B 70ᶜ clite V 41 (*cf.* L 15/36 lappa clitæ) 614 toh C 1207, D 432/24 617 þreatmelum C 1265 618 conposito geregnade C 1301, gerenode D 443/14 619 earbetlicust C 1320; *cf.* Cl.I 444/16 *marg.* molestissimum earfoðlicost 620 burgliod *only* C 1334 621 munifica cystigan C 1335 622 anuualda C 1321 623 miri-fillo gearwe C 1315 mirefilon i. gearwe B 70ᵛᵇ mirofilon millefolium T 98ᵛᵃ; *cf.* 639 624 gespon *only* C 1336 *etc.*

ÉPINAL		ERFURT	
mancus	anhendi	mncus	anhaendi
mafortae	scybla	maforte	scybla
morgit	milciþ	morgit	milcid
mossiclum	ragu	mossuclum	ragu
mimoparo	thebscib	630 mimoparo	thebscip
manica	gloob	manica	glob
momentum	scytil	momentum	scytil
manile	lebil	manile	lebil
manitergium	liin	manutergium	lim
f. 8ᵃᵇ malagna	salb	635 malagma	salb
(641)		635a mastigia	suibæ
malus	apuldur	malus	apuldro
martus	uuyr	melarium milc apuldr	
melarium	milsc apuldr	myrtus uuyr	
(646)		638a marcus grima	
millefolium	gearuuae		
molibus	ormetum	640 molibus	ormetum
mastigia	suipan	(635a)	
manubium	uuaelreab	manuuium	uuelreab
melodium	suinsung	melodium	ruinsung
mustacia	granae	murtacia	granæ

f. 8ᵛᵃᵇ

y
627 sciblae *with* e *erased*
    i
631 manaca *with* a *erased*
    l
638 miscapuldr   639 mille-
folium] *curve of* e (?) *before first* i

637 apuldr   638 myrtus
after 637; uuyr *after* 636 *on line*
above   638a *on same line*
as preceding item, 372/7
      lo
643 medium

---

626 mancus C 1266 *etc.*   627 maforte C 1267, D 442/21; *cf.* A* 268/6
mauors scyfele   629 mosiclum C 1324 *etc.*   mossiclum D 443/
25   630 mimopora, -para ðeofscip C 1316, D 443/18   633 *cf.* C
193 aquemale lebel, D 350/10 aquemanile læuel   634 manitergium lin
C 1270   manitegrum lim D 442/25; *cf.* A* 281/36 maniteorium handlind,
D* 445/10 maniterium handlin   635 malagma C 1272 *etc.*   636 apuldur C 1273 *etc.*   637(8) myrtus C 1356, D 444/2, A* 269/25; uuir C
wir DA*;   wirtreow *ad.* D   638(7) mircapuldur C 1302   milisc
apuldor A* 269/28   639 millefolium ł myrifilon R 133/31 (*cf.* 623)
millefolium *only* A 278/27, D* 445/5, A² 297/31, Æ 311/1, B² 239;   *om.* CD
641 mastigium suiopan C 1276   mastigia swipe A 477/11   642 manubium C 1277, D 442/27   643 suinsung C 1303   644 mustacia C
1343, T 46/26 mustatia V 44   mustacra L 47/32;   granae C   grane V
gronae L   grana que uino expressa remanent T

manticum	handful beo-uuas	645	manticum handful beo-uaes
mascus grima			(638a)
mergulus scalfr			mergulus scalfr
marsopicus fina			marpicus pina
musiranus screuua			
mustella uuesulae		650	mustella uuesulae
maruca snegl			
maialis bearug			
mordacius clofae			mordacius clofæ
maulistis scyhend			
mastice huuitquidu		655	
malua cotuc *uel* geormant-lab			
marrubiu*m* hunae *uel* biouuyrt			
merx merze		657a	
mulio horsthegn			
margo mengio			
mugil haecid		660	mugil hecid
matrix quiða			

f. 8ᶜᵈ mergus scalfr

mars martis tiig   mars martis tiig   f. 8ᵛᶜᵈ

651 ::::snegl   653 *between*
                    lab
the lines   656 geormant *with*
first curve of a *before* m
      a
657 m*u*rrubium *with* ụ *erased*

---

645 hondful beowes C 1278   handful beowæs D 442/28   hondful baeues L 47/34   handful *only* A 477/12   646 mascus C 1280, D 442/29 muscus T² 245/12; *cf.* C 1279 masca grima   648 marsopicus fina C 1281 *etc.* 651 marruca C 1283, D 443/1   maruca L 47/90   murica T² 245/11 654 scyend C 1286 scyhend D 443/3, L 47/35   656 hocc cottuc ł gear-wan leaf C 1288 hocc cottuc *only* D* 444/39 *marg.* germanlef *only* B 70ᵛᵃ; *cf.* A* 271/16 malna, D* 444/38 malua hocleaf, A² 301/27 malue herratice geor-menleaf   657 biowyrt ł hune C 1289 hune ł beowyrt D 443/5 hune *only* A* 271/17; *cf.* A² 298/6, Æ 311/5 marubium harehune, R 136/12 marrubium ł prassinum harhune   659 mango C 1285 margo D** 449/18; *cf.* Cl.I 449/12 mango ic menge   660 ł heardra *ad.* D 443/32 (*cf.* C 1347 mugil heardhara)   661 *cf.* R 161/6 matrix cwið ł cildhama 662 *om.* C *etc.*; *cf.* R 131/18 mergus scealfr, Æ 307/6 mergus ł mergulus scealfra *and* 647

mus muris	mus		mus	muris mus	
merula	oslae	665	merula	oslae	
megale	hearma		megale	hearma	
mulcet	friat	666a	mulc*et*	friad	

f. 8ᵛᵃᵇ Nausatio   uomitus *uel*   Nausatio   fom*i*tus *uel*   **f. 8ᵛᵉᶠ**
       uulatung   uulating
nauiter   horsclicae   nauit*er*   horsclicae
ninguit   hsniuuith   ninguit   sniuidh
nomisma   mynit   670 nomysma   munit
nux   hnutbea*m*   nux   hnutbeam
nigra spina   slachthorn   nigra spina   slachdorn
noctua   naechthraebn ali   noctua   nechthraebn
   dicunt nectigalae   (673a) alii dic*un*t   nacthegelae
nycticorax   naechthraebn   nicticorax   nethhræbn
netila   hearma   675 netila   hearma
nasturciu*m*   tuuncressa   nasturciu*m*   leccressae
napta   blaec teru   napta   blaec teru
nugacitas   unnytnis   nugatitas   unnytnis   **f. 9ᵃᵇ**
n*on* subsciuu*m*   unfaecni   non subciuu*m*   unfecni
negotio   unemotan   680 negotia   unemo
nebulonis   scinlaecean   nebulonis   scinlecan
nimb*us*   storm   nimb*us*   storm
nequiquam   holunga   nequicqua*m*   holunga

666a *in lower margin*
            h
673 naechtraebn;   nectigalae
                    u
above line   681 nebolonis
   i
scnlaecean   683 nequiquam]
curve of c (?) *before* i

                    s
668 horclicae   670 *followed*
by [de]leramentum (374/1)
673a alii dic̄t (§ 11) nacthegelae
*written as separate item on line
below* 673   674 nicticorax] '*first* c
looks like an unfinished x' S

665 oslæ, -e C 1306, A* 260/26   ðrostle D 443/12 *etc.* (*cf.* A* 260/25 turdella
ðrostle)   666a lenit friat C M350 (*cf.* Abol. MU 30 mulcet lenit ł
placat)   667 uulatunc *only* C 1357   669 sniuwið C 1379
sniweð D 452/25   670 nomisma C 1383   numisma Æ 302/2;
mynit, -et CÆ   671 ł walhhnutu *ad.* D 452/34   672 *cf.* 957
673 naehthraefn *only* C 1384   nechthrefn *only* L 47/54   674 nocticorax A* 261/12, D* 453/12, A² 287/2   nicticorax R 132/3; *om.* CDA
676 leaccersan tunc̄ A* 270/32   leaccærse idest tuncærse D* 453/16
tuuncressa *only* C 1359   tuncærse *only* D 452/15, A² 298/10   tunkerse
only R 135/36   678 nugacitas C 1395, D 452/35   679 subsciuum
C 1386, D 452/27   680 negotia unemetta C 1371   683 nequiquam C 1373

	ÉPINAL			ERFURT		

(688)

nepa   habern

napta   genus fomenti

   idest tyndir

nauat   frangat

f. 8ᵛᶜᵈ nanus   *uel* pumilio duerg

napi   naep

nodus   ost

683a nodus   ost

nepa   hafern

685 napta   genus fom*e*nti idest

   ryndir

685a nauat frangat

nanus *uel* punilio   duerg

napi   nep

(683a)

---

f. 8ᵛᵉᶠ Oscillae   totridan

oscitantes   ganaendae

origanu*m*   uurmillae

osma   suicae

oppillauit   gigiscdae

obliquum   scytihalt

obnixus   strimaendi

obreptione   criopungae

oridanu*m*   elonae

orcus   orc

opere plumari bisiuuidi

   uuerci

Oscille   totr*i*dan   **f. 9ᶜᵈ**

690 oscitantes   ganendæ

ori*g*anum   uurmillæ

osma   suicae

oppillauit   g*i*scdae

obliquum   sestihalth

695 obnixus   str*i*mendi

obreptione   criupungae

oridanu*m*   elonae

orci   orc   **f. 9ᵉᶠ**

opere plum*ario*   bisiuuisidi

   uerci

---

685 tyndir *above line*

685 napta] *first* a *from* e;   idest
ryndir *on line below followed by*
685a   687 *followed by* nequam
from 374/42   690 *followed by*
odo uia [= 16 ef 5]   693 gisc-
dae] ǧ (§ 11) scdae
     ı
696 crupungae   697 elonae]
second e *from* t (?)

---

684 haebern C 1370   hæfern D 452/22   685 tynder *only* C 1361, D
452/20; *cf.* L 16/10 nappa genus fomitis   686 nanus pumilio C 1362
nanus *only* A 477/25, D* 453/21, Æ 302/3; *cf.* R 190/16 pygmaeus ł nanus
(? Isidore, *Ety.* xi. 3/7 ut nani uel quos Graeci pygmaeos uocant) ł pumilio
dweorg   687 napis C 1363, D 452/17 *etc.*   napus D 452/18 *marg.*,
R 135/30   688 wrasan ost C 1387; *cf.* Cl.I 454/7 *marg.* nodus ost
(§ 35 fn. 7)   689 *cf.* A 276/27 oscida totrida   691 wurmille C 1452,
D* 460/32, -æ D** 463/15   wurmelle B 71ᵇ   wyrmella A* 271/20   war-
melle R 136/30   692 suice C 1468   swice D 460/6   693 clausit
gegiscte C 1447 (*cf.* Cl.I 463/6 betynde gegiscde)   gigisdae *only* L 47/26
694 scytehald C 1403   698 orcus C 1454, D 459/31   orca R 123/18;
þrys ł heldeofol *ad.* D (*cf.* C 1457 orcus ðyrs heldiobul)   699 plumario
C 1450, D 459/27;   bisiudi werci C   bisiwed feðergeweorc D

ÉPINAL		ERFURT	
olor	suan	700 olor suan	
f. 9ab obuncans	genicldae	obuncans genyccilde	
oligia	nettae	oligia nectae	
obestrum	beost	obestrum beoth	
ogastrum	aeggimang	ogastrum aeggimong	
oresta	thres	705 oresta thres	
obtenuit	bigaet	obtenuit bigaet	
ordinatissimam	ðgisettan	ordinatissimam agirettan	
obnixe	geornlice	obnixæ geornlicet	
omnimoda	oeghuuelci	omnimoda oeghuelci	
ðinga		hadga	
orbita	huueolrad	710 orbita hueolraat	
obligamentum	lybb	oblicamentum libb	
occupauit	onettae	occupauit onete	
occas	fealga		
ortigomera	edischaen	ortigomera edischenim	
occiput	hreacca	715 occipud hræca	
ostriger	bruunbesu	ostriger bruunbesu	
		occupauit geomette f. 9vab	
f. 9cd olor grece latin	cignus	olor grece latinae cignus	
aelbitu		æbitu	
omentum	maffa	omentum naffa	
occipitium	snecca	720	

---

700 suān   701 genicldae]
                        h
second e *indistinct*   705 tres
                        t
707 ðgisetan   709 ði:nga
    u
716 brunbesu

700–1 *on same line*
701 genycclde] *cf.* § 11 fn. 2
              c
712 ocupauit;   onete *above line*
715 *followed by* [occul]tantur (376/32)

---

700 ilfetu swan *ad.* D 459/22 (*cf.* 718)   701 genyclede C 1408   gecny-clede D 458/33   702 oligia C 1437, D 459/21 obligia R 160/1; nettae, -e CD   nytte R   703 beost C 1406 *etc.*   706 forcuom bigaet C 1409 (*cf.* C 1420 obtinuit ofercuom) begeat *only* D** 463/16   707 þa gesettan C 1458, D** 463/17   708 obnixe geornlice C 1410, D** 463/18   709 omnimodo . . . ðinga C 1442 omnimoda . . . þinga D 459/24   710 hueol-, hweoglrad C 1459, D 460/1   711 obligamentum lyb lybsn C 1413, lyfesn D 459/5 obligamentum lyb *only* D** 463/19   712 onette C 1425, D 459/12   713 *sic* D** 463/20; *om.* CDA   714 edischen C 1460 erschen D 460/2   715 occiput C 1429, D** 463/21 occipui D 459/14; hrecca C hracca D** hnecca D   717 *om.* C *etc.*   718 grece latin[e] *om.* C 1439, Æ 307/5–6; aelbitu C ylfette Æ   719 maffa C 1443 massa D 459/25   720 hnecca A* 263/19; *om.* C *etc.*

ÉPINAL

f. 9ef promulserit lithircadae
profusis genyctfullu*m*
promulgarunt scribun
prouehit gifraemith
perfidia treulesnis
pro captu faengae
pro maritima saegesetu
percommoda matunos sua cendlic morgenlic
praetextatus gigeruuid
9vab partim sume daeli
pudor scamu
p*ro*propera fraehraedae
priuigna filia sororis id*est* nift
palpitans brocdaettendi
piraticum uuicingsceadan
percrebuit mere uueard
perduelliu*m* þorgifect
proscribit ferred
paludamentum genus uestimenti bellici id*est* haecilae

er
722 promulsit 723 genyctfullum] r *erased above* ge
726 treuleusnis *with second* u *erased* 729 percommoda] a *from* o (?); morgenlic] lic *above line*
l e
735 papitans brocdattendi
740 haecilae *above line*

ERFURT

P*ro*curatio scur f. 9vcd
promulserit lithircadæ
p*ro*fussis genyctfullum
p*ro*mulgar*un*t scr*i*bun
725 proueh*i*t gifremit
perfidia treulesnis
p*er* capta faengae
p*er* mar*i*tima saegaesetu
p*er*co*m*moda matutinos sua cendlic morgendlic
730 pretextatus gigarauuit
partim sumae dæli
pudor scoma
p*ro*pepera fraehraedae
priuigna filia sororis id*est* nift
735 palpitans brogdaethendi
piraticam uuicingsceadae
p*er*crebuit mere uuard
p*ro*duelliu*m* dorhgifecilae
740 paludam*en*tu*m* gen*us* uestim*en*ti bellici id*est* hecæli

721 *followed by* [de]cipere (377/49)
724 promulgarī (§ 11) 727 capta] second a *from* u (?) 729 [mor]gendlic *after* 728 *on line above*
733 propepera] *first* e *from* o (?)
736 *followed by* [a]quæ (378/17)
740 hecæli *after* 378/20 *on line above*

---

721 sciir C 1625 scir A 276/33, R 183/27 723 profusis C 1627
726 treuleasnis C 1533 727 pro captu C 1630 728 pro C 1631, D 469/27; saegeseotu C sægesetu D 729 percommoda sua cenlic, matutinos morgenlic C 1534–5 730 gegeruuid C 1632 gegirwed D 469/28
732 scomo C 1679 733 propropera C 1633 propera D 469/29; fraehraeðe C freahræde D 734 filia sororis idest *om.* C 1634, L 42/7
735 brogdetende C 1472 brodetende D 468/7 736 piraticam C 1579 piratici D 469/6; wicincsceaðan C wicingsceaþan sæsceaðan æscmen D
738 perduellium þorhgefeht C 1537 739 proscripsit C 1635, D 469/30; faerred C forrædde D 740 haecile C 1474

per seudoterum þorh ludgaet			percitus hrad		f. 9ᵛᵉ¹

per seudoterum   þorh lud-   percitus   hrad   f. 9ᵛᵉ¹
  gaet
percitus   hraed   *per* seuduterum   dorh ludgaet
propensior   tylg   *pro*pensior   tylg
profligatus   forsleginu*m*   *pro*fligatis   faerlslaeginu*m*
pelices   cebisae   745 pelices   caebis
phisillos   leceas   phisillos   leceas
praerupta   staegilrae   praerupta   stegelræ
probus   ferth   prob*us*   fert
proterunt   treddun   *per*ter*unt*   treodun
permixtum   gimengidlicæ   750 p*er*mixtum   gimaengidlicæ
particulati*m*   styccimelu*m* particulatim   scyccimelu*m*
proterente*m*   naetendnae   *pro*terentem   naetendnae
pertinaciter   anuuillicae   pertinatit*er*   anuuillicae
penduloso   halði   penduloro   hahdi
pessu*m*   spilth   755 pessum   spilth
petisse   sochtae   petisse   scochtae
per anticipatione*m*   þorch   p*er* anticipatione*m* dorh
  obust   obust
prouectae   frodrae   prouectae   frodrae
f. 9ᵛᶜᵈ prouetæ   gifraemid   *pro*uecta   gifremid
per uispellones þorh byrgeras 760 per uispellones dorh buyr-
                                   genas

parcas   burgrunae   parcas   burgrunæ
pliadas   sifunsterri   pliadas   funsterri
perpendiculu*m*   colþred   perpendiculu*m*   coldraed

742 hraed] h *added in margin*   743 propensior] *or altered from* us

                                   u
757 ob'st   758 pro͡fectae;
  r   u
fodrae   759 profetę;
gifra͞emid   760 þorh]
                                   r
c *erased after* r;   bygeras

741(2) seudoterum C 1538, D 468/25   742(1) hraed C 1539
744 profligatis C 1637, D 469/31;   forslaegenum C, -slægenum D
745 cebise C 1540   748 ferht C 1639   749 proterunt tredun C 1640
750 gemengetlic C 1542   751 styccimelum C 1473; *cf.* H F825 frustra-
tim i. particulatim . . . sticmælum   753 pertinaciter C 1543
754 penduloso haldi C 1541   756 sohte C 1545   757 obst
C 1546   758 praefectae C 1642 preuectue D 470/1   759 profecta
C 1643 prouecta D 470/2   760 byrgeras C 1547, D 468/26   761 *cf.*
R 189/12 parcae hægtesse   762 sibunsterri C 1599

	ÉPINAL			ERFURT	
	parcae	uuyrdae		parce	uuyrdae
f. 9ᵛᵉᶠ	parabsides	gabutan	764a	parapsidam	gabutan	f. 10ᵃᵇ
f. 10ᵃᵇ	petigo	tetr	765	petigo	tetr	f. 10ᶜᵈ

<table>
<tr><td colspan="2">puncto foramine in quo pedes
uinctorum tenentur in
ligno cubitali spatio inter-
iecto idest cosp</td><td colspan="2">puncto foramine in quo pedes
uinctorium tenetur in ligno
cubitalis spacio interiecto
idest cosp</td></tr>
</table>

	ÉPINAL			ERFURT	
	pulenta	briig		pulenta	briig
	papilio	fifaldae		papilici	uiualdra	f. 10ᵉᶠ
	pice seuo	unamaelti sperwi		pice seuo cinamelti spreui
	pustula	angseta	770	pustula	angreta
f. 10ᶜᵈ	papula	uueartae		papula	uearte
	praxinus	aesc		praxinus	esc
	pampinus	cros		panipinus	crous
	perna	flicci		perna	flicci
	pituita	gibrec	775	pituita	gibreec
	pres et uas	byrgea		praes et uas	byrgea
	pus	uuorsm		pus	uuorsin
	pedo	uel paturum fetor		pedo uel paturum	fetor
	prætersorim	paad		praetorsorum	paad
	prifeta	thriuuuintri steor	780	prifeta	triuumtri steur
	pullentum	fahamae	780a	pulmentum	fahamae
	papiluus	ilugsegg		papiluus ilugseg

765-6 *order reversed in* S
     tur
767 tenen; in ligno . . . cosp
across both columns on line below
770 angseta] n (?) *erased before* g
778 pedo] *vertical stroke before* o
   r
780 steo   781 papiluus] l (?)
erased before uu

        t
765 ter   766 tenetur *after* 765
on line above; in ligno . . . cosp
across both columns on line below
773 panipinus] *second* i *over* a

764a parabsides gauutan C P27; *cf.* A* 280/23 parabsidis gabote 765 tetr
afa (ἀλφός?) L 35/74 teter *only* C 1550, D 468/28 766 cosp *only* C
1680 768 papilio C 1484, D 468/9 pampilio A* 261/10; fiffalde CD
fiffealde A* 769 unamaelte smeoruue C 1581 770 oncseta C 1682
ang-, ongseta D 470/14, A 277/10 772 uiridus color ł aesc C 1651 (*cf.* 19 ab
25 praxinus uiridis color) 773 pampinus crous C 1486 776 *cf.* R 190/11
sponsor ł praes... ł uas...borhhand 777 uuorm C 1683 worms D 470/15
778 *cf.* L 46/42 paturum fctor 779 pretersorim, praetersorium C 1654,
1676 pretersorim (*twice*) D 470/3-4; paad C, waad D (*both places*)
780 prifeta C 1655, D 470/5 priueta A* 274/29; ðriuuintra C þrie wintre
D þriwintre A* 780a polentum, pullentum C P562, 874 781 illucseg
B 71ᶜ eolugsecg D468/11 eolxsegc A* 271/21 wiolucscel C 1487

ÉPINAL

puntus   brord
palingenesean edscaept
patena   holopannae
pingit   faehit
patena   disc
f. 10ᵉᶠ pila   thothor
prorigo   gycinis
pittacium   clut
ptysones   berecorn
  berændae
papula   *uel* pustula spryng
  uel tetr
populus   birciae
plantago   *uel* septenerbia
  uuaegbradae
pastinaca   uualhmorae
paperu*m*   eorisc
pictus acu   mið naeðlae
  asiuuid
pangebant   faedun
polimita   hringfaag
f. 10ᵛᵃᵇ pronus   nihol
prodimur   birednae
palla   rift
penitus   longe
platisa   flooc

ERFURT

puntus   broord
palingeneseon edscaept
785 pingit   faethit
patena   disc
pila   thorr
prurigo   gycinis   f. 10ᵛᵃᵇ
pittacium   clut
790 ptysones   berecorn
  berendæ
papula *uel* pustula spryng *uel*
  tetr
populus birciae
plantaga *uel* septinerbia
  uuegbradæ
pastinacia   uualhmorae
795 papirum   eorisc
pic*tis* acu   mid nedlæ
  asiuuid
pangebant   fædum
polimita   hrnigfaag
*p*ronus nihol
800 *p*rodimur   biraednae
palla   ritf
801a penitus   longae
platissa   floc

786 pa*e*tena]   790 bericorn
796 naeðlae] na *from* m;
a
siuuid

792 *preceded by* significantia (381/
52)   799 *on same line as*
preceding item, 382/12

782 puntus C 1685, D 470/16 punctus A 277/12   783 palingenesean C 1488
785 faehit C 1582 fegð D 469/8   786 *cf.* R 124/7 patena huseldisc
787 thothr C 1584 ðoþor D 469/11 þoþor A* 273/14; *cf.* R 150/28 pila ł sfera
(?Isidore, *Ety.* xviii 69) ðoðer, Æ 320/12 pila pilstoc oððe ðoðer   788 prurigo C 1658, D 470/6; *cf.* L 35/3 prorigo urido cutis i. gyccae   789 os
peri clut cleot C 1585   790 *cf.* R 114/27 tipsana beren gebered corn
791 papula spryng *only* C 1492; *cf.* 175   793 plantago C 1601, D 469/15 *etc.*;
uuegbrade *only* C *etc.* ł septineruia wegbræde D   794 pastinaca C 1502
etc.   795 papirum C 1503   796 pictus C 1591   797 faedun C 1504
798 hringfaag C 1612, -fag D 469/20; *cf.* R 125/36 polimita ł oculata hring-
fagh, 188/13 polimita ł orbiculata wingfah   801 rift C 1505   801a longe
C P310; *cf.* Cl.I 466/20–1 procul longe, penitus longe (§ 35 fn. 7)
802 platisa C 1602 platissa D 469/16, A*261/21, A² 293/23, -u L 47/9

ÉPINAL			ERFURT		
pessul	haca			pessul	haca
perna	flicii				
petra focaria	flint		805	petra	focaria flint
parrula	masae			parrula	masae
porfyrio	felofor			porfirio	felusor
picus	fina *uel* higrae			picus	fina *uel* higrae
porcopiscis	styria			porcopiscis	styria
porcaster	foor		810	porcast*er*	for
porcellus	faerh			porcellus	faerh
peducla	luus			peducla	luus
pulix	fleah			pulix	floc
proflicta	forslaegæn			pr*o*flicta	forslaegæn
prouentus	spoed		815	pr*o*uentus	spoed
pendulus	ridusaendi			pendulus	ridusendi
papilo	buturfliogae			papilo	buturfliogo
pella	sadulfelgae			pella	sadulfelgae
palurus	sinfullae			palliurus	sinfullæ
pix picis	id pic		820	pix picis	id*est* pic
pollux	thuma			pollux	thumo
prunus	plumae			prunus	plumae
pullis	grytt			pollix	grytt
popauer	popaeg			papauer	papoeg
pecten	camb		825	pecten	camb
pauo	pauua			paud pauua	

f. 10^{vcd} (left margin, beside *pauo pauua*)
f. 10^{vcd} (right margin, beside *picus fina uel higrae*)

810 porcaster] s *erased after* o
     i
813 pulṳx   816 pend:ulus;
ridusaendi] g *erased before first* d
     r
823 gytt

                o
817 buturfligo   820 pic] x
erased before c   826 *on same*
line as following item, 382/51

804 *om.* CD (*cf.* 774)   805 fyrstan flint D 469/2   flint *only* C 1561
806 parula C 1506 *etc.*   807 porfyrio C 1613, D 469/22, A* 259/5;
feolufer C fealfor D, -uor A*   808 higre fina C 1592   higræ, -ere *only*
L 47/66, A* 260/14   higera ł gagia A² 286/9   fina *only* R 132/14, Æ 307/8
812 peducla C 1560, A* 274/10   peduculus Æ 310/5–6   pediculus ł sexpes R
122/1   813 flaeh C 1684 fleo, -a R 121/38, Æ 310/6   815 prae-
uentus C 1663   prouentus D 470/7, R 191/9   817 papilio buterflege
C 1507, buttorfleoge R 121/18   818 sadolfelg D 469/3   radolfelt A 283/4
sadulfelge C 1563   819 paliurus C 1508   pariulus D 468/17   820 pix
picis C 1593 pix picia D 469/13; id[est] *om.* CD   821 pollux ẋuma C
1617 pollex þuma A* 264/39 *etc.*   822 plumæ C 1664 plyme D 470/8, A*
269/31   823 pollis C 1620, L 46/21, A* 281/28;   grytt C grot L grut A*
824 popauer popæg C 1621 papauer popig D 468/19 *etc.*   826 pauo C 1509 *etc.*

(829)

826a palumpes   cuscotae

phitecus   apa

phitecus   capa

progna   suualua

progina suualuuæ

palumbes   cuscutan

(826a)

pastellas   hunaegaepl

830 pastellus   cænegaepl

pulium   duuergaedostae

puleum   duergaedostae

f. 11^ab pansa   scabfoot

pansa   scaabfot   f. 11^ab

pituita   gillistrae

pedetemtim   caute quasi
  temtans pede

pedetemptim caute quasi pede f. 11^cd
  temptans uel fotmelum

petulans   uel spurcus
  uuraeni

835 petulans uel purcus ureni

f. 11^cd perpendit   aectath

perpendit   aechtath

perstromata   ornamenta
  stefad brun

perstromata ornamenta staefad brum

pendulus   ohaelði

pendulus   oheldi

838a peltam   auram del   f. 11^ef

f. 11^ef Qualns   mand

Qualus   mand

quisquiliae   aehrian

840 quisquiliæ   aegrihan

quadripertitum   cocunung

quadripertitum   cocunung

quacumque modo   gi-
  huuuelci uuaega

quocumque modo gihuelci
  uuegi

quacumque   suae suithae

quacumque   suue suidae

828 suualuae [*dot intended for* a?]
    g
830 hunaeçaepl *with* ç *erased and
second* e *from* p
    t
836 aectah   837 brun *above*
                 d
line   841 quaripertitum
842 quacumque] a *from* o

828 progina] in *from* m
830 pastellus *after* ueteres (382/10)
from column b
834 ł fotmelum *after* 384/52 *on*
                 u
line above   835 purcos

---

827 phitecus C P386, D 469/5   plutecus A 277/14;   apa CDA
828 progna suualuue C 1665, swealwe D 470/9   829 palumbes cuscote
C 1511; cf. A* 260/7 pudumba cusceote, A² 286/2 palumba cuscote
ł wuduculfre   830 pastellus C 1512, D 468/18 passtellus A 279/25;
hunigaeppel C, -æppel DA   831 pulleium duergedostle C 1686 puleium
dweorgedosle B 71^c   833 om. C etc. but cf. C 1575, D 469/12 petuita sped
834 om. C etc.   835 ł spurcus om. C 1569, T² 246/25; wraene C uure-
nisc T²   837 steba only C 1571   838a om. C etc. but cf. D 468/29
pelta scyld   839 qualus C 1689   840 aegnan C 1696   841 cocunung C 1690 cocormete A* 281/6   842 quocumque. . . wega C 1700

quantisper	suae suithae		quantusper	suue sidae
quoquomodo	aengi þinga	845	quoquemodo	aengi dinga
quin etiam	aec þan		quin etiam	aec don
quaternio	quatern		quaterno	quaterni
quinquefolium	hraebnæs		quinquefolium	hræfnæs
foot			foot	
quinqueneruia	leciuuyrt		quinqueneruia	leciuyrt

f. 11vab

Renunculus	lundlaga	850	Renunculus	lundlaga
radium	hrisil		radium	hrisl
rictus	graennung		rictus	graemung
runcina	locaer uel sceaba		runtina	locaer uel sceaba
rabulus	flitere in ebhatis		rabulus	flitere in ebhatis
rema	stream	855	rema	stream
reuma	gibrec		reuma	gebrec
roscinia	nectaegalae		roscinia	necegle
resina	teru		resina	teru
respuplica	cynidom		respuplica	cynidom
rien	lændino	860	rien	lendino
radinape	lelothrae		rodinare	lelothre

f. 11vcd

rostrum neb uel scipes   rostrum neb uel scipes cæle
 celae

robor aac   robor aac
reciprocato gistaebnændrae reciprocato gistaebnen
reclines suae haldae 865 reclines suuaeldae

f. 11val

   d
850 lunolaga *with* o *erased*

852 graen:nung 857 roscina

  p
862 sci::es

   n
845 aegi

        i
859 cynidom] i *over* o
865 suuaeldae] '*first* a *may be* o' S

---

844 quantisper . . . suiðe C 1692 845 quoquomodo C 1701 847 quaternio quatern C 1693; *cf.* R 164/1, Æ 304/6–7 quaternio cine 848 *cf.* A²
299/18 quinque fila hræfnes fot, B² 269 pentafilon refnes fot 851 radius
C 1704 radium A* 262/10, A² 294/2   852 grennung C 1738
853 runcina C 1755;   *uel om.* C; *cf.* A* 273/10–11 olatrum scafa,
runcina locor 854 eobotum C 1705 855 rema C 1714 reuma
L 47/31; *cf.* A² 289/8 reuma gytestream, R 183/18 ebbe ł gytestream
856 *cf.* R 112/28 reuma bræc 857 ruscinia L 47/62 roscinia C 1746;
naectegale C nectigalae L 861 rodinope C 1747; *cf.* A² 300/15 rodinaps
ompre docce, B 71ᵛᶜ rudinaps i. ampre 862 cæli C 1748 863 arbor
aac C 1749 ac *only* A* 269/2 864 gestaefnendre C 1721 865 suae
halde C 1722

rationato	ambect	
recessus	helustras	
rostratu*m*	tindicti	
relatu	spelli	
remota	fram adoenre	
rigore	heardnissae	
reserat	andleac	
rostris	forae uuallu*m* *ue*l	
	tindu*m*	
rancor	throh *ue*l inuidia	
*ue*l odiu*m*		
remex	roedra	
rumex	edroc	
ridimiculae	cyniuuithan	
rastros	ligones id mettocas	
ruscus	cnioholaen	
ramnus	thebanthorn	

f.12ᵃᵇ

Salebrae	thuerhfyri
sibba	sigil
scalbellu*m*	bredisern
scrobib*us*	furhum
sartago	bredipannae
sarcinatu*m*	gisiuuid
sarculum	ferru*m* id
	uueadhoc

866 rationato] *second* o *from* i
874 inuidia] a *erased before* d;

            r
odium *above line*   887 saculum

ERFURT column

rationato	ambaet	
recessus	helustras	
rostratum	tindic*ti*	
relatu	spelli	
870 remota	fram adoændrae	
rigore	heardnissae	
reserat	andleac	
rostri*s* fore uuallu*m* *ue*l		
tindum		
rancor throch *ue*l inuidia *ue*l		f.11ᵛᶜ
odiu*m*		
875 remex	roedra	
rumex	edroc	
ridimiculi	cyniuuithan	
rastros	ligones id metticas	
ruscus	cniolen	
880 ramnus	thebanthron	

Salebrae	thuerhfyri	f. 11ᵛᵉᶠ
sibba	sigil	
scabellum	bredisaern	
scrobibus	furhum	f. 12ᵃᵇ
885 sartago	breitibannæ	
sarcinatum	gesiuuid	
surculum id*est* ferru*m*		
uueadhoc		

       r
884 scobibus

866 ambaect C 1706   870 adoenre C 1724   872 onlaec C 1725
874 troh *only* C 1708   876 edric C 1756; *cf.* R 157/45 rumen wasend (=A*
264/19) ł edroc   877 ridimiculae cynewiððan C 1743   878 mettocas
only C 1709   879 cnioholen C 1759 *etc.*   cneoholen fyres A* 269/22
880 ðeofeðorn C 1710   þefeðorn A² 299/25   þifeþorn R 139/20   þifþorn
B 71ᵛᶜ thyfethorn B² 258   coltetræppe þefanðorn A* 269/21; *cf.* R 149/32
ramnus ł sentix ursina (Isidore, *Ety.* xvii. 7/59) ðyfeþorn   882 sigl C 1856;
cf. 408 (?)   883 scalpellum C 1793, A 276/17; bredisern C brædisen A
885 brediponne C 1762 bredingpanne A 276/13; *cf.* C 407 cartago braadponne,
D 363/11 brædepanne   886 *cf.* A 276/26 sarcidis geseped is   887 sarculum uueodhoc, sarcum weodhoclu *only* C 1764, A 277/24

f. 12^{cd}	sternutatio	fnora
	sartatecta	gifoegnissae
	sentina lectha ubi multae 890	
	aque colliguntur in naue*m*	
	scalpru*m* byris *ue*l ut ali	
	thuear*m*	
	salix salch	
f. 12^{ef}	sambucus ellaen	
	scirpea lerb de qua mata	
	conficitur	
	serpillum bradaeleac 895	

sternutatio   huora
sartatecta   gefegnessi
sentina lechta ubi multae
  aquae colligunt*ur* in una*m*
  naue*m*
scalbrum   byris *ue*l ut alii
  duæra*m*
salix   salh   f. 12^{cd}
sambucus   ellae
scirpea   lebrae de qua m*a*ta
  conficit*ur*
serpillu*m*   bradelec syle-
  noru*m*

ÉPINAL		ERFURT
stabula seto		stabula seto
surum sparuua		surum sparua
sagulu*m* loda		sagulum loda
struere stridae		struere streidæ
seditio unsibb	900	seditio unsib
secessum helostr		secessus helostr
scena sceadu		scena sceadu
sanguinis cneorissa		sanguinis cneorissae
scina grima		scina grima
seta byrst	905	seta byrst
scarpinat scripit haen		scarpinat scripit hæn

890 aque *above line*   891 ɫ
above line; thueaꝛ (§ 4 fn. 1)
893 ellaen] ellaer Q and *Schlutter,*
but MS. clearly has tagged n (§ 3)
          u
902 sceado

890 inunam nauem *after* 889 *on*
line above   894 conficitur
after 893 *on line above*

---

888 fnora C 1909, A 277/26   nor L 19/65; *cf.* H C383 cartilagines coriza
sternutatio ... fnora, C1808 coriza i. sternutatio cartilagines nebgebrǣc ɫ fnora
889 gefoegnisse C 1765   890 lectha *only* C 1833; *cf.* L 39/50 sentina
dicitur ubi multe aquæ fiunt collecte in naui   891 scalprum C 1795;
ut ali(i) *om.* C; *cf.* A 277/25 scalprum bor (? = C 1803 scalpro bore) *and* 907
893 ellaern C 1775   ellen A* 269/41; *cf.* A² 303/3 actis i. sambucus ellen, E²
1131 sambuca lignum elle sāx, W² (Gallée 352) ellæ sāx   894 scirpea
C 1804 sciripea B 72ᵃ scirpia A 278/29 scippio A² 301/19; lebr C leuer
B lǣfer AA²; unde ... conficitur *om.* C *etc.*   895 bradelaec *only* C 1835,
A² 300/8   899 struerer streide C 1910   901 secessus C 1838
903 cniorisse C 1780   904 *om.* C *etc. but cf.* 953   906 scripið C 1805
scribid L 47/39 scribit V 46;   haen *om.* CLV

ÉPINAL		ERFURT		
scalpellum	byris		scalpellu*m*	byris
sturnus	staer		sturnus	sterm
scorelus	emer		scorelus	emer	f. 12ᵉᶠ
sardinas	heringas	910	sandinas	heringas
scira	aqueorna		scira	aquorna
scrofa	sugu		scrofa	ruga
strigia	haegtis		str*i*ga	heg*tis*
scabris	pisces similes	913a	scabris	pisces sim*i*les
lopostris			lopostr*is*	
sullus	otor		sullus	otr
f. 12ᵛᵃᵇ suspensus	anhaebd	915	suspensus anhæbd	
scnifes	mygg		scnifes mycg	
sinapio	cressae		sinapio cressa	
sicalia	rygi		sycalia ryg	
simbulu*m*	herebaecon		symbulum	herebecon
scilla	gladinae	920	scilla	gledinae
sequester	byrgea		sequester	byrgea
			sinapio	cressae
situla	ambaer		situlae	emb*er*
stornus	dropfaag		stronus	drofaxg
sualda*m*	durhere	925	sualdam	durhere
sella	sadol		sella	satul
scasa	eborthrotae		scasa	eborthrotae

917–18 *on same line*

    r
912 scofa   920 gladinae] e
                  e
added in same hand   921 byrga
925 durhere] e *erased after* u

---

907 biriis L 47/48 bor C 1806 (*cf.* L 48/66 scalpeum boor) 908 staer
C 1911 *etc.*; *cf.* A² 286/29 stirnus stær ł fulix, R 132/7 stronus stærn *and* 125
909 scorelus C 1810, L 47/58 scorellus A* 260/27, T² 245/22; omer C
amer T amore A* emaer L 910 sardinas C 1781 sardinus L 47/74;
cf. A* 261/36 sardina hæring 911 scirra aqueorna C 1811 scira acurna L
47/88; *cf.* R 119/1 scirra aquilinus sciurus acwern 912 sugu C 1812, *etc.*
913 striga C 1913, L 47/80 913a scabri...lopostum C S174; *cf.* L 36/8
scabros pisces sunt 916 scniphes C 1814 917 sinapian cressa C
1860; *cf.* A² 301/1 sinapdones cærsan, E² 1133 sinapiones cressa sax. qui in
aqua crescit 918 sicalia ryge C 1861 919 sim-, symbulum C
1873, 1971 920 glaedine C 1815 *etc.* 922 *om.* C *etc.*;
cf. 917 923 situla omber C 1859 924 stornus C 1914 stronius
A278/12; dropfaag C, -fag A 926 sadol C 1839, -ul R 120/4
sotol A 278/8; *cf.* Æ 317/14 sella sadol oððe setl 927 ł scapa ł sisca
eoforðrote B² 301 (*cf.* C 27 scisca eoforðrote) eborðrote *only* C 1816

strepitu	brectme *ue*l cli-derme		strepitu	bretme *ue*l cli-drinnae
stipatorib*us*	ymbhringen-du*m*		stipatorib*us*	ymbdringen-du*m*
saginabant	maesttun	930	saginabant	mestum
semigelato	halbclungni		semigelatu	halbclungn*i*
spatiaretur	suicudae		spatiareti	suicudae
squalores	orfiermae		squalores	orfermae
suffragator	mundbora		suffragator	mundbora
suffragiu*m*	mundbyrd	935	subfragium	mundbyrd
sollicitat	tychtit			
spiculis	flanum		spiculis	flanu*m*
subsciuum	faecni		subsciuum	faecni
sinuosa	faetmaendi		sinuossa	faedmendi **f. 12^vab**
successus	spoed	940	successus	spoed
f. 12^vcd sublustris	sciir		sublustrus	sciir
sopitis	ansuebidu*m*		sopitis	ensuebitum
scindulis	scidu*m*		scindulis	scidum
seuo	smeruui		seuo	smeruui
serio	eornæsti	945	ser*i*o	eornesti
strenuæ	framlicae		strenuae	fromlicae
spina	bodæi		spina	bodæi
scrobib*us*	groepum		scropib*us*	groepum
sardas	smeltas		sardas	smeltas
sandix	uueard	950	sandix	uueard

       l   u
931 hab clungni   933 sqalores
       ga   h
934 suffrator   936 tyctit
945 *between the lines*

932 spatiareti] *see* § 11   934 suffra-
                                    c
gator] *second* a *from* o   938 faeni
941 *followed by* sermo (391/4)
942 sopitis] p *from* b
948 *followed by* / (tempera)mentum
                                 a
(391/18)   950 uuerd

928 braechtme *only* C 1916   929 ymbhringedum C 1915   930 maestun C
1782   931 semigelato C 1844   932 spatiaretur C 1893   933 orfeorm-
nisse C 1902   935 *om.* C *etc.*   938 fraecni C 1950   939 sinuosa
faeðmendi C 1862   941 sublustris C 1952   942 onsuebdum C 1882
943 *cf.* A* 266/33, A² 294/33 scindula scid   944 smeoru C 1846
smero A* 267/2   946 strenue C 1917   948 scrobibus C
1819; *cf.* L 46/22 scropis groop   949 *cf.* A* 262/4 sardina smelt
950 uueard C 1783   wyrt A 277/31, A* 281/29   wad A 278/17, A² 300/35, R
136/25, Æ 311/8, B 72^b vad B² 296; *cf.* Cl.III 513/14 sandix wyrt ł wad

	ÉPINAL			ERFURT		
	soccus	sooc		soccus	sooc	
f. 12^{vef}	scienicis	scinneras		scien*i*cis	scineras	f. 12^{vcd}
	scina	nitatio *uel* grima		scina	nitatio *uel* gri*m*a	
f. 13^{ab}	stiria	gecilae		stir*i*a	gecile	
	sponda	selma	955	sponda	selma	f. 12^{vef}
	spina alba	haeguthorn		spina	alba heguthorn	
	spina	nigra slaghthorn		spina nigra salachthorn		
	singultus	iesca		singultus iesca		
	stabulu*m*	falaed		stabulu*m* falaed		
	scrirpea	eorisc	960	scirpea	eorisc	
	sabulcus	suan		subulcus	suam	
	stagnu*m*	staeg *uel* meri		stagnum	staeg *uel* meri	
	scapula	sculdur		scapula	sculdra	
	sceda	teac		sceda teag		
	scifus	bolla	965	sciffus	bollae	
	salu*m*	segg		salu*m*	seg	
	stiliu*m*	*uel* fusa spinil		stilium *uel* fusa spinil		
	senon	cearruccae		senon	cearricae	
	smus	uuellyrgae		simus	uuellyrgae	
	slens	milti	970	splenis	milti	
	spatula	bed		spatula	bed	
	suesta	suina suadu		siuesta	suina suadu	

952 *followed by* absque uino (392/
12)   958–9 *on same line*
964–5 *on same line*   966–7 *on
same line*

---

951 socc slebescoh C 1879 (*cf.* A 277/29 soccus slypescos)   952 scienices
C 1822 scinici L 39/55;   scinneras C scinnenas L   953 nititio *only*
C S137 imitatio ł grina L 27/5   954 *cf.* R 117/14 stiria stillicidia
(Isidore, *Ety.* xiii. 20/5) ises gicel   955 benc selma C 1895 (*cf.* A* 280/13
spondeus benc)   956 *cf.* 19   957 slahðorn C 1898; *cf.* 672
958 *cf.* R 179/4 singultus geocsung   960 scirpea C 1823;   leber *ad.*
C (*cf.* 894); *cf.* R 135/17 scirpus ærisc   961 subulcus snan C 1953;
cf. A* 272/12 bubullus swan, Napier 1/2450–1 bubulcos cuhyrdas, sub-
ulcos swanas   962 mere *only* C 1921 *etc.*   963 sculdur C 1824,
-er R 159/15 sculdra Æ 298/11   964 taeg C 1821 teah A 278/21
965 sciphus bolla C 1826   966 seeg ł mare C 1786 segc *only* A 276/22
967 stilium spinel *only* C 1922; *cf.* C 933 fusum spinel, H F1003 fusa spinl
968 cearricgge C 1849   969 smus C 1876 sinus A 278/19; wellyrgae
C wellere A   970 splenis C 1896 splen A* 266/15, R 160/35,
Æ 298/9 splena A² 293/1   972 suesta C 1954, A* 272/10;   sceadu
C swaþu A*

ÉPINAL	ERFURT
sisca snidstreo	sista snidstreu
salsa surae	salsa surae
sinfoniaca belonae	975 sinfroniaca belonae
senecen gundaesuelgiae	senecen gundaesuelgae
sorix idest mus	sorid idest mus
scurra leuuis	977a scurra leuuis
stilio uel uespertilio hreathamus	stilio uespertilio hreathamus
seru huaeg	seru huaeg
f. 13^cd spoma pomo	979a spoma ponma f. 13^ab
f. 13^ef sortem condicionem id uuyd	980 sortem conditionem id uyrd
f. 13^vab sceuus strabus torbus idest sceolhegi	sceuus strabus torbus id f. 13^cd sceolegi
serum liquor casei id huaeg	serum liquor casei id huuaeg
f. 13^vcd Trux palpitat uel hunhieri	Trux palpitrat uel unhyri f. 13^ef
tonica polimita hringfaag a rotunditate circulorum	tonica polimita hrinfag a rotunditate circulorum
torta auunden	985 torta auunden
tonsa rothor	tonsa rohr

973 s:::nidstreo   978 hreath^amus   981 s:ceuus   983 hunhie^ri   984 [hringfaa]g . . . circulorum *above line*

973–4 *on same line*   977 *on same line as preceding item,* 393/2   977a *after* potest (392/12) *from column* d   979 *on same line as preceding item,* 393/9   984 circulorum *after* 395/34 *on line above*   985–6 *on same line*

———

973 sisca C 1868; cf. 927   974 sure C 1787 etc.   975 sinfoniaca C 1869   simfoniaca A 278/23   simphonica A² 300/4   simphoniaca B 72ª   976 senecen C 1850, A 278/24, B 72ª   senecio A² 300/3, B² 303   sintea ł senecion R 135/11;   gundesuilge C   grundeswylige A² etc. om. A   977 sorix C 1884   sorex R 120/16;   idest om. CR;   cf. A 477/16 sorex scrifemus, Æ 309/11 mus ł sorex mus   977a leuis C S146   978 hraeðemuus only C 1924 (cf. 1098); cf. E² 335/58 uespertilio et tilio unum est   979 om. C etc. but cf. 982   979a pomo C S476; cf. Affatim 571/35, Werden I (CGL i. 156) spuma poma   980 wyrd condicionem C 1885   981 om. C etc. but cf. C 1939 strabus scelege, R 162/2 scyleagede, E² 331/30 scebus tortus strambus   982 hwæg only C 1847 etc.; cf. E² 331/45 serum liquor casei, Affatim 566/10 care   983 unhiorde only C 2040   984 hringfaag C 2029   986 roðr C 2031

f.13^vef

ÉPINAL		ERFURT	f 13va
titio	brand	titio brond	
trutina	*uel* statera helor	trutina *uel* statera helor	
trulla	crucae	trulla crucae	
traductus	georuuierdid	990 traductus georuuierdid	
tempe	scaedugeardas	tempe sceadugeardas	
tropea	signa *uel* sigbeacn	tropea signa *uel* beanc	
tortum	coecil	tortum coecil	
trocleis rotis modicis *uel* stricilu*m*		trocleis rotis modicis *uel* stricilu*m*	
triplia	lebil	995 tr*i*blia lebil	
tignarius	hrofuuyrcta	tr*i*grarius hrofhuyrihta	
testudo borohaca *uel* sceld-reda *uel* ifaenucæ		testudo brodth*a*ca *uel* sceldhreða *uel* fænucæ	
tessera	tasol quadrangu-lu*m*	tessera tasul quadrungu-lu*m*	
tertiana	lectinadl	tertiana lenctinadl	
teris	distulis	999a teris distulis	
tubo	thruuch	1000 tuba thruch	
tragelafb*us* *uel* platocerus elch		tragelafus *uel* platocerus elch	

f.14^ab

ÉPINAL		ERFURT	
torqu.t	uuraec	torquet*ur* uuraec	
tridens	maettoc	tri*d*ens mettoc	
tilia	lind	tilia lind	
taxus	iuu	1005 taxus iuu	

　　　　　g　　　　　　r
996 tinarius hrofuuycta
　　　　　cæ　　　　　　u
997 ifaenu　　　　1000 tabo *with*
　　　　　　c
a *erased*;　　thruuh

987 *on same line as preceding item,*
395/51　　　995 triblia] b *from* p
997 ł fænucæ *after* 396/19 *on line
above*　　　999a–1000 *on same line*

987 *cf.* R 127/8 titio ł torris (Isidore, *Ety.* xvii. 6/27) brand　　　　988 heolor *only*
C 2041; *cf.* E² 334/6 trudina statera　　　　989 turl scofl *ad.* C 2051 (*cf.* 1022)
990 georuuyrde C 2042　　　　992 sigebecn *only* C 2043; *cf.* L 35/126 tropia
signa　　　994 stricilum *only* C 2044　　rotis modicis ł stricilum V 47; *cf.* L 35/40
troclei rotis modicis　　　995 triplia C 2045　　　996 tignarius C 2020, -is A*
280/8;　　hrofuuyrhta C　　hrofwyrhta A*; *cf.* R 111/41 sarcitector ł tignarius
(Isidore, *Ety.* xix. 19/2) hrofwyrhta　　　　997 bordðeaca *only* C 1999
998 tasul *only* C 2000; *cf.* L 35/35 tesseras tesulas　　　　999 lenctinald
C 2001　　lencteladl A 279/8　　　1000 tubo C 2067　　　1001 tragelaphus elch
only C 2054　　　1002 torquet C 2033　　　1003 auuel meottoc C 2047
(*cf.* R 127/10 fuscinula ł tridens awel)　　mettac *only* A 279/9

ÉPINAL			ERFURT		
tremulus	aespae		tremulus	espæ	
thymus	haeth		thymus	haedth	
toculus	brooc		taculus	broa	
trifulus	felospraeci		trufulus	feluspreici	
tabula	fala	1009a	tabulo	fala	
terrebellus	nafogar	1010	terebellus	naboger	
turdella	throstlae		turdella throstlae		
tilaris	lauuercae		itilaris lauuercæ		
turdus	scric		turdus	screc	f.13 vcd
talpa wand			talpa	uuond	
tincti	sli	1015	tincti	sli	
tabunus	briosa		tabanus	briosa	
tilio	lind uel baest		tilio	lind uel best	
tuber	tumor uel suollaen		tuber	tumor uel assuollan	
toreum	eduella		toreuma	eduelli	
tapeta	ryae	1020	tapeta	hryhae	
transtrum	ses		transtrum	ses	
trulla	scofl		trulla	scolf	
tabetum	bred		tebe	bred	
tignum	tin		tignum	tin	
tenticum	sprindil	1025	tenticum	sprindil	
telum	uueb		telum	uueb	
torax	felofearth		torax	felufrech	

1010 nabfogar   1014 *between
lines*   1016 tabunus] n *faint*
1017 uel   1025 tenticum] ten
faint

1010 naboger] b *from* o
1011–12 *on same line*
1020 tapeta] *first* a *from* e

1006 aespe C 2048   æspe A* 269/10   1007 haet C 2012   hæþ A* 269/42
1008 taculus brocc C 1974; *cf.* R 119/2 taxus ł meles ... broc   1009 tru-
fulus C 2049 truffulus L 47/18;   feluspreci C felospric L   1009a tubolo
fala C T321, L 47/41   tubulo fealo A 279/10   1010 terebellus C 2002,
L 47/46;   nabogaar C   næbugaar L   1012 tilares C 2026   tilaris L
47/61, A* 260/23, A² 286/17;   lauricæ C laurice L lauwerce A* lawerce
ł alauda A² (*cf.* C 142 allauda lauricae)   1013 scric C 2069, A* 260/29,
A² 286/22, R 131/36   scruc L 47/63   1015 tincti C 2021 tinct L
47/71   tinctus A* 261/24, A² 293/28   tinca R 180/36   1016 tabunus
C 1976, A* 261/2; *cf.* L 47/82 tabanus brimisa   1017 baest *only*
C 2022 (*cf.* 1004)   1018 tumor asuollen C 2071   1019 toreuma
eduuaelle C 2034   1020 rye C 1977   reowu A 278/35; *cf.* L 42/2 tapetibus
rihum   1022 scofl A 278/4; *om.* C *but cf.* 989   1023 tabetum C
1978; *cf.* A 279/1 tabetum cecin(?)   1026 *cf.* L 13/34 telam orditus
inuuerpan uuep   1027 feoluferð C 2035   feolufor A 278/2

ÉPINAL			ERFURT	
	titule	gata loc	titulae	gatan loc
	tudicla	thuerae	tudica	thuere
	textrina	uueb	1030 textri*n*a	uuæb
	tibialis	baanrift	tibialis	baanryft
	talumbus	giscaduuyrt	talumbus	gescanuuyrt
	torrentib*us*	streum	torrentib*us*	streaumu*m*
	tuta	orsorg	tuta	orsorg
	taxatione	raedinnae	1035 taxatione	redinnae
f. 14cd	tabuisset	asuand	tabuiss*et*	assuant
	tantisp*er*	þus suiþae	tantisp*er*	dus suidae
	tutella*m*	sclindinnae	tutellam	scildinnae
	triquarum	ðrifedor	tr*i*quadru*m*	tr*i*foedur
	taberna	uuinaern	1040 tab*er*na	uuinaern
	trans	biginan	trans	bigenan
	termofilas	faestin *ue*l anstigan	termopilas	fes*tin ue*l an- stiga
	temonib*us*	dislum	temonibus	dixlum
	tractata	tangi	1043a tractata	zangi
	tabida *et* putrefacta aduinen- danan afulodan asuundnan		tabida *et* putrefacta afulat ond asuunden	
	talpa	uuandaeuuiorpae	1045 talpa	uuondæuuerpe f. 13v
	tuber	ofr	tuber	ofr
	teres	sinuurbul	teres	sinuulfur
f. 14ef	tipo	droco	tipo	draco

          e
1030 uub   1032 giscaduuyrt] gi
added in margin   1036 tabuisset] i
indistinct   1038 sclindi::nnae
1044 aduinendanan, [asuund]nan
          o
above line   1045 uuandaeuuir-
          b
pae *with* n *rubbed*   1047 sinuurful

1044 āfulat;   ondasuunden   *in*
                    f
lower margin   1046 or

1028 titule C 2024 titula A 275/31;   gata CA   1029 tudicla thuaere
C 2072   1030 tela web A* 262/7, web ł telum A² 293/38 (*cf.* 1026) webb
only C 2005   1031 baanrist C 2025 banrift A 277/37   1032 ge-
scadwyrt C 1979 gescaldwyrt A 278/25   1033 streamum C 2036
1036 asuond C 1981   1038 scildenne C 2073   1039 triquadrum
ðrifeoðor C 2052   1041 begeonan C 2053   1042 termofilas faesten *only*
C 2006   1043 *cf.* A* 267/26 themon þisl, R 106/29 temo ł arctoes þisl
1043a tangi C T300   1044 tabida et putrefacta *only* C T30   1046 hofer
C 2074   1047 siunhuurful C 2008   1048 draca ł inflatio (*cf.* L 39/71
typum inflationem) C 2027; *cf.* W² (Gallée 355) tipo dracho

ÉPINAL

f. 14^{vab} Uerruca uueartae
uia secta iringaes uueg
uerbere torta auundre suipan
uenabula eborspreot
ua . . . durheri
uentriculus stomachus auis uel cesol
uescada mundleu
urciolum crucae
uicatum libr
uestibulum cebærtuun
uoluola wiuwindae herba similis hederae q*uae* utib*us* et frugib*us* circu*m*dari sol*et*
uittas thuelan
uulgo passim uel oghuuaer
uitelli suehoras
uscidae tholicae

1052 eborspreot] f *erased before* b
1053 ua . . . Q: a *still visible in Brown's infra-red photograph*; duėrheri *with* ė *erased*
1054 uentriculus Q: ent *no longer visible*; stomachus] o *from* a; cesol *above line* 1055 mundleu] *second* u *very faint* 1056 urciolum Q: i *no longer visible*, o *shows up faintly in infra-red photograph*; crucae] cru *very faint* 1059 circumdari solet *above line*
1060 uittas] ta *faint*
1063 urcide Q: *tops of* usc *still visible*

ERFURT

Verruca uuertae f. 14^{ab}
1050 uia secta iuuuringes uueg
verbere torto auundenre suipan
venabula eborspreot
ualba durheri
uentr*i*culus stom*a*chus auis *ue*l cesol
1055 uescada munleuu
urciolum cruce
(1099a)
uestibulu*m* caebertuum
uoluola uuidubindae herba similis hedere q*uae* uitib*us* *et* frugib*us* circumdar*i* sol*et*
1060 uitas thuelan
uulgo passim *ue*l oeghuuer
uitelli sueoras
uiscide tochtlicae

u
1050 iuuaringes 1054 cesol *after* 398/47 *on line above*
1059 similis . . . frugibus *on line below*; circumdari solet *on line below* similis . . . frugibus

---

1049 wearte C 2088, R 114/5 1050 iringes C 2118, L 27/28 1051 torto awundere C 2087 1053 ualba C 2075; *cf.* A* 280/11 ualua duru 1054 stomachus auis uel *om.* C 2090 1055 mundleu C 2091 mundlan A* 281/33 1056 waetercruce C 2165 cruce A* 281/32 1058 caebrtuun C 2094 cauertun A* 279/35 1059 uuduuuinde *only* C 2158; *cf.* A 279/13 uoluula hymele 1060 uittas C 2120 1061 passim oeghuer C 2173 1062 sueoras C 2121; *cf.* L 36/22 uiteleos iuuenes 1063 uscide tohlice C 2170; *cf.* C 1033 huscile tolice

ÉPINAL		ERFURT	
uene.um	geolu	uenetum	geholu
uatilla	gloedscofl	1065 uatilla	gloedscofl
uillis	uulohum	uillis	uulohum
unibrellas stalu to fuglum		unibrellas stalu to fluglum	
uertigo	edwalla	uertigo	edualla
uiciligo	blectha	uitiligo	blectha
uitricius	steupfaedaer	1070 uitricius	staupfotar
uespas	waeffsas	vespa	uuaeps
uorago	hool	vorago	hool
uarix	amprae	uarix omprae	
f. 14ᵛᶜᵈ uerberatorium	cortr	uerberatorium	cordr
uerberatrum	fleti	1075 uerberatrum	fletu
urna	ambaer	vrna	ombar
uessica	bledrae	uessica	bledrae
uerbenaca	sura magna	1077a uerbæraca	sura magna
ueneria	speruuuyrt	ueneria	smeruuuyrt
ulmus	elm	ulmus	elm
uillosa	ryhae	1080 uillosa	ryhae
uilla	linnin ryhae	uilla	linin ryhae
uiburna	uuiduuuindae	uiburna	uuidubindae

f. 14ᶜᵈ

1064 uene.um] ne *visible in infra-red photograph* 1067 *between the lines;* fuglum] *first* u *from* l 1069 uiciligo *with third* i *over* a Q: a *still faintly visible;* blectha] a *faint* 1073 uarix] *curve of* a (?) *before* i oi 1074 uerberatrum

1066 *followed by* humant (399/11) 1072–3 *on same line* 1075–6 *on same line* 1077a uerbærạta 1079 *followed by* umguentum: *cf.* C 2154 unguentum smeoru (§ 14)

1064 uenetum geolu C 2095 1067 unibrellas . . . fuglum C 2153 umbrellas . . . fuglam L 47/14 1068 eduelle C 2096 eduallæ L 47/16 1069 uitiligo C 2123; *cf.* C 2117, L 36/10 uitiginem bleci 1070 steopfaeder C 2124 *etc.*; *cf.* R 174/6 uitricus ł patraster (= Lib. Gloss. VI 458) steopfæder, L 36/14 uitricum steuffeder 1071 uespas uuaefsas C 2098 uespa wæfs R 121/14, Æ 307/13; *cf.* C 859 fespa waefs 1073 *cf.* L 46/29 uarix ompræ in cruribus hominum 1074 uerberatorum corthr C 2099; *cf.* A* 280/31 uerberaturium þwiril 1075 uerberatrum C 2100 uerberatum A* 280/28; flete C fliete A* 1076 amber C 2166 1077 uesica C 2101, R 160/3 1077a uerbenaca C U97; *cf.* B 72ᵛᶜ uermenaca i. escþrote 1078 smeoru wyrt C 2102 smerewurt B 72ᵛᶜ smerovyrt B² 331 1081 linin C 2128, T² 245/38 1082 uuduuuinde C 2129 wuduwinde A* 270/16 vudebinda B² 335

ÉPINAL		ERFURT	
uiscus	mistil		
quinquefolium	hraefnaes		
	fot		
uicium	fuglaes bean	1085 uicium	flugles bean
uaricat	stridit	uaricat stridit	
uangas	spadan	uirecta cuique	
uirecta	quicae	uangas	spadan
uericundiæ concesserim gi-		uerecundiae concesserim gi-	
lebdae		lepdae	
uadimonium	borg	1090 uadi borg	
uitiatum	auuaerdid	uitiatum	auuerdid
uimbrat uel dirigat borættit		uibrat uel dirigat boretit	
uitiato oculo	unþyctgi	uitiato oculo undyctis ægan	
egan			
uesica	blegnae	uesica	blegnæ
ut..muis	uterque	1094a utrumuis	uterque
undecumq.e	huuanan-	1095 undecumque	huuonan-
huuoega		huuoega	

q
1088 çuicae   1091 auuaerdid]
ti (?) *erased before second* d
   i   t
1092 umbrat;   borętit
    c
1093 unþyotgi egañ
1094 uesica Q: u *and* s *indistinct*
1094a *Schlutter reads* aenig man
above ut..muis, *perhaps as a
scratched gloss, but only a slight
roughness is apparent in MS.*
1095 undecumq.e] *stroke over second*
u *faint*; huuananhuuoega] u *erased
before first* a

1086-7 *on same line*   1090 uadi
after 1089;   borg *after* 1088 *on
line above*   1093 uitiato oculo
after 1092;   undyctis ægan *after*
1091 *on line above*

1083 mistel C 2127   mistellam A 279/15   mistelta B² 336   1084 *om.* C *etc.
but cf.* 848   1085 fugles C 2125, B 73ª; *cf.* L 13/35 uiciam pisas agrestes
idest fugles beane, 47/33 uicias fuglues benae, A² 300/6 uiumum fugeles-
leac, B² 337 uiuinum fugeleslec   1087(8) spaedun L 39/12   spadan
C 2079; *cf.* R 106/12 uanga spada, Æ 318/16-17 uanga ł fossorium spadu
1088(7) quicae C 2130, -e B 72ᵛᶜ wice A* 269/16; *cf.* 464   1089 *om.* C *etc.
but cf.* 1090   1090 uadimonium C 2080, A 279/16, T² 245/39;   borg
gilefde C (*cf.* 1089) borgwed A   borg *only* T²   1092 uibrat borettið ł dire-
gað C 2147; *cf.* C 2132 uibrat brogdetteð, E² 336/2 uibrat diregit ł micat
1093 unðyhtge egan C 2133   1094 *om.* C *etc.* (*cf.* 1077?)   1094a utrum-
uis C U305   1095 undecumque C 2155

f. 14^vef

ÉPINAL	ERFURT	
usurpauit agnaettae	usurpauit agnetæ	
uris urum	uris urum	f. 14^ef
uespertilio hreadaemus	uespertilio hreadamus	
	uetellus sueor	
(1057)	1099a uicatum libr	f. 14va
	1100 Yripeon heresearum	

       i
1096 usurpaut

1097–8 *on same line*
1098 hreadaṁs   1099 *on*
same line as following item, 400/44

1096 agnette C 2171   1097 *cf.* R 118/38 urus wesend *and* 160   1098 hraeðemuus C 2103   hreaþemus A* 261/4; *cf.* Æ 307/10 uespertilio hreremus
1100 yryseon C 2175

NOTES

1. ? VL Exod. 30: 4 *erunt arcus amitibus* (Augustine, *Quaesitiones in Heptateuchum*, ii. 132, *PL* xxxiv. 641): cf. the following item, 1 ab 4 *archontus principes* (? VL Ps. 2: 2 *archontes*). *loerg(a)e* is presumably a jō-stem variant of *lorh*, -g 'weaver's beam', pl. *lorgas* (BT 646, TS 621).

2. ? A gloss on Vulg. Exod. 29: 22 *adipem* . . . *et aruinam*: cf. Karlsruhe MS. Aug. 99 (SS v. 156/10) *aruinam exungiam* and Jun. 159/5 *aruina* . . . *uel axungia* . . . *hrysel*.

3. *argillus* may be a corruption of *argillosa*, from Vulg. III Reg. 7: 46 *in argillosa terra*: cf. Cl.I 348/11–2 *argillosa ðoihte*, *argilla ðo* (in an Old Testament batch according to Lübke, *Archiv*, lxxxv. 403). Erf.II 268/13 *argilla terra in qua figuli operantur* may come from the same source. For *thohae* 'clay' cf. Hl. C2062 *creta* . . . *þoe*.

3a. ? Vulg. Exod. 26: 5 *ansulas cortina habebit in utraque parte, ita insertas ut ansa contra ansam ueniat*: cf. Erf.III 566/31 *ansa auris fibola anostola* (for *ansula*?). *ansa* 'handle' or 'ear of a jug' here = AV 'loops' (cf. Cl.II 266/23 *ansa hringe*); *fibulae* (OE. *fifele*?) refers to the clasps by which the *ansae* were fastened (cf. 410 n.).

4. *andeda* = ML. *andena*, *anderia* 'andiron': perhaps a gloss on *arula* immediately following. *brandrad* and Cl.II *brondrida* are otherwise unrecorded.

5. ? Vulg. Exod. 27: 5 *subter arulam altaris*: cf. Cl.I 348/31 *arula fyrpanne* (Lübke, *Archiv*, lxxxv. 403). *fyrpannae* 'brazier' is recorded only in these glosses.

6–7. (1 ab 36–7) ? Philox. AL 15 *alea* κότιος (-ττος) κύβος κυβ(ε)ία, 19 *aleator* κοττιστής κυβευτής: cf. Erf.III 1141–2 *aleator tebleri, alia tefil* (§ 34 fn. 1, p. lv) and the dicing terms in 178, 998, combined with the present items in Aldhelm, *Metr.* 164/7–8 *alea unde aleator calculis et tesseris ludens per aleam*. Ép. *teblae* beside Erf. *tefil* 'die' (also Trier *taflæ*) may be a weak fem. like ON. *tafla* 'draughtsman'.

8. *axedones* and *lynisas* = 'lynch-pins' (Schlutter, *Angl.* xlv (1921), 195 ff.): cf. Herm. 195/58 *paraxonia asinodes*, etc. Bodl. MS. Auct. F. I. 16 *axedones idest humeruli* supports Schlutter's suggestion of a scholion on Vulg. III Reg. 7: 30 *quatuor rotae* . . . *et axes aerei, et per quatuor partes quasi humeruli subter luterem fusiles*, where *humeruli* really means 'supports' (AV 'undersetters'). The Berne scholion on *Geo.* iii. 7, *Oenomai currui cereos axedones* (MS. *saxidones*) *imposuit*, cited by Schlutter, *Angl.* xlix (1925), 95, is also a possibility in view of 9 immediately following, below which was room for this item in Erfurt (cf. § 10).

9. ? *Geo.* iii. 25 *purpurea . . . aulaea*: cf. Servius, *aulaea autem dicta sunt ab aula Attali regis. strel* 'bed-cover' is an alternative explanation, as in Abba AU 33 *auleum et aulea stragulum uel genus cortinae regalis.*

10. A misinterpretation of Vulg. IV Reg. 21: 6 *ariolatus est: ariolatus* is the pret. part., correctly glossed in Placidus III H7 *hariolatus est diuinauit coniectauit. frictrung* 'divination' is otherwise unrecorded, but cf. *fyrht, friht* in the same sense (BT 353, TS 267).

11. *amites* = 'poles' (cf. 1), not 'rafters', as Schlutter pointed out (*Angl.* xx (1898), 385). There may have been confusion here with *asseres*, e.g. VL (Robert) Exod. 27: 19 *assares atrii aerei.*

12. ? Vulg. Lev. 21: 20 *si alburginem habens in oculo*: cf. Cl.I 348/33 *albugo eagflea* (Lübke, *Archiv*, lxxxv. 403).

14. Cf. Abol. AP 5 *aplustria ornamenta nauis* (v.l. *armamenta*), Philox. AP 7 *aplustra πτερὸν πλοίου* (Festus 103 *aplustria nauium ornamenta*): *aplustre* = the stern-ornament of a ship, so *πτερὸν πλοίου* and *giroedro* 'oarage' (also Jun. 181/24 *aplustre gerepru uel scipgetawu*) presumably translate the variant *armamenta.*

17. ? A combination of Herm. 500/69 *nessa aneta* and Isidore, *Ety.* xii. 7/51 *an(a)s ab assiduitate natandi aptum nomen accepit*: cf. 18 immediately following.

18. Cf. Isidore, *Ety.* xix. 22/28 *armilausia uulgo uocata quod ante et retro diuisa atque aperta est, in armos tantum clausa: armilausia* was therefore a sort of tabard; the scholion on Juvenal v. 43, *'thoraca' armilausiam prasinam ut simiae*, applies it to a child's pinafore.

21–4. (1 ef 1–4) ? *Ecl.* ii. 48 *bene olentis anethi*, *Geo.* ii. 291 *aesculus in primis*, 152 *nec miseros fallunt aconita legentis*, *Ecl.* vi. 68 *apio crinis ornatus amaro* (Lindsay, *Gloss.* 105 f.), attracted into the Hermeneumata batch by Herm. 88/67 *anethon anetum*, etc.: *pungas* 'poisonous plants' (BT 1078) fits the sense of Virgil's *aconita. merici* 'smallage, water parsley' = ModE. *march* (*OED* sb.¹).

25–6. (1 ef 5–6) ? *Geo.* iii. 338 *litoraque alcyonen resonant, acalanthida dumi*: cf. Servius, *per dumos uero acalanthis, quam alii lusciniam esse uolunt, alii uero carduelim quae spinis et carduis pascitur, ut inde etiam apud Graecos acalanthis dicta sit ab acanthis idest spinis quibus pascitur*, whence Aldhelm, *Aenig.* 68/6–7 *aut arguta simul cantans luscinia ruscis | quam lingua propria dicunt acalantida Graeci.* Holthausen, *Literaturblatt* x (1889), 446, interprets *isærn* as 'ice-eagle', i.e. the kingfisher, because of its colour, but the spelling (also Cp. *isern*, Cl. *isen*) suggests confusion, perhaps only graphic, with *īse(r)n* 'iron'. *luscin(i)a* 'nightingale' may have been confused with *acalanthis* 'goldfinch' because Virgil described the latter as singing in thickets (Lindsay, *CP* xiii (1918), 13). For *roscini(i)a* see 857 n.

27. (1 ef 7) ? *Geo.* iii. 147–8 *plurimus Alburnum uolitans, cui nomen Asilo | Romanum est, oestrum Grai uertere uocantes*: cf. Abstr. AS 12 *asilum quem Graeci oestrum, rustici tabanum appelant*, Abavus AS 1 *asilo oestrus e(st) tabanus*, and 1016. OE. *brīosa* 'gadfly, breeze' is found only here and in 1016.

29. ? VL (Robert) Exod. 38: 3 (23) *phyolas et harpagones aereos*, etc. (Vulg. *fuscinulas*): cf. 30 immediately following. For *auuel* 'meat-hook' cf. Jun. 127/10 *fuscinula uel tridens awel* and W. A. Craigie, *TPS* 1906, 261–4.

30. ? Vulg. Cant. 5: 13 *genae illius sicut areolae aromatum*: cf. 1 cd 6 *areoli aromatum horti* and the Trier marginal glossary (§ 23. 2), 47/23 *areoli idest aromatum horti uel scauos. areolae* = 'garden beds'; *sceabas* 'sheaves', if not a mere guess, may be a corruption of *seaðas* 'cisterns', the interpretation of *areola(e)* in Abol. MS. A (*post CGL* iv 4/18) *areole id est collectiones aquarum que in hortis deriuantur pro utilitate olerum* and Ld. 10/22 *areola dicitur ubi aqua diriuatur in ortum et stat in modico stagnello*.

31. ? Jerome, *Chronicon* a.c. 713 (*PL* xxvii. 382) (*Numa*) *congiarium dedit asses ligneos et scorteos*, whence Chronographus Anonymus (*MHG Auctores Antiquissimi*, ix. 144/14) *scortinos asses*, v.l. *scortinas*. The ultimate source is Suetonius, *De Regibus* (*Reliquiae*, ed. A. Reifferscheid (Leipzig, 1860), 319). *trimsas* = the gold *tremisses* copied from the Franks, which were the earliest English coins (G. F. Brooke, *English Coins* (London, 1932), 3).

32. *ansueop*: 'inspired'; also Cp. 1143 *instincta onsuapen*, Cl.I 420/1 *inswapen*.

33. *acerabulus* = Fr. *érable* 'maple', dim. of *acer* (Hessels, *Leiden* 52).

34. *acrifolium* is apparently a species of maple (cf. Herm. 192/2 *sfendamnos acrifolium*, etc.); *holegn* is an obvious guess. Trier 54ª *acrifilon arbor folia dura uel aspera habe(ns)* suggests that the original gloss was a tautological one like *eptefilon septifolium* (379), *mirifilon millefolium* (639).

36. *alneum*: ? for *alnetum* (Goetz, *CGL* vi. 53) or *alneium* 'plantation of alders' (DuCange); *fulaetrea* = Ger. *Faulbaum* 'black alder' (Lindsay, *Corpus* 192).

37. *saeppae* 'spruce' (L. *sappīnus*) is otherwise unrecorded.

38. *ocusta*: 'armpit'; cf. Cl.I 356/1 *ascella ohsta*, Cl.II 263/29 *ascilla oxtan*, and ModE. dial. *oxter*.

39. *auriculum* is probably a mistake for *aurichalchum* 'brass' (Hessels, *Leiden* 67 f.): cf. Cl.I 353/20 *auriculum dros*, following 353/15 *argentum uiuum cwicseolfor* in a series of marginal additions from Isidore, *Ety.* xvi. 19 'de argento', where sub-paragraph 4 reads *argenti purgamenta λιθάργυρος, quam nos spumam argenti appellamus* (cf. 603). Trier 59ᵛᵇ

auriculum purgamentorium aurium may be a corruption of Isidore's *argenti purgamenta*. *dros* 'dross' is unrecorded elsewhere in Old English, but cf. *drōsna* 'dregs'.

40. *arpa* = Gr. ἅρπη, a predatory sea-bird according to Pliny x. 204, 207. For *earngeat, -geuþ* cf. OHG. *aringreoz* 'haliaëtos albicilla' (Suolahti, 349) and Jun. 132/19 *uultur earngeap*. D. von Kralik, *Göttingische gelehrte Anzeigen* 1914, 159 f., takes *-gēap* as the original form, relating it to *gēopan* 'swallow', but his explanation of the name, 'a bird that attacks even the eagle', is fanciful.

41. Herm. 319/24, etc. identifies *acceia* with Gr. ἀσκάλαφος 'a nightbird, probably a kind of owl', but *holthana* 'woodcock' is the correct interpretation: cf. It. *acceggia*, etc. (P. Barbier, *Revue*, ii (1910), 182).

42. *dieperdulum* = It. *perdigiorni* 'day-waster' (Barbier, *Revue*, ii. 189), referring perhaps to the heron's static posture.

43. *aquilium*: for *aculeus* 'prick, sting'; cf. Philox. AQ 2 *aquilio* κέντρον βοῶν καὶ σκορπίων. For OE. *anga* 'sting' (BT *onga*, TS *anga*) cf. ON. *angi* 'spike, prickle' and Frankish *angones* 'barbed spears' (DuCange).

44. *auriculum*: 'earwig'; cf. Fr. *oreillere* < L. *auricularius* (sc. *uermis*).

45. Cf. Trier 58vb *ara stabula porcorum, ariola locus ubi saginantur uerres* and the Trier marginal glossary, 47/13–14 *ara stabulum porcorum inde areola stigu*: *auriola* 'sty' is presumably identical with OF. *oriol*, ML. *oriolum* 'porticus, atrium' (DuCange), perhaps by dissimilation from **auleola*, dim. of *aula*. Barbier, *Revue*, ii. 184, compares Fr. *(pere)loriot* 'inflammation of the eyelid', but *sty* in this sense is first recorded in 1617 (*OED*).

46. *alnetum*: 'plantation of alders'; cf. PP 9 *aldyrkyr alnetum, viz. locus ubi alni et tales arbores crescunt. alerholt* is otherwise unrecorded.

50a. Sweet, *OET* 667 and *Second Reader* 6, takes *uncenos* as OE., but cf. Eucherius 149/9–10 *anconiscos incastraturas, aspidiscas uncinos* ('hook(ed)'), cited by Brown, A149.

51–2. (2 ab 33–4) ? Orosius i. 5/6 *dimissi altrinsecus montes*, iii. 17/9 *Aegyptus addicta sit* or Aldhelm, *VP* 232/16 *altrinsecus sequestrasse*, 250/5 *naturae legibus addicti*, whence Cl.I 338/8 *altrinsecus on twa healfa* (Lübke, *Archiv*, lxxxv. 400), Napier 1/1452 *addicti gescriuene*.

53. *argutie* = *argu(i)tio* 'rebuke': cf. Augustine, *Enarrationes in Psalmos* (*PL* xxxvi. 923) *argutio correptio est: qui arguitur, corripitur*, on VL Ps. 72: 14 *argutio mea in matutinis*. Presumably drawn into the Hermeneumata batch by 54 immediately following.

54. *asfaltum*: ? for *aspaltum* 'balsam' (Herm., e.g. 560/36 *diaziron* (*-ξυλον*) *aspaltum*); cf. Ld. 12/18 *aspaltum spaldur* (VL (Sabatier) Ecclus. 24: 20 *aspaltum aromatizans*) and Schlutter, *ESt.* xxxvii (1906), 186–7. ÉE *asfaltum* may indicate confusion with *asphaltum* 'asphalt' (Herm.

194/45 *asfalton bitumen*, etc.), however, as Hessels, *Leiden* 66, suggests. Flasdieck, 95 ff., derives *spald(u)r* from a Gmc. *spalðuz, related to *speld* 'splinter, torch' (Gmc. *spalðiz); alternatively, it might be borrowed from lL. *aspaltrus* 'balsam' (Holthausen, *ESt.* l (1917), 335) or 'asphalt' (cf. lOE. *spelter* Pogatscher, § 191. 1), with *-ld-* after § 70.

55. Goetz, *CGL* vi. 47, takes *albipedius* (here only) as a bird-name, *TLL* as a translation of Gr. ἀργίπους 'swift-footed, white-footed'; a gloss on Isidore, *Ety.* xii. 1/52 (*equi*) *qui autem albos tantum pedes habent petili appellantur* is another possibility. *huitfot* 'white-foot(ed)' is otherwise unrecorded in Old English.

57. ? Vulg. Dan. 14: 32 *intriuerat panes in alueolo*, attracted into the Hermeneumata batch by *aluium* immediately preceding. *aldot* (? -*þ* § 70) 'trough' is otherwise unrecorded, but cf. Norwegian dial. *olda* < IE. **aldh-* (*IEW* 31) and IE. **-tom* as a concrete suffix in *hēafod*, etc. (Kluge, § 99(b)).

58. *scaldthyflas*: lit. 'plants growing in shallow water'; cf. Cp. 1491 *paupilius* (for *papiluus* 'papyrus') *scaldhulas* and ME. *scold* 'shallow' (Schlutter, *ESt.* xliii (1911), 318–19), whence ModE. *shoal*.

59–60. *actula, acitelum*, and *accitulium* 63 are presumably forms of *acidula* adj. used as a plant-name (sc. *herba*): cf. Trier 53ᵛᵇ *acitula genus cicutae, acitulium genus herbae, acitelum genus item cicutae* and *salsa* 974. The plant intended is uncertain: *hramsa* is wild garlic (cf. Erf.II 1107 *ca(e)pinica hramsa*), *geacaes surae* wild sorrel.

62. *ascolonium = Ascalonia* sc. *caepa* 'scallion' (Pliny xix. 101 *Ascalonia ab oppido Iudaeae nominata*); *hynnilaec* (*ynni-*) 'onion-leek' is also recorded glossing *unio* and *caepa* (BT 1300).

64. *ambila* may be a corruption of Gr. ἕρπυλλον or L. *serpyllum* 'wild thyme', which is confused with a variety of leek in 895.

66. Erf. *uermodae* may be a weak variant of *wermōd* 'wormwood' (BT 1209), corresponding to OHG. *uuermuota*.

68. *anguens* 'the worrier' could be a nickname for the briar (Lindsay, *Corpus* 193), although Cl. *bremel* has no independent authority. Goetz, *CGL* vi. 69, suggests a misinterpretation of *Aen.* ii. 379–80 *improuisum aspris ueluti qui sentibus anguem | pressit*, in which case an interlinear or marginal gloss on *sentibus* may have been wrongly applied to *anguem*.

69. *hindberiæ* 'raspberry' does not fit *acinum* 'grape': could it be a mistake for *winberige*?

70. Vulg. Dan. 14: 2 *similae artabae duodecim*: *sibaed*, lit. 'sifting' (cf. pl. *siuida* 428), translates *similae* 'flour', not *artabae* 'measures'. For the latter cf. 26 cd 2 *tres artabae x. modius* (*-os*) *faciunt* (= Eucherius 159/8–9).

71. Presumably Orosius v. 17/5 *uirum acrem et integrum* in view of the

preceding item, 2 cd 31 *auspic(i)a cantationes auium* (? Orosius iv. 13/14 *contemptis auspiciis*), and the Orosius batch immediately following; but the form of the lemma suggests that the Orosius gloss was supplanted by Erf.II 260/51 *acris fortis uelox* (? Philox. AC 73 *acres* σφοδ(ρ)ούς δριμεῖς), whence Cp. *fortio*.

72. Orosius v. 19/10 *Cn. Pompeius, qui a senatu cum exercitu arcessitus . . . diu sese nouarum rerum aucupatione suspenderat* ('had delayed, watching for political changes'): *setungae* 'plotting' is a reasonable inference from the context.

73. Orosius ii. 12/13 *se . . . honoribus abdicauit: biscerede* 'deprived' (BT, TS *bescerian*) appears to be used reflexively with *hine* understood.

75. *staefnændra*: 'alternating'. *stefnan* is not recorded elsewhere in this sense, but cf. *emb stemn* 'uicissim' (Meritt, *PG* 54) and *gistaebnændrae* 864.

77. Erf. *blidi* was taken as OHG. by Sweet, *OET* 4, but cf. Cl.II *blīðe*; it may have been a marginal addition to the archetype.

80. *misbyrd* 'abortion' is otherwise unrecorded, but cf. *misbyrdo* 'congenital deformity' (BT 690).

86. Orosius v. 18/28 *cum ipsa Roma . . . praecipuas sui partes auctionabatur*: cf. 5 ab 13 *actionabatur puplice uendebat*. BT *scīran* III(e) takes *scirde* as 'accused', Meritt, *FL* 2 B 23, as 'administered' (cf. Jun. 109/3 *actionator folcgerefa*), but a pret. part. 'distinguished, excellent' glossing *praecipuas* would fit the Orosius context better.

87. ? Orosius vi. 9/2 *nauibus . . . onerariis atque actuariis* (v.l. *actuaris*): cf. Cp. 1032 *honeraria hlaestscip*. Schlutter, *ESt*. xliii. 337, and Lindsay, *Gloss.* 23 fn. 1, take *uuraec* as an abbreviation of **wræcscip* 'a light, swift vessel' (cf. SS ii. 45/13 *actuarius drifskiffon*); but an item such as Abol. AC 17a *actuarius acta qui facit* (= 4 ab 15 *actuaris*) may have supplanted the Orosius gloss, in which case *uuraec* would = Go. *wraks* 'persecutor' (*AEW* 406).

91. ? Orosius i. 10/3 *plurimi auctores consentiunt regem Bocchorim, adito Hammonis oraculo remedium petentem, . . .id genus hominum . . . alias in terras auehere iussum* +Abol. AU 8 *auehit exportat: aferidae* as pret. subj. in a *þæt*-clause (sc. *man*) would = the Latin infin. after *iussum*.

93–4. Orosius vii. 7/8 *centies centena milia sestertium annua ad expensas*: *gerlicae* is probably the adverb glossing a Lat. adj. as in 205, etc. (§ 87).

95. Orosius vii. 18/8 *Ulpiano usus adsessore*: the OE. dative mechanically glosses a Lat. ablative, unless the construction was mistaken for an ablative absolute.

97. Orosius i. prol. 15 *sub apparitione Antichristi: gitiungi, getiong* therefore = 'appearance' (cf. *tēon* 'show'), not 'preparation' (*OET* 617) or 'arrangement' (TS 438).

99. Lindsay, *Gloss.* 24, suggests Orosius vii. 22/12 *collecta agresti manu* or 25/2 *agrestium hominum . . . manum*, but the precise form of the lemma occurs in Vulg. IV Reg. 4: 39 *herbas agrestes*, whence Cl.I 345/23 *agrestes wudulice uel wilde*.

102. ? Orosius ii. 17/16 *adempta . . . libertate* (Lindsay, *Gloss.* 24): *binumni* could be explained as depending on a masc. *freodome*, but cf. 104 n.

104. Cf. Codex Vaticanus 1469 (*CGL* v. 530/31) *adimpta ablata* (Terence, *Andria* 837 *ea causa . . . adempta*) and *ade(m)pta* 102: such a gloss (perhaps a lost Abolita item: cf. R. Wier, *CQ* xv (1921), 44 ff.) might have attached itself to *ade(m)pto* 100, to which *binum(i)ni* originally belonged. Erf. *binoman* is OHG.

106. *sceptloum* is dat. pl. of *scaeptloan* 'straps for launching a spear' (489), glossing Orosius v. 15/16 *hastilia telorum quae manu intorquere sine ammentis solent*.

108. *fosturbarn*: 'fosterlings' (also Cl.I 347/5 Cl.III 516/6); cf. *fostorcild*. For Erf. *foe(s)tri-* cf. *cildfōstre, -fēstre* 'nurse' (BT 154).

109. Perhaps a conflation of Orosius ii. 18/5 *seseque toto mentis affectu . . . causis bellisque permisceat* and vii. 28/26 *punitionem . . . in proprios egit affectus* ('relations'): both the sense of the lemma and the sequence of adjacent items seems to require the latter, as Brown points out (A240), which suggests that the Orosius glosses used by the compiler were already arranged alphabetically in *a* order, like the Rufinus glosses of Leiden v (cf. 187, 370 and notes).

112. *uulanclicae*: 'arrogantly' (here only); cf. *wlanc* 'bold, proud' and *tohlicae* 1063 (n.). Erf. *gelplih* is OHG. in form (Sweet, *OET* 4), but both *gilplic* adj. and *gilplice* adv. are recorded in Old English.

114. ? Abol. AR 28 *arcistes sagittarius* (= 1 ef 34 *arcistis sagittarus*): cf. Aldhelm, *Aenig.* 60/3 *arcister contorquens spicula ferri*, *Epist.* 493/6–7 *utpote belliger . . . arcister*. 'arcister', a corruption of *arcites* 'bowmen' (cf. Festus 117 *arquites . . . qui nunc dicuntur sagittarii*), exemplifies Aldhelm's 'glossary Latin' (Lindsay, *Gloss.* 97), and *strelbora* (here only) may reflect Abol. *sagittarius*.

115. ? Vulg. I Reg. 22: 2 *oppressi aere alieno*: cf. the Trier Bible gloss 7ᵇ *ere alieno usurato tributo quod aliis debebant*. *gaebuli* fits *tributo* better than *aere alieno* 'lent or borrowed money', as in 4 cd 35 *alienum aes pecunia faeneraticia* (= Abstr. AL 43).

115a. Gen. sg. *alum(i)nis* suggests Charisius 38/10 *acumen acuminis, agmen agminis, alumen στυπτηρία*, or possibly Cassius Felix, *De Medicina* (ed. V. Rose, Leipzig, 1879), 125/14 *aluminis upari id est liquidi*, whence Herm. 597/45 *alumen upari alumen liquidus* (Goetz, *CGL* i. 49). Förster, *Angl.* xli (1917), 138 fn. 1, takes *aelifnae* as gen. sg. of *ælefn 'alum', borrowed from L. *alumen* via Celt. *alīfn* (so Pogatscher, p. 14).

116. *anate* might be a corruption of *amite* instr. sg. 'rod' (Goetz, *CGL* vi. 66): cf. *HF* 275 *perculam amite amiclios*. If so, *cladærsticca* 'rattle' (cf. *claedur* 218, *cliderme, -drinnae* 928) may be a misinterpretation of Abol. AM 4 *amites fustes aucupales* (= 4 ef 16 *fustis aucupalis*). *aneta* 'duck' (cf. 17) in the sense of 'clapper' would be another possibility: cf. *OED corn-crake* 2.

116a. Cf. Erf.II 264/6 *alapiciosus caluus* (= Abol. AP 6), Affatim 471/17 *alapiciosa calua*: the compiler of the *ab*-order exemplar apparently took the Latin n.s.f. *calua* (Schlutter, *Angl.* xxxv. 152) as a weak form of OE. *calu* 'bald' (cf. Cl.II 276/31 *caluus calo*) or a noun *calwa* 'alopecia', cognate with OHG. *cal(a)wa* f.; cf. Cp. *ule* 378 for Erf. *ulule* (§ 14) and 287 n.

116b. ? A corruption of *aliter elles* or *aliter alio elles* (Bradley, *CQ* xiii. 104): if so, the source might be Philox. AL 30 *aliter ἄλλως* or Aldhelm, *VP* 248/20-1 *aliter sedet in carruca praefecturae dignitas, aliter mulionis utilitas*, etc., whence Napier 1/1380 *aliter elles*.

117. ? Phocas 415/24 *anser anseris* or Herm. 187/60 *chin (χήν) anser*, etc.: Lindsay's second Phocas batch (*Gloss.* 16) ends two lines above, but cf. 118 immediately following.

118. ? Herm., 11/20 λύψ *africus*, etc.: one of the small group of wind-names which occur at the end of the *a*-order sections under A, B, C, and F (cf. 162, 311, 452 n.). *westsuþwind* 'south-west wind' is found only in this gloss and 452, but cf. *westansuþanwind* (BT 1211).

119. *atticus* (*-acus*): 'a kind of locust' (Gr. ἀττάκης); presumably a Leviticus gloss, on 11 : 22 *bruchus in genere suo et attacus*, which attached itself to the Hermeneumata glosses immediately preceding, like *bruc(h)us* 150 (in the Hermeneumata batch).

120. Cf. Abavus BU 2 *bucula bucca*: *bucc* (? also *-cc* in the exemplar of Erfurt, mistaken for 'horned' *a*) may be a strong variant of OE. *bucca* 'buck' (cf. ON. *bukkr*) or simply a scribal error for Latin *bucca*. Schlutter, *JGP* 1 (1897), 332, takes the latter as a corruption of *uacca* (cf. Abol. BU 2 *bucula bacca*), but it could be a genuine borrowing from Celt. *boukkā* 'cow', whence Old Welsh *buch*, etc. (*IEW* 483). If Cp. *buuc* = OE. *būc* 'pitcher', *bucula* would presumably = *buc(c)ula* 'a "boss-like" vessel' (cf. Erf.II 318/2 *patera fiola* (= Abstr. PA 67 *fiala*) *uel bucula calicis* and Souter, 33), but Ép. *bucc* is supported by Cleopatra; the Corpus form is presumably an eccentric spelling like *sooc* 951 for *socc* (§ 37 fn. 2). This is one of the *ab*-order glosses which stand before the *a*-order section in Épinal (§ 25); the Erfurt order is confirmed by Corpus and Cleopatra.

121. *balus*: ? for *bolas*, a by-form of *boias* 'fetters'; cf. Codex Vaticanus 1468 (*CGL* v. 493/4) *bole uincula lignea et ferri* (Festus 135 *boiae id est*

genus uinculorum tam ligneae que ferreae dicuntur) and Cl.III 499/35
boias beagas (Aldhelm, *VP* 274/21–2 *boias in collo . . . nectunt*).

121a–2. *bothana, bothonicula* may be latinized forms of Gr. πυτίνη
'a wicker-covered flask' (Goetz, *CGL* vi. 150): cf. Herm.
194/11 *ydria uictine* and IL. *buttis* 'cask', *buticula* 'bottle'. *embrin* 'jar' is a
derivative of *amber* (L. *amphora*), formed with the dim. suffix **-ina-*
(Sievers, *ESt.* viii (1885), 154; Kluge, § 58(b)).

123. Lindsay, *Corpus* B4, takes *bacidones* as a corruption of *pactiones*,
but *bacido* 'botrus' (related to *bacca* 'berry'?) was accepted by the
compiler of the Junius 'nomina arborum' list. For *redisnae* 'bunches
of grapes'(?) Wehye, *PBB* xxx (1905), 61, compares OHG. *rādo*
'cockle', but a borrowing from L. *racēmus* with IL. assibilation (§ 71)
and assimilation to Gmc. **-isnō* (Kluge, § 86) would fit the meaning
better.

124–5. (5 ef 29–30) *bicoca, beacita* may be corruptions of **beccatia*
'(long-)beak' (cf. *beccus* 'beak'), whence It. *beccaccia* 'snipe', *beccaccia
di mare* 'oyster-catcher' (Lindsay, *Corpus* B61, 96). *hraebrebletae* (*hae-*)
'goat-bleater' (Suolahti, 276) = Sc. *heather-bleater* 'snipe'. OE. *stearn*
is a sea-bird in *Seafarer* 23–4 *him stearn oncwæð | isigfeðera*, presumably
identical with ModE. dial. *starn* 'tern' (Norfolk). Ép. *stearno* and
Voss. *sterno* may represent a weak **stearna*: cf. ON. *þerna* f., whence
ModE. *tern*.

126. *briensis* is apparently some form of boring parasite: cf. Cp. 1193
ladasca piae (= Cl.II 274/12 *pie*) *briensis hondwyrm*, Napier 25/1
uerme i. briensis hondweorm; Brown, B7, compares Marcellus Empiricus
(ed. G. Helmreich, Leipzig, 1889), 80/32–3 *brigantes, qui cilia arare et
exulcerare solent* (Gallo-Latin **vrigantes* < IE. **wer-* 'twist, bend'
IEW 1152). *handwyrþ* (here only) might be an error for Cp. *honduyrm*,
but *-uyrþ* could be an ablaut variant of **-werþō* in *uuandaeuuiorpae*
1045 (§ 44. 1).

127. *bagula*: ? for (*re*)*pagula*; cf. 20 ef 39 *pagula frena* (= Erf.II
317/28, Affatim 548/50) and the Brussels Aldhelm gloss, *ZfdA* ix.
406/26–7 *lupatis repagulis midlum* (*VP* 230/18 *aureis . . . lupatis*).
repagulum 'bar, bolt' (cf. 803 n.), hence 'check, restraint' (*VP* 243/13
pudicitiae repagula . . . seruare, etc.), = 'bridle' in Ennodius (ed.
G. Hartel, Vienna, 1882), 68/9–10 *nemo enim taciturnitatis repagulo
ora porrigit*, 494/2–4 *nescit probatae qualitatem uirtutis expendere qui de
cartarum freno superbit armatis; adquiescant istis inertia corda repagulis*,
the latter of which might be the source of (*re*)*pagula frena*.

128. *ba(l)sis*: ? for Gr. ψωρίασις 'scabies' (Holthausen, *AB* xxxiv
(1923), 273); Lindsay, *Corpus* B6, compares Sp. *bolsa*, It. *borsa* 'abcess'.

129. *bobellum*, for *bouile* 'cattle-pen' (Herm. 313/45, etc.), is a 'Hisperic'
form (§ 35): cf. *HF* 312 *septa que irriunt bouella*.

130–1. (6 ab 2–3) Cf. Trier 60va *bratum unde conficitur ceruesia, bratigapo herba quae admiscetur* and Bodl. MS. Auct. F. 1. 16 (SS iv. 245/42, 45) *bracium malt, bradigabo feldhoppo* (Schlutter, *Angl.* xxxv. 153): *bradigabo* may be a compound of IL. *bradia* 'campus uel ager suburbanus' (DuCange) and Gmc. **gab(b)-*, whence OF. *gab*, It. *gabbio* 'mockery' (*REW* 3626), which would correspond semantically with *felduuop* (?*-hwōp*). The meaning of both words is uncertain, but their context favours 'wild hops' over 'grasshopper' (OHG. *feldhoppo*), suggested by Lehmann, *AB* xvii (1906), 297; Bodl. MS. *-hoppo* may be a mistake for *-hopfo* 'hops', prompted perhaps by an OE. **feldhopp* in its exemplar.

132. *beta*: ? for *betula* 'birch'; confusion with *beta* 'beet' (Herm. 16/17, etc.) could have taken place when the class lists were alphabetized, but the influence of Ir. *beithi* 'birch' (Schlutter, *AJP* xxi (1900), 191) is also a possibility.

133–4. (6 ab 5–6)? Vulg. Gen. 6: 14 *bitumine linies*, Jud. 8: 21 *ornamenta ac bullas quibus colla regalium camelorum decorari solent*: cf. Karlsruhe MS. Aug. 99 (SS v. 140/4, 176/17) *bitumen genus gluti* (= OE. *lim*), *byllas sigillas uel ornamenta cinguli*, and the following item, 6 ab 7 *bullas ornamentum cinguli*. In this context *sigil* presumably = 'seal' (cf. Jun. 126/2 *sigillum uel bulla insegel*).

136. Orosius iv. 8/11 *ballistas deferri imperauit*: *staeblidrae* 'catapult' is otherwise unrecorded, but cf. ME. *stafslynge*. It presumably meant a hand weapon like the latter, since the ballista was unknown to the Anglo-Saxons: the OE. Orosius, 174/9–10, translating this passage, borrows and explains the Latin word: *palistas mid þæm hie weallas bræcon*.

137. Orosius iv. 20/34 *Basternarum gens ferocissima*, etc.: the gloss confuses the German tribal name with *basterna* 'litter', as in 5 ef 31 (Erf. 348/5) *basterna similis curro de corio tota et portatur semper ab hominibus uel asinis nullam ratam (ro-) habens* (= Ld. 42/21 *asinis uel hominibus*, on *Vit. Eug.* 3 *pertranseunte basterna*). Cp. 270 *basterna scrid* ('cart') and Cl.III 507/30, *ZfdA* ix. 504/15 *basterne scrides* (*VP* 297/1 *basternae uehiculo*, paraphrasing *Vit. Eug.*) may reflect *similis curro*.

139. *bitiligo* = *uitiligo* 'white leprosy' (Abol. VI 39 *uitiligo macula alba in corpore*); for *blecthrustfel* (**blǣci-* H. Osthoff, *ESt.* xxxii (1908), 81 ff.) cf. *blectha* 1069.

141. Cf. 5 ef 5 *bileso passus* (? = *bile suffusus* 'jaundiced') *a amaritudinem(-e?)* and Hl. B223–4 *bile felle attre, bile passus passus amaritudine*, Affatim 489/13–14 *bilem amarum, bilem passus amaritudinem passus*: *atr* 'poison' is not recorded elsewhere in the sense of 'bitterness', but cf. **aterlic* 'bitter' (?) in Cl.I 414/34 *gorgoneo aterlicum uel biter* (*VC* 2635 *gorgoneo . . . cruore*).

143. *bucina*: for *uaccinia* 'whortleberries' (? *Ecl.* ii. 18 *uaccinia nigra leguntur*); cf. Cp., Cl. *baccinia* and the confusion between *bucula* and *uaccula* in 120. *bucinus* is properly the sea-trumpet (Herm. 355/27 *bucini κήρυκες*). For *begir* 'berry' (here only) cf. *winbegir* 'grape' (BT 1231).

144. *blitum* (βλίτον) is a sort of beet, so *clatae* (also Cp. 2066 *tubera clate*) is presumably a different word from *clate* 'burr', although both are combined in Jun. 134/3 *blitum uel lappa clate uel clyfwyrt*.

147–8. *broel* = Gallo-Latin *broilus* 'park' (DuCange *broilum*); *broelarius* and *ediscueard* 'park-keeper' are otherwise unrecorded.

149. Cf. Codex Vaticanus 1468 (*CGL* v. 492/46) *bataclat (h)alat, Glossae Scaligeri* (*CGL* v. 601/18) *hippitare oscitare badare*: Loewe, 412, emends *badare* to *bataclare*, but Meyer–Lübke, *WS* xxv (1903), 92, compares It. *badare* 'attend' < **batare*.

152. *brunchus*: 'pig's snout'; cf. Trier 62ᵃ *bruncus porci[l]labrum superum*, and Sardinian *brunku* (*REW* 1336). For *uurot* cf. Jun. 118/34 *promuscida (proboscis) ylpes bile uel wrot* and *wrōtan* 'root'.

155. *lediruuyrcta* 'tanner' is otherwise unrecorded.

156. *berna* = *uerna* 'shrike, butcher-bird': cf. It. *(a)verla* 'auis uernula' (Meyer–Lübke, *WS* xxv. 92–3). The greater butcher-bird is said to lure other birds by imitating their cries, which may account for its identification with *higrae* 'jay' (808), described as mimicking other birds in *Riddles* xxiv.

157. ? A conflation of Herm. 274/12–13 *ὑπάρχοντα bona, χρήματα pecuniae* (also 202/29–30): it comes immediately after the second Hermeneumata batch.

158. *cian*: 'gills' (here only); cf. OS./OHG. *kio* and *cīnan* 'gape' (*AEW* 47).

160. *bubalus* = 'gazelle', not 'aurochs' (cf. 1097 n.), but the mistake is an old one: cf. Pliny viii. 38 *uros quibus imperitum uolgus bubalorum nomen imponit, cum id gignat Africa uituli ceruique quadam similitudine*.

161. ? Vulg. Lev. 11:17 *bubonem et mergulum*: cf. the preceding item, 6 cd 29 *bruc(h)us genus locustae quod uolat* (= the Trier Bible gloss 4ᵛᵃ *que necdum uolat*, on Lev. 11:22) and 1098 n. For *bufo* cf. Codex Leidensis 67F⁵ (Loewe, 421) *bubo nomen auis quem quidam bufum dicunt*.

162. *eastnorþwind*: 'north-east wind'; cf. Cp. 460 *chorus eostnorðwind* (452 n.) and the OE. *Apollonius* (ed. P. Goolden, Oxford, 1958), 16/20 *eastnorðerne windas*.

163. ? A Virgil gloss, e.g. on *Aen.* i. 12 *Tyrii tenuere coloni*: cf. the following item, 6 ef 16 *cellis apothecis* (Servius, *Geo.* ii. 96 '*cellis*' *autem apothecis dicit*). Erf. *uicinus* is unparalleled and may simply re-translate *gibuur*.

165. ? Abstr. CA 83 *calculus lapillus calx enim lapis est unde et calculare dicitur id est numerus*: cf. the preceding item, 6 ef 19 *calcis finis* (?Abstr. CA 69 *calce fine*), and 172. *calc* therefore = 'counter', not 'chalk' (TS 115): cf. Cl.III 517/7 *calculus cealcstan* (Aldhelm, *Metr.* 69/12 *supputationum calculus*).

166. *clibecti* is probably 'steep' (Schlutter, *Angl.* xix (1896), 110) rather than 'sticky' (Sweet, *OET* 504), although the latter would be possible in the metaphorical sense of 'difficult': cf. Festus 170 *omnia enim difficilia cliuia uocabant unde et cliui loca ardua* and *Maxims* II 13 *wea bið wundrum clibbor*.

167. ? Isidore, *Ety.* xix. 22/24 *colobium dictum quia longum est et sine manicis* (= Hl.): cf. the four previous items, 6 ef 22–5 *constillatio notatio siderum* (*Ety.* viii. 9/24 *constellationes*), *censor dignitas iudicalis, censere iudicare* (*Ety.* ix. 4/13), *ciliarchus qui mille praeest* (*Ety.* ix. 3/30 *chiliarchae*), and *armilausia* 18 n.

171. *crocha*: 'crock' (also Cp. 1254 *luteum crohha*), presumably from IE. **gr(e)uk-* beside **gr(e)ug-*, whence *crocc(a)* (*IEW* 389); cf. *crōg* < IE. **grōk-* (*IEW* 385).

172. Cf. Erf.II 274/28 *calculus lapillus et sententiam et numerus* and Abstr. CA 83 (165 n.): *tebelstan* 'draught' may come from a gloss on Juvenal xi. 132 *nec tessellae nec calculus*, like the preceding item, 6 ef 37 *cintia luna* (=Abstr. CI 4), on Juvenal vi. 7 *haud tibi similis Cynthia*. The Juvenal passage may also be echoed in Aldhelm, *Metr.* 164/8 *calculis et tesseris ludens* (cf. 6–7 n.). For *sententia* 'vote' cf. Vulg. Apoc. 2: 17 *dabo illi calculum candidum*.

174. ? Vulg. Job 40: 13 *cartilago illius quasi laminae ferreae*: cf. Ld. 19/59 *cartillago uuldpaexhsue* (OHG. *waltowahso* 'neruus' Hessels) *uel grost* and the preceding item, 7 ab 4 *carauma scriptura lintea* (VL Apoc. 19: 20 *caragma*). For *naesgristlae* cf. Cl.I 427/26 *internasus nosgrisele*.

176. Lindsay, *Gloss.* 21, suggests a gloss on Rufinus ix. 9/3 *signum . . . crucis ex auro fabrefactum*, but the lemma occurs in Vulg. III Reg. 7: 36 *sculpsit . . . cherubim et leones et palmas quasi in similitudinem hominis stantis, ut non caelata sed apposita per circuitum uiderentur*: it may have been attracted into the Rufinus glosses by *fabrefacta* in the preceding verse. For *utathrungaen* 'embossed', lit. 'forced out', cf. Ælfric, *Lives of the Saints* (ed. Skeat, London, 1890–1900), xxiii(b). 409 *ut aþrungen fram eallum þam folce*.

177. *haam* = Cp., Hl. *aam* 'cautery' (?), connected with *ǣmyrge* 'embers' by Schlutter, *MLN* xiii (1898), 149, as referring to the cinders which replaced hot iron as a cauterizing agent in later medical practice (562 n.). If so, it must be distinguished from *aam* 'weaver's reed' in LR 8 *ni mec ouana aam sceal cnyssa* (= *Riddles* 35/8 *amas*), from L. *hāmus* (*AEW* 3).

178. *cot(t)izat* = Gr. κοττίζει 'dices': cf. Trier 68ᵛᵃ *cotizat alea(m)*

ludit (Philox. AL 16 *aleam ludit* κοττίζει κυβεύει) and Erf.II 264/39 *aleatur* (? = Philox. AL 19 *aleator*) *cotizat graece*. For Class I *teblith* beside Hl. *tæflaþ* and ME. *tavelin* cf. ON. *tefla*.

178a. *cyprinus* (Polemius 'item natancium' 544/9) is presumably a seafish in Pliny ix. 58 *hoc et in mari accidere cyprino putant. fornaeticli* is a dim. of *forn(e)* 'trout' (Kluge, §§ 60 a., 63): cf. Jun. 180/39 *turnus forn* and OHG. *forhana*.

179. *conuexum*: 'vault, sky'; cf. Isidore, *Ety.* iii. 39 *conuexum enim curuum est, quasi conuersum seu inclinatum, et in modum circuli flexum.* The semantic development of *hualb* 'hollow' as adj. (*Judith* 214 *hwealfum lindum*) and as a noun in the phrase *heofenes hwealf* (*Beowulf* 576, etc.) parallels that of *conuexum* in *Aen.* iv. 451 *caeli conuexa*, etc. and may have been influenced by it.

180. *cercylus* = a light, swift ship (Nonius 533/25 *nauis est Asiana pergrandis* is a misinterpretation of Plautus, *Stichus* 368 *cercurum quo ego me maiorem non uidisse censeo*), which was presumably the sense of *aesc* before it came to mean a viking ship (ON. *askr*): cf. Br. 287/31 *dromo æsc* (Isidore, *Ety.* xix. 1/14 *dromo autem a decurrendo dictus*).

181. Cf. Cl.III 483/22 *cahus dwolma* (Vulg. Lk. 16: 26 *chaos magnum*), Napier 17/9 *chaos idest tenebre saxonice dwolma* (Aldhelm, *VC* 511 *chaos obstrusum et torpens confusio rerum*): *dwolma* also translates *chaos* in the West-Saxon Gospels, whence BT 221 'chasm, gulph', but its cognates *dwelian* 'wander' and *gedwol* 'error' suggest that the root meaning was 'confusion'; if so, it may replace an interpretation like Abstr. CA 73 *confusio rerum* (cf. Corpus), which also underlies the Aldhelm passage.

182. *uuilucscel*: 'whelk'; cf. pl. *weolescylle* in the OE. Bede, i. 26/8 *missenlicra cynna weolcscylle* (*BH* i. 1 *uariorum generibus conchyliorum*).

183. *camellea* = *chamelaea* 'dwarf olive', which glosses *dipsacus* 'teazel' in Herm. 560/10 *dipsaga idest camillea*, so *uulfes camb* is not 'a mere guess' of the English compiler, as Lindsay imagined (*Gloss.* 110): Förster, *Angl.* xli. 136, identifies it with *wulfes tæsl* (BT 970).

187. ? A combination of Orosius v. 1/12 *quod illis erat debita pensio seruitutis, nobis est libera conlatio defensionis* and iv. 16/19 *priuata conlatione* (cf. 7 ef 17 *conlatione comparatione*): *ambechtae* 'service' could refer to *seruitutis* in the first passage (Brown, C 72), but the dat./ instr. ending suggests the second. Cl.III 490/22 *collationes ymbeahtas* (also Cl.I 371/9, on Aldhelm, *VP* 242/10 *collationes patrum*) and Napier 53/22 *ex conlatione ol (ob) ymbeactæ* (Donatus 379/15), from which Schlutter, *ESt.* xlii (1910), 182, inferred a noun *ymbeaht* 'consideration', may be misapplications of the Orosius gloss.

198. Orosius v. 11/2 *cum . . . locustarum multitudines coaluissent*: *suornodun* (Erf. *suarnadun*) may be a mistake for **swearmodon* 'swarmed' (Schlutter, *JGP* i. 323), but cf. *āswārnian* 'confudi, erubescere' (BT 56, TS 53), related to *swǣr* 'heavy', *swǣran* 'oppress' (*AEW* 331).

199. Meritt, *HG* 73, points out that the interpretation of the next item, 7 cd 30 *creacas recessus* (= Cp. C295), is a further or alternative explanation of *cuniculos*: cf. 7 ef 14 *cereacas tubicines* (Orosius vii. 7/1 *cerycas*) and Cp. C353 *cereacus hornblauuere* (possibly the interpretation missing in 7 cd 30), Hl. C647 *cereacos idest tubicines uel recessus cornicini*. For *smygilas* 'burrows, tunnels' and Hl. *smygels* cf. *smūgan* 'creep'.

200. Orosius vii. 35/20 *fortasse concedam ut non haec fidei Christiani ducis concessa uidetur*: *lytisna* 'almost' may translate *fortasse*, but the sense is still inexact.

203. *gimaengiungiae* (*-ungae*): dat. sg. of **gemengung* 'confusion'; cf. *gimengidlicæ* 'confusedly' 750 n.

205. Cf. Ab Absens 408/20 *compar partim potens conueniens*: BT 337 records an adj. *gehæplic* 'convenient, orderly' here and in Cp. 1462 *ordinatus gehaeplice*, but an adv. formed directly from *gehæp* 'fitting' (BT 398) like *gimengidlicæ* 750 and *tohlicae* 1063 (n.), glossing a Latin adj. as in 94, etc. (§ 87), seems more likely.

206. Lindsay, *Gloss.* 25, suggests a gloss on Orosius v. 7/14 *potione . . . recalescentes* or vi. 10/4 *testas feruentes* (cf. Abol. CA 27 *calent feruent*), but the lemma occurs in Sedulius, *Carm. Pasch.* i. 202 *ardore calentes* and Aldhelm, *VC* 2323 *thermas . . . calentes*. Erf. *hattendæ* may be a mistake for Ép. *haetendae* (cf. Ép. *obtt* 421 for **obet*) or Cp. *hatende*, which is the normal form (cf. Chadwick, *TCPS* iv. 211 fn., and BT, TS *hātian*).

207. Orosius i. prol. 14 *ut . . . claruerit regnasse mortem auidam sanguinis dum ignoratur religio quae prohibet a sanguine*; *ista inlucescente illam constupuisse* (v.l. *constipuisse*): the Latin acc. and infin. are replaced by an OE. finite construction as in 353, 365, 756 (§ 87). For Erf. *-suderadae* (*-suedr-*) without *i*-mutation cf. *gesuedradum* (*-n*) 368 and § 86.

210. Orosius vi. 5/10 *inuoco qui est cum conuenio qui non est*: *adiuro* glosses *inuoco* rather than *conuenio* (Brown, C109).

213. Lindsay, *Gloss.* 25, suggests a gloss on Orosius vii. 39/13 *tamquam magnum cribrum*, but cf. Herm. 263/9 κοσκινίζω *cribro*, Cl.III 484/3 *cribraret sifte* (Vulg. Lk. 22: 31 *ut cribraret*). Erf. *crefrat* is noted as a popular form by Loewe, 421.

214. ? Orosius iii. 18/8 *Amyntas consobrinus occisus* (Lindsay, *Gloss.* 25) or Abstr. CO 204 *consobrini qui de singulis sororibus nascuntur*: the latter is supported by pl. *gesuirgion* (§ 80), *-an* (also Cp.) and the two following items, 7 ef 20–1 *consocierant coniunxerunt* (? Abavus CO 239 *consociant coniungunt*), *cieuo reuocabo* (? Abstr. CI 28 *uocabo*). *gesuirgion*, *gisuirgian*, and Cl. *geswiria* are etymologically correct spellings for **giswirjō* 'nephew, cousin' (*IEW* 1051); Cp. *gesuigran*, Hl. *geswegran* may be influenced by *sweger* 'stepmother'.

215. ? Abstr. CA 10 *caulem fruticem*: cf. 214 and 7 ef 20–1 immediately preceding.

216. ? Aldhelm, *Metr.* 159/20 *capita clunibus per uices sustinent*: d.p. *lændnum* (= Hl. *renibus*) indicates that the lemma was originally *clunibus*.

218. Cf. Trier 69ᵇ *crepacula tabulae per quas aues territantur*, Erf.II 282/28 *crepaculum tabula per quam passeres terrentur*: the common source may have been a lost Abolita gloss on Apuleius, *Metamorphoses*, xi. 4 *aureum crepitaculum* (for the Apuleius glosses in Abolita see Weir, *CQ* xv. 41), but the form of the lemma corresponds to Aldhelm, *Aenig.* 31/3 *faxo crepacula rostro. claedur* 'rattle' is otherwise unrecorded, but cf. *cladærsticca* 116.

219. *caumeuniae = chameuniae* 'pallet-beds' (Gr. χαμαιευναι): cf. Jerome, *In Aggeum*, i. 11 (*PL* xxv. 1398c) *chameunias idest humi dormitiones. eordrestae* 'earth-beds', otherwise unrecorded, may have been coined from Jerome's *humi dormitiones*.

220. Dat. sg. *clustorlocae* suggests that the lemma was originally *clustello* (cf. 216), perhaps from Gildas 66/23 *penurii clustello . . . obseratos*, whence Ld. 6/28 *clustello claustro*, or Aldhelm, *VP* 319/7 *in arto carnis clustello* (*ZfdA* ix. 527/71–2 *clustello loce uel fæstene*). *clustorloc* = 'enclosure' (*OET* 581), not 'bar, bolt' (BT 160, TS 129); BT would emend to -*loca*, which gives the desired meaning, but cf. Cp. *clustor*-, Cl., Hl. *clusterloc* and pl. -*locu* in Cl.III 520/11 *crustra clustorlocu* (*VC* 2152 *uerbi clustella resoluens*). Lindsay's note, 'Since Gildas glosses are peculiar to Corpus, Gildas . . . cannot be the source' (*Gloss.* 110) begs the question.

221. ? *Aen.* ii. 381 (*anguem*) *caerula colla tumentem*: cf. Affatim 494/17 *cerula colla* (one of the 'English' Virgil glosses cited by Dall, § 33 fn. 3) and the preceding item, 8 cd 23 *cant(h)arus genus uassis* (*Ecl.* vi. 17). For *haeuui* 'blue, grey' beside *hæwen* cf. Ld. 22/3 *aeri ha(e)ue* and 473; the form is presumably *casus indefinitus* as in 495, 939.

222. ? Vulg. Lk. 9: 17 *cophini duodecim*: cf. Cl.III 485/14 *cophinus mand* and 223 immediately following.

223. ? VL IV Reg. 18: 18 *Ioahe . . . commentariensis scriptor* (*TLL*, from Codex Legionensis): *commentariensis* 'recorder' (Vulg. *a commentariis*) was the title of the clerk of a law-court, particularly that of the praetorian prefect, under the early Empire. 'Reeve' was often used to render the Latin titles of non-English officials (TS *gerēfa* II), as in 197; Hl. *uilicus* translates it (§ 19).

224. ? Aldhelm, *VP* 284/6–7 *apertis clatrorum obstaculis* or *VC* 1235 *leo de clatris . . . mittitur*: cf. Cl.I 372/30 *clatrorum pearroca*, Cl.III 501/32 *de clatris of pearrocum. clatrum* (-*us*?) = 'bar, bolt' in Philox. CL 9 *clatri* κανόνες οἱ ἐν θυρίσι ὀβελίσκοι (cf. Gr. κλεῖθρον, Abol. CI 25 *clitri ligna uolubilia in caueis*), but the meaning 'enclosure' (? by metonymy, as in 220) seems peculiar to Aldhelm.

225–7. (8 cd 33–5) Part of an Aldhelm batch noted by Bradley, *CQ* xiii. 91 (§ 35 fn. 2, p. lvi), on *Aenig.* 74/7 *ferrata cuspide contis*, *VP* 298/4 *adulterinae titillationis calcar*, 256/18 *torrido dogmatum cauterio*: cf. Cl.I 378/11 *cuspide palstre*, Cl.III 508/17 *calcor spura*, Napier 2/61 *cauterio mercisene*, and the preceding item, 8 cd 32 *cautum scriptum* (= Abstr. CA 42), applied to *VP* 263/7 *de illo cautum sit* in Cl.III 495/7. *palester* 'spike, spear' (also Meritt, *OEG* 28/230 *cuspide pale(s)tre*, glossing Sedulius, *Carm. Pasch.* ii. 215 *confossus cuspide uerbi*) may be a Celtic loan-word: cf. Welsh *paladr* 'hastile' (*IEW* 545); if so, the suffix was presumably assimilated to Gmc. *-*stra*- (Kluge, § 94(a)). For *mear(c)isern* 'branding-iron' cf. the Trier Bible gloss 32va *cauterium ferrum candens unde nota pro signo uel morbo animalibus imprimitur* (on 1 Tim. 4: 2 *cauteriatam . . . conscientiam*, whence Aldhelm's metaphor).

228. Cf. Festus 161 *clauata dicuntur aut uestimenta clauis intertexta aut calciamenta clauis confixa*, Cl.I 375/41 *clauatæ gebyrde uel gestefnde* (Aldhelm, *VP* 318/3 *manicae sericis clauatae*): the source, if not Aldhelm (cf. 239), may have been a lost Festus gloss of Abolita or Philoxenus (cf. Lindsay, *CR* xxxi (1917), 158 ff.). For *gebyrdid* 'striped'(?) cf. Cp. 479 *clauia* (-*us*?) *borda* and *bord* 'board'; the semantic development is parallelled in L. *clauus*.

229. *catasta* 'scaffold on which slaves were exposed for sale' (Gr. κατάστασις) had two distinct developments in later Latin. (1) An instrument of torture similar to the rack: cf. Abstr. CA 41 *catasta genus poenae est eculeo similis* and Gildas 84/29 *ad carcerem uel catastam poenalem*, Aldhelm, *VP* 301/23 *catastarum crudelitatem exercuit*; fire was placed beneath it according to the gloss on Prudentius, *Peristephanon*, i. 56 '*catastas igneas*' *genus tormenti idest lecti ferrei quibus impositi martyres ignis supponebatur* (*PL* lx. 286a). (2) A hostile crowd, perhaps by metonymy for the crowd surrounding a slave-sale or a martyr's torment: cf. Gildas 39/1–2 *satellitum canumque prolixiorem catastam*, whence Cl.I 379/8 *catasta werod*, and Aldhelm, *Epist.* 493/5 *ceu aper truculentus molosorum catasta ringente uallatus*. The present gloss has been explained in both ways. (1) Schlutter, *Angl.* xix. 485, and Meritt, *FL* 4 D 22, take Ép. *gloed* 'hot coal' as the original form of the interpretation, and Holthausen, *AB* xxxv (1924), 249, emends to *gloedþolla 'pan of coals' after Napier 1/4485 *catastarum hyrdla fyrþollena.* (2) Schlutter, *JGP* v (1903–5), 467, infers a noun *gelæd 'crowd' from Hl. *geled*, Cl.II *gæleþ*; alternatively, Erf. *geleod* could be taken as a collective noun with the same meaning related to *lēode* 'people'. In either case Ép. *gloed* would be taken as a scribal conjecture, but its form is closer to Erf. *geleod*, which is also supported by Cp. *geloed*.

230. Cf. Ld. 46/30 *celox nauis* (Phocas 421/22–3 *haec celox quod scapham significat nauis*) and Erf.II 275/14 *caelox nauis genus*, Abba

CE 68 *celox genus nauis uelocrioris*: *ceol* 'long ship' (cf. Gildas 38/19–20 *tribus ut lingua eius exprimitur cyulis* (v.l. *ciulis*), *nostra nauibus longis* and Hl. C1037 *ciula ceol*) is therefore not just 'another of these identifications based on a similarity of sound' (Lindsay, *Gloss.* 110).

231. ? Aldhelm, *VC* 73 *auratis . . . capsis*: cf. Cl.III 517/5 *capsis cystum* and Hl. *cestum*.

232. ? Aldhelm, *VP* 237/10 *tubo cataractisque uorantibus*: cf. *tubo* 1000 and the preceding item, 8 ef 9 *crustu ornato*, (§ 35 fn. 4, p. lvi). *cataractae* = 'sluice, floodgate': cf. Vulg. IV. Reg. 7: 2 *si Dominus fecerit etiam cataractas in caelo* and *PP* 206 *cataracte in plur. sunt fenestre celi, nubes, uel meatus pluuiarum*. For *uuaeterthruch* cf. Cp. 372 *canalibus waeterőruum*.

233. The identification of *cer(u)us* 'stag' with *elch* 'elk' (cf. 1001) suggests Isidore, *Ety.* xii. 1/20 *tragelaphi . . . quum eadem specie sint ut cerui, uillosos tamen habent armos*, etc.

234. ? Herm. 240/42 ὁ κύαθος *cyathus cotula*: cf. Hl. C1697 *cotula uel c(y)atus bolla*. The first Hermeneumata batch begins with the next item.

235. ? Herm. 192/18 *melandrus robur*, etc. +Isidore, *Diff.* i. 492 *rubor coloris est, robur uirtutis, robor arboris* (from Agroecius, *De Orthographia*, Keil, vii. 118/19): cf. Cp. 1749 (R206) *robor arbor aac* (= 863), R207 *robor uirtus rubor coloris est*.

236. ? Abstr. CO 208 *corillos auellanas uel nuces*: cf. Erf.II 278/52 *corilus arbor abellanus* (= Trier 68ᵇ *abellana*), Cl.II 268/40 *abellanus uel colurnus hæsl*.

237. *cisirbeam* and Jun. *cyrstreow* 'cherry-tree' are otherwise unrecorded.

238. *cariscus* is also recorded in Eucherius 149/8–9 *troiscos uel cariscos quasi in nucis modum deformatos* (VL Exod. 25: 33 *c(h)arys(s)os*, translating Sept. καρυΐσκους 'nut-like'), but this is a tree-name: it could be related to *carex* 'sedge' or to *carica* 'fig', in which case *cuicbeam* 'mountain ash' (ModE. *quicken*) might be a mistake for *ficbeam*.

239. ? Aldhelm, *VP* 318/2–3 *capitium et manicae sericis clauatae*: cf. *clabatum* 228. Not Vulg. Exod. 28: 32 (*tunicam*) *in cuius medio supra erit capitium* (so K. W. Gruber, *Romanische Forschungen*, xx (1907), 451), where *capitium* means 'hole' (*AV* 'and there shall be a hole in the top of it, in the midst thereof').

241. *cornacula*: 'crow'; cf. It. *cornacchia* (Barbier, *Revue*, ii. 188).

245. *cappa*: 'a cape with a hood'; cf. 8 ef 17 *cappa uel capsula* (*cas-*) *cocula* and Erf.II 320/58 *penulam cocula sine* (*-ue*) *cappa*. It already = the liturgical cope in Gregory of Tours, *Vitae Patrum*, viii. 5 (*PL* lxxi. 1045a) *cappa . . . dilata erat atque consuta ut solent in illis candidis fieri quae per paschalia festa sacerdotum umeris imponuntur*. For *scic(c)ing* 'cloak' (here only) cf. OE. *sciccel(s)*, ON. *skikkja*.

246. *cunillae* = 'wild thyme' (L. *cunīla*), not *cerefolium* 'chervil'; *cer(e)folium*, *-fillon* (Herm. 497/26 *kerefillon cerfolium*, etc.) may have been confused with *serpyllon* (cf. 895), or with OE. *fille* 'wild thyme' as in Dur. 111 *ceruillum fille* (Brown, C244).

247. *leactrogas*: ? 'leek-troughs', i.e. 'vessels with foliated ornamentation', glossing *Ecl.* iii. 36 ff.:

> pocula ponam
> fagina, caelatum diuini opus Alcimedontis,
> lenta quibus torno facili superaddita uitis
> diffusos hedera uestit pallente corymbos.

Other interpretations are 'clusters of berries carved for the ornamenting of a ship' (TS 608), after Cp. C661 *corimbus nauibus uel cacumen* (Ld. 47/5 *corimbis nauibus*+Abstr. CO 67 *corymbus cacumen*), and 'herb-jugs' (Meritt, *HG* 118–19), from Pliny xix. 175 *corymbiam hanc uocant, corymbosque quos condunt* (of the herb *ferula*, stored in jars); various emendations were proposed by Schlutter, *Angl.* xix. 114, xx (1897), 386–7, *JGP* i. 316, and Holthausen, *AB* xxxii (1921), 64.

248. Cf. Servius, *Ecl.* ii. 36 '*disparibus . . . cicutis*' *inaequalibus cannis, nam et harmonia inaequalis est*: *uuodaeuistlae* 'hemlock' is recorded elsewhere only in Jun. 135/42 *elleborum uel ueratrum wodepistle* (*-wistle?*), but cf. (*w*)*oedibergæ* 388 n.

249. *cistimbeam* (*cistin-*): 'chestnut-tree' (this gloss only), from L. *castanea* with WGmc. **-innjō* replacing **-annjō* (Campbell, § 518 fn. 2).

250. *calta*: 'marigold'; the interpretation may be an inference from *Ecl.* ii. 50 *mollia luteola pingit uaccinia calta*, whence Cp. *genus floris* (= Abstr. CA 116). The confusion is carried a stage further in Jun. 134/42 *calta uel trifillon clæfre*, where the present gloss is combined with one like Dur. 324 *trifolium rubrum reade cleaure*.

252. *uuryd* = *wrīd* 'stalk' (BT 1274), not *wyrð* 'worth' (*OET* 564, after Corpus), whence Lindsay's suggested emendation of *culmus* to *culmen* (*Corpus* C942).

253. *popeg* 'poppy' may have been inferred from πέπων *pepo* ('melon'), which follows σικύδια *cucumeres* in Herm. 16/23–4, 88/46–7 (Lindsay, *Gloss.* 9); the two items are combined in Herm. 594/12 *peponus cucumeres*, etc., influenced perhaps by Num. 11 : 5 *cucumeres et pepones*. *popeg*, the normal OE. form with *o* for L. *a*, may represent a lL. *popāuer* (Luick, § 666 a.) with pretonic rounding: the Latin word is so spelt in 824.

254. *calcesta*: ? 'nomen a colore calcis simili tractum' (*TLL*).

256. Presumably Herm. 188/16 *tetrix cicada*, etc. (§ 28 fn. 3), but the pls. *cicade* and *haman* (also Cp.) suggest a gloss on *Ecl.* v. 77 *pascentur . . . rore cicadae*.

258. *hafaern*: 'crab' (§ 38); cf. *wæterhæfern* (BT 1161).

261. Cf. Erf.II 278/61 *colustrum lac concretum in mammis* (Nonius 84/8 *colustra*), Cl.III 527/27 *colobostrum beost* (Aldhelm, *VC* 1601 *candescens lacte colostrum*): *colobostrum* may show contamination with *obestrum* 703.

262. *ciscillus*: ? for *acisculum* 'stone-cutter's mallet' (cf. 4 ab 12 *acisculum quod habent instructores quasi mallioles ad cedendos lapides*) or 1L. **cisellum* 'chisel' (L. *cīsorium*).

heardheui: ? 'chisel'; it glosses *foratorium* 'borer' in Hl. F557 *foratorium heardheawe uel nafogar* (cf. 1010), but cf. *hēawan* 'hew'. Holthausen, *AEW* 159, accepts **-hīewe* as a genuine inflexional variant of *-hēaw(a)*, *-e*, presumably a neut. *ja*-stem, but it depends solely on Erfurt, which sometimes confuses *-æ*, *-e*, and *-i* (§ 63).

263. *calciculium*: ? for *calcularis* 'henbane' (Herm. 539/50 *simfoniaca siue caliculâria*); *TLL* and von Lindheim, 35–6, suggest a corruption of *accitulium* 63, which is itself obscure.

264. *cucuzata* = **cucutiata* 'crested' (Barbier, *Revue*, ii. 188); It. dial. *cucugghiata* (Thompson, *CP* xiii. 16) is the crested lark, but the name may have been used for other crested birds.

laepaeuincæ: 'lapwing'; Suolahti, 267, compares North Frisian *liap*, regarding Cl. *hleape-* as due to popular etymology, but initial *h* is often omitted in the early glossaries (cf. § 72). For the second element cf. OE. *wancol* 'skittish' and ModE. *wince* (Gmc. **wankjan* through NF. *wencir*).

266. *thistil*: for *þisteltwige* 'goldfinch, thistle-finch'; cf. *linaethuigae* 309 n.

268. *cacomicamus* = Gr. κακομήχανος 'mischievous' (? Herm. 'de moribus hominum'). For *logdor* 'deceitful' (Gmc. **lug-þr-*, ? < IE. **leugh-* 'lie') cf. Cl.I 443/9 *marsius logeþer* (? Aldhelm, *VP* 279/8 *marsorum machinas*).

269. *caloma(u)cus* = Gr. καλυμαύκιον 'cap' (Schlutter, *JGP* i. 326): cf. Trier 62vb *calomaucus pilleus*, Affatim 553/25 *pilleum calamaucum*. Cp. *haet*, Ld. *het* is therefore the correct reading, and Hl. *genesta* (*-ista*) must be a re-translation of *hæþ* (cf. § 19).

270. *heardhara*: 'mullet'; cf. Cp. 1347 *mugil heardhara*, Jun. 180/31 *mulus uel mugilis heardra*.

272. ? Herm. 581/37 *castorius* (for *castoreum* 'musk') *idest e castor(e) et sunt testiculi bebiris* (= OE. *bebir*).

273. ? Abstr. CO 137 *compos optatae felicitatis effectum consecutus*: if so, *faegen* would = 'pleased, satisfied' (cf. TS *fægen* 2a) as in Cl.III 505/35 *uoti compos wilfægen*, and Hl. *facetus* would be a mistranslation (§ 19).

274. Perhaps a lost item from Abstrusa (cf. Abavus CA 116 *cauma aestus aequor*), whence 273 immediately preceding; but Cl.I 379/6

caumate swole (? = Cp. 415 -*i suole*) glosses Gildas 35/9 *incalescenteque caumate* (Schlutter, *AJP* xxix (1908), 445).

275. ? Herm. (cf. 255) or Abstr. CA 112 *crabro uespa longa*: it begins Lindsay's second Hermeneumata batch, but cf. 273–4 immediately preceding, and 276 immediately following.

276. Holthausen, *IF* xlviii (1930), 267, takes *ginehord* as a variant spelling of Cp. *geneorð* with intrusive *h* (cf. § 72 fn. 6), and the latter as an adj. 'content, satisfied', related to ON. *Njǫrðr*, the sea-god, and OE. *neorxnawang* 'paradise': cf. Nonius 263/24 ff. *contentus dicitur cui res etiam parua abunde est*: *Vergilius lib. vii* (736) *'patriis sed non et filius aruis contentus'* and Ld. 2/32 *contentus patiens* (= Abstr. CO 187) *sufficiens*. For other suggestions see Krogmann, *Angl.* lv (1931), 398–9; Meritt, *FL* 4 D 17, *HG* 61.

279. Cf. Herm. 581/34 *cardamomus uel cardamus idest nasturcius siue crissonus* (*h*)*ortensis*: *cartamo* = Gr. κάρδαμον 'nasturtium', the seed of which, Gr. καρδάμωμον, was used as a cathartic (OE. *lybcorn*).

281. Cf. Abavus CO 329 *cohors* (v.l. *coors*) *castra uel numerus militum* (Abstr. CO 41 *cohors numerus militum sexcentorum*): Corpus may preserve the original form of the gloss, which was abbreviated independently in Épinal–Erfurt and Cleopatra I, II; Hl. *uilla* is presumably a re-translation of *tuun* (§ 19).

282. *cummi*: for *gummi*; cf. Herm. 544/65 (*c*)*liorro* (? = *chlora* 'poltice') *gummi*.

283. *carpella* 'pommel' (?) may be related to L. *corbus* (? *coruus*, ? *corbis*) in Cl.I 379/31, Jun. 120/3 *corbus sadel-, sadolboga*; Lindsay, *Corpus* 197, compares Sc. *curpel*.

287. *coacas*: for *cloacas* 'sewers' (Schlutter, *AJP* xvii (1896), 85–7), perhaps a gloss on VL (Robert) Jud. 3: 24 *in recessu culinae cubiculi*. Cp., Cl. *cocas* and Cl. *culini* (? for *culinarii*) look like scribal conjectures, but could be due to confusion with Vulg. Ez. 46: 24 *domus culinarum, in qua coquent ministri*.

288. *halstan* = **heallstān* 'flat cake' (TS 522, *AEW* 151): cf. ON. *hella, hellusteinn* 'flat stone'. Holthausen, *AB* xv (1904), 349, compares Ger. *Pflasterstein* 'paving-stone', used for a hard, round spiced cake.

289. *cemetum* = *cal*(*a*)*metum* 'a place full of reeds' (302): cf. the *Itinerarium Antonini Placentini* (*Itinera Hierosolymita*, ed. P. Geyer, Vienna, 1898), 181/9 *inter calmita uel palmita ambulante* (the only other example in *TLL*). Lindsay, *Gloss.* 32, suggests a gloss on Vulg. Exod. 2: 3 *in carecto ripae fluminis*, but Jos. 16: 8 *de Taphua pertransit contra mare in uallem arundineti* (referring to the same region as the *Itinerarium*) is a more likely source.

289a. *lipidium*: for Cp. *lapidum*; cf. Hl. C1049 *cimentum stanlim*.

291. *cimbing*: 'joining'; cf. Hl. C1196 *commisura siue dicitur tabularum coniunctio gefeg cimbing* and ModE. *chimb* 'rim of a cask' (*OED chime* sb² 1).

294–5. (354/37–8) ? Herm. 270/19 ἀκόνη *cos*, 311/62 μερός (μη-) *coxa*; *cox* might also be from Phocas 419/4 *haec cos, haec dos*, whence Ld. 46/4 *cos ueostun* and *dos* 324.

297. *pung*: 'purse' (here only); cf. Go. a. s. *pugg*, ON. *pungr*.

298. Vulg. Esther 1: 6 *tentoria aerii coloris et carbasini ac hyacinthini*: cf. Ld. 22/7 *carbasini color gemme idest uiridis. carbasini* = 'linen' (cf. Sept. βυσσίνοις καὶ καρπασίνοις τεταμένοις); *græsgroeni* 'grass-green' may be due to confusion with *prasinum* 'leek-green', as in the Ld. jewel-name gloss, 41/10 *smaragdus uiridem colorem habet hoc est prasinum* (*smaragdino . . . lapide* occurs later in the same verse). The text, however, is uncertain: AV has 'white, *green*, and blue hangings', and the first Targum version has sapphire, *green*, and violet (L. B. Paton, *Critical and Exegetical Commentary on the Book of Esther* (Edinburgh, 1908), 138).

299. ? Vulg. Jn. 19: 31 *frangerentur eorum crura* or Herm. 249/13 κνήμη *crus*: it comes at the end of the Bible batch (§ 32 fn. 5), followed immediately by 300–1. For *scīa* (otherwise unrecorded) beside *scinu* 'shin' (*AEW* 276) cf. OHG. *bīa*: *bini* 'bee' (*IEW* 920).

300. Goetz, *CGL* vi. 165, takes *caldica* as a corruption of *calautica* 'turban' (cf. Nonius 537/1–2 *calautica est tegmen muliebre quod capiti innectitur*), but *TLL* accepts *cladica* 'weft' on the authority of this gloss. The weaving terms in Épinal–Erfurt and related glossaries may derive ultimately from Herm. 'de suppellectile', but include a number of obscurities: cf. *depoline* 328, *stilium* 967.

303. W. H. Stevenson (Lindsay, *Corpus* 199) takes *colicum* as a corruption of Gr. χάλκειος 'carline thistle' (= OE. *eoforðrote*), *TLL* as 'a remedy for colic' (sc. *medicamen*). For the latter cf. Cp. 595 *cocilus* (*-licus*) *ampre* and 1073 n.: *Leechdoms*, iii. 70/23–4 prescribes a drink made from *eoforðrote* and other herbs *wið breosta hefignesse and hrifes apundennesse*.

305. *couel* is probably an error for Cp. *cauuel*, Cl. *cawel* 'basket' (lL. *cauellum*), but cf. *popeg* < L. *papāuer* (253 n.).

306. *uuilmod* = Hl. *wulmod* 'distaff': cf. OHG. *wollameit*. The second element corresponds to ON. *meiðr* 'pole, beam', with *o* for Prim. OE. *ā* under reduced stress (Campbell, § 336).

309. *linaethuigae* (*-tuigae*): 'linnet'; cf. Sc. *lyntquhit* and *thistil*(*tuige*) 266. The second element is related to *twiccan* 'pluck' (Hessels, *Leiden* 74).

311. *uuestnorduui*(*n*)*d*: 'north-west wind' (here only); cf. *be westannorðan* OE. Orosius 22/4–5, etc.

312. Cf. Erf.II 274/35 *cartilago grurzapa dicitur rusticae*: *grundsuopa* has been taken as a plant-name 'ground-soap' (*OET* 584, BT 492) or the etymon of ME. *growndesope* 'dregs' (TS 489, Meritt, *HG* 9 ff.), but neither interpretation fits *cartilago*. Erf. *-suopa* suggests a compound 'ground-sweepings', the second element related to *ǣswǣpa* (BT *swǣpa* 941), *geswǣpa*, *-swāpa* (BT 447), with *o* for Prim. OE. *ā* under reduced stress as in *uuilmod* 306; if so, *cartilago* may = Gr. χορτολογία 'foraging': cf. Philox. PA 9 *pabulatio* χορτολογία.

313–14. (355/50–1) ? Aldhelm, *VP* 321/19 *quantum distat dulcis sapa* (v.l. *dulcisapa*) *a merulento temeto*, Metr. 159/11 *sapa, id est defrutum*, etc.: *dulcis sapa* (? *dulcisapa*) is peculiar to Aldhelm and *defrutum* is a favourite Aldhelmism, e.g. *VC* 2512 *nunc potius metuat defruti pocula uirgo*, whence Cl.III 532/35 *defruti cerenes*. Both drinks consisted of new wine boiled down with spices and sweet herbs to preserve it, the difference being in the amount boiled off: cf. Pliny xiv. 80 *nam siraeum* (σίραιον), *quod alii hepsema* (ἕψημα), *nostri sapam appellant, ingeni non naturae opus est, musto usque ad tertiam mensurae decocto; quod ubi factum ad dimidiam, defrutum uocamus*. *cæren* (L. *carēnum*) was a similar decoction: cf. Isidore, *Ety.* xx. 3/15 *carenum eo quod feruendo partem careat, tertia enim parte musti amissa quod remanserit carenum est*. Erf. *oe* (also Cp. 628) may reflect pretonic rounding as in *pop(a)eg* 253 n., 824.

316. *dodrans* 'three-quarters' = Hisperic 'flood, surge' (*HF* 402 *dodrante inundat freta*, etc.): cf. Napier, *Modern Language Quarterly* i (1897), 51, and Raby's and Ehwald's notes to *Altus* 103–4 (*ex*) *oceani dodrantibus* | *maris* and *Carm. Rhythm.* i. 107–9 *oceanus cum* . . . *dodrantibus pulsat* | *promontoria*; could there be some connection with the triangular shape of the earth (1039 n.)? For *aegur* 'flood' (TS *ēgor*) cf. Napier 7/159 *cataclismi genus fluctus egores*.

317. Cf. Lib. Gloss. DU 122–3 *dumis locis siluestris, dumis (-us) spina in qua nascitur morum siluestre id est rubus* (= Abol. DU 6 *dumis locis siluestris uel spinae*, on Geo. iv. 130 *rarum tamen in dumis olus*, etc.): such an interpretation would explain OE. *thyrnae* 'thorn-bush'.

318. ? Gildas 27/16–17 *magi deuoturi* (v.l. *deuotaturi*) *populum dei* (cf. Cp. D180 *deuotaturi maledicturi*), or Aldhelm, *VC* 58 *deuotaturus populum* . . . *uatis* (cf. Cl.I 387/42 *deuotaturus wiergende*, in Lübke's first Aldhelm batch).

319–20. Vulg. Is. 60: 5 *dromedarii Madian et Epha*: cf. Ld. 13/60 *dromedariæ castrati cameli, dromedarius unus*. *dromidus* may be a corruption of *dromedarius* or of *dromeda* (cf. Jun. 119/7 *camelus uel dromeda olfend*); for wk. *obbenda* (*olb-*) beside *olfend* 'camel' cf. OS *olƀundeo* (m.), OHG. *olfenta* (f.). *se oritmon* is a corruption of Cp. *se eoredmon* 'rider', i.e. the 'camel-driver', a meaning of *dromedarius* recorded in inscriptions (*TLL*); *-rit* is presumably the German scribe's interpretation of *-red* < *-rǣd* (Campbell, § 336).

321. (356/5) *dalaturae* presumably = *dolatorium* 'stone-cutter' (cf. Jerome, *Epistles*, cvi. 86 (*PL* xxii. 867) λαξευτήριον *autem, pro quo Latinus asciam uertit*, . . . *dolatorium dici potest* and Werden I (Gallée, 338) *dolatorium grece acsia latine aetsa* (? = *adesa* 'adze') *saxonice*), but the interpretation suggests confusion with *dolabra* 'pick-axe': cf. Erf. II 287/53–4 *dolabrum est dolaturia, dolabella deminutiu(u)m* and Ld. 47/47 *dolabella bradacus*. In any case the source was probably VL Ps. 73 : 6, where the Cassino Psalter (ed. A. M. Amelli, *Collectanea biblica latina*, i, Rome, 1912) reads *in securi, ascia, et dolatorio conciderunt* and Augustine (*PL* xxxvi. 935) *in dolabro et fractorio deiecerunt eam* (Sept. ἐν πελέκει καὶ λαξευτηρίῳ κατέρραξαν αὐτήν).

braedlaestu: 'broad' (Cp. *braadlast*); cf. *wīdlāst* 'extensive'. -*laestu* may be the nom. sg. fem. of an *ija/ō*-stem variant, like *earfeðe*, -*u* beside *earfoð* (Campbell, § 648. 4). For *braed*- beside *braad*- cf. *bredisern* 883, *bredipannae* 885 and notes.

322. *dob(g)endi*: 'crazed, doting'; cf. ON. *dofinn* 'numb, dead' and *dofunga* 'deliramenta, stoliditates' (TS 153).

323. ? Orosius v. 1/14 *ubi dissidebat diuersitas potestatum*: cf. 356/31 *dissidebat discordabat*, beginning Lindsay's Orosius batch. For **unsibbian* 'disagree' cf. Hl. D283 *unsibbaþ* 'desidet, discordat'.

324. *uuituma* = 'bride-price', not 'dowry' (*OET* 514, BT 1258): cf. the Laws of Alfred (F. Liebermann, *Gesetze der Angelsachsen* (Halle, 1903), i. 16–89), 12 ðæt *weorð sie hire mægðhades, ðæt is weotuma, agife he hire þone* (Exod. 21: 10 *pretium pudicitiae non negabit*), 29 *agife he ðæt fioh æfter þæm weotuman* (Exod. 22: 17 *reddet pecuniam iuxta modum dotis quam uirgines accipere consueuerunt*).

325. ? Abstr. DE 52 *delibutus delicatus unctus perfusus* or Aldhelm, *VP* 230/9 *delibutus . . . nardo*: cf. Erf.II 283/58 *delibutus perunctus uel perfusus* (= Affatim 503/33), Hl. D105 *delibutus idest perunctus linitus perfusus*, and the Brussels Aldhelm gloss, *ZfdA* ix. 405/44–5 *delibutus gesme(rod) perunctus*. Sweet prints *gisalbot* as OHG., but OE. **sealfian* is attested by Cl.I 406/13 *fotam sealfode* and ME. *salfen* 'anoint'.

326. *delumentum*: 'soap'; cf. Peterhouse MS. 2.4.6 (§ 9 fn. 3) 592/1 *sapo delumentum quo sordes abluuntur* and Cl.I 439/21 (*de)lumentum sape* (in an Isidore batch, possibly glossing *Ety*. xvi. 2/7 (*nitrum*) *ex quo . . . sordes corporum uestiumque lauantur*). OE. *þwēal* normally means 'washing' (BT 1082), but cf. ON. *þváll* 'soap' (Schlutter, *ESt*. xliii (1911), 334).

327. *gifyrdro* is otherwise tr. 'advance, promote' (TS 331).

328. *depoline* (-*ponile*): 'weft'(?); cf. Cp. 1735 *reponile gearnuuinde*. OE. *weft(a)* is also recorded in Hl. C1110 *clatica wefta*.

331. *ymbdritung* (Cp. -*ðriodung*): 'deliberation'; cf. Hl. C976 *circumuenientium embðrydiendra* and *þreodian, þreodung*.

333. Lindsay, *Gloss.* 25, suggests a gloss on Orosius v. 22/18 *eadem celeritate . . . euanuit*, but cf. Aldhelm, *VP* 295/8–9 *ut fumus euanescens disparuit* (Cl.I 388/29 *disparuit gedwan*); Gregory, *Dial.* iii. 7 *malignorum spirituum turba disparuit. ungiseem (-ni)* 'unseen' is otherwise unrecorded, but cf. *ungesīnelic* 'invisible'.

334. ? Orosius vi. 14/1 *uelut forma Oceani maris, quae . . . naturali damno et* defectu *interio*re *subducitur*: if so, *aspringendi* 'failing' presumably represents *quae . . . subducitur* (§ 87).

337. *hondgong*: 'surrender' (TS 507); cf. *on hand gān* 'to surrender' (TS *hand* VIII 5b (δ)).

338. *ue(a)rnuislicæ*: 'with difficulty'; cf. *wearn* 'hindrance, obstacle' (BT 1178), whence **wearnwīs* 'difficult', like **lēawīs* 977a (n.).

339. ? Orosius vi. 7/6 *cum diu exercitus . . . pugnam detrectasset*: cf. 356/50 *detrectasset recussasset* and Abstr. DE 22 *detrectat . . . recusat.*

340. Lindsay, *Gloss.* 25, suggests Orosius v. 23/5 *per deuia oberrans*, etc., but cf. Sedulius, *Carm. Pasch.* ii. 103–4 *per loca mutati gradientes deuia callis | in patriam rediere suam*: the glossator apparently took *deuia*, acc. pl. neut. with *loca*, as a nom. sg. fem. (?) with *callis*, influenced perhaps by Vulg. Jud. 5: 6 *ambulauerunt per calles deuios*, which Sedulius is paraphrasing. For other probable Sedulius glosses cf. 576, 578; but the *Carmen Paschale* has not proved the major source that Meritt expected (*OEG*, p. viii).

342. Orosius iv. 5/5 *libertini . . . dominos procul abigunt, qui miseri exules egentesque Romam deferuntur*: *deferuntur* = 'went away', not 'informed against' (OE. *meldadun*). *roactun*, taken as a corruption of Cp. *wroegdun* 'accused' by Sweet, *OET* 650, and BT 1273, may represent OIr. *roachtatar*, prototonic third plural of *rosiacht*, the reduplicated preterite of *saigid* 'seeks, prosecutes' (Thurneysen, § 682 and n.); if so, it was presumably an interlinear or marginal gloss in an Irish manuscript used by the English glossator (cf. § 35 fn. 2, p. lvii).

343–4. Lindsay, *Gloss.* 25, suggests Orosius iv. 11/7 *(aedificia) quae segnior redundatio tenuit madefacta dissoluit et quae cursus torrentis inuenit impulsa deiecit*, but cf. Abol. DE 2 *de(h)iscit patescit* (= Abavus DE 126 *fatiscit*) and Orosius vi. 1/4 *ubi ratiocinatio deficit* (cf. 866). For *tecinid* 'cracks, gapes' cf. *ZfdA* ix. 529/10 *rimosa tocinan (-en)*; *tedridtid* is taken as a corruption of Cp. *tetridit* from **totredan* 'trample' by BT 1009, of Hl. *tetreþ* for *tydreþ* 'fails' by Meritt, *HG* 117, but its form suggests rather *(*to)ðri(u)tið* impers. 'it wearies': cf. BT, TS *(ā)þrēotan.*

345. *detriturigine* = *detrita rubigine* (Orosius vii. 25/10 *detrita regii fastus rubigine*), so Cp., Hl. *agnidine*, pret. part. of **āgnīdan* 'rub away', is the correct form of the gloss, and *āgniden(n)* 'rubbing' (*OET* 515, TS 29) is a ghost-word.

345a. Abstr. DA 4 *dracontia gemma ex cerebro serpentis*: for *gimrodr* 'bright gem' cf. *Beowulf* 2749 *swegle searogimmas* and inverted compounds such as *cyningwuldor*. Bradley, TS 767, reads *gim (ex cereb)ro d(icitu)r* after Abstr. *gemma ex cerebro*; Meritt, *FL* 3 A 17, emends to *gimhrōðor 'gem splendour' after Aldhelm, *VP* 244/22 *sine topazio et carbunculo et rubicunda gemmarum gloria uel sucini dracontia* whence Cl.III 491/16 *dracontia gimrodor*, etc., but *dracontia* 'draconite' is there used simply for 'precious stone' (after Abstr. *gemma* ?).

346. Brown, D99, following a suggestion of Professor Meritt's (cf. his thesis, p. 58), cites Pliny xxv. 160 *duo genera eius (cotyledontis)*, *maius (genus)* . . . *digitillum, alterum minusculum*, which would confirm Bradley's interpretation of *fingirdoccuna* as 'foxgloves' (*CQ* xiii. 105), rather than 'finger-muscles' (*OET* 582, TS 219).

346a. *eola* beside *elch* 'elk' (233, 1001) is otherwise unrecorded, but cf. OHG. *elaho*. For its identification with *damma* 'fallow deer' cf. Isidore, *Ety*. xii. 1/20 (233 n.) and 22 *dammula*.

347. ? *Vit. Ant.* 16 *quasi echo ad extrema uerba respondent* (Lindsay, *Gloss*. 114): cf. the preceding item, 357/18 *explosi extincti* (= Ld. 28/14, on *Vit. Ant*. 26 *explosi* . . . *prodigii*). For *uuydumer* 'wood-sprite' cf. *mera* 558 and Jun. 108/21–2 *satiri uel fauni* . . . *wudewasan*. BT 1278 cites Grimm ii. 452, iv. 1412–13, on ON. *dvergmál* 'echo', but a classical allusion is also possible: cf. the *uocalis nymphe* of Ovid, *Metamorphoses*, iii. 357 f.

348. *uuidouuindae* 'convolvulus' (cf. 1059 n.) suggests Vulg. Jonah 4: 6 *praeparauit Dominus Deus hederam* rather than II Mac. 6: 7 *hedera coronati* (Lindsay, *Gloss*. 33): Jonah's quick-growing vine (AV 'gourd') is similarly interpreted in *Patience* 443 ff.

> þe whyle God of his grace ded growe of þat soyle
> þe fayrest bynde hym abof þat euer burne wyste.
> When þe dawand day Dryȝten con sende,
> þenne wakened þe wyȝ vnder wodbynde . . .

349. *ceapcnext*: 'bought slave' (Exod. 12: 44 *seruus empticius*, etc.); cf. *cypecnihtas*, Ælfric, *Homilies* (ed. B. Thorpe, London, 1844–6), ii. 120/18, translating *pueros uenales*, *BH*., ii. 1 (p. 79).

352. *erimio* = Gr. ἠρύγγιον 'eryngo, sea-holly' (Stevenson in Lindsay, *Corpus* E271), e.g. in Herm. 611/13 *eringio idest cardo panis*; but Cp., Cl. *hindber(i)ge* 'raspberry' suggests confusion with *acinus* (cf. 69), perhaps from Vulg. Ecclus. 33: 16 *qui colligit acinos*, since it comes immediately after the Bible batch. Erf. *hindbrere*, Hl. *-brer* 'hind-briar' (here only) is presumably the raspberry plant.

353. ? *Aen*. ii. 229 f. *scelus expendisse merentem | Laocoönta ferunt* (cf. Abol. EX 112 *expendisse exsoluisse*) or Orosius ii. 4/10 (*certamina*) *quam breuissime strinxerim*: . . . *pace disrupta Mettum Fufetium* . . . *duplicis animi noxam poena diuisi corporis expendisse* (cf. 365): in either

case the OE. pret. (subj.?) renders a Lat. infin. of indirect discourse (§ 87) and *araebndae* = 'suffered for, expiated', not 'pondered' (TS 46).

354. Orosius v. 6/5 *egerere foras non facile potest intestinum malum*: *ascrepan*, lit. 'scrape off' (BT 52), = 'remove' here and in 375.

358. *athraestae*: 'wrenched out'; cf. *awræste* 'extorsit' (Cl.I 397/37).

362. *euiscerata*: fig. 'plundered' (Orosius vi. 14/3 (*Roma*) *usque ad medullas paene euiscerata et exesa est*); hence *aeohed* = Cl. *æthyd*, p.p. **æthȳðan* 'spoil, plunder' (cf. *āhȳðan*), not **æthȳdan* 'flay' (TS 23), *āþēodan* 'separate' (Lindsay, *Corpus* 268), or **āȳðan* 'destroy' (Meritt, *FL* 3 I 1).

366. *āræddun*: 'made ready'; *ārædan* is not recorded elsewhere in this sense, but cf. *geræde* 'ready' and *rædan* 'prepare' (BT VII and add *Maldon* 18 *rad and rædde*).

367. *stæb*: for *endestæf* 'end, death' (Cp., Cl., Hl.).

369. Orosius vi. 7/8 *pugna maxime grauis ex phalange Germanorum fuit* (paraphrasing Caesar, *De Bello Gallico*, i. 52 *phalange facta*): *ob* therefore = 'because of' (TS *of* IIIa).

370. *e uestigio* = 'immediately' (cf. Abstr. EV 11 *e uestigio statim*) in Orosius vi. 15/20 *e uestigio prorumpens*, but Cp., Cl., Hl. *on laste* translates Orosius iii. 2/9 *e uestigio secutus*, to which *an landae* may also refer as an alternative interpretation.

371. *exauctorauit*: 'cashiered' (Orosius vi. 18/33 *uiginti milia militum exauctorauit*); Erf. *giheldae* 'bent, subjected' (?) and Cp. *geheende*, Cl., Hl. *geh(i)ende* 'humbled, disgraced' are both inexact.

372. The original gloss may be preserved in Cp. 817 *arydid*, p.p. **āryddan* 'strip, plunder' (TS 48), to which *aþry(i)d* 'crushed' (cf. Hl. *conquassatam*) was added as a further explanation.

373. Orosius v. 15/11 *expeditio ad cauendum (telorum nimbum) compressione multitudinis deerat*: *expeditio* here = 'freedom, opportunity', not *f(i)erd* 'campaign, expedition'.

375. ? Vulg. Deut. 23: 13–14 *cumque sederis, fodies per circuitum et egesta humo operies quo releuatus es* (Lindsay, *Corpus* E98); if so, Erf. *ascrepaeni* beside Cp., Cl. *ascrepen* is presumably the instr. sg. neut. used substantively or with *greote* 'humo' understood.

376. *echinus*: 'sea-urchin'; cf. Isidore, *Ety.* xii. 6/57 ('de piscibus') *echinus . . . cuius testula* (= OE. *scel*) *duplex, spinis aculeata in modo castanearum, quando adhuc coopertae de arboribus cadunt*.

377. Cf. Ld. 20/6 *extentera inicium excoriandi* (Vulg. Tob. 6: 5 *exentera hunc piscem*): *ans(c)eot* therefore = 'rip open, gut', not 'unbar' (TS 672.)

378. Cf. Ld. 43/30 *emblema fodor* (Donatus 379/12–13 (*nomina*) *quae a Graecis sumpsimus, ut emblema*): if *fothr* = Go. *fōdr* 'sheath' (TS 259), it may refer to appliqué work on vases, as in Abstr. IN 5 *imblemata ornamenta uasorum*.

NOTES 85

379. *gilodusrt (-uyrt)*: 'septfoil, tormentil'(?); cf. OHG. *lodwurz* 'comfrey'.

380. *exagium* = Gr. ἐξάγιον 'weighing': cf. Cyrillus 301/16 ἐξάγιον *pensatio*, Aldhelm, *Metr.* 199/16–17 *aequamentum uel exagium trutinae.* *handmitta* = *anmitta* 'scale, balance' (TS 43), lit. 'that in which one measures', which may reflect Aldhelm's *trutinae.*

381. Cf. Ld. 35/203 *extale snedildaerm* (? a Bible intruder in the Ld. Rufinus list, from Vulg. I Reg. 5: 9 *conputrescebant prominentes extales eorum*): the present item comes immediately after Lindsay's second Rufinus batch, followed by 359/6 *exetri scabelli ad cibos* (= Ld. 35/61 *exedræ*, on Rufinus xi. 23). *snaedil uel thearm* = *snædelþearm* 'rectum' (BT 891).

382. Cf. the Trier Bible gloss 3ᵛᵃ *emunctoria quibus candelae mundantur* (Exod. 25: 38 *emunctoria . . . fiant de auro purissimo*): *candelthuist* (*-tuist*), otherwise unrecorded, therefore = 'candle-trimmers' (AV 'tongs'), not 'a pair of snuffers' (*OET* 504, BT 145); for the second element cf. ME. *twist* 'branch'.

383–4. (359/13–14) ? On I Reg. 21:15 (Sept. ἐπιλήπτων, Vulg. *furiosi*), Lev. 1: 15 (Sept. στραγγιεῖ, Vulg. *decurrere faciet*): cf. Karlsruhe MS. Aug. 99 (SS. v. 207/4) *epilempticos cadiuos (-ucos)*, Hesychius, *In Leviticum (PG* xciii. 802d) *decurrere faciet uel secundum LXX esculat.* For *uuoda* sb. 'madman' (BT 1261) cf. Cp. 1044 *inergumenos* (ἐνεργουμένους) *wodan.*

385. ? Rufinus viii. 14/5 *exta uisceribus reuulsa perscrutabantur*: cf. Ld. 35/202–3 *exta intestina, extale snedildaerm* (= 381). It is clear from the examples in BT 65, TS 61 that *bæcdermi (-ðearm)* = 'rectum' (cf. *snædelþearm*), not 'entrails'.

386. *elothr (-htr)* = *elehtre* 'lupin' (BT 246), from L. *electrum* 'amber' (*AEW* 89) because of its yellow colour according to von Lindheim, 47: could *electrum* itself have been a popular name for the flower?

387. *eptafolium* = Gr. ἑπτάφυλλον 'septifolium' (cf. 379); its identification with *sinfullae* 'house-leek' (also 819) may be due to graphic similarity.

388. ? Isidore, *Ety.* xvii. 9/24 (*elleborum*) *Romani alio nomine ueratrum dicunt pro eo quod sumptum motam mentem in sanitatem reducit*: cf. the preceding item, 359/30 *ebenum arbor quod decrescit cesa in lapidem* (*Ety.* xvii. 7/36 *ebenus . . . qui caesus durescit in lapidem*). (*w*)*oedibergæ* 'mad-berry' (cf. adj. *w(o)ede*, BT 1181), recorded elsewhere only as a gloss in *Leechdoms*, i. 258/23, may be derived from this passage.

389. *epimemia (-nia)* = Gr. ἐπιμήνια '(monthly) provisions': cf. Herm. 14/20 ἐπιμήνια *cybaria*, etc., Abstr. EP 7 *epimenia xenia quae dantur per singulos menses* (VL (Robert) Gen. 45: 21).

390. ? *Vit. Ant.* 23 *lauit ependyten suum*: cf. Ld. 3/56 *ependiten tonica*

8111649 M

uel cocula uel omnis uestis desuper aliis uestibus pendens. For *cop* 'over-garment' cf. Jun. 188/14–15 *ependeton cop uel hoppada uel ufrescrud*; it is otherwise unrecorded.

391. ? Isidore, *Ety.* xvii. 7/28 *fagus et esculus arbores glandiferae ideo uocatae creduntur quod earum fructibus olim homines uixerunt cibumque sumpserunt escamque habuerunt, nam esculus ab esca dicta*: cf. the following item, 359/36 *exsul qui extra solum suum uoluntatem peregrinatur* (*Ety.* v. 27/28 *exul dicitur qui extra solum est*).

392. ? An alternative interpretation of Jonah 4: 6 (348 n.): cf. Ld. 17/11 *hederam ibaei.* Herm. 192/21 *cissos edera*, etc. is another possible source, since this item is in a Bible-name list (359/39–44) just before the Hermeneumata batch, like 892.

393. *uualhuyrt*: ? a mistake for *weallwyrt 'wall-wort, dwarf elder' (Förster, *Angl.* xli. 133); cf. Cl. *wealwyrt*, etc. and 518, where *uualhuyrt* glosses *inula* 'elecampane'.

394. *gebles monung*: 'tax-collecting'; cf. *gafolmanung* (TS 279).

395–6. *erpica* = (*h*)*irpex* 'harrow' (Festus 227 *irpices genus rastrorum ferreorum quod plures habet dentes ad extirpandas herbas in agris*; Servius, *Geo.* i. 95 '*crates*' *quam rustici irpicem uocant*): cf. SS iii. 273/26, 28 *erpicarius egidare, erpica egida* and 719/57–8 *erpica egethe, erpicarius egethere. erpicarius* and *egderi* 'harrower' are recorded only in these glosses.

396a. ? Abol. EX 129 *expediam dicam explicabo narrabo*: cf. the following item, 359/57 *excubiae spolia* (? Abol. EX 91 *exuuiae spolia quae occiso hosti tolluntur*). *arectio* (Cp. *arecio*) = *areccio, the Angl. 1 sg. pres. of *āreccan* 'narrate', which renders a Latin future as normally in Old English (§ 87).

397. Phocas 413/20 *haec . . . aerugo*: one of the small batch of Phocas glosses (359/58–60) which follow the *ab*-order section (§ 25) here and are correspondingly placed in Corpus; Lindsay's second Phocas batch under A (5 cd 18–21) also follows immediately after the *ab*-order section, before 117–19. For Hl. *uel tinea* cf. Vulg. Mt. 6: 20.

400. *flustra* 'ground-swell' (cf. Isidore, *Nat. Rer.* 44/3 *flustra* (*sunt*) *motus maris sine tempestate fluctantes* and Cl. *sigend*) = Hisperic 'billows': cf. HF 389 *garrula fatigat Nothus flustra* and Aldhelm, *VP* 232/15 *spumantis pelagi flustra*, whence Cl.I 399/14 *flustra flod uel hærn*.

401. ? A lost Abstrusa/Abolita item (§ 33): cf. Abba FO 29 *forfices de quibus aliquid inciditur*, AA F516 *forcipes de quibus inciditur aurum aut quodlibet aliud huiusmodi*, and the following item, 9 ab 10 *fastes libri* (? Abstr. FA 79 *fastos libri consulatus*). *scereru* 'shears' (also Cp. 903 *forfex isernsceruru*) is an old *es/os*-stem pl. (Campbell, § 636) beside the usual *ō*-stem pl. *scēara* (BT 824).

403–4. ? Vulg. Exod. 2: 3 *fiscellam scirpeam*, Lev. 13: 30 *capillus flauus*, 36 *in flauum colorem*: cf. Meritt, *OEG* 34/1 *fiscellam sportam thenil*, 36/12 *reod* and Meritt's note (p. 44). 403 falls in a Rufinus batch (Lindsay, *Gloss.* 21) which 404 immediately follows, like 381.

405. Presumably Abol. FI 13 *fibrae uenae iecoris* (§ 33 fn. 6), but *librlaeppan* 'folds or lobes of the liver' (otherwise unrecorded) may reflect Isidore, *Ety.* xi. 1 126 *fibrae iecoris sunt extremitates, sicut extremae partes foliorum in intibis* (Brown, F23): cf. Trier 78ᵛᵃ *fibrae iecoris extremitates*.

407–8. (9 ab 25–6) ? Aldhelm, *VC* 2329 *fax et fomes*, *Aenig.* 100/25 *dum fulget fibula*: cf. Cl.III 531/8 *fax fæcele*, 518/2 *fibula sigel*.

409. ? Isidore, *Ety.* v. 27/34 *patibulum enim uulgo furca dicitur*: cf. Trier 79ᵛᵃ *furca patibulum* (= Lib. Gloss. FU 237).

410. ? Vulg. Exod. 26: 11 *fibulas aeneas, quibus iunguntur ansae*: cf. Karlsruhe MS. Aug. 99 (SS v. 154/17) *fibulas hrincas uel fiblas* and *ansa* 3a. For *hringiae* 'buckle' cf. *gyrdislrhingae* 582 and ON. *hringja*.

411. Cf. Isidore, *Ety.* xix. 22/10 *russata* (*uestis*) *quam Graeci phoeniciam uocant, nos coccinam*: possibly a marginal addition to the next item, 9 ab 34 *fenicum cocimum* (Abol. FE 22 *foenicium coccineum*).

412. Cf. Ab Absens 411/40 *flegmata umores*: ? a continuation of the Abstrusa/Abolita batch, like 413 immediately following.

414. *afigaen*: 'fried' (here only); cf. L. *coctus*, Gr. πεπτός (*IEW* 798). The Épinal order is confirmed by Corpus and Cleopatra.

415. ? *Aen.* i. 215 *pinguisque ferinae*: cf. Trier 78ᵇ *ferina* (-*a* from -*æ*) *caro a feris sumpta*. *hold* is normally 'carcass, body' (BT 550, TS 557), but cf. ON. *hold* 'flesh' and OIr. *colainn* 'meat' beside Welsh *celain* 'body' (*IEW* 924).

418. *fusarius*: 'spindle-tree' (WW 270 fn. 6); cf. SS iii. 37/37 *fusarius spinnelbovm*. Hl. *trabs uinee* is due to the corrupt *winbeam* (§ 19). For *uananbeam* (otherwise unrecorded) Holthausen, *AEW* 383, compares OS. *wānan* 'gleaming', so called because of its yellow wood; if so, it must be an ablaut variant, since OS. *ā* before *n* = OE. *ō*.

419. Lindsay, *CP* xiii. 5–6, explains glosses equating *fulica* 'coot' with sea-birds such as the gannet as misinterpretations of *Geo.* i. 362–3 *cumque marinae | in sicco ludunt fulicae*; but *fulix* translates Gr. αἴθυια 'gull' in Cicero, *De Diuinatione*, i. 8/14 *cana fulix itidem fugiens e gurgite ponti. dopaenid* (also Jun. 132/18 *fulica dopenid*) is the bald coot or water coot (Suolahti, 161).

421. Presumably Herm. 316/26 κοκκύμηλα *fraga*, where μιμαίκυλα 'strawberries' (cf. Philox. FR 2 *fraga* μαμίκυλον) was replaced by the lemma of the next item, κοκκύμηλα *pruna*; but *obtt* (-*et*) suggests Abol. FR 8 *fraga poma agrestia* (v.l. *pomus agrestis*).

422. *sugga* presumably = *hægsugga, hegesugge* (*-a?*) 'hedge-sparrow':
cf. Jun. 131/34 *cicada uel ficetula hegesugge* and *OED haysugge*. The
identification with *ficedula* 'fig-sucker' may have been suggested by Gr.
συκαλλίς in Herm. 89/72 *sycallis ficetula*, etc. (Lindsay, *Gloss.* 9).

424. *uuorhana*: 'cock-pheasant'; cf. Cl.I 380/18, Hl. C2021 *cracinus*
(? = OE. **crāca*) *worhen*.

425. Cf. Werden III (Gallée, 359) *felis ferunculus merth*, Herm. 320/49
αιλιουρος *forunculus*: αἴλουρος 'cat' also meant 'weasel' (= OE. *mearþ*)
in later Greek; *furunculus* is a diminutive of *furo* 'ferret' according to
Cl.I 411/1–2 *furo mearþ itidem diminutiue furunculus a furuo dictus unde
et fur* (Isidore, *Ety.* xii. 2/39 *furo a furuo dictus unde et fur*).

426. *famfaluca*: 'bubble' (cf. 447 n.), whence It. *fanfaluca* 'fable,
trifle' (= OE. *leasung*).

427–9. (9 cd 14–16) ? Herm. 184/6 *mucitis* (μύκητες) *fungi*, etc., 27/27
πίτυρα *furfures*, etc., 573/33 *uitellus idest me(d)iolus oui*, etc., continuing
the Hermeneumata batch interrupted by 9 cd 13 *furcifer cruci dignus*
(= Ld. 42/26, on *Vit. Eug.* 14). *aegergelu* 'egg-yolk' is otherwise
unrecorded, but cf. *Leechdoms*, ii. 130/12 *æges geola*.

430. ? Isidore, *Ety.* xx. 14/4 *falcis est qua arbores putantur et uites*:
falcastrum (cf. 449) is the next item in Isidore. *uudubil* 'bill-hook' is
recorded only here and in 449.

430a. Cf. Ld. 35/63 *fucum colorem* (Rufinus xi. 25 *adulterii fucum*),
306 *fuco pigmento* (Rufinus iv. 7/14 *adulterino maledicorum fuco*, etc.):
Erfurt, confirmed by Corpus and Cleopatra, places this item in the
Rufinus batch (§ 31 fn. 2), supporting Mrs. Turville-Petre's suggestion
that *fex* (Cp. *faex*) = OE. **fæhs* 'colour', related to *fāh, fǣgan*.

431. *flabanus*: 'swineherd'(?); cf. *Glossae Scaligeri* (*CGL* v. 600/26)
flabarius custos porcorum (= Hl.) and Meritt, *HG* 83 ff.

432–3. (9 cd 32–3) ? Vulg. Lev. 13: 36 *in flauum colorem*, Gen. 30:
32 *furuum et maculosum*: cf. Karlsruhe MS. Aug. 99 (SS v. 143/31)
furuum brunus and 403–4 n.

435. *fenus*: ? for *penis* 'membrum uirile', glossed 'sparrow' after
Festus 408 *strutheum* . . . *uocant obscenam partem uirilem a salacitate
uidelicet passeris, qui Graece* στρουθός *dicitur*; cf. Martial xi. 6/16
donabo tibi passerem Catulli. Alternatively, *fenus* might = *foenus* 'gain'
and *spearuua* an otherwise unrecorded noun 'savings, gain', related
to *spær* 'frugal' and *sparian* 'save'.

438–9. (9 ef 1–2) Orosius v. 7/1 *pudorem Romae frontis oneraret*, 22/2
duo bella funestissima, continuing the Orosius batch immediately
preceding (§ 30 fn. 1, p. xlvii).

440. Cf. Eucherius 147/1–2 *framea hastae longissimae sunt quibus etiam
nunc Armorici utentes hoc nomen tribuit*: perhaps a lost Abstrusa
Eucherius gloss (cf. *GL* iii. xx). For *aetgaeru* 'halberd' (§ 77) cf. Cp.
839 *falarica ætgæro* (MS. *ægtẹro*) and *ætgār* (TS 22), ON. *atgeirr*.

441. ? *Geo.* ii. 495 *non populi fasces, non purpura regum* (Lindsay, *Gloss.* 115): cf. Servius, *'populi fasces' honores qui a populo praestabantur; proprie autem locutus est, ut fasces populi, regum purpuram diceret* and Abstr. FA 78 *fasces honores,* Hl. *honores ... uel godweb.* The original form of this gloss may have been *fasces honores uel purpura goduueb.*

442–3. (9 ef 7, 11) Orosius v. 9/2 *super Calpurnium fornicem,* vi. 17/4 *feriatisque inimicis:* cf. the adjacent items, 9 ef 5–6 *fauonio zephyro, flagratione petitione* (Orosius i. 2/57 *a fauonio,* etc., i. 14/4 *flagitatione*) and 8–10 *fudit prostrauit, flamminibus sacerdotibus, fanogorio deuano* (Orosius iv. 16/12, etc., v. 18/27 *flaminibus,* vi. 5/2 *Phanagorio*), resuming the Orosius batch interrupted by 440–1 (§ 30 fn. 1, p. xlvii).

445. ? Isidore, *Ety.* xix. 6/6 *flamma uero proprie fornacis est dicta quod flatu* (= OE. *blǣd*) *follium excitetur:* Cl.I, II *flamina* may reflect Erf.II 295/21 *flamina uenti* (= Affatim 517/11), and Cl.I *biscophadas* shows further conflation with an interpretation like Hl. *episcopali gradu uel sacerdotali bisceophadas uel sacerd(hadas)* (Aldhelm, *VP* 255/19 *pontificum flaminia*).

447. *famfaluca* = Gr. πομφόλυξ 'water-bubble': cf. Herm. 244/56 ἡ πομφόλυξ *bulla aquae* and Aldhelm, *Aenig.* 62 'Famfaluca', glossed *bulla aquatica* in several manuscripts. For *uuapul* 'bubble' (here only) cf. *wapolian* 'foam, bubble up'.

448. *loca:* 'lock of wool' (here only); cf. *locc* (? < IE. **lugn-,* whence Lithuanian *lùgnas* 'pliant', ON. *lykna* 'bend the knees' (*IEW* 685)).

449. ? Isidore, *Ety.* xx. 14/5 *falcastrum a similitudine falcis uocatum; est autem ferramentum curuum cum manubrio longo ad densitatem ueprium succidendam:* cf. Hl. *ferramentum curuum a similitudine falcis uocatum* and 430 n. Gregory, *Dial.* ii. 6 *ferramentum ... quod ad falcis similitudinem falcastrum uocatur,* if not Isidore's own source, must draw on a common one, possibly 'Placidus' (cf. 554 n.).

450. *ferula* 'fennel' is confused with *aescthrotae* 'vervain' (*Leechdoms,* i. 8/1 *herba uermenaca ðæt is æscþrotu*).

452. *uuestsuduuind* 'south-west wind' (118 n.) here glosses *fauonius* 'west wind'. The same discrepancy occurs in Herm. 172/9 ff.

> nothus africus
> lips fauonius
> zephyrus septentrio, *etc.*

where *auster,* the interpretation of *nothus* (νότος 'south wind') in Herm. 11/21, etc., presumably dropped out and was replaced by *africus,* the interpretation of *lips* (λίψ 'south-west wind'), replaced in turn by *fauonius,* the interpretation of *zephyrus* (ζέφυρος 'west wind'), and so on: cf. the Junius wind-name list, 144/2 ff., where *uulturnus* 'south-south-east wind' is glossed *eastan suðan wind,* which belongs with the next lemma *eurus,* etc., see Wright's note. A similar confusion may underlie Cp. 460 *chorus* (*corus* 'north-west wind') *eostnorðwind.*

453-4. (10 ab 19, 21) These two items, which interrupt the *ab*-order section (§ 26), may derive from a common source, possibly Philox. FO 8 *follex* θύλακος καμίνου ἀσκός, 35 *fornax* κάμινος οψις (i.e. ἁψίς 'arch, vault'). For *blestbaelg* 'bellows' cf. Cp. 28 *sub(f)latorium bloestbaelg* and ON. *blástrbelgr*.

455. Cf. Affatim 518/12 *fellitat sugit*, Erf.II 294/23 *fellitat fingit figit*: *suggit* is probably Latin, as Holthausen pointed out (*Literaturblatt*, xi. 446), but the Erfurt scribe or his exemplar apparently took it as a form of OE. *sūgan*. It is treated as Latin, however, in Hl. F271 *fellitat i. decipit suggit beswicþ* (BT 932).

457. Cf. Festus 219 *gurgustium genus habitationis angustum a gurgulione dictum* (? a marginal addition to 456): *cesol* 'hut' < L. *casula*, *-ella* (Pogatscher, § 193; E. Lidén, *IF* xix (1907), 327 fn. 2) = 'gullet' in 1054; it apparently had the same range of meaning as *gurgustium*. *chelur* 'creel' in Ld. 39/38 (Job 40: 26 *gurgustium piscium*) = OHG. *kelur* 'throat', a different word, related to *celae* 862 (Holthausen, *AB* xxxiv (1923), 275); but the two may have been confused.

458. ? Isidore, *Ety.* xii. 1/50 *giluus autem melinus color est subalbidus*: cf. Cl.I 415/28 *giluus gioluhwit* (in an Isidore batch).

459. ? Vulg. Lev. 21: 20 *si gibbus* (AV 'crookbackt'): cf. SS iv. 257/43 *gippus hover*, Cl.I 413/30 *gibbus hoferede* (in the Old Testament batch) and Ælfric, *Gloss.* 321/16 f. *gibberosus uel strumosus hoferede, gibbus uel struma hofer*.

460. *spa(e)raen*: 'spar, gypsum' (*OET* 472, *OED* spar sb.[2]); BT *spæren* takes it as an adjective 'of plaster, of mortar', but cf. *(a)suollaen* 'swelling' (1018 n.), with Gmc. substantival *-ainiz* (Kluge, §§ 148-9), and Ælfric *spærstan*.

461. ? Vulg. Job 30: 6 *in desertis habitant torrentium et cauernis uel super glaream*: cf. Trier 82[a] *glarea minuti fluminum lapilli* and the Trier Bible gloss 16[b] *glarea lapilli fluminum quos aqua defluens trahit. cisil* is a suffix-variant of *ceosol* 'gravel', like OHG. *kisil*.

462. ? Aldhelm, *VP* 249/9 *granigera spicarum glumula*: cf. Cl.I 412/3 *glumula gewrid egenu uel scealu* and the preceding item, 10 cd 23 *gabulum patibulum* (? *VP* 276/20 *gabuli patibulo*). *glumula*, dim. of *gluma* 'husk' (Festus 218 *gluma hordei tunicula*), is first recorded in Aldhelm and was probably coined by him.

464. *gramen* 'couch-grass' (Herm. 27/28 ἄγρωστις *gramen*, etc.) = OE. *cwice* 'quitch' (BT 179), but cf. 1088 n.

466. *galluc* = 'comfrey' (Br. 299/20 *sinfitum gallac*), presumably identified with *galla* 'oak-apple' because of graphic similarity: cf. 253, 422.

467. *ferhergænd*: 'ravager'; cf. *forhergian* 'ravage, destroy', *forhergung* 'devastation'.

468. ? Aldhelm, *VC* 124 *metens ex aequore garbas*: cf. Cl.III 517/11 *garbas manipulas sceafas*. *garba* 'sheaf', the etymon of OFr. *jarbe*, Fr. *gerbe* (Barbier, *Revue*, ii. 189), is first recorded in Aldhelm.

469. *grallus* = *grac(c)ulus* 'daw': cf. Isidore, *Ety*. xii. 7/45 *graculus a garrulitate nuncupatus* and St. Gall MS. 913 (SS iv. 460/8) *garrula hroc*, added to the bird-names of Leviticus 11 (§ 32 fn. 4).

469a. *muscellas*: 'mussels'; cf. Erf.II 1117 *genesco musscel* and n.p.f. *muscule*, OE. Bede i. 26/8 (?= Erf. *muscellae*), beside wk. *mu(c)xle* (Cl.I, II), the normal OE. form (BT 702). *genisculas* (also Ld. 47/75 *ginisculas*) and Erf. II *genesco* (*-a*?) are otherwise unrecorded; *TLL* compares Herm. 187/28 *chaldices* (*-cides*) *corricule*.

470. *eglae* = 'ear of grain, stalk' (Schlutter, *Angl*. xix. 474): cf. Cl.I 347/29 *aristis eglum uel earum*, Cl.III 479/25 *fistucam . . . strewu eglan*. *glis* is therefore *glis*, *glitis* 'thistle', as in Aldhelm, *VC* 2725 *praua seges glitibus* (v.l. *gliribus*) *densescet acerbis*, whence Cl.III 532/33 *gliribus eglum*, not *glis*, *gliris* 'dormouse' (*OET* 524).

471. *galmaria* and *galbalacrum* 476 n., *galmum* 477, *galmilla* 486 n. appear to be corruptions of *galbanus* 'lac ferulae'. *caluuer* 'paste made of curds' (also 476) may be due to Herm. 579/6 *tetanus* (τίτανος 'lime') *galbanus*, etc.: cf. *liim* 486.

472. *cleouuae*: 'clew'; otherwise only Cp. *cleouue* beside *cleowen*, but cf. OHG. *kliuwa*.

475. *glus*: ? for *glutus* 'throat, gullet'; cf. Isidore, *Ety*. x. 114 *glutto* (v.l. *gluttus*) *a gula id est gulosus*. *frecnis* = 'greediness, gluttony' (TS 263): cf. *frec*, *fræc* 'greedy' (? *fræc* Förster, *ESt*. xxxix (1908), 331 ff.).

476. *galbalacrum*: ? for *galba lac*; Cyrillus 261/13 γαλβάνη ἢ χαλβάνη *galba* also confuses *galbanus* 'lac ferulae' (471 n.) and *galba* 'maggot'.

477. *galmum*: ? for *galbanus* or *galba* (476 n.); cf. Trier 80vb *galmum lac* and *galmilla* 486 n. *molegn* 'paste made of curds'(?) is otherwise recorded only in 486 and Cp. 953 *molegnstycci*.

479. Orosius v. 22/15 *tantam uel in bello saltim extinctam modo fuisse gregariorum militum manum quanta tunc caesa est in pace nobilium*: *aedilra* beside Cp. *unaeðilsa*, Cl. *unæþelra* may be due to *nobilium* (Lindsay, *Gloss*. 26), but cf. 10 cd 20 *gregarius dux militum* (? Abol. GR 21 *gregarius homo dux*).

482. ? Abstr. GE 13 *genae uultus maxillae*: cf. the following item, 10 ef 21 *grassator latro* (Abol. GR 7 *latro depraedator*).

483. ? Abol. GI 2 *giluus color in equo medius inter rufum et album*: cf. the preceding items, 10 ef 24–5 *gymnos nudos, gymnasia exercitatio palestrae* (Abstr. GI 5 *gymnasium locus ubi athletae nudi exercitantur; gymnos enim nudus dicitur, gymnasia exercitatio*).

486. Cf. Trier 80vb *galmilla a galmo diminutiuum* and *galmum* 477 n.: the Erfurt order is confirmed by Corpus and Cleopatra.

487. Cf. Erf.II 297/54 *genuinum initium uel dens qui interius in ore hominis* (= Affatim 522/36 *intimum*): Cp. *genuino tusc naturale* conflates the present item with 480 and Abstr. GE 6 *genuinum naturale de genere tractum.*

489. *scaeptloan*: 'straps for launching a spear'; cf. d.p. *sceptloum* 106 and *lōhsceaft* 'stick with a strap to it' (TS 620).

490. Orosius iv. 4/5 *ita cum horrendo fragore terra tremuit, ut stupore miraculi utrumque pauefactum agmen hebesceret*: indic. *asuand* for the Latin subj. in a result clause is good Old English syntax (cf. § 87).

492. Orosius v. 7/4 *ipsa qualitate habitudinis suae apparatus aliorum praecellerat*: *habitudinis* = 'character', not 'manners' here. *habitudines* (also Cp.) may be due to pl. *geberu.*

493. ? *Geo.* i. 138 *Hyadas claramque Lycaonis Arcton*: cf. the following item, 11 cd 2 *hyalinum uitreum uiridi colore*, and Servius, *Geo.* iv. 335 *'hyali (colore)' pro hyalino uitreo uiridi.* Holthausen, *AB* xxiv (1923), 279, takes *raedgaesran* as a mistake for *rǣdgǣsnan 'desperate', comparing Horace, *Odes* i. 3/14 *tristes Hyadas*; Brown, H13, suggests a corruption of OIr. *rétglainn* 'stars' (cf. 342 n.).

495. Cf. Abol. HI 1 *hiulcum patens apertura*, 29 *hialca soluta uel aperta* (*Geo.* ii. 353 *hiulca . . . arua*): the present gloss is applied to Aldhelm, *VP* 265/15–16 *hiulco . . . rostro* in Cl.I 416/22 *hiulca cinende. cinaendi* is presumably the *casus indefinitus* as in 221, 939.

496. *biscopuuyrt* = 'betony' in *Leechdoms*, i. 2/1 *betonica ðæt is biscopwyrt* and Ælfric, *Gloss.* 310/15 *betonica seo læsse biscopwyrt*, but the name was derived from L. *hibiscum* 'wild mallow' (Pogatcher, § 381; Förster, *Angl.* xli. 130), so this again is not 'a mere guess suggested by similarity in sound' (Lindsay, *Gloss.* 41): cf. 183 n.

497. Cf. Vulg. Job 39: 13 *penna struthionis similis est pennis herodii et accipitris* and Ld. 19/35–6 *herodion ualchefuc, accipitres haefuc*: confusion of *herodius* 'heron' and *wealhhafoc* 'peregrine falcon' (Förster, *Angl.* xli. 121), e.g. in the St. Gall 913 Leviticus gloss (SS. iv. 460/21) *erodionem ualuchaebuc*, stems from this passage.

499. ? Aldhelm, *VP* 246/15–16 *ista stolidis ornamentorum pompis indruticans*: cf. Cl.III 491/32 *indruticans wrǣstende*, Cl.I 419/6 *wrǣstende uel wlancende. indruticans* is found only here, and its sense in the context is 'flaunting' (of a bride bedecked, compared with the Scarlet Woman of Apoc. 17). Lindsay, *Corpus* 203, suggests a corruption of *infruticans* 'sprouting', glossing Rufinus iv. 30/1 *haeresibus . . . pullulantibus*, and Bradley, *CQ* xiii. 105–6, compares It. *drudo* 'gallant'. The latter, however, appears to be borrowed from OHG. *drut* 'friend', and it may be that Aldhelm simply latinized OE. *drūtian* 'swell' in the sense of 'behave insolently'. *uuraestendi* 'is derived from *wrǣst* 'fine, delicate' by Bradley and BT 1270, but the pres. part. of *wrǣstan* 'twist' (*OET* 596) is possible in the sense of 'strutting, posturing'.

501. ? Vulg. Deut. 28: 57 *illuuie* (v.l. *illuuies*) *secundarum*, lit. 'filth of afterbirths': cf. Trier 90va *illuuies folliculus in quo paruulus fit*, Isidore, *Ety.* xi. 1/144 *secundae dicuntur folliculus qui simul cum infante nascitur continetque eum*, and 502 n.

502. Cf. Ld. 35/74 *petigo tetr afa* (? ἀλφός, ? *alba*) and 765: ? a Bible intruder in the Ld. Rufinus list, from Vulg. Lev. 21: 20 *si impetiginem* (*habens*) *in corpore*, like 381 and 501 immediately preceding.

505. *neuunseada, -sida* (*neowan-*?) = *neweseoða* 'paunch' (BT 717, TS 650). Holthausen, *IF* xlviii (1930), 266, connects the first element with *niwol, neowol* 'prostrate' (cf. § 45 and fn. 4) and the second with OIr. *sōim* 'twist', but *sēod* 'pouch' (BT) or *sēoðan* 'boil' would be more likely cognates to 'paunch'. Schlutter, *Angl.* xix. 103–4, identifies Erf. *-sida* with the second element of *heortgesidu* 'entrails' (BT 531, TS 536); if so, Ép. *ea* would = *eo* < Prim. OE. *i* by back mutation, but the failure of back mutation of *i* elsewhere in Épinal (§ 56) makes this unlikely.

506. ? Vulg. Jn. 11: 44 *ligatus . . . instita*: cf. Ld. 25/12 *institis suethilon* and the preceding item, 12 ab 3 *iuniperum similis taxo* (? III Reg. 19: 4 *subter unam iuniperum*).

508. ? Orosius ii. 7/6 *regina . . . non muliebriter increpitans*: cf. 12 ef 6 *increpitans insonans*, following 552 at the end of the Orosius batch.

509. ? Nonius 446/34–5 *inlix et inlex hoc discernuntur: ab inliciendo inlix, inlex a quo lex non seruetur*: Nonius glosses were included in the 'Abstrusa–Abolita' material used by the compilers of Erfurt II and Affatim (Lindsay, *CQ* xi. 188–9); cf. 261, 568, 712.

510–14. (12 ab 12–16) Orosius iv. 17/4 *infestus accessit*, etc., i. 20/5 *fulmine interceptus*, iv. 9/8 *infando naufragio*, etc., ii. 10/11 *escarum inlecebris*, v. 10/9 *ab improbis et ingratis* (§ 30 fn. 1, p. xlvii): cf. the two preceding items, 12 ab 10–11 *index testis, interdiu tempus inter diem et noctem* (Orosius v. 12/2 *indices*, etc., iv. 15/1 *interdiu duas lunas ortas*), and 516 two lines below. The basic meaning of *flach* is 'false, deceitful': cf. ON. *flá-, flátt* and TS 223. *araepsid* = 'interrupted' (cf. *raebsid* 523, *raefsed* 526); Cp. 1067 *arasad* 'snatched away' is an alternative interpretation, like 1083 *fornoom* (526 n.)

516a. *iota* = *iuta* 'broth, gruel' (Meritt, *FL* 4 D 48): cf. Cl.II 281/10 *iuta awilled milc* and ME. *ioutes* 'soup or pottage made chiefly of vegetables' (*OED*). For *soctha* 'juice, broth'(?) cf. *gesoc* 'sucking' (BT 443) and *sūcan* (Meritt).

517. *TLL* takes *iuncetum* in this gloss as a popular form, presumably diminutive, of *iuncus* 'rush', but *riscthyfil* 'clump of rushes' (BT 806) is sufficiently well attested: cf. Cl.I 422/39–40 *iuncus risc, iungetum riscþyfel* and Schlutter, *ESt.* xliii. 319 (58 n.).

518. *uualhuyrt*: 'elecampane', lit. 'the foreign root' since it was introduced into Britain from Southern Europe (Förster, *Angl.* xli. 133). Apparently confused with **weallwyrt* 'ebulum' in 393 (see note).

521–6. (12 ab 33–7, cd 1) Orosius v. 15/17 (*elephanti corio*) *cuius ea natura est, ut acceptum imbrem tamquam spongia ebibat ac perhoc intractabile . . . fiat*, v. 17/2 *euoluere . . . seditionum causas incommodum simul ac longum uidetur*, i. 20/5 *fulmine interceptus* (cf. 511), ii. 15/10 *pro quadam insimulatione*, i. 5/7 *fluuius . . . augmentis ubertatis impendebatur*, i. 21/17 *interpellari . . . uoluptates* (§ 30 fn. I, p. xlvii): the main Orosius batch follows immediately after the next item, 12 ab 38 *inuitiandi negandi* (= Ld. 28/5 *infitiandi*, on Vit. Ant. 28 *inficiandi . . . delicto*), which may have been attracted to the Orosius glosses by *interpellari*; cf. Ld. 28/17 *in(ter)polastis . . . inpinguastis* and Hessels's note. *raebsid, raefsed* = 'interrupted', not 'seized, reproved' (BT 784): cf. *ræps* 'response' (L. *responsorium*) and Cp. 1082–3 *intercepit ræfsde, intercepit fornoom* (? Philox. IN 607 *intercepit* ὑφαίρεται ἀπαγορεύει).

529. *a fordh*: 'always, continuously' (TS *ā* II); cf. *Christ* 299 f. (*þæt þu sceolde) þe, Maria, forð | efne unwemme a gehealden.*

531. ? Abol. IN 239 (*iners*) *inertia affectus uel læsus* (? *lassus* Goetz, *CGL* vi. 568): for *asolcaen* 'slack', pret. part. of *āsealcan* 'languish' OE. *Genesis* 2168 (= WS. **āseolcan*), cf. Jun. 190/14 *accidiosus uel tediosus asolcen*, etc.

535. *anslegaen[g]rae*: 'struck in'; cf. *onslege* 'blow' (BT 758) and *onaslean* (TS *āslēan* II). ? A nonce-compound like *uuidirhliniendae* 537.

536. Orosius iii. 2/9 *contexui indigestae historiae inextricabilem cratem*: *unofaercumenrae* (here only) = 'untamed, unruly'.

538. *oberuuaenidae*: pret. of **oferwennan* 'grow haughty, insolent'; cf. *wenian* 'accustom' (once in an intransitive sense, TS 743) and *feruuaenid* 548.

539. Orosius vii. 6/15 *Iudeos impulsore Christo adsidue tumultuantes*: d.s.f. *baedendrae* (also Cp., Cl.) may be due to the -*re* of *inpulsore*, but cf. lWS. *wealdendras, -rum* (Campbell, § 633).

540. Lindsay, *Corpus* I211, proposes Orosius, *capitula 2/2 (Roma) assiduis fracta fuerit et infecta criminibus*, but Cp. *ungeuuemmid* suggests Servius, *Aen.* xii. 1 f. '*Turnus ut infractos (aduerso Marte Latinos | defecisse uidet)' postquam Turnus uidet bello defecisse Latinos, semper antea infractos namque ita maior est sensus quam si 'infractos' ualde fractos acceperis* (*infractus* 'shattered' normally = 'unbroken' in later Latin).

541. Orosius iii. 5/3 *satisfecit inprobis faucibus praecipitio suo* M. Curtius *. . . iniecitque crudeli terrae inopimam satietatem*: *unaseddae* = 'unsatisfied'; cf. ON. *úseðjanligr* 'insatiable'. The glossator may have misunderstood the rare *inopimam* 'very rich', with intensive *in-* like *infractus* 540, as a negative, 'poor, needy' (cf. *inops, inopiosus*).

542. Orosius v. 18/8 *ciues Romanos indicta caede iugularunt*: did the glossator's text read *indictos*?

543. Orosius i. 5/4 *halitu lacus infici terram et corrumpi reor*: *gimaengdae* 'contaminated' might be taken as a.s.f. of the past part. with *eorðan* understood, or as pret. subj. after *þæt* in an active construction.

544. *torhtendi*: pres. part. of **torhtian* 'make clear, indicate'; cf. adj. *torht* 'bright, clear' and adv. *torhte* 'clearly'.

548. *feruuaenid*: 'ill-bred, insolent'; cf. *oberuuaenidae* 538 and *forwenednes* 'insolence' (TS 257).

554. ? Abstr. IU 2 *iubar solis radius uel stella quae ante solem apparet*: cf. Trier 89vb *iubar uel lucifer uel splendor solis lunae et stellarum* (Placidus I I38 *iubar splendor solis*, etc.), Isidore, *Ety.* iii. 71/18 *hic (lucifer) proprie et iubar dicitur eo quod iubas lucis effundat, sed et splendor solis ac lunae et stellarum iubar uocatur*. *earendil* is properly 'day-star', not 'shining light, ray' (BT 232): cf. *Christ* 104 *Eala earendel, engla beorhtast* (paraphrasing the Advent antiphon *O Oriens, splendor lucis aeternae*), *Blickl. Hom.* 163/29–31 *ond nu (wæs) seo Cristes gebyrd æt his æriste, se niwa eorendel Sanctus Ioannes*, and the ON. PN *Aurvandill* (*Skáldskaparmál* 26). Erf. *oerendil* (? *eo-* as in *Blickl. Hom.*, etc.) may represent a Gmc. ablaut variant **euz(a)wandilaz* beside **auz(a)wandilaz* (K. Kärre, *Nomina agentis in Old English* (Uppsala, 1915), 55–6).

555. *isic* = lL. *isicius*, for *esox* 'salmon': cf. abl. sg. *issicio*, BH i. 1; acc. pl. *isicios*, Ælfric, *Coll.* 106. Isidore, *Ety.* xx. 2/30 *isocem piscem quendam dictum, ex quo primum isicia facta sunt* shows confusion with *isicium* 'a kind of sausage' (Herm. 314/47 ἰσσικίον *isitium*), which may also underlie the form *isicius*.

556. *ign(i)arium* = Gr. πυρεῖον 'a stick rubbed against another until they caught fire': cf. Pliny xvi. 207 *calidae* ('inflammable') *et morus, laurus, hedera, et omnes e quibus igniaria fiunt . . . teritur ergo lignum ligno ignemque concipit adtritu*. For *algiuueorc* 'fire-making'(?) cf. *weall(ge)weorc* 'wall-building': such an interpretation might be derived from the passage in Pliny.

557. ? Herm. 323/46 ἐνιλεμα (-είλημα) *inuolucrum* + Vulg. Ez. 27: 24 *inuolucris hyacinthi*: cf. SS i. 640/15–16 *inuoluclis dicitur quando inuoluitur vestimentum idest vulluch* and 558 immediately following. *uulluc* therefore = 'wrapper, shawl' (Holthausen, *AB* xxxii (1921), 22), not 'whelk' (BT 1191).

558. ? Herm. 451/34 *incubo* ἐφιάλτης + Jerome, *In Isaiam*, 13: 21 (*PL* xxiv. 159b) '*pilosi saltabunt ibi' uel incubones uel satyros uel siluestres quosdam homines quos nonnulli fatuos ficarios uocant aut daemonum genera intellegunt*: cf. St. Gall MS. 299 (SS i. 589/25) *pilosi incubi monstri idest maerae* (= Ld. 13/24 *menae*). Ép. *mera* beside Erf. *merae*, Cp., Ld. *maer(a)e*, and later OE. *mare* (BT 660) is most probably a scribal error, since ON., OHG. *mara* is also wk. fem.: cf. ModE. *nightmare* 'a *female* monster supposed to settle upon people and animals in their sleep, producing a feeling of suffocation' (*OED* 1).

559. *inuoluco*: 'convolvulus'; cf. *uoluola* 1059 n. For *uuidubindlae*, †-*blindæ* (also Ld.) beside Cp. *uudubinde* 'woodbine' cf. *bindele* 'binding, bandage' (BT 102, TS 92).

560. ? Vulg. Job 39: 1 *ibicum in petris* or I Reg. 24: 3 *solis ibicibus*: cf. Ld. 19/29 *hibicum firgingata*, Cl.I 423/11 *ibices fyr(g)engatum. firgingaett* is the mutated pl. of *firgengat* 'ibex' (Campbell, § 627).

561. For Ép., Cp. *infridat* cf. Cl.I 427/5 *infridat cælþ* (a marginal addition to the *nīg* (§ 12 fn. 3) section) and IL. *infrigdo* beside *infrigido* (Souter, 205); Erf. *infrigidat* is presumably a scribal correction.

562. Cf. Trier 89ᵛᵇ *isca genus fomenti unde inuri solemus*, referring to the use of cinders for cauterizing wounds (177 n.). G. Gundermann, *ZfdW* viii (1907), 116 f., distinguishes *esca, is(i)ca* 'tinder' (= late Gr. ἴσκα) from *esca* 'food', taking it as a Gmc. loan-word related to ON. *eisa* 'embers' like *aam* 177. This gloss belongs to the Hermeneumata batch in Erfurt.

tyndirm, tyndrin (also Cp.) are derivatives of *tynder* with Gmc. -*ma* (Kluge, §§ 152–3) and -*unnjō, -innjō* (Kluge, § 150): cf. *cliderme, clidrinnae* 928 beside *cladær*- 116, *claedur* 218.

564. Cf. Abavus LE 22 *lepor sermo subtilis uel leuis*: perhaps a lost Abstrusa–Abolita gloss, in view of 565 immediately following.

565. ? Abstr. RA 12 *rastri ligones* (cf. 878) or Vulg., e.g. Joel 3: 10 *concidite . . . ligones uestras in lanceas* (= Ld. 17/2 *ligones ferrum fusorium(foss-) idest tyrfhaga*): Cl.I 433/33 *lagones mattucas* is a marginal addition to 433/32 *ligonem mattuc* (I Reg. 13: 20).

566. ? Orosius vi. 19/8 *triremes uelocitate liburnicis pares*: BT 392 takes *gerec* as 'pinnace', presumably related to *reccan* 'drive' (cf. Abstr. LI 8 *liburna (b)arca uel nauis*). Meritt, *FL* 2 A 31, reads *grec(e)* 'Greek' as in Werden I (Gallée, 338) *dor(i)cus girec sāx* (Abstr. DO 9 *dorica graeca*, etc.), suggesting a similar gloss on Orosius i. 2/59 *insulas Liburnicas*; but the analogy is inexact, since *dorica = graeca* by synecdoche in *Aen.* ii. 27 *Dorica castra*, etc.

567. ? Rufinus ix. 9/3 *signum . . . in militaria uexilla transformat, ac labarum quem dicunt in speciem crucis dominicae exaptat*: cf. Ld. 35/69 *uixilla et labrum idem sunt idest segin*, Cp. 2093 *uexilla seign*, and Trier 91ᵛᵃ *labarum uexillum*. Apparently a straggler from the Rufinus batch which ended four lines above.

568–9. (13 ab 35–6) ? Aldhelm, *Aenig.* 69/7 *lurcones rabidi quem carpunt rictibus oris*, etc., 100/9 *me larbula terret*: Affatim 535/45 *lurcones auidi deuoratores* (? Nonius 10/27–8 *lurcones dicti sunt a lurcando; lurcare enim est cum auiditate cibum sumere*) would provide a common source for *lurcones*, but *larbula* is first recorded in Aldhelm.

sigiras: 'gluttons'; cf. the participial noun *sigirgend in Cl.III 489/14 *lurconibus sigirgendum*, presumably from a Class I wk. *sigirjan, and *sīgan* 'sink'.

egisigrima: 'spectre'; cf. the *Old English Martyrology* (ed. G. Herzfeld, London, 1900), 54/1 *larbo þæt is egesgrima* and *grima* 646 n.

570. ? Vulg. Is. 3: 19 *lunulas et torques*: cf. St. Gall MS. 299 (SS i. 589/10–13) *lunulas quas mulieres habent de auro uel argento similitudine lunæ diminutiuae sic dicuntur idest hlibas uel scillingas* (= Ld. 13/6 Latin only). *menescillingas* 'necklace-pieces' may be a nonce-word coined to translate *lunulas*, described as *bullulae aureae dependentes* in Isidore, *Ety.* xix. 31/17.

571. ? *Aen.* vii. 187 *Quirinali lituo*: cf. Servius, *lituus est incuruum augurum baculum quo utebantur ad designanda caeli spatia* and Lib. Gloss. LI 573 *lituum baculum incuruum quo augures utuntur*.

573a. Schlutter, *JGP* v. 139, takes *laxhe olor* as *la(n)x heolor*, but cf. Gr. λάγκη in Herm. 93/56 *mazonomos lanche*, etc. In any case, the interpretation is presumably *helor* 'scale of a balance' (607 n.).

576. ? Sedulius, *Carm. Pasch.* i. 52 *liuida mortiferis uellatis toxica sucis* (cf. 578): the present gloss is misapplied to Aldhelm, *VP* 318/17 f. *liuida . . . uibex*, where *liuida* is the nom. sg. fem., in Cl.III 514/25 *libida þa wannan* (= Cl.I 431/22).

577. Orosius i. 18/1 *ludi litterarii disciplina*: *staebplegan* is clearly a nonce-word coined to gloss *ludi litterari(i)* 'primary school'. For the latter cf. Ld. 35/53 *ludus literarum scola paruulorum legentium* (= Ép. 13 ab 11 *scola legentium*).

579. *scocha*: 'enticement'(?); cf. Go. *skohsl* 'demon' and *scȳan* 'tempt' (*AEW* 285).

580. Cf. Erf.II 306/38 *lacessit prouocauit* (? Abstr. LA 5 *lacessit prouocat uel inuriis agit*), possibly applied to Orosius vii. 17/2 *bellis lacessitus* (cf. 593).

581. ? Orosius vii. 28/3 *lenta illa paganorum poena sed certa*: if so, *toch* is presumably an additional interpretation, which may have been borrowed from 614.

582. ? VL (Robert) Jos. 7: 21, 24 *ligulam auream* beside Vulg. *regulam*, whence Karlsruhe MS. Aug. 135 (SS i. 375/15) *regulam auream idest hringan gyrdisles*. Trier 95ᵛᵃ *lingula cingulum uel fibula* (cf. 410) appears to be an analysis of *gyrdislhringae* 'buckle or clasp of a girdle' (here only, but cf. *hringae* 410).

583. ? *Aen.* iv. 137 *picto chlamydem circumdata limbo*: cf. Cp. 1264 *lymbo ðresi*. Holthausen, *AB* xxxv. 247, takes *thres* as sb. 'fringe' (cf. 705), related to *þrāwan* 'twist'.

584. Cf. Ld. 29/47 *lagonam uas lapideum ollo (-a) idest crog* (Jerome, *In Mattheum*, 26: 18 (*PL* xxvi. 193b) *portantem lagenam aquae*): Jerome paraphrases Mk. 14: 13 *lagenam aquae baiulans*, whence Cl.III 484/28 *lagenam wætercrog*.

585. *lutrus* (*-ra*): 'otter' (Polemius 543/8 *ludra*); cf. Jun. 118/42 *lutria otor*.

586. This item begins Lindsay's Hermeneumata batch (*Gloss.* 19), but cf. 565 n.

587. *lucius*: 'pike'; cf. Polemius 'item natancium' 544/17 *lucius*, Herm. 318/31 τυρνες (?) *luciolus*.

588. *mearh*: 'sausage'; cf. *mearh(ge)hæcc(a)*, *mear(h)hæccel* 'pudding, sausage' (BT 674). Lidén, *ESt.* xxxviii (1907), 342, distinguishes *mearh* 'sausage' from *mearg* 'marrow' with etymological *g* (cf. OHG. *marag*, ON. *mergr*), but Jun. 159/32 *medulla uel lucanica mearh* combines both meanings.

589. ? Herm. 330/35 λορδός *pandus cloppus*, etc.: *laempihalt* 'limping' (*OED limphalt*) = lL. *cloppus*; the second element is presumably *healt* 'lame, limping', which Leiden confused with *-heald* 'inclined' as in *tohald* 96, *scytihalt(h)* 694, though λορδός and *pandus* mean 'bent'.

590. *lendina*: dim. of *lens*, *lendis* 'nit' (Herm. 190/13 *lendes*, etc.), formed with lL. *-īna* < Gmc. *-īnaz* (K. Vossler, *Einführung ins Vulgärlatein* (Munich, 1954), § 288).

592. *baers*: 'perch' (here only); cf. ModE. dial. *barse*.

596. *ludari(u)s*: ? 'bullock'; cf. *Vita Sancti Maedoc* (C. Plummer, *Vitae Sanctorum Hiberniae* (Oxford, 1910), ii. 141–63) 26 *occurrit ei ibi quidam leprosus petens ab eo elymosinam, cui rex ludarium caluum* (? 'polled') *et fuluum dedit in elymosinam*. Presumably a Hisperic word like *prætersori(u)m* 779, *prifeta* 780: Schlutter, *AJP* xxi. 192, compares Welsh *lhudon* 'young animal', Cornish *lodzon* 'bullock'.

597. *lacunar*: for *lacuna* 'cistern' (cf. Ld. iii. 53 *lacuna floda*), confused with *lacunar* 'panelled ceiling' in Erf.II 306/6 *lacunar locus aquarum* (= Abavus LA 23 *locus aquarum quasi lacus*) and 609.

599. ? Herm., e.g. 568/21 *lolium idest auena agrestis*: for *atae* 'wild oats' cf. Li. Mt. 13: 38 *ata* 'zizania'.

601. *pupistil*: ? for *pūfe pistel* 'sow-thistle' (BT 1075), confused with *lactuca agrestis* 'wild lettuce' (Herm. 558/23, etc.) because of its white, milky juice.

602. ? Vulg. I Par. 11: 23 *ut liciatorium texentium*: cf. the Trier Bible gloss 24ª *liciatorium a liciis dictum et licia sunt quibus stamina ligantur* (= Isidore, *Ety.* xix. 29/7 *licia . . . ligantur quasi ligia*), which would explain the confusion between *hebild* 'weaver's thread' (Cp. 1232 *licium hebeld*) and *liciatorium* 'weaver's beam', Cp. *hebelgerd*, Cl. *hefeldgyrd* (Brown, L98).

603. Schlutter, *Angl.* xix. 109, took *lihargum* as *lethargus* 'lethargy' (cf. Abstr. LE 20 *letargus uitium quo comprimuntur aegri ad falsum somnum*) and *slægu* as 'stroke', or later (*Angl.* xxxiii (1910), 387) as

*slægu 'slowness', which would be closer in meaning to lethargus but etymologically very doubtful. OET 471, BT 881 take slaegu as an otherwise unrecorded cognate of Middle Dutch slagge, whence ModE. slag, glossing λιθάργυρος 'spuma argenti' (cf. 39 n.), which seems more likely: cf. Bd. 70ᶜ lithargirus idest spuma argenti.

604. licidus: ? for liquidus or lucidus; cf. Affatim 534/2 liquidum splendidum (uel) lucidum (= Abba LI 62) and Cl. licidus, liquidus. Since licidus is found in both Corpus and Cleopatra, Erf. lucidus must be a scribal correction, due perhaps to Affatim. hu(a)et is presumably hwæt 'sharp, keen' (§ 38), but may have been confused with wæt 'wet' in the archetype: cf. the forms with 'inorganic' h in 62, 177, 340, 669, 983 (§ 72 fn. 6). For the latter interpretation cf. the Echternach Glosses (Jenkinson, Hisperica Famina, 35–41) 36 liquidis humidis (? Aen. v. 525 liquidis in nubibus).

605. lectidiclatum = Cl.I, II lac tudicl(at)um, perhaps from Hermeneumata 'de escis' (cf. 315/15 πηκτή lactancia). For fleti 'curds' cf. ON. flautir, n.p.f. i-decl., beside the OE. wk. pl. flētan (BT 293).

606. lelodrae: ? for *lēa(h)loðre 'meadow-bur' (Lehmann, AB xvii (1906), 298), presumably a form with Angl. smoothing (§ 57. 1). Lehmann relates the second element to ON. loða vb. 'stick' and MHG. lodw(u)rz 'comfrey' (cf. gilodu(y)rt 379); if so, its association with λάπαθον 'sorrel' may be due to confusion of the latter with lappa 'bur'.

607. helor: 'scale of a balance' (also 573a, 988); Holthausen, IF xlviii (1930), 264, connects it with L. cālix.

609. lacuna: for lacunar 'panelled ceiling' (cf. 597). Possibly a split from 595 (cf. Phocas 415/9 hoc laquear, hoc lacunar, whence Ld. 46/12 lucunar camera), but lacuna = 'roof, sky' in HF 144 apricat lacunas rogus ('sun'): cf. heofenhrof 'sky'(?) in Cl.I 432/8 lacunar hushefen (= Cp. 1180 hebenhus 'attic') uel heofenhrof.

610. ? Vulg. Lev. 11: 16 noctuam et larum: cf. St. Gall MS. 913 (SS iv. 460/52) larum hragra, adrianus dixit meum esse, presumably referring to the Abbot Hadrian who accompanied Theodore of Tarsus (§ 32 fn. 4, p. lxix). 610–13 form Lindsay's Bible batch under L.

611–12. ? Aldhelm, Aenig. 100/37 lumbricus et limax et tarda testudo palustris (cf. 997); but Aldhelm's own source may have been a class-list like Herm. 'de serpentibus', e.g. 305/32 limax, 35 lubricus, or Polemius 'nomina insectorum siue reptantium' 544/2 lumbricus . . . limax. regenuuyrm = 'earth-worm, rain-worm'; the first element is *ragin- 'mighty' as in regnheard 'very hard', referring to the animal's size, not regn 'rain'.

613. ? Vulg. Osee 9: 6 lappa in tabernaculis eorum, etc.: cf. Ld. 15/36 lappa clitæ and the preceding item, 14 ab 11 labrusca uitis agrestis (= the Trier Bible gloss, 9ᵛᵃ, on Is. 5: 2 fecit labruscas). For Ép. clipae

'burdock' (*OED clithe*) cf. **clīðan* 'stick' (Bede Glosses (OET 181/64) ad(*ha*)*erentem ætcliðende*) and *cliðwyrt* 'clivers'.

614. *toch*: 'pliant, sticky' (BT *tōh* II); cf. Cl.I 343/15 *alulentis ðæm ton* (*VP* 306/9 *alii lentis*), 430/15 *lento þæm ton*, and *tohlicae* 1063.

615. ? Abstr. LI 22 *ligustra et uaccinia florum genera crocei coloris*: the confusion between *ligustrum* 'privet' and *hunaegsugae* 'honeysuckle' (also Cl.III 517/35 *ligustra hunigsuge*, on Aldhelm, *VC* 193 *ceu fronde ligustra fatiscunt*) may be due to such a vague interpretation.

616. Orosius v. 12/2 *stipites . . . a lupis reuulsos mordicus* (v.l. *mordicos*) *conrososque*: *bibitnae* 'gnawed' (here only) may be a guess at the ghost-word *mordicos* for adv. *mordicus*, but it fits *conrosos* exactly.

617. *threatmelum*: 'troop by troop'; here only, but cf. *floccmælum*, *heapmælum*.

618. *geradnodae*: ? 'arranged'; cf. *gerád* 'order' (TS III) and *gerádian* 'arrange, prepare' (BT 429, TS 390).

621. Cf. Abol. MU 5 *munificus honorificus magnificus*, possibly applied to Orosius iii. 19/5 *castra . . . plus solito magnifica* (Lindsay, *Gloss.* 28).

624. ? Jerome, *In Mattheum*, 6: 28–30 (*PL* xxvi. 46a) *uiolae uero purpuram nullo superari murice*: cf. Ld. 29/11 *mauria de auro facta in tonica idest gespan*, Trier 99ᵛᵃ *murica fibula purpurea auro texta*. For *gespan* 'clasp' Michiels, 18 f., compares DuCange *mauria* 'spinarum genus' and Tacitus, *Germania* 17 *tegumen omnibus sagum fibula aut . . . spina consertum*; but Trier *auro texta* suggests a misinterpretation of *Aen.* iv. 261–4:

atque illi stellatus iaspide fulua
ensis erat, Tyrioque ardebat *murice* laena
demissa ex umeris, diues quae munera Dido
fecerat, et tenui telas discreuerat *auro*.

625. ? Vulg. III Reg. 7: 33 *canthi et modioli*: cf. Karlsruhe MS. Aug. 135 (Meritt, *OEG* 43/2–3) *canti . . . felei* (*-ei*), *modioli nabæ* and 292. This and the preceding item, 14 ef 12 *myro unctio chrismatis* (Judith 10: 3 *unxit se myro*), = Lindsay's Bible 'batch' under M (§ 32 fn. 5).

626. ? Herm. 330/33 κυλλός *manchus* + 37 μονόχειρ *unimanius*: cf. Trier 97ᵃ *mancus vnanimus* (*-imanus*) and Jun. 162/3 *unimanus anhende*, Cl.I 441/16 *mancum anhende* (*VP* 273/20 *mancum et debilem*). *ānhende* glosses *debilis* 'crippled' in Rushworth Mt. 18: 8 (where the context implies 'one-handed') and 15:30.

627. *mafortae* (*-e*) = 'kerchief, veil': cf. Lib. Gloss. MA 153 *maforte matronale operimentum quod in capite inponitur* ('de glossis'); Isidore, *Ety.* xix. 25/4 (*ricinium*) *uulgo mauortem dicunt*. For *scybla* (? w.f. *-e* as in Cl.II) cf. Cl.III 514/7 *mafortibus scyfelum* (Aldhelm, *VP* 318/4–5 *candidis et coloratis mafortibus*) and ON. *skupla* 'a woman's hood hiding the face'.

628. Cf. Philox. MU 8 *mulget* ἀμέλ(γ)ει (*Ecl.* iii. 5 *ouis* . . . *bis mulget in hora*): *morgit* is one of the 'purely colloquial, half-Romance forms' noted by Sweet, *OET* 10; cf. 667, 886, 906 nn.

629. *mossiclum*: ? for *musculus, dim. of *muscus* 'moss' (*REW* 5771).

630. *mimoparo* = μυοπάρων 'a light vessel used by pirates': cf. Abba MI 9 *myoparon nauicula scapha piratarum* (Abstr. MI 18 *scapha aut nauicula* only). *the(o)bscip* (this gloss only) may be a nonce-word coined from *scapha piratarum*.

632. *momentum*: 'bar of a balance' (Abstr. MO 14 *momentum stilus in quo momentana exaequatur, quia cito admodum inclinatur si aequaliter non pensetur uocabulum sumpsit*); cf. the next two items, 14 ef 26–7 *murex regalis purpura* (Abstr. MU 26), *magnetis lapis qui ferrum rupit* (Abstr. MA 13 *magnes . . . rapit*). *scytil* therefore means the lever or beam of a balance (lit. 'the part that moves', like Lat. *momentum*), not the tongue or pointer (BT *scutel*); the latter derives from DuCange's misinterpretation of *momentum* as 'languette de balance'.

633. *manile* = *aquiminale* 'ewer, basin': cf. Erf.III 567/19 *aquiminalium ubi aqua pisilo dimitti et obstrui potest ad lauandus* (*-as*) *manus*, Nonius 547/6–7 *urceolum aquae manale uocamus, quod eo aqua in trulleum effundatur*. *lebil* 'cup, bowl' (also 995) < L. *labellum* (*AEW* 191) is the historically correct form, corresponding to OHG. *lebil*; later OE. *læfel* may represent a by-form **labul-* with *i*-mutation due to suffix-interchange (Pogatscher, § 261), or a later reborrowing without umlaut.

636. *malus*: 'apple-tree'; cf. Cyrillus 370/58 μηλέα *malus* and 638 n.

638. *melarium*: 'apple-tree' (Souter *-ius*); cf. Herm. 428/19 μηλέα κοκκυμηλιο *melario pronum* (for μηλέα *melaria*, κοκκυμηλέα *prunum*), Aldhelm, *Metr.* 152/22 *arbor fructifera . . . quae melarius uocatur*. For *milsc apuldr* 'pomegranate-tree' cf. *milsc treow* in Jun. 118/4–5 *quintinas grece caducas milscre* (*-ra*) *treowa blostman* (Isidore, *Ety.* xvii. 7/6 *flores malorum a Graecis appelati sunt* κύτινος; *Latini caducum uocant*); *milsc æppel* in Napier 1/3844 *nicolaos mylisce appla*, *ZfdA* ix. 496/65 *melscappla* (*VP* 290/5–6 *mala punica, quae et mala granata nuncupantur, cum palmeti dactilis, quos nicolaos uocant*) refers to *mala granata* 'pomegranates', not *nicolaos* 'dates' as BT 688 assumes (cf. 1088 n.).

640. ? Orosius vi. 9/8 *magnis . . . malorum molibus* (cf. 940): BT 766 infers a noun *ormet* (*-mætu*?) 'a very great mass, something immense' from this gloss, but *ormetum* may be simply adj. *ormæte* 'immense' used substantively or glossing *magnis*.

641. *mastigia*: 'whip' (Souter, 244); the nom. sg. fem. is also treated as neut. pl. in Affatim 537/30 *mastigia flagella* (Abstr. MA 43 *mastigiae tauriae flagella*), Ld. 41/17 *mastigia lora cum uncis ferreis* (Sulpicius Severus (ed. C. Halm, Vienna, 1866), 183/23–4 *Gallicas . . . mastigias*). The Épinal order is confirmed by Corpus.

643. ? Vulg. Ecclus. 40: 21 *tibia et psalterium suauem faciunt melodiam*:
cf. the preceding item, 15 ab 16 *manzyr filius meretricis* (Deut. 23: 2
mamzer, hoc est de scorto natus).

644. *mustacia*: ? for Gr. μύσταξ 'upper lip, moustache' (Herm. 175/
15 *mistax infra nares*, etc.). *granae* would then correspond to ON.
granar, Go. *granōs* 'moustache(s)', in which case Trier *grana qui uino
expresso remanent* would presumably be a scribe's conjecture (so
Schlutter, *Angl.* xxxv. 152), due perhaps to confusion with *mustaceum*
'must-cake'; the word was treated as OE. in Ld. 47/32 *gronae*.

645. *manticum*: ? for *mantica* 'wallet', confused with *manua* or *manipulus*
'sheaf' in an alphabetical list like Herm. 455/54–6 *manipulus, manipulum,
manua* δράγμα, 59 *mantica* πήρα. For *handful* 'sheaf' cf. the Lambeth
Psalter (ed. U. Lindelöf, Helsingfors, 1909), 128: 7 *handfulla* 'manipulos' and *MED hondful* I(c); *OED handful* 1.A does not distinguish
this meaning, but cf. the quotations from Wycliff and Usk, and add
More's *Dialogue of Comfort* (*Works*, 1557, 1154h), 'They shal come
agayne more then laughyng, wyth greate ioye and exultacion wyth
theyr handfuls of corne in theyr handes' (translating Ps. 125: 6
portantes manipulos suos). *beouua(e)s*, g.s. of **beō(w)* 'barley' (= ON.
bygg), suggests Gildas 76/11 *manum plenam hordei*, quoting VL(?)
Ez. 13: 19 (Vulg. *pugillum hordei*), cited by Schlutter, *AJP* xxix. 443.

646. ? Aldhelm, *VC* 2859 *cum larbam et mascam miles non horreat
audax*: *masca*, from Arabic *maskara* 'buffoon' (*REW* 5394), = both
'mask' and 'spectre', like OE. *grima*; for the latter cf. *Riddles* 40/16 f.
mec bealdlice mæg | gearu gongende grima abregan, translating *Aenig.*
100/9 *me larbula terret* (569 n.), and 953 n.

647. *scalfr*: 'cormorant'; cf. MHG. *skalver* (Förster, *Angl.* xli. 111).

648. *marsopicus* (*marto-*) = *picus marticus* 'woodpecker' (Herm. 319/25
marsicus), It. *pico martico* (Barbier, *Revue*, ii. 192).

649. Cf. Jun. 122/20 *mus araneus screawa*: 'shrew' is otherwise unrecorded in Old English.

651. *maruca*: ? for Bd. *murica*, a by-form of *murex* (Schlutter, *JGP* v.
151 fn.), as in 624; cf. Peterhouse MS. 2.4.6 (*CGL* ii. 587/45) *mur(i)ca
genus piscis*.

653. *mordacius*: ? 'clove'; otherwise unrecorded, but cf. Sp. *mordaza*,
etc. (Meyer–Lübke, *WS* xxv. 103). For OE. *clofae* cf. *clufu* (TS 129),
pl. *clufe* (BT 160). Other possibilities are DuCange *mordacium*
'ornamenti genus quod cingulo assuitur' (Hessels, *Leiden* 150) or the
etymon of Fr. *mordaunt* 'indenture' (Barbier, *Revue*, ii. 193), which =
OE. *geclofa* (TS 304).

654. *maulistis* = Gr. μαυλιστής 'pander' (Herm. 179/61 *maulistis
leno*, etc.). For *scyhend* 'seducer, pimp' (here only) cf. *scyan* 'tempt'
(Schlutter, *Angl.* xx. 382) and *scocha* 579.

656. *geormantlab* (*-leaf*) 'mallow' is too well attested to be taken as an error for Cp. *gearwan-*. W. Krogmann, *ESt.* lxix (1934–5), 161 ff., connects it with L. *Germanus*, which he derives from **germana-* 'spike', IE. **gher-* 'stick out' (cf. *hocc, hocleaf*); J. Schuetz, *Zeitschrift für Ortsnamenforschungen*, ix (1933), 225 ff., connects it with Ger. *gären* 'make slimy', comparing Dur. 227 *malua crispa smerig vyrt*. Both Krogmann and Schuetz assume a participial stem *geormant-* (*-d-*?), but the *t* is peculiar to Épinal and may be a scribal error or a secondary development (§ 75).

657. *marrubium*: 'horehound' (Jun. 136/12 *marrubium uel prassiun harhune*, etc.); *biouuyrt* 'balm-mint, sweet-flag' (cf. 20) may be due to confusion with *melisphyllon* or *melissa* 'horehound'.

657a. *merx = merces* 'payment', confused with *merx* 'merchandise' in later Latin (Souter, 250): cf. 15 cd 8 *merx mercis a mercando non merces mercides* (Phocas 412/2 *mercedis*). For *merze* cf. Jun. 145/28 *teloneum* ('toll') *scipmanne* (*-a*) *mertse ceping*.

659. Cf. Cl.I 449/12 *mango ic menge* (after *merx med* in a miscellaneous batch): *mango =* 'dealer' (cf. 15 cd 7 *mango negotiatur*), but the glossator apparently took it as a verb, like lL. *mangonare* 'trade' (DuCange). *mengio* is apparently 1st sg. pres. indic. (cf. Cl. *ic menge*) of a verb *meng(i)an*, presumably a variant of *mangian* 'trade, traffic' (BT 667) and therefore distinct from *mengan* 'mix, mingle', although it may have been confused with it. There is a curious logic in this, since *mangian* was itself formed from L. *mango* (*AEW* 214).

660. *mugil =* 'mullet' (cf. 270 n.), not *haecid* 'pike' (587).

662. *mergus* 'diver' is applied to various sea-birds, including the cormorant (cf. 647 n.) in Ovid, *Metamorphoses*, xi. 751 *spatiosum in guttura mergum*.

663. *tiig =* ON. *Týr*, the Germanic war-god: cf. *Gylfaginning* 25 *hann er djarfastr ok best hugaðr ok hann ræðr mjǫk sigri í orrostum*.

665. *oslae*: 'blackbird, ousel'; here only in Old English.

666. *megale =* Gr. μυγάλη 'shrew': Herm. 320/44 μυγάλη *talpa* may be due to Vulg. Lev. 11: 30 *mygale . . . et talpa*. For OE. *hearma* 'stoat'(?) cf. *hearmascynnene* adj. 'ermine' *Chron.* 1075D and Plummer's note; it glosses *nitela* 'field-mouse' in 675.

666a. Cf. Erf.II 312/2 *mulcet spoducet lenet* (Abstr. MU 2 *mulcet producit*+Abol. MU 30 *mulcet lenit uel placat*): Schlutter, *JGP* v. 142, takes *friat* as OE. *frēoð*, Nh. *friað* 'love' (cf. Erf. *friad*); Lindsay, *Corpus* 205, takes it as L. *friat* 'nurse, fondle'.

667. Cf. Trier 100ª *nausia fastidum uomitus, nausacio nausia*, Lib. Gloss. NA 187 *nausia uomitum* ('de glossis'): *naus(e)atio* 'nausea', first recorded by DuCange in the ninth century, may be a colloquial form like *morgit* 628.

668–70. (16 ab 7–9) Cf. Abstr. NA 17 *nauiter studiose*, Affatim 541/58 *ninguit niuem mittit*, Abol. NU 6 *numisma nummi percussura moneta*: presumably a continuation of the Abstrusa–Abolita batch which ended two lines above.

672. Cf. Trier 100ᵛᵃ *nigra spina vbi prunellas* ('sloes') *crescunt*, Herm. 586/5 *agazea* (*acacia*) *idest sucus prunellæ ex nigra spina*, and *OED* sloethorn.

673. ? Vulg. Lev. 11: 16 *noctuam et larum*: cf. Abba NO 14 *noctua eadem et nocticorax quasi noctis coruus* (Eucherius 157/10 ff. *nycticorax noctua: multi bubonem esse contendunt; sunt etiam qui adserunt esse orientalem auem quae nocturnus coruus appelletur*), St. Gall MS. 295 (SSi. 342/32–5) (*noctuam*) *id est quæ nocte uolat* ... *alii lusciniam uoluerunt esse, id est nahtagala*. *noctua*, the short-eared owl, is confused with *bubo*, the great horned owl, which follows in Lev. 11: 17, and *nycticorax*, the tawny or screech-owl (cf. 674); *luscinia* 'nightingale' may be a misinterpretation of Ambrose, *Hexameron*, v. 24 (*PL* xiv. 239c) *habet et noctua suos cantus; quid autem de luscinia dicam*. OE. *naechthraebn* 'night-raven' may simply translate *nycticorax* 'noctis coruus', but cf. Ger. dial. *Nachtrabe* 'bittern, night-heron' (Suolahti, 380–2; C. H. Whitman, *JGP* ii (1898), 175). The Bible gloss apparently displaced Herm. 90/4 *g(l)aux noctua*, etc. here and in Ld. 47/54 (cf. § 28).

674. ? A Bible gloss, like 673 two lines above: cf. Cl.I 453/12 *nocticorax nihthremn*, following *noctua ule* in the Old Testament batch. *nycticoracem* in Vulg. Deut. 14: 17 corresponds to *bubonem* in the Leviticus list, which may explain the confusion between these two species of owl (637 n.) in Herm. 18/9 νυκτικόραξ *bubo*, etc.

675. *netila*: for *nitela* 'field-mouse' (Polemius 543/13).

676. *tuuncressa*: 'garden cress'(?); cf. OHG. *gartcressa*. -*cressa* may be an error for -*cressae* (cf. *sura(e)* 1077a), but cf. OHG. *cresso* masc. beside *cressa* fem.

leccressae: 'a cress with an onion-like smell, *alliaria officinalis*' (BT 624).

677. ? Another Bible intruder in the Hermeneumata batch: cf. 685 n.

680. *unemotan*: 'want of leisure, business'; here only beside Cp. *unemetta*, but cf. OS. *mōta*, OHG. *muoza* 'leisure'.

684. Cf. Festus 283 *nepa Afrorum lingua sidus quod dicitur nostris cancer*, Nonius 145/12 *nepam quidam cancrem putant*: the same interpretation underlies Aldhelm, *Aenig*. 37 'De cancro quae nepa uocatur', beginning *Nepa mihi nomen ueteres dixere Latini*, whence Cl.I 455/29 *nepa crabba uel hæfern*.

685. ? Vulg. Dan. 3: 46 *non cessabant* ... *succendere fornacem naphtha*: cf. Karlsruhe MS. Aug. 135 (Meritt, *OEG* 58/2) *nasta genus fomitis est idest tyn(der)* (= Ld. 16/10 *nappa genus fomitis*) and Jerome, *In*

Danielem (*PL* xxv. 510b), *Sallustius scribit in historiis quod napta sit genus fomitis apud Persas, quo uel maxime nutriantur incendia*, whence Aldhelm, *VP* 252/15 f. *incendia naptarum fomite* ... *succensa.* This gloss and 16 ab 40 *nardum spicatum species nardi in modum spicæ infusa conficitur* (Mk. 14: 3 *nardi spicati*), after 685a, form Lindsay's Bible 'batch' under N (§ 32 fn. 5).

685a. *nauat* = (*g*)*nauat* 'perform with vigour or diligence': cf. Erf.II 312/46 *nauat instat continuat*, Abavus GN 1 *gnauat fortiter ex(s)equitur*. Schlutter, *JGP* v. 143, reads *nauant framgath* 'advance', but *framat(h)* 'proficit' (TS *framian* II) would fit *gnauat* better; the form *frangat* (also Cp. N34) may have arisen from the misinterpretation of *m* as *ni*.

686. ? A lost Abolita gloss from Festus 293 *nani pumiliones* (cf. 228 n.), whence Erf.III 1176 *humiliamanus duerh* (Philox. PU 62 *pumilio νᾶνος*), Aldhelm, *Metr.* 159/18–19 *nanus idest pumilio*.

687. *napi* = Gr. νᾶπυ 'sinapi', perhaps a gloss on Phocas 412/14 *sinapi* (cf. 922). For the confusion with *napus* 'turnip' (= OE. *naep*) cf. Herm. 593/18 *napius idest sinapi*, Isidore, *Ety.* xvii. 10/10 *sinapis appellatur quod foliis sit similis napis.*

689. Cf. Lib. Gloss. OS 25 *oscilla genus ludicri propriae funis ligatus agitatione perducens sedentem* (*Geo.* ii. 389 *oscilla ex alta suspendunt mollia pinu*). For *totridan* 'swings' cf. ModE. *totter* (Meritt, *FL* 4 E 2), first recorded by *OED* as a verb *c.* 1200, and *rīdan* 'hang, swing' (BT III).

691. *uurmillae* (*wy*-): 'wild marjoram'; cf. OHG. *wurmeli* 'vermiculus' (BT 1285) and 697 n.

692. *osma* = Gr. ὀσμή 'smell, scent': cf. Ld. 47/24 *osma odor*, Herm. 429/28 ὀσμή *odor*, etc. Dahl, 162, takes *suicae* as dat./instr. sg. of an *i*-stem **swice* beside the *ja*-stem *swicce* (*Panther* 66), in ablaut with *swæcc*, *swecc* 'taste, smell'; if so, its source may have been a gloss on Ez. 20: 41, where the Septuagint reads ἐν ὀσμῇ εὐωδίας.

693. Cf. Ld. 47/26 *opilauit gigisde*, Cl.I 463/6 *oppilauit betynde gegiscde* (Aldhelm, *VP* 284/10 *huilcas faucium gurguliones opilauit*): Meritt, *FL* 3 A 15, takes Aldhelm as the common source of the Épinal–Erfurt and Leiden glosses, but cf. the Trier Bible gloss 20ᵇ *opilauit obclusit* (Brown, O21), on Ps. 106: 42 *omnis iniquitas oppilabit os suum* (v.l. *oppilauit*). *gigiscde* 'choked' may represent a causative **gegiscan* beside *giscan* 'sigh'.

694–5. (16 ef 23–4) ? Abstr. OB 30 *oblicum* ... *de angulo in angulum ductio*, Abol. OB 77 *obnixus obstinatus uel perseuerans*: cf. the following item, 16 ef 25 *obstinatus perseuerans.* Sievers, *PBB* ix. 282, derives *strimaendi* 'striving, persisting' (also Cp. 1132 *innixus strimendi*) from a Class IV **striman*, like *niman*; Holthausen, *AEW* 326, proposes a Class I **strīman*, from the same root as *strīdan*, IE. **strei*- 'be stiff, walk stiffly' (*IEW* 1026), and of similar meaning (cf. 1086 n.).

696. *criopungae*: dat./instr. sg. of **creopung* 'creeping', otherwise un-recorded in Old English.

697. *oridanum*: ? for *origanum* 'wild marjoram' (cf. 691); if so, *elonae* 'elecampane' may be a mistake for *ælere* < L. *alarus* 'puleius maior' (Merrit, *FL* 2 B 2) as in Br. 299/19 *origanum ælere*, Dur. 260 *origanum curmelle* (*wu-*) *uel elere*, or L. *colena* (Brown, O28) as in Herm. 555/36 *colena idest origano*, etc. But *oridanum* might also be a corruption of Gr. ὀρέστ(ε)ιον (sc. φυτόν) in Herm. 571/48 *orestimi idest eleniu*, in which case *elonae* would be the correct OE. equivalent.

698. *orcus* is presumably *Orcus* 'god of the underworld, death' as in Abol. OR 32 *Orcus secundum stultitiam gentilium deus inferni ab urgendo mortem* and Cp. 1457 *orcus ðyrs heldiobul*. *orc* may be a borrowing from *Orcus* corresponding to the first element of *orcneas* 'evil spirits' (*Beowulf* 112), or it may = *orc* 'flagon' after Isidore, *Ety.* viii. 11/42 *Pluton . . . quem alii Orcum uocant quasi receptorem mortium, unde et orca nuncupatur uas quod recipit aquas* (cf. Jun. 123/18 *orca orc*). Lindsay's emendation of *orcus* to *urceus*, citing Eccles. 2: 8 *scyphos et urceos*, etc. (*Gloss.* 33), is therefore unnecessary.

701. *obuncans*: 'accosting'; cf. Ld. 35/214 *obuncans obiurgans* (= 16 ef 8), on Rufinus x. 18 *tunc illa, ut mulierum se talium procacitas habet, obuncans Timotheum* (v.l. *obiurgans*). Aldhelm interpreted it literally as 'hooked, embraced' in *VP* 274/3 (*Timotheum*) *nefandis ulnarum gremiis procax obuncabat*, whence Napier 1/2956 *obuncabat idest reflectebat beclypte*. For *geniclde* (*-yclde* § 54) cf. Cl.III 530/17, Hl. C355 *carper(r)abat geniclede, -elde* (Aldhelm, *VC* 2178 *fronte caper-rabat* 'frowned'): TS 305 equates it with ModE. *knuckle* (cf. Cl.I *gecnyclede*); Schlutter, *Angl.* xxx (1907), 133, and Holthausen, *AB* xxxiv. 276, with OE. *hnocc* 'knot', *gehnycned* 'drawn, pinched' (IE. **kn(e)ug- IEW* 559), for which cf. Gmc. **hnekk- (IEW* 558), whence *h(n)eacca* 715, (*h)necca* 720. In either case its root meaning would be 'bent', giving an interpretation of *obuncans* like Aldhelm's.

702. ? *Lorica* 72 *fithrem cum obligia*: cf. LG 64 *cum obligia nettan*. *nettae* also means 'caul' in Br. 293/6 *reticulum nette* ('de membris hominum').

703. *obestrum* might represent lL. **bestum* (?< Gmc. **beustam*) or a corruption of *colostrum* (Meyer–Lübke, *WS* xxv. 104): cf. *colobostrum* 261.

704. Schlutter, *AJP* xxi. 192, takes *ogastrum* as a Gallo-Latin word related to Ir. *og* 'egg'. For *aeggimang* 'egg-mixture' cf. *Leechdoms*, iii. 38/2 *aagemo(n)gc* and Cl.II 281/11 *ocastrum gemenged æg*.

705. *oresta*: ? a corruption of *oraria* 'fringe' (e.g. Rufinus vii. 30/9 *theatricale more oraria moueri*) or of *ora uestis* (Lindsay, *Corpus* O229); for the latter cf. *Glossae Vergilianae* (*CGL* iv. 450/11) *limbis* (*-us) ora uestis auro texta* (*Aen.* iv. 137) and 583.

709. ? Vulg. Is. 66:11 *ab omnimoda gloria* (Lindsay, *Corpus* O162) or Rufinus x. 9b (*coepit*) *omni modo gestire, ut Christianorum inibi semen exurgeret* (cf. Cp. *omnimodo*): *oeghuuelci ŏinga* 'by all means' (cf. *Blickl. Hom.* 221/21 *ælce þinga*) fits the latter. Erf. *hadga* may be a mistake for *hāda* 'ways'; cf. *Azarias* 98 *þurh monigne had. oeghuuelci* (also VP 64: 3 *oeghwelc*) is a weakly stressed form (§ 52).

710. Orosius i. 10/17 *tractus curuum rotarumque orbita*: *huueolrad* 'track of a wheel, rut' is otherwise unrecorded, but cf. *hweollast* 'orbit' (TS 580).

712. Lindsay, *Gloss.* 28, suggests Orosius vi. 5/2 *arcem occupauit*, but *onettae* 'anticipated' (BT *onettan* II) corresponds to Erf.II 315/56 *occupauit praeuenit* (? Nonius 355/3–4 *occupare est proprie praeuenire*). Schlutter, *Angl.* xlvii (1923), 43, emends to (*ge*)*agnettae* as in 1096.

713. ? Aldhelm, *VC* 225–6 *laeti cespitis occas | depopulare studet*: cf. Cl.III 518/14 *occas fealge*, Napier 15/1, 17/2 *occas idest felga*. *occas* = Gallo-Latin *olca* 'cultivated land' (J. Hoops, *PBB* xxxvii (1912), 320), also *VP* 264/16 *fecunda conuersationis occa*; the form is peculiar to Aldhelm.

fealga: 'fallows', pl. of *fealh* 'fallow land', recorded in glosses on *VP* 264/16 (TS 206).

714. Cf. Placidus I O11 *ortygometra genus auium id est coturnices*, Abol. OR 16 *ortigometra coturnices*: the ultimate source of these glosses may have been VL Exod. 16: 13, where Sept. has ὀρτυγομήτρα 'corncrake' (D'A. W. Thompson, *CP* xiii. 19) for Vulg. *coturnix* 'quail' (= OE. *edischaen*), or VL (Robert) Num. 11:31, Vulg. Sap. 16:2 *ortygometram*, Vulg. Sap. 19: 12 *ortygometra*.

715. ? Abstr. OC 3 *occipitium posterior pars uel summitas capitis*, continuing the Abstrusa–Abolita batch immediately before (cf. Lindsay, *Gloss.* 41). *hreacca* may be an error for *hnecca* 'back part of the head' (cf. *snecca* 720) or an ablaut variant **hnacca*, corresponding to ON. *hnakki* (*IEW* 558): cf. 701 n.

716. ? Geo. i. 207 *ostriferi fauces . . . Abydis* (Lindsay, *Gloss.* 118) or Aldhelm, *Aenig.* 98/1 *ostriger en aruo uernabam* (cf. Napier 26/64 *ostriger brunba*(*so*)): *ostriger* is first recorded in Aldhelm, but the two preceding items, 17 ab 31–2 *orchi graece testiculi, opus balsami* (for *opobalsamum*) *sucus balsami* are probably Virgil glosses (cf. *Geo.* ii. 86 *orchades*, 118 f. *sudantia . . . balsama*), and another Virgil gloss may have been Aldhelm's own source.

718. Cf. Servius, *Aen.* xi. 580 '*olorem*' *latine ita dicimus, nam cycni graece dicuntur*: ? another of the 'English' Virgil glosses used by the compilers of Erfurt II and Affatim (cf. § 33 fn. 3 and 221).

719. Cf. Erf.II 1122 *omentum maffa* (= Abstr. OM 9 *mappa uentris* 'caul'): *maffa* is probably a corruption of L. *mappa* (Schlutter, *Angl.* xix. 464).

722. *lithircadae*: 'soothed, appeased'; cf. Hl. B461 *blanditur . . . liþercaþ*. Lit. 'make gentle', from *līðe*+causative suffix *-rcian* (? after *gearcian* 'prepare').

723. *genyctfullum*: 'abundant'; here only, but cf. Cp. 38 *abunde genycthlice* and Cl.I 340/25 *affatim genihtsum*, 342/36 *affatim genihtsumlice*.

727. Orosius iv. *praef*. 5 *quamuis apud omnium sensus pro captu temporum ita uideri queat*: *captus* here = 'nature, condition' (cf. Ammianus, *Res Gestae* (ed. J. A. Wagner, Leipzig, 1808), xvi. 10/1 and note), but the glossator interprets it literally.

728. *saegesetu*: 'maritime regions'; cf. Li. *sæburug*, Ru. *sæceastre* for Vulg. Mt. 4: 13 (*in*) *Capharnaum maritimam*.

729. Orosius iv. praef. 7 *e mollissimis stratis cubiculoque percommodo matutinus egrediens*: *sua* 'very' (BT *swā* IV (4)) renders the Latin intensive *per-*, and *cendlic*, for *cynlic* 'fitting, convenient' (§§ 54, 75), renders *-commodo*.

730. Cf. Isidore, *Ety*. xix. 24/16 *praetexta puerile est pallium quo usque ad sedecim annos pueri nobiles sub disciplinae cultu utebantur, unde et praetextati pueri apellati sunt*: perhaps a word like *scyrtan* 'praetextā' (Meritt, *PG* 362) should be understood with *gigeruuid* 'arrayed'.

733. Orosius v. 5/7 *ut praepropera pugna iniretur*: *fraehraedae* 'too quick(ly)' may be a weak n.s.f. or, more probably, an adv. (§ 87). For the prefix *frae-* cf. *fracod (fra-cūþ), fræfel, fr-etan (AEW* 114).

734. Orosius v. 10/7 (*Ptolemaeus*) *priuignam uero suam, hoc est filiam sororis et coniugis, coniugem adsciuit*: *priuigna* = 'stepdaughter', not 'niece' (OE. *nift*, from L. *neptis*), although the stepdaughter of Ptolemy IX was also his niece (Justin xxxviii. 8/5).

736. *uuicingsceadan (-ae)*: 'piracy' (here only); taken as *wīcingsceaða 'pirate' by Cleopatra. The first element presumably = ON. *víking* f. 'piracy' rather than OE. *wīcing* m. 'pirate' (= ON. *víkingr*). The latter is recorded before the viking period in the OE. *Exodus* 333 *sæwicingas* and also, apparently as a tribal name, in *Widsith* 47, 59, 80; but the Norse invasions gave it a new meaning, as they did to *aesc* (180 n.).

738. Cf. 18 ab 35 *perduellum dicitur bellum eo quod ex utraque parte geritur*: *þor(h)gifect* 'war' (here only) may be a nonce-word coined from *perduellum*.

739. *ferred*: pret. of *forrǣdan* Class VII 'condemn'; here only beside wk. *forrǣdde* (BT 316, TS 250).

740. Cf. Erf.II 317/47 *paludamentum uestimentum belli sunt, toga pacis*, Abavus 547/38 *uestimentum belli sicut toga pacis* (= 21 ab 5 *uestimentum belli* only).

741. *þorh* (also 757, 760) and *þor(h)*- 738 are normal Anglian forms of *þurh(-)* with *o* for Gmc. *u* under reduced stress (Luick, § 326. 2).

For *ludgaet* 'postern' cf. Karlsruhe MS. Aug. 135 (SS i. 382/1) *postica ludgete* (Jud. 3: 24 *per posticum egressus est*) and *lȳðre*, OHG. *lotar* 'deceitful' (**l(i)uþr(i)- IEW* 963).

743. Orosius iii. 1/3 *Conon praebet industriam in hoc propensior ciuibus* (sc. *quam sociis*): *tylg* 'rather (than)', comparative of *tulge* adv. 'very' (BT 1018), is used for a Latin adjective (§ 87).

747. Orosius vii. 7/7 (*Nero*) *auaritiae autem tam praeruptae extitit, ut post hoc incendium Urbis* . . . *neminem ad reliquias rerum suarum adire permiserit*: *staegilrae* 'steep' (also *Christ* 678 f. *heanne beam,* | *stæglne* (MS. *stælgne*) *gestigan*) corresponds to the literal rather than the figurative meaning of *praerupta* 'sheer'.

748. *ferth* (*-ht*): 'honest, just'; cf. OS. *feraht* 'wise' (Holthausen, *Angl.* lxx (1952), 5) and *ferhtlic* (Paris Psalter 95: 10 *he ferhtlic riht folcum demeð*, translating *iudicabit populos in aequitate*).

749. *treddun*: pret. of Class I wk. **treddan* 'tread upon', not Class IV *tredan* (*OET* 605); cf. Paris Psalter 118: 161 *ðær ic ðin halig word* . . . *tredde* and *for-, oftreddan*.

750. ? Orosius i. 10/12 *post grandinem cum igne permixtam* or v. 19/12 *cum permixtim corpora ad sepulturam discernerentur*: TS 370 records both an adj. *gemengedlic* 'mixed together' (cf. Cp.) and an adv. *gemengedlīce* 'confusedly' from this gloss; the latter seems more likely, formed from pp. *gemenged*+the adv. suffix *-lice* (1063 n.)

754. *penduloso halði* = *pendulos oha(e)lði* (Orosius iv. 15/2 *Sarnus late redundans pendulos et dissolutos campos reliquerat*): cf. Schlutter, *JGP* i. 63, and 838. *pendulos* in this context = 'unsteady'; (*o*)*ha(e)lði* 'sloping' (cf. BT *ōheald* and *āhyldan, -hildan* 'incline') is presumably the *casus indefinitus* as in 221, 495, 939.

755. Orosius v. 16/5 *pessum dederunt*: for *spilth* 'destruction' cf. Abstr. PE 106 *pessum deorsum uel praecipitium idest perditum*, Ld. 35/305 *pessum interitum* (on Rufinus iv. 7/2 *pessumdarent*).

757. ? Augustine, *Quaesitiones in Heptateuchum*, ii. 177/4 (*PL* xxxiv. 659) *fortasse enim per anticipationem aliquid dicit de his uelis capillaciis, quod ad illa proficiat, de quibus nondum locutus est*: *anticipatio* = the rhetorical figure *prolepsis* (cf. Cyrillus 418/49 πρόληψις *anticipatio occupatio praesumptio prædictio*; Quintilian, *Institutio oratoria* (ed. E. Bonnell, Leipzig, 1895–6), ix. 2/16 *praesumptio quae* πρόληψις *dicitur, cum id quod obiici potest occupamus*), inadequately explained by *þorch obust*.

760. Orosius vii. 10/7 (*Domitianus*) *cuius cadauer populari sandapila per uespillones exportatum* . . . *est*: cf. 28 ab 32 *uespelliones fossarios qui corpora humant*. Aldhelm, *Metr.* 174/27 f. *uespellones idest fossarios qui corpora humant, unde* Orosius '*per uespellones*' inquit '*in Tiberim tractum est*' confuses this passage and its gloss with Orosius vii. 8/8 (*Vitellius*) *in Tiberim mersus etiam communi caruit sepultura. byrgeras* 'buriers' is not recorded elsewhere in Old English.

761. Cf. Erf.II 318/6 *parcus qui facta* (? *fata*) *dicunt*, perhaps a re-casting of Abstr. PA 38 *parcas fata (dictae) sunt (per) antifrasin* (cf. 764). *burgrunae* = 'wise woman, sybil': cf. Jun. 188/34 *pythonissa helle-rune uel hægtesse*; *lēodrūne* (BT 630–1) is a parallel formation.

762–3. (18 cd 12, 14) ? Vulg. Job 38: 31 *stellas Pleiadas*, Is. 34: 11 *extendetur . . . perpendiculum*: cf. Ld. 44/22 *pliadæ uii sunt stelle in cauda tauri* (on the same passage quoted by Isidore, *Nat. Rer.* 26/1), 13/40 *perpendiculum modica petra de plumbo qua licant in filo quando edificant parietes pundar*, and the intervening item, 18 cd 13 *protelata prolongata* (? Deut. 5: 33 *protelentur dies in terra possessionis*). *sifunsterri* 'the seven stars' = OHG. *sibunstirri*, ON. *sjaustirni*: for the collective *-sterri* cf. OHG. *gistirri* 'constellation' (Kluge, § 66). For *colþred* 'plumb-line' (here only) cf. Cl.III 522/27 *perpendicula walðræd idest rihtnesse* (Aldhelm, *VC* 802 *similare . . . perpendicula patris*); Holthau-sen, *AB* xxxii (1921), 68, takes *col-* as referring to the practice of blackening the thread with a coal to mark the perpendicular, but it may = Ld. *modica petra*, i.e. the plummet (Meritt, *HG* 67–8).

764. Cf. Erf.II 318/47 *parce facta uel fortune melioris* (= 21 ab 15 *par(c)e facta* only), Abstr. PA 38 *parcas fata sunt antifrasin* (761 n.).

764a. Abol. PA 19 *paropsis gabata uel catinus*: cf. SS i. 721/16 *parapsis kebita uel catinus uel acetabulum maius* (Vulg. Mt. 23: 25 *calicis et paropsidis*); the original case of the lemma may be preserved in Cl.II *parabsidis*. *gabote* 'serving dish' (lL. *gabata*) is recorded only in this gloss, but cf. OHG. *kebita*.

766. ? Rufinus v. 1/27 *septimo, ut dicunt, puncto in neruo pedes . . . distenti*: cf. Ld. 35/27 *puncto foramine in quo pedes uinctorum in ligno tenentur cubitali spatio interiecto inter uinctos* and 765 (= 502) im-mediately preceding. *cosp* 'fetter' here = lL. *cuspus* (DuCange) 'the wooden sandal, a form of torture inflicted on slaves', perhaps a borrow-ing from Gmc. **kuspa-*.

768. Cf. Erf.II 318/33 *papilio animal sicut apis tenuis quas dicitur ani-mulus* (= 21 ab 28 *papilo animal quomodo apes tenuis quas dicunt animula*) and Ld. 43/47 *animulus* and Ld. 43/47 *animulus fifaldae* (? Donatus 376/18–19 *pumilio uel papilio*). The former comes in an Abstrusa batch (Lindsay, *Gloss.* 63), suggesting that the common source was a lost Ab-strusa gloss, since Abstrusa and Abolita were apparently used to gloss Donatus: cf. Ld. 43/6 *notha adultera eo quod incerti generis* (Abstr. NO 15 *nothi generis incesti ex adultero et adultera nati*), 13 *agrippa qui in pedes nascitur* (Abol. AG 9 *in pedibus*), 22 *forinnadas interior pars nauis* (? Abstr. FO 11 *fori mediae partes nauium*), 23 *comicus qui comedia scripsit* (Abstr. CO 64 *scribit*), 31 *manes anime mortuorum* (Abol. MA 64), 32 *mactus magis auctus* (? Abstr. MA 5 *macte magis aucte*), 34 *horno hoc anno* (Abol. HO 16), 43 *quidni quare non* (Abstr. QUI 10), 48 *cedo dic uel perdono* (Abol. CE 7 *dic quaeso*), and 378.

769. ? Orosius vi. 11/26 *cupas pice, sebo, et scindulis repletas* (cf. 943–4): the interpretation applies only to *sebo* 'tallow'. For *unamaelti* 'unmelted' (here only) cf. *āmiltan* tr. 'melt' (TS 36).

771. Vulg. Lev. 22: 22 *si papulas (habens)*: cf. Karlsruhe MS. Aug. 99 (SS v. 163/5–6) *papulas uerrucas* (= OE. *uueartae*) *quæ in leprosis apparent*.

773. *cros*: pl. of **crōh* 'vine-shoot'; cf. OHG. *cruoh* 'fruticem' (SS i. 357/57). Erf. *crous* (also Cp.) may represent an uncontracted **crōas* (§ 59. 4).

778. *pedo*: for *pedum* 'shepherd's crook' (Phocas 412/15); cf. Ld. 45/18 *pedum fustis quem pastores habent in modum* ⌒. *paturum* (also Ld. 46/42 = lL. *pastorium* (DuCange) 'clog or hobble by which animals were tethered while grazing'; its presence in the Phocas lists may be due to confusion of *pedum* with *pedica* 'fetter, snare', e.g. Ld. 19/19 *pedica fezra ligamen* (Job 18: 10 *abscondita est in terra pedica eius*).

779. *prætersori(u)m*: ? 'stray animal'; cf. Adamnan, *Vita S. Columbae* (ed. J. T. Fowler, Oxford, 1920), i. 38 *homouncio . . . tria apud se uicinorum praetersoria in una retentabit maceria unamque electam de uaccis praetersoriorum occidi iubebit sibi*. Schlutter, *AJP* xxi. 192, connects the second element with Ir. *scor* 'paddock'.

paad: ? for *wād* 'hunting, prey'; cf. Cl. *waad* and ModE. *waif* (? ON. *veiðr*). For other suggestions see Loewe, 411; Schlutter, *Angl.* xix. 107; Sievers, *ESt.* viii. 156 f.; Holthausen, *AB* xxxii. 65.

780. *prifeta*: ? for **trieta*, from Gr. τριέτης adj. 'of three years'; cf. the participle τριετίζων, applied to a heifer in Sept. Gen. 15: 9 λάβε μοι δάμαλιν τριετίζουσαν (Vulg. *vaccam triennem*). Schlutter, *AJP* xxi. 192, suggests a form **triueta* connected with OIr. *triath* 'boar', presumably a Hisperic word like *prætersori(u)m* immediately preceding. *thriuuuintri* = *þriwintre* adj. 'three-year-old' (BT 1071).

780a. Cf. Karlsruhe MS. Aug. 135 (SS i. 375/1–2) *polenta idest subtilissima farina sineduma* (sm-) *uel gisistit* (-*ftit*) *melo* (Vulg. Jos. 5: 11 *polentam eiusdem anni*) and Cp. 1606 *polenta smeodoma: fahama*; may be a conflation of *farina* and *smeduma*. For another view see Meritt, *HG* 82–3.

781. Cf. Cp. 1491 *paupilius scaldhulas* (? = *scaldthyflas* 58): *papiluus* and *papilius* may be genuine popular forms of *papyrus* (e.g. Herm. 428/14), but evidence is lacking. For *ilugsegg* 'sword-grass' cf. the *Rune Poem* 41 ff.:

> (eolhx)secg eard (MS. seccard) hæfð oftust on fenne,
> wexeð on wature, wundaþ grimme,
> blode breneð beorna gehwylcne
> ðe him ænigne onfeng gedeð.

AEW 187 and BT 253, TS 191 identify the first element with *eolh* 'elk', but *ilug-* and Cl. *eolug-* suggest a different word, possibly identical with the obscure *eoletes* (? for *eoleges*) in *Beowulf* 224, meaning 'water'.

783. Cf. Cyrillus 392/48 παλιγγενεσία *regeneratio recreatio renatio*: perhaps a lost Philoxenus gloss in view of the following item, 19 cd 19 *palin iteratum* (? Philox. IT 9 *iteratum* πάλιν σκαφέν); for the connection between Cyrillus and Philoxenus see Lindsay, *CR* xxxi (1917), 190–1. A scholion on Mt. 19: 28 *in regeneratione*, where the Greek text has παλιγγενεσίᾳ, is another possibility.

784. *holopannae*: ? for **he(o)lorpanne* 'scale of a balance' (cf. *he(o)lor* 573a, 607, 988 and Schlutter, *Angl*. xix. 112) or **holdpanne* 'frying-pan, meat-dish' (cf. Herm. 24/10 *lopás patena*, etc. and *bredipannae* 885 n.).

785. ? Herm. 414/3 *pingit zografi* (cf. *pangebant* 797) or Vulg. Jer. 22: 14 *pingitque sinopide* (Schlutter, *JGP* i. 332): for *faehit* 'paints' < **fæhan* beside *fægan* (TS 197) cf. *faedun* 797 and OHG. *gifēhen*, ON. *fá*.

786. ? Isidore, *Ety*. xx. 4/10 *patena quod dispansis patentibusque sit oris*: cf. the preceding item, 19 cd 30 *praestigium quod prestringit aciem oculorum* (*Ety*. viii. 9/32–3 *praestringat*).

787. *thothor* 'ball' may be related to *þodettan, þyddan* 'strike': cf. Isidore, *Ety*. xviii. 69 (*pila*) *et sfera a ferendo uel feriendo dicta*.

788. ? Rufinus i. 8/9 *prurigo . . . intolerabilis per omnem corporis diffusa superficiem*: cf. Ld. 35/3 *prorigo urido cutis idest gyccae*. For *gycinis* 'itchiness' (here only in Old English) cf. *gyce* sb., *gyccan* vb. 'itch'.

790. ? Vulg. Prov. 27: 22 *quasi ptisanas feriente desuper pilo*: cf. KG 1036–7 *quasi tipsonas swa berecorn, feriente þercce(n)dum*. Schlutter, *Angl*. xx. 382–3, takes *berændae* as Class I wk. **berian* 'strike' (OHG. *berien*, ON. *berja*), whence pret. *berode* (J. C. Pope, *Homilies of Ælfric* (London, 1967–8), xxi. 446), p.p. *gebered* (Jun.), and ME. *berien*; but the form belongs to Class IV *beran* (cf. Cp. 1677 *beorende*), presumably translating a variant reading *ferente* (Holthausen, *Angl*. xxi. 243).

791. ? Vulg. Lev. 13: 2 *diuersus color siue pustula*: cf. the Karlsruhe MS. Aug. 99 marginal gloss (SS v. 119/18) *pustela gisprinc* and Stuttgart MS. Herm. 86 (SS v. 246/30–3) *pustulæ sunt bulle turgentes in cute . . . pupula autem est paruissima cutis erectio circumscripta cum rubore et dicitur quasi papula* (= Isidore, *Ety*. iv. 8/21) *. . . sed hieronimus unum esse pustulam et papulam dicit*. The statement attributed to Jerome could be an inference from *In Nahum* 2: 10 (*PL* xxv. 1250c) *papulae quoque quae post aegrotationem nascuntur in labiis uocantur ἐκβράσματα* ('eruptions').

795. Cf. Herm. 511/56 *bibola papirum* (Isidore, *Ety*. vi. 10/1 *bibulam autem papyrum dixit quod humorem bibat*): Lindsay, *Gloss*. 34, places this item at the beginning of his second Bible batch, citing Vulg. Is. 18: 2 *in uasis papyri*, whence Ld. 13/31 *papiri unde faciunt cartas*; but the case of the lemma suggests that it belongs to the Hermeneumata batch immediately preceding. *eorisc* (*ēa-* § 40) 'water-rush, bulrush' (cf. 960) may reflect the same interpretation.

796. *asiuuid*: 'sewn'; here only, but cf. *bisiuuidi, gisiuuid*.

797. *pangebant* = *pingebant* 'they were painting', probably from the alphabetical section of Hermeneumata, where *pingere* was extensively conjugated: cf. 142/25 *zografusin pingent (-unt)*, 414/7 *pinxerunt ezografesan*, and *pingit* 785. For the confusion between *pangere* 'join' and *pingere* 'paint' cf. Cl.III 526/27 *pangit fægde* (Aldhelm, *VC* 1387 *glus . . . moenia pangit*) and It. *pingere* 'push, thrust'.

798. *hringfaag* 'marked with circles' refers to the circular patterns in which damask (*textus polymitus*) was woven: cf. 984 n.

800–1. (20 ab 3, 5) ? *Aen.* i. 251–2 *unius ob iram | prodimur*, 648 *pallam signis auroque rigentem*: cf. the intervening item, 20 ab 4 *praeuertitur praeuenit* (= Lib. Gloss. PR 1182, on *Aen.* i. 317 *fuga praeuertitur Hebrum*). *birednae* 'betrayed' is an isolated example of the strong pret. part. beside wk. *berædde, -on* (BT 88), with *sind(on)* understood (§ 87).

801a. *penitus*: 'far' (? *Ecl.* i. 66 *penitus toto orbe diuisos Brittanos*). *longe* is treated as Latin in Épinal (cf. § 37), but it was presumably regarded as Old English in Cl.I 466/21 (? misapplied to Aldhelm, *VP* 256/13 *penitus abdicare et procul eliminari*), and perhaps also in Erfurt; L. *longe* is not recorded elsewhere as a gloss on *penitus*.

802. Cf. Werden I (Gallée, 342) *platesa genus piscis floc saxonice*: *platis(s)a* 'plaice' is also equated with *floc* 'fluke' in Ælfric, *Coll.* 107.

803. *pessul* = *pessulus* 'bar, bolt' (cf. Trier 107ª *pessulum obex repagulum*), but its position between *platissa* and *perna* (see next note) suggests that *pessulus* may also have been a fish-name, in which case *haca* could represent ModE. *hake* (cf. *haecid* 587, 660). *haca* is taken as a cognate of OE. *hæc(ce)* 'hatch, gate' and ON. *haki* 'hook' by BT 497, TS 493, *OET* 470, and *AEW* 143, but the semantic connection is unexplained.

804. ? Another fish-name: cf. *pernae* 'sea mussels' (Pliny xxxii. 154) and 802–3. Ld. 47/13 *perna flicci* follows 9 *platissu folc*, 10 *balera hron* (= 802, 146), 11 *uiuarium piscina*, 12 *caefalus haerdhera* (= 270); but *flicii* presumably = *flicce* 'flitch of bacon' (ON. *flikki*) as in 774.

806. *parrula* = 'crested lark' in Herm. 18/3 κοριδαλλός (κορυ-) *parrumla* (the only other example recorded), but *parra* 'barn-owl' (?) is equated with *parus* 'tit' in Herm. 17/48 αἰγίθαλλος *parra* (cf. Thompson, *CP* xiii. 20). OE. *masae* 'titmouse' is found only here, but cf. OHG. *meisa*, etc. (*AEW* 215) and ME. *mose*.

807. ? Vulg. Lev. 11: 18 *onocrotalum et porphyrionem*: cf. St. Gall MS. 913 (SS iv. 460/18–20) *onocratulum auis que sonitum facit in aqua raredumlæ uel felofor*; *porphirionem non fit in Brittania* and Cp. 1445 *onocratallus feolufer*. For the St. Gall gloss cf. the note in the same MS. quoted by Baesecke, p. 10, *scotum esse auctorem prodit modus quo de aliquibus animalibus loquitur, dum de porphyrione ait 'non fit in Britannia'*; its juxtaposing of *onocrotalus* 'pelican' (Thompson, *CP* xiii. 18–19) and *raredumle* 'bittern' misled TS 209 f. OE. *felofor* 'pelican'

(L. *porphyrio*) may be influenced by *scalf(o)r* 'cormorant' (Suolahti, 300–1).

808. *picus* 'woodpecker' (Herm. 18/4 δρυοκολαψ (-άπτης) *picus*) = OE. *fina* (cf. 648); *higrae* 'jay' (cf. 156 n.) shows confusion with *pica* (Herm. 188/25 *cissa pica*, etc.).

809. *porcopiscis* = Fr. *porpois* (Meyer–Lübke, *WS* xxv. 106), but it was applied to the sturgeon in Medieval Latin (Köhler, 82).

810. Cf. Ld. 47/92 *porcastrum foor*, Napier 20/4 *porcaster for* (Aldhelm, *VC* 2779 *stratis recubans porcaster pausat obesus*): *porcaster* 'an immature or gelded boar' (Hessels, *Leiden* 170) is otherwise recorded only in Aldhelm, but the latter may have found it in the 'de suibus' list from which he took *Metr.* 180/14 *porcelli* (cf. 811 immediately following). For *foor* 'young pig' cf. Napier 22/3 *porca idest for* (also glossing *VC* 2779 *porcaster*).

811. *faerh* 'young pig' (cf. Jun. 119/27 *suilli uel porcelli fearas*) may also be intended in *Beowulf* 305b, where the manuscript reads *ferh wearde heold* (cf. Hoops, 55).

812–13. (20 ab 23–4) ? Herm., e.g. 260/10–11 ἡ ψύλλα *pulex*, ὁ φθείρ *pedunculus*, resuming the Hermeneumata batch which ended three lines above. Erf. *floc(h)* = OHG. *flōh*.

814–16. (20 ab 24–6) ? Orosius iii. 17/8 *deciens nouiens milia profligata*, etc., iii. 21/7 *externos prouentus*, vi. 2/17 *pendulo . . . cinere*: for *proflicta* beside *profligata* cf. Abba PRO 36, Abavus PR 124 *proflixit prostrauit* and Gellius, *Noctes Atticae* (ed. P. K. Marshall, Oxford, 1968), xv. 5/2 *'profligatasque' res quasi 'proflictas'. ridusaendi*, pres. part. 'swinging, dangling', may represent a Class II wk. *rid(u)sian*, formed from an *es/os*-noun like *hlēoðrian* from *hlēoðor* (cf. W. von Unwerth, *PBB* xxxvi (1911), 33).

817. *buturfliogae* 'butterfly' is otherwise unrecorded in Old English.

818. *pella*: ? 'pommel'; cf. Sp. *pella* 'ball' < L. *pila* (BT 808). But Herm. 273/20–1 ἐφίππιον *phalera sella*, ἱπποκόσμοι *phalera* suggests a conflation of *sella* 'saddle' (cf. 926) and *phalera* 'saddle-boss(es)', the latter of which would suit *sadolfelgae* 'saddle-felly' or '-fellies' (? wk. n.s.f. or str.f.p. like *felge* 292) better than 'pommel'.

819. Cf. Ld. 13/41 *paliurus (h)erba quæ crescit in tectis domorum grossa folia habens (sin)fullae* (Vulg. Is. 34: 13 *orientur in domibus eius spinae et urticae, et paliurus in munitionibus suis*): *sinfullae* 'house-leek' (BT 876) for *paliurus* 'Christ's thorn' (Herm. 264/58) may be due to Is. 37: 27 *facti sunt sicut . . . herba tectorum*.

822. *plumae* beside Cl. *plyme* 'plum-tree' (L. *prūnea AEW* 248) may be due to *prūnum* 'plum'.

828–9. (20 cd 8–9) ? Geo. iv. 15 *manibus Procne pectus signata cruentis*, *Ecl.* 1. 57 *raucae . . . palumbes*: in a Hermeneumata batch like 21–6 and 857. The second *u* in Ép. *cuscutan* beside Erf., Cp. *cuscot(a)e* 'dove' (cf. ModE. dial. *cowshot*) may be dittography after the preceding *u*.

830. *hunaegaepl*: 'lozenge, pastille' (this gloss only); for OE. *æp(p)l* in this sense cf. *Leechdoms* i. 250/10 *cnuca tosomne þam gelice ðe ðu anne æppel wyrce*.

831. *duuergaedost(l)ae*: 'penny-royal'; so called because it was used as a remedy for *dweorg* 'cramp' (Holthausen, *AB* xxix (1918), 253).

832. Cf. Erf.II 317/55 *pansa qui ambulat pedibus in diuersa tendentibus* (= Abol. PA 10): *scabfoot* 'splay-footed' is otherwise unrecorded, but cf. OHG. *scěffuoz* and ON. *skeifr* 'crooked, awry', etc. (*AEW* 271).

833. *gillistrae* and *gillister* (BT 476) are by-forms of *geolstor* 'phlegm, pus' (**gel(l)ustr-* Geldner, ii. 22); the double consonant also appears in *gealla* 'gall' from the same root, IE. **ghel-* 'gleam' (*IEW* 429 ff.), and OHG. *gillister*.

834–5. (21 ab 38–9) Cf. Erf.II 319/61 *peditemptim leniter ambulat uel cautae quasi pede temptans* (Abstr. PE 9 *pedetemptim quasi pede temptans*), 70 *petulans impurus spurcus* (= Lib. Gloss. PE 1316 'de glossis', i.e. Abstrusa?): *fotmelum* 'gradually' (cf. Cl.I 412/28 *gradatim fægre uel fotmælum*) and *uuraeni* 'lascivious' may replace *leniter ambulat* (*-ans* ?) and *impurus*, since the common source of Erfurt II and the *ab*-order sections of Épinal–Erfurt does not appear to have been glossed in Old English (§ 26).

836–7. (21 cd 14–15) Cf. Erf.II 319/20 *perpendit intellexit intelligit aestimat* (? Abstr. PE 78 *perpendit aequauit uel aestimauit*), 23 *peristromata gemina* (*tegmina*?) *accubitus* (Abol. PE 3 *perstromata gemina stibadii*), and Codex Leidensis 67E (*CGL* v. 636/23) *perstromata ornamenta stafediorum*: Loewe, 347, and Schlutter, *Angl.* xix. 101, take *st(a)efad brun* as a corruption of *stibadiorum*, but *st(a)efad* 'striped' (= ON. *stafaðr*) suggests a gloss on Plautus, *Pseudolus* 145–6 *ita ego uostra latera loris faciam ualide uaria uti sint | ut ne peristromata quidem aeque picta sint Campanica*.

838a. *auram*: ? for *auri unam* (Vulg. III Reg. 10: 17 *trecentae minae auri unam peltam uestiebant*). *del* = OE. *ðel*, as Schlutter pointed out (*JGP* i. 318), but the sense is 'metal plate', not 'board': cf. Cl.I 360/33 *bratea gylden þel arlægen* (*asl-*) and the *laminas* mentioned in the preceding verse.

839. ? Isidore, *Ety.* xx. 14/13 *qualos corbes*: cf. the following item, 21 ef 9 *quaestor quaesitor qui quaestionibus þreest* (*Ety.* ix. 4/16 *quaestores quasi quaesitores eo quod quaesitionibus praesunt*). *mand* 'basket' = ModE. dial. *ma(u)nd*.

840. ? Vulg. Amos 8: 6 *quisquilias frumenti*: cf. Abba QUI 28 *quisquilias paleas minutissimas quas faluppas (famfalucas?) dicunt* and Cp. 1526 *paleae aegnan*. For *aehrian* pl. 'chaff' cf. *ēar*, Nh. *æhher* 'ear of corn' (§ 50. 3 and fn. 3); Cp. *aegnan* and Cl.I. 412/3 *egenu* (462 n.)

represent another development of the same root, corresponding to Go. *ahana* and ON. *ǫgn*, the etymon of ModE. *awn*.

841. *quadripertitum*: ? for *quadripartitus* (sc. *panis*); cf. Gregory, *Dial.* i. 11 *in hac prouincia crudi panes ligno signari solent, ut per quadras quattuor partiti uideantur* (L. G. Hallander, *Stockholm Studies in English*, xv (1966), 138 ff.). But a gloss on Gr. τετραφάρμακον, 'a dish made of four ingredients' favoured by the Emperor Hadrian (Spartianus, *Vita Adriani* 21/4 *tetrapharmacum quod erat de fasiano, sumine, perna, et crustulo*), would fit OE. *cōc(u)nung* 'seasoning, seasoned food' (TS 131) better.

843–4. (21 ef 15–16) ? Philox. QUA 49–50 *quanticumque* ὅσον δήποτε, *quantisper* πόσως: *swa swiþe (swa)* = 'as much (as), however much'; cf. *þus suiþae* 1037 and BT *swiþe* III.

846. ? *Aen.* iv. 309 *quin etiam, hiberno moliris sidere classem*: cf. Affatim 559/38 *quin etiam insuper uel magis*. For *aec þan* 'moreover' (TS 163) cf. *eac þæm*, OE. Orosius 72/12.

847. *quaternio* 'the number four' is recorded as (1) a dicing term (cf. Isidore, *Ety.* xviii. 65 *iactus quisque apud lusores ueteres a numero uocabitur, ut unio, trinio, quaternio* and 6–7, 178, 998), (2) a gathering of four leaves (= Jun., Ælfric *cine*), and (3) a squad of four soldiers (Vulg. Acts 12: 4 *quatuor quaternionibus militum*). *quatern* may be a learned borrowing from *quaternio* (Pogatscher, § 186), perhaps in sense (2), or an error for L. *quaterni* 'four each' as in Erfurt.

849. *quinqueneruia*: ? 'germander'; cf. Codex Vaticanus 1468 (*CGL* v. 517/22) *traxaginem (tri-) quinque neruia*. Its confusion with *leciuuyrt* 'ribwort' (also Trier 113ᵃ *quinqueneruia plantago*, Br. 299/14, Dur. 282 *quinquenerbia, -uia ribbe*) may be a misinterpretation of *septineruia* 'plantago' (793), written *vii. neruia*: cf. *vii folia* 'heptafolium' 379 and *quinquefolium* 1084, where the exemplar must have read *v. folium*.

851–2. (22 ab 19–20) ? Aldhelm, *VP* 287/16 *radiis stridentibus*, 300/7–8 *ursinae rapacitatis rictus*: cf. Napier 1/3739 *radiis (h)rislum*, 5017 *rictus ceaflas*. For *graennung* 'baring the teeth' (here only) cf. *grennian* 'ringere' (BT 488) and ModE. *grin(ning)*.

853. *locaer*: 'carpenter's plane'; here only, but cf. ON. *lokarr*.

854. *rabulus (-la)*: 'cheap lawyer, demagogue'; cf. Festus 377 *rabula dicitur in multis intentus negotiis . . . quia acrior est in negotiis agendis, et quasi rabiosus. ebhatis* = Cp. *eofotum*, d.p. of *eofot* 'charge, lawsuit': cf. Werden III (Gallée, 359) *ephiphonima* (ἐπιφώνημα) *causa contentio efat*.

857. *roscinia*: 'nightingale' (cf. 26); from *russus, russeus* 'russet' according to Barbier, *Revue*, ii. 195, but Aldhelm, *Aenig.* 68/7 *cantans luscinia ruscis* implies another derivation.

861. ? Herm. 547/45 *lapacio rodenape*: cf. *lapatium* 606 and Br. 300/ 15 *rodinaps ompre docce*. *rodinape* looks like a form of *rāpanāpus* 'turnip'

(Souter, 340), in which case its connection with λάπαθον 'sorrel' might be due to confusion in a list of edible roots. *lelothre* 'bur'(?) was probably introduced through confusion between λάπαθον and *lappa* as in 606, but the turnip is associated with a similar plant in Jun. 134/3–4 *blitum uel lappa clate uel clyfwyrt.*

862–3. (22 cd 1–2) Lindsay, *Gloss.* 34, assigns these glosses to Vulg. Is. 41 : 15 *quasi plaustrum . . . habens rostra serrantia,* Ez. 19 : 12 *marcuerunt et arefactae sunt uirgae roboris eius,* but the interpretations point rather to Orosius vi. 19/8 *(naues) sine rostris* (cf. 868), vi. 8/12 *naues solido robore intextae*: Lindsay's Orosius batch *(Gloss.* 30) begins with 864 on the next line below. Ép. *celae* would correspond to *ceole* 'throat' (BT 151, TS 121), used for the neck or stem of a ship (Schlutter, *Angl.* xix. 482 : cf. ON. *kjǫlr* 'keel' *IEW* 365), but Erf. *cæle,* Cp. *caeli* may represent an ablaut variant **kaliz* (Dahl, 159) with *æ* as the *i*-mutation of Prim. OE. *a* before intervolcalic *l* (§ 50. 2), in which case *celae* might be a scribal error like Erf. *-gela* 26. For Cp. *arbor* see 235 n.

864. Orosius v. 10/11 *insula . . . in tantum efferbuit, ut . . . homines . . . reciprocato anhelitu calidi aeris adustis introrsus uitalibus, suffocarit*: for *gistaebnændrae* 'corresponding' cf. *staefnændra* 75.

865. Orosius v. 18/20 *ita ut attoniti . . . steterant, alii stirpibus uel saxis reclines, alii armis suis innitentes*: *suae = swa (swa)* 'as it were' (cf. BT *swā* V (11)), translating *ita ut.*

866. ? Orosius vi. 1/4 *ubi ratiocinatio* (v.l. *rationato) deficit, fides subuenit*: a verb such as *lǣstan* may be understood with *ambect* 'service' as in *Genesis* 518–19 *lǣste þu georne | his ambyhto,* paraphrasing *subuenit,* or *ambect* itself may represent a form of *ambeht(i)an* 'serve' (TS 35).

868. *tindicti*: 'pronged, spiked' (BT 987–8); cf. *tindum* 873.

870. *fram adoenre*: pret. part. of *fram-ādōn* 'take away' (BT 330), a quasi-compound of prepositional adverb+verb (Campbell, §§ 78–80).

872. Orosius vii. 35/3 *claustra deseruit* or Abstr. RE 82 *reserat patefacit* (misread *-fecit*?): Lindsay's Orosius and Abstrusa–Abolita batches overlap at this point (cf. *Gloss.* 30, 42). *andleac* = Cp. *onlaec* 'unlocked', with stressed *and-* substituted for the normal *on-* (Campbell, § 73 fn. 1).

873. ? Orosius v. 19/23 *interfectorum ciuium capita . . . conlata Rostris,* influenced by Isidore, *Ety.* xv. 2/27 *haec loca* (the Roman Forum) *et prorostra uocantur ideo quod ex bello Punico captis nauibus Carthaginiensium rostra ablata sunt et in foro Romano praefixa* (Brown, R40): *forae uuallum* may translate Isidore's *prorostra* or *pro rostris* in Aldhelm, *VP* 264/2 *qui pro rostris . . . contionantur,* whence Napier 1/2322 *pro rostris idest muris for heahseldum on(d) weallum* and Cl.I 470/10 *prorostris heahseldum* (= Cp. 1667) *foreweardscip* (!); *OET* 487 and TS 241 take it as dat. pl. of *foreweall* 'bulwark', which is clearly wrong.

874. Cf. Affatim 560/36 *rancor inuidia odium*, echoed by Aldhelm, *VP* 274/5 *rancida liuoris inuidia*: *throh* is otherwise recorded as an adj. 'rancid' (= Modern Icelandic *þrár AEW* 370) glossing *VP* 274/5 and 272/10 *rancidis fletuum questibus* (BT 1072); there is no other evidence for the noun 'rancour' inferred by BT 1071 from this gloss.

875–6. (22 cd 25–6) ? Isidore, *Ety.* xix. 1/6 *remex uocatus quod remum gerit*, xi. 1/59 *rumen proximum gurgulioni* . . . *hinc bestiae quae cibum reuocant ac remandunt ruminare dicitur*: the apparent confusion between *rumen* 'gullet' and *rumex* 'sorrel' (Herm. 317/17, etc.) may be merely graphic, caused by *remex* on the line above. The true meaning of *edroc* may have been 'cud', not 'gullet' (TS 179): cf. Cl.III 534/3 *rumen edreced roc* (Aldhelm, *VC* 2778 (*sus*) *alternare nequit crasso sub gutture rumen*) and *edreccan, eodorcan* 'ruminate'.

877. Cf. Erf.II 328 14 *redimicula auri cincilla* (= Affatim 561 16): perhaps a lost Abstrusa gloss on *Aen.* ix. 616 *habent redimicula mitrae* in view of the following item, 22 cd 28 *reduces incolumi* (Abstr. RE 25 *reduces saluos uel incolumes reuersos*, on *Aen.* i. 390 *reduces socios*), which begins the second Abstrusa–Abolita batch. For *cyniuuithan* 'fillets' cf. Napier 1/5241 *redimicula wrædas cynewiþþan lofas* (Aldhelm, *VP* 316/22, quoting Virgil) and **wiðu-* in *uuiduuindae* 348, 1059. The geminated forms may be due to a *jōn*-stem variant like OHG. *witta*, ON. *viðja* 'withy' beside Go. d.p. *kunawidom* 'chains', etc. (*AEW* 402).

878. ? Abstr. RA 12 *rastri ligones*: cf. Abavus RA 12 *rastros ligones* (= 23 ab 3) and 565.

879. *cnioholaen*: 'knee-holly, butcher's broom' (*ruscus aculeatus*), also identified with *uictoriola* 'daphne' (Br. 300/21 *uictoriale*) and *mustelago* 'periwinkle' (Cl.I 448/30 *mirstellago*).

880. Cf. Erf.II 327/30 *ramnus ramus spinae albe* (= 22 ef 40): *thebanthorn* = 'buckthorn' (*rhamnus catharticus*), ModE. dial. 'theeve-thorn'; Schlutter, *ESt.* xxxviii. 27, connects the first element with dial. *theave* 'ewe of the first year', BT 1075 with *þúfe* 'tufted' (cf. *þuþistil* 601 n.), presumably with Kentish *e* for *ȳ*.

881. ? Abstr. SA 16 *salebrae loca lutosa*: cf. the preceding item, 23 ab 11 *salebrosus asper* (= Abstr. SA 15). *thuerhfyri* pl. 'cross-furrows', i.e. 'difficulties'(?) is also recorded in Aldhelm glosses which may derive from this interpretation: cf. Cl.III 493/16–17 *salebrosos ða unsmeþan, anfractus ðwerhfuru* (*VP* 253/26 *salebrosos complanans anfractus*), whence Cl.I 340/20 *anfractus ðweorhfyro* and Cl.III 503/28 *anfractus þwyrhfero*, applied to *VP* 286/18 *errabundis anfractibus*; and related interpretations in Cl.III 520/12 *salebroso þwyres fura* (*VC* 469 *sed genus explanat salebroso pagina uersu*, where *þwyres fura* appears to be misapplied) and SS ii. 22/35 *salebras furihi* (*VC* 2399–2400 *celydrum . . . in uacuas iussit reptare salebras*). *VC* 2400 *salebras* may reflect *loca lutosa*, while *VP* 282/3–4 *per obliquos anfractus* recalls *thuerhfyri*

itself. -*fyri* is a fem. root-consonant noun (Campbell, § 628. 1), but was apparently treated as neut. in the later glosses.

882. *sibba*: ? for *fibula* 'brooch' as in 408 (Lindsay, *Corpus* S319) or *Phoebus, Phoebe* as in Hl. F320–1 *fibus sol, fibea luna*; *sigel* (BT 873) could be either 'jewel' or 'sun'.

883. *bredisern* = 'pen-knife': cf. Ld. 14/20 *scalpellum ferrum est quod habent scriptores unde incidunt cartas et pennas acuent ex altera parte latum sicut graphium*. Meritt, *FL* 3 D 2, connects the first element with *bred* 'writing tablet' (TS 104), but Cl.II *brædisen* suggests *bræd(e)* 'broad' as in *braedlaestu* 321 (cf. Ld. *latum*).

884. Cf. Abol. SC 15 *scrobibus fossulis* (*Geo.* ii. 288–9 *forsan et scrobibus quae sint fastigia quaeras.* | *ausim uel tenui uitem committere sulco*), Napier 1/2018 *scrobibus idest fossulis on furum; scrobes sunt fosse* (Aldhelm, *VP* 257/12 *propagines . . . scrobibus pastinantem*): hence *furhum* 'furrows' glosses *scrobibus* 'ditches' (cf. 948).

885. *bredipannae*: 'frying-pan' (also Cl.I 428/6 *in frixorio on brædepannan*); cf. Cl.I 386/15 *de sartagine of bradre pannan*. The first element is presumably *bræde-*, related to *bræde* 'roast meat', *brædan* 'roast' with Gmc. *æ* (§ 39); but Cp. 407 *braad-* and Cl. *bradre* show confusion with *brād* 'broad', which would also account for Erf. *breiti-* (cf. Ger. *breit*).

886. *sarcinatum*: ? for *sar(ci)tum* 'patched, mended' (cf. Cp. S32 *sarcitum consutum*), perhaps a split from 889. *sarcinare (also Cyrillus 427/34 ῥάπτω *sarcino . . . sarcio*) appears to be a colloquial development from *sarcire*; cf. *sarcinare* 'a mender of old clothes' and *scarpinat* 906.

887. *sarculum*: 'hoe, rake'; cf. Ld. 13/18 *sarculum ferrum fossorium duos dentes habens*, on Is. 7: 25 *omnes montes qui in sarculo sarrientur, non ueniet illuc terror spinarum et ueprium. uueadhoc* (*wēo-*) 'weed-hook' (here only) may be a misinterpretation of Isaiah.

889. Vulg. IV Reg. 12: 5 *instaurent sartatecta domus*, etc.: cf. the Trier Bible gloss 9ᵃ *sarta tecta reparatio fabrice, sartum enim consutum dicitur a sar(c)ire uerbo* and 886. For *gifoegnissae* 'repairs' cf. *gefēg, gefōg* 'joining' and OHG. *gefuognissa* 'nexus' (TS 324); such an interpretation may underlie Æthelwulf, *De Abbatibus* (ed. A. Campbell, Oxford, 1967), 452 *plumbea sarta tegunt case cum culmina summae*, where *sarta* appears to be used as a noun meaning 'joints, patches' (*RES* xix (1968), 417 fn. 8).

890. *lectha*: 'bilge'; cf. (*h*)*lec* 'leaky' (= ON. *lekr*) and *leccan* 'irrigate'.

891. ? Isidore, *Ety.* xix. 19/13 *scalprus dictus quod scalpturis et foraminibus sit aptus quasi scalforus, cuius diminutiuum scalpellus* (cf. 907): this would explain the confusion between *scalprum* 'chisel' and *byris* 'auger' (Cp. 11 *foratorium buiris*). *thuearm* 'chisel' (?), otherwise unrecorded, is presumably a derivative of *geþweran* 'forge' (*AEW* 373).

892. ? Vulg. Job 40: 17 *salices torrentis* (cf. Ld. 19/61 *salices salhas*) or Herm. 264/31 *ἰτέα salix*, etc.: it precedes a Bible-name batch (23 cd 34–9), followed immediately by *sambucus* 893, which begins the Hermeneumata batch (§ 28 fn. 3); cf. 392 n.

894. ? Vulg. Exod. 2: 3 *fiscellam scirpeam* (cf. 403)+Festus 422 *scirpus . . . unde tegetes fiunt*: Erf. *lebrae* could be either acc. sg. fem. or nom./ acc. pl.

895. ? *Ecl.* ii. 11 *alia serpyllumque herbas contudit olentis*: cf. AA S338 *serpyllum puleium uel alia siluatica*, Philox. SE 120 *serpyllum ἕρπυλλον εἶδος βοτάνης ἀγριοπράσιον*, both of which confuse *serpyllum* 'wild thyme' and *al(l)ium* 'garlic'. *bradaeleac* 'broad leek' (here only) is presumably the broad-leaved or winter leek (von Lindheim, 69); Erf. *sylenorum* may be a corruption of AA *siluatica* (cf. Brown, S73).

897. *sparuua*: 'calf of the leg'; here only, but cf. *spærlira*.

899. (23 ef 18) ? *Aen.* v. 54 *strueremque suis altaria donis*: *str(e)idae* 'strewed', pret. (subj. ?) of *strēgan* or *stregdan* (§ 59. 2 fn. 1), for *struere(m)* 'heap up' may be due to the similarity in sound, but cf. *bestregdan* 'cover' (TS 85)

900–1. (23 ef 19–20) ? *Aen.* i. 148–9 *cum saepe coorta est | seditio*, 159 *in secessu longo*: cf. Abol. SE 16 *seditio dissensio discordia*, 10 *secessu remoto loco*, and the adjacent items. Taken together, these glosses and 21–7 make impressive Virgil batches (§ 34).

902–3. (23 ef 21–2) ? *Aen.* i. 164 *siluis scaena coruscis*, 329 *nympharum sanguinis una*: cf. Servius, '*scaena*' *inumbratio, et dicta scaena ἀπὸ τῆς σκιᾶς*, '*sanguinis*' *generis*, and the following item, 23 ef 23 *sertis coronis* (? *Aen.* i. 417 *sertisque recentibus*, etc.). *cnēoris* 'generation, family' (§ 65. 4 fn. 3) is similarly used in the OE. *Genesis*, 2319–20 *monna gehwilc | þære cneorisse*, paraphrasing Gen. 17: 12 *omne masculum in generationibus uestris*.

904. *scina*: ? 'illusion' (953 n.).

905. ? Isidore, *Ety.* xii. 1/26 *porcorum pilos setas uocamus*: cf. Erf.II 1132 *setes byrsti saxonice*. 904, immediately preceding, belongs to an Isidore chapter in Leiden (cf. 953 n.).

906. *scripit haen* 'the hen scratches' (Schlutter, *Angl.* xix. 474) may reflect Plautus, *Aulularia* 467 *gallus gallinaceus . . . occepit scalpurrire ungulis*, cited by Nonius, 171/29 f., to illustrate *scalpurrire*. *scarpinat* 'scratches' may be a colloquial form from **scarpere* beside Classical *scalpere* (Schlutter), like *sarcinatum* 886 (n.) beside *sar(ci)tum*. *scripit* is 3rd sg. pres. of **screpan* 'scrape': cf. Cp. 1828 *scalpio scriopu* and *ascrefan* (*-pan*) 354, *ascrepaeni* 375.

907. ? Isidore, *Ety.* xix. 19/13 *scalprus . . . cuius diminutiuum scalpellus*: cf. 891 n. and Ld. 48/66 *scalpeum boor*, applied to Cassian viii.

NOTES   121

19/2 *contra calamum* . . . *contraue scalpellum*, where *scalpellum* = 'pen-knife' as in 883.

908. Ép. *staer* = ModE. dial. *stare* 'starling' (*EDD* v. 732); it also glosses *turdus* and *passer* (BT 909). Erf. *sterm*, Jun. *stærn* (i.e. **stearn*) = ModE. dial. *starn* 'starling' (Shetlands, Somerset).

909. *scorelus*: ? for *sc(i)uriolus*, dim. of *sciurus* 'squirrel' (911 n.), used as a bird-name. For *emer*, etc. cf. Ger. *Ammer* 'bunting' and ModE. *yellow-hammer* (= Ger. *Goldammer*).

910. *heringas* 'herrings' is also used for other salted or pickled fish in Jun. 181/3 *allec uel iairus uel taricius uel sardina hæring* and Ælfric, *Gloss.* 308/5 *taricus uel allec hærinc*: cf. *smeltas* 949 n.

911. *scira* = *sciurus* 'squirrel': cf. Polemius 543/11 *scirus*, Herm. 569/76 *meogalis* (? μυγάλη) *idest scuriolus. aqueorna* = Ger. *Eichorn* 'squirrel': cf. Werden I (Gallée, 338) *dispredulus* (? *dieperdulus) acuaerna uel sciron.*

913. ? Philox. ST 87 *striga* λωστυγων (? = ἀπὸ στυγῶν 'hateful things') καὶ γυνὴ φαρμακίς: cf. Festus 410 *strigem Graeci* στρίγγα *appellant, unde maleficis mulieribus nomen indutum est quas uolaticas etiam uocant*; Isidore, *Ety.* xi. 4/2 ('de transformatis') *quidam adserunt strigas ex hominibus fieri.*

913a. Orosius i. 3/4 (*lapides*) *conchis et ostreis scabros*: cf. Ld. 36/8 *scabros pisces sunt. lopostris* = Cp. *lopost(r)um*, d.p. of **lopost(e)r* 'lobster': cf. the Milan Bible gloss on Mark 1 : 16 *locustas, sunt locustæ marinæ quas lopustras uocant* (F. C. Robinson, *Philologica Pragensia*, viii (1965), 306–7). The gloss presumably refers to *conchis et ostreis*, which are shell-fish like lobsters.

914. *sullus*: ? for ὕλλος (Goetz, *CGL* vii. 315) or *suillus* (Brown, S108) 'ichneumenon'; the latter is confused with ἔνυδρις 'otter' in Isidore, *Ety.* xii. 2/37 (*enhydros*) *ichneumon Graece uocatus* . . . *de quo Dracontius ait 'praecidit suillus uim cuiuscumque ueneni'; suillus autem a saetis est nuncupatus.*

915–16. (24 ab 3, 5) ? Vulg. Esther 7 : 10 *suspensus est* . . . *in patibulo*, Exod. 8 : 16 *sint sciniphes in uniuersa terra Aegypti*: cf. the intervening item, 24 ab 4 *stibium unguentum de herbis* (? IV Reg. 9 : 30 *depinxit oculos suos stibio*, etc.). *anhaebd* 'raised up' beside *-hefed*, the lWS. wk. pret. part. of *hebban* (Campbell, §749), may represent an old Class III wk. verb corresponding to OHG. *enthabēn* (§ 86).

917–18. (24 ab 6–7) ? Herm. 430/7 βρίζα *secale*, 67 σίνεπιν (? -ηπυ) *sanapi*: Lindsay, *Corpus* S338–9, assigns both items to Phocas 427/22–3 *haec frumenta hordea, farra*, etc., where neither actually appears, presumably because 922 belongs to his Phocas batch (§ 29 fn. 2). *sinapi* 'mustard' is also confused with watercress in Erf.II 1133 *sinapiones cressa saxonice qui in aqua crescit* and 922. Erf. *cressa* may be Old High German, but cf. *tuuncressa* 676 n.

920. Cf. *Leechdoms*, i. 144/22–3 *þas wyrte þe man bulbis scillitici and oðrum naman glædene nemneþ*: *scilla* 'sea-leek' (*bulbus scilliticus*) is confused with *glædene* 'gladden' or 'sword-lily' (TS 473), another bulbous plant; *cf*. Br. 301/15 *scilla et gladiola glædene*.

923–4. (24 ab 14–15)? Herm. 368/7 *situla ὑδροφόρος*, 188/12 *psaros sturnus*, etc.: *dropfaag* 'speckled' (cf. *Leechdoms*, i. 242/14 *stillatus, ðæt is on ure geþeode dropfah*) = Gr. ψαρός adj., from ψάρ, ψαρός 'starling'. 924 begins a rather tenuous Hermeneumata batch (Lindsay, *Gloss*. 20).

925. *durhere*: 'door-fold' (also 1053); cf. Cl.III 517/8 *uualbas dureras*, Karlsruhe MS. Aug. 135 (SS i. 382/20) *fores dureras*. It may be related to *heorr(e)* 'hinge' (Meritt, *HG* 57) and *L. cardo*,? < IE. *kŏr- 'hang' (*AEW* 156, *IEW* 573).

926. Sweet, *OET*, prints Erf. *satul* as German, but cf. Cl.II *sotol*, Meritt, *PG* 361 *sella sotelas* (? *sa-*, ? *seo-*). OE *satol 'seat', presumably an ablaut variant of *setl*, would be an alternative interpretation of *sella*, like Ælfric's *sadol oððe setl*.

927. *scasa*:? for *scaria*, recorded as a plant-name in Lib. Gloss. SC 46 *scaria arbuscula spinosa ponum rubeum affert*, Herm. 546/28 *fisalida* (φυσαλίς 'nightshade') *iscaria*; both names are apparently identified with *sisca* 'thistle'(?) 973 in Dur. 301 *scasa uel scapa* (*-ra*?) *uel sisca*. For *eborthrotae* 'carline thistle' cf. 303 n.

928. *cliderme, -drinnae*:? otherwise unrecorded derivatives of *cladær-*116, *claedur* 218 'clatter'. Ép. *-me* has been taken as an error for *-ine* (Dahl, 153), but cf. *tyndirm* 562 n. and Kluge, §§ 152–3.

929. Erf. *ymbdringendum* may be an alternative interpretation: cf. *ymbþringan* 'throng round' (BT 1299).

931. Orosius ii. 9/10 *crasso et semigelato sanguine*: *halbclungni* 'half-congealed' (Schlutter, *Angl*. xlvii (1923), 47) is taken as 'shrunken together from cold' by TS *clingan*, but 'stuck together' would fit the context better; cf. p.p. *beclungen* (*Elene* 696 *clommum beclungen*) and *OED cling* 1 (but Cp. 1744 *rigentia forclingendu*, if from Gildas 29/10–12 *portenta . . . rigentia*, means 'stark').

933. *orfiermae*: pl. of *orfiermu* 'filth' (§ 80); cf. *orfirme* 'filthy' (BT 765) and *feormian* 'cleanse, polish'.

936. Cf. Abba SO 9 *sollicitat suadet*:? applied to Orosius ii. 10/1 *sollicitare*, 11 *sollicitate*, etc. (Lindsay, *Gloss*. 30).

939. *faet(h)maendi*: pres. part. of *fæðmian* 'embrace' as adj. 'curving, winding'; cf. Cl.III 486/4 *sinuosis ðæm fæðmlice* (Aldhelm, *VP* 230/8–9, *sinuosa laterum flexibus*). Its semantic development from *fæðm* 'embrace' parallels that of L. *sinuosus* from *sinus* 'bend, fold'.

941. Orosius vi. 4/6 *rex inter tumultus belli fuga lapsus, adiutus etiam beneficio sublustris noctis euasit*: *sublustris* = 'dim' rather than 'bright'

(cf. Trier 120va *sublustris luna parum lucens*), but the context could easily be misunderstood.

947. Orosius iv. 8/11 *molare saxum spinae eius incussum compagem totius corporis soluit*: *bodæi* translates *corporis*, not *spinae* 'spine'. *spina* 'body' in Aldhelm, *VC* 2852 *spinam lorica noscit defendere prosae* (contrasted with *capiti* in the preceding line), etc. may reflect this interpretation.

948. For *grōep(e)* 'ditch, drain' (TS 485) cf. infl. *feltungrepe* 'dung-pit', *Vercelli Homilies* (ed. M. Förster, Hamburg, 1932), vii. 96, and Förster's note.

949. *smeltas* 'smelts' is used generically for *sardas* 'anchovies', like *haeringas* for *sardinas* in 910 (n.): cf. Cl.II 264/4 *sardina smelt*.

950. *sandix* 'a plant producing scarlet dye' (cf. Servius, '*sandix*' *herba de qua sandicinus tinguitur color*, on *Ecl*. iv. 45 *sandix pascentis uestiet agnos*) is equated with *wād* 'woad' in Cl.III 513/14 *sandix wyrt uel wad* (on the same line of Virgil, quoted by Aldhelm, *VP* 316/9). Sievers, *ESt*. viii. 157, and Lübke, *Archiv*, xxxv. 388 fn. 2, take *uueard* in this gloss as a corruption of *wad* (? due to confusion with *wyrt*), but the Continuation of Philoxenus (*CGL* ii, p. xiii) *sandix herba apta tincturae quam uulgus uuarantiam uocant* suggests a Germanic plant-name, perhaps from IE. **wer-* 'twist' (*IEW* 1152 ff.), whence Gr. ῥάμνος, L. *uerbena*: 'warantia' is also recorded in Herm. 579/30 *uuarantia idest rubea*, etc. Schlutter's attempt to relate *weard* to *wād* as *meord* is related to *mēd* (*Angl*. xxx. 249–50) is a phonological impossibility, since *wād* = OHG. *weit* (Gmc. **waid-*).

951. ? Herm. 194/29 *eyrnia* (? φώρμα, *CGL* vii. 275) *soccu(s)*: cf. Abba SO 29, AA S540 *soccos calciolos uel furnia* (a lost Philoxenus gloss according to Laistner, *GL* v. 356).

952. Cf. Ld. 39/55 *scinici scinnenas* (*Canones Conciliorum Africanorum* 45 *scenicis atque histrionibus*): Leiden xxxix 'de dialogorum' contains several intruders from the *Canones* (cf. Hessels, *Leiden*, p. xl), e.g. 73 *autenticum auctorale* (= Ép. 3 ab 25). For *scinneras* 'illusionists, magicians' (?) cf. Cp. 746 *emaones* (? *Haemonides) scinneras* and *scinna* 'demon' (Sievers, *ESt*. viii. 157), *scin(n)* 'phantom' (Cl.III 530/34 *fantasma scin idem et nebulum*, Cp. 1831 *scenis scinnum*).

953. Cf. Ld. 27/5 ('de libro rotarum') *scina imitatio uel grina*. The 'Liber Rotarum' (Isidore's *De Natura Rerum*) offers no suitable context, but Brown, S96, points out that this and the following item in Leiden, 27/6 *explosi extincti*, belong to the *Vita Antonii* section of the related Codex Ambrosianus glossary, *CGL* v. 426/20, 27. *explosi extincti* (also Ld. xxviii 'in libro antonii' 14) glosses *Vit. Ant.* 26 *explosi . . . atque enecati prodigii*, and the present item may refer to the same passage or to *Vit. Ant.* 20 *daemonum ludos . . . expellens* (Brown, S219), in which case the lemma might represent a disguised OE. *scin* 'illusion'

(cf. 952 n.), and *grima* would = 'spectre' (cf. 646 n.). The two preceding items in Épinal–Erfurt, 24 ef 28–9 *sophismatum quaestionem(-um)*, *sputacum sputum*, correspond to Ld. 28/8, 22 (*Vit. Ant.* 46 *sophismatum*, 20 *sputaculum*).

955. *selma*: 'bedstead'; cf. OS. d.s. *selmon* (*Heliand* 4007). OE. *sealma, d.s. *sealman* (*Beowulf* 2460) is presumably an ablaut variant with IE. *o*.

962. Cf. Festus 411 *stagnum quidam dici putant quod in eo aqua perpetuo stet, ali quod is locus a Graecis στεγνός dicitur, quia bene contineat aquam*: *staeg* might be a corruption of Gr. στεγ(α)νός 'watertight' or an otherwise unrecorded cognate of *stig* 'enclosure' < IE. **stēi-* 'thicken, coagulate' (*IEW* 1010–11). For other suggestions see Schlutter, *Angl.* xix. 465; Holthausen, *AB* xxxii. 68.

964. *sceda*: ? for Gr. σχεδία 'cramp, holdfast' (= OE. *tēag* 'tie').

966. *segg* 'sea' is otherwise unrecorded, but cf. *gārsecg* 'ocean'.

967. *stilium*: ? for *stilus* 'style'; the interpretation suggests that a gloss like Lib. Gloss. ST 168 *stilo radio ut ueteres* was confused with a list of weaver's tools such as Herm. 322/3–4 κερκίς *radius*, ἄτρακτος *fusus*, but another obscure weaving term may be involved (cf. 300, 328).

968. *senon*: ? for σίσων 'rock parsley'; cf. WW 46 fn. 7 and Herm. 628/65 *sinonus idest siriacus uel mella*. *cearruccae, -icae* might then be taken as a corruption of *siriacus* or a derivative of Celt. **karruk-* 'rock', whence OE. *carr* (Förster, 126), rather than a word meaning 'carriage' from L. *carrūca* (*AEW* 45) or lL. *carrigium* (TS 120). ModE. *carriage* is a later borrowing, from Norman-French *cariage* 'carrying', first recorded in the fourteenth century (*OED*).

969. *smus*: ? for *sinus* 'churn'; cf. 25 ef 15 *sinum uas quo buterum conficitur* (= Affatim 567/33 *in quo*) and Cl.II 280/32 *sinum cyrin* (= Cp. 1867 *sinnum cirm*). *uuellyrgae* (here only) could then be explained as a derivative of *wealwian, wiellan* 'roll' (*IEW* 1142) + Gmc. **-uzjō(n)* as in *æmyrge* 'embers' (cf. Kluge, § 85).

970. Cf. Trier 122ᵛᵃ *splen splenis lien*, presumably from a grammatical source like Charisius 38/7 *lien* σπλήν *lienis* (Brown, S252).

971. *spatula* = 'mattress, pallet' in Felix of Crowland, *Vita Guthlaci* (ed. B. Colgrave, Cambridge, 1956), 19 *agresti de spatulo* (v.l. *spatula*) *surgens*, one of the exotic words noted by Colgrave (p. 17, fn. 1); it could be identical with *spatula* 'palm-branch' in Lev. 23: 40 *spatulasque palmarum*, possibly confused with *psiathium* 'mat', e.g. in Cassian v. 35 *incubantem psiathio*, whence Ld. 34/3 *spiathio mattae*, Cp. 1901 *spiato matte*. It is chronologically improbable that the *Vita Guthlaci*, written between 716 and 749, was itself the source of the present gloss, as Schlutter thought (*Angl.* xxxiv. 268, *Facs.* vii); his other supposed *Vita Guthlaci* gloss, 27 cd 4 *triuerunt scripserunt*, is a misinterpretation of Orosius i. 1/6 *se inter actores scriptoresque omnium*

otia negotiaque triuerunt, which Felix presumably borrowed from a glossary.

972. ? *HF* 314 *atritas hirti lustrant suistas porci* (Schlutter, *ESt.* xliii. 326): Lindsay, *Corpus* 209, reads **suistar* 'pigsty' after *bustar,* etc. (cf. Cp. *scadu* 'shelter'), but ÉE *suadu* 'paths' (also Cl.II *swapu*) and Cp. *scadu* both fit *HF suistas,* as Meritt points out (*FL* 3 G 1).

973. *sisca* (also Cp. 27 *scisca eoforprote*) is presumably a thistle-like plant (cf. 927 n.); Lindsay, *Corpus* S358, compares Ir. *seisg* 'sedge', BT 892 Sp. *sisca* 'sugar-cane'. *snidstreo* (*snið-* Cp. 1868) 'cut-straw' (also Cp. 13 *gacila*(?) *snithstreo*) would fit a type of thistle.

974. *salsa* (sc. *herba*) presumably = OE. *sūre* 'sorrel': cf. Br. 'nomina herbarum' 300/16 *salsa sure,* Bd. 72ᵃ *salsa idest sure.*

975. *sinfoniaca*: for *symphoniaca* (sc. *herba*) 'a variety of henbane' (Souter, 410).

976. *gundaesuelgiae*: 'groundsel', lit. 'pus-swallower', from *gund* 'pus, matter' + **swalgiōn* 'swallower' (cf. ON. *svelgr*), perhaps because it was used to cleanse wounds (*Leechdoms* i. 180/14–15); later OE. *grund-* is due to popular etymology.

977. Cf. Phocas 420/29 *hic codex codicis,* after which Jensen's edition (Venice, *c.* 1475) adds *latex, sorex.*

977a. Phocas 412/21 *hic scurra*: cf. Ld. 45/26 *histrio* (Phocas 413/8) *scurres* (? for *scurre saxonice*) *lees,* where Hessels, *Leiden* 123, reads *leas* 'false, deceitful'. *leuuis* also appears in Hl. C652 *cereuma* (*cel-*) . . . *idest leta cantatio lewisplega,* which Meritt, *FL* 4 D 35, interprets as *lēws*(*a*) 'misery' after Lib. Gloss. CE 186 *celeuma carmen quod nauigantes cantare solent siue quod supra mortuos uel ad lacu*(*m*) *cantatur*; but the present gloss suggests an adj. **lēawīs* 'scurrilous', which would fit Hl. *l*(*a*)*eta cantatio.*

978. *stilio* = *stellio* 'newt' (Phocas 413/8 *hic stellio*), which is also confused with *uespertilio* 'bat' (cf. 1098) in Erf. II 335/58 *uespertilio et* (*s*)*tilio unum est* and Karlsruhe MS. Aug. 99 (SS v. 162/14) *stelio uespertilio id calua s*(*a*)*uricis* (Lev. 11: 30 *stellio et lacerta*), KG 1111 *stelio hryremus* (Prov. 30: 28 *stellio manibus nititur*). Lindsay, *Corpus* 208–9, explains this confusion by assuming that *uespertilio* was added to the text of Phocas (cf. 977 n.), but it might well have arisen in a list of glosses on Leviticus 11, where *uespertilio* also occurs (19 *upupam quoque et uespertilionem*), which would better explain its wide currency.

  hreathamus: 'bat' (also 1098); cf. Ælfric, *Gloss.* 307/10 *hreremus* (= KG *hryremus,* with Kt. *y* for *ē*). *IEW* 623 derives *hrēatha*(*e*)- (§ 67 fn. 1) from IE. **kreut-* 'shake, move quickly', like *hrēre-* from the root of *hrōr, hrēran* (*AEW* 175).

979a. *pomo*: ? for OE. *fa*(*a*)*m*; cf. Jun. 178/12 *spuma fam.* Affatim 571/34 and Werden I (*CGL* i. 156) both read *spuma poma,* but there is no reason to connect foam with apples, so this is presumably a scribe's guess.

980. ? Abstr. SO 32 *sors condicio uel euentus*+37 *sortilegus qui dat sortem*: cf. 25 cd 28 *sortilegus qui dat sortem* and Erf.II 333/32, 34 *sortilegus qui dat sortem, sortem condicionem,* Cp. 1885–6 *sortem wyrd condicionem, sortilegos hlytan.*

981. Cf. Erf.II 331/30 *scebus tortus strambus,* Abol. SC 25 *strabo qui unum oculum tortum habet*: *sceol(h)egi* = 'cross-eyed, squinting' (also Cl.III 524/19 *strabos sceolige*); cf. *sceolh-eagede* 'strabo, strabus' (BT 829).

982. Cf. Erf.II 331/45 *serum liquor casei,* Affatim 566/10 *care(i)* (? *Geo.* iii. 406 *sero pingui*).

983. ? Abstr. TRU 6 *trux dirus aut terribilis*+AA T496 *trux palpitans* (v.l. *palpitat*) *in quacumque causa.*

984. Vulg. Gen. 37: 3 *fecitque ei tunicam polymitam*: cf. St. Gall MS. 295 (SS v. 145/2–5) *polimeta propter ipsas imagines rotundas quæ fuerunt in ea, siquidem a rotunditate polum dicitur.*

985–6. (26 cd 27–8) ? Virgil glosses on *Geo.* iii. 106 *uerbere torto* (cf. 1051), *Aen.* vii. 28 *in lento luctantur marmore tonsae* (= Abol. TO 16 *tonsae remi*), attracted to the Bible batch by Vulg. Jud. 16: 9 *filum de stuppae tortum putamine.* Lindsay, *Gloss.* 34, assigned 985 to Jer. 37/20 *torta panis,* for which see 993 n.

988. ? Vulg. Lev. 19: 36 *statera iusta*+Abstr. TRU 4 *trutina statera*: cf. St. Gall MS. 295 (SS v. 245/4–5) *statera trutina* and the following item, 26 ef 5 *tolor* (*stolo*?) *hasta* (= Abstr. TO 3).

989. Vulg. IV Reg. 25: 14 *ollas quoque . . . et trullas*: *crucae* 'crock' (cf. 1056) translates *ollas* rather than *trullas* 'ladles'. Lindsay assigned this item to Amos 7: 7 *trulla caementarii* (1022 n.)!

990. *georuuierdid*: 'shamed, disgraced'; cf. Cl.III 508/12 *traducta georwyrðed* (Aldhelm, *VP* 297/18 *nominis praesagio traducta*) and *orweorð, orwierðu* 'shame, disgrace' (BT 768).

991. ? *Geo.* ii. 469 *frigida Tempe*: cf. Lib. Gloss. TE 167–8 *Tempe locus in T(h)essalia amenissimus nemorosusque, locus quidam frigidas* (*-us*) *nebulis semper tectus in ualle cuius cacumina saxosa et alta multum.* For *scaedugeardas* 'abodes of shade' cf. the poetic compounds *ēador-geard* 'abode of veins' (*Andreas* 1181), *windgeard* 'abode of winds' (*Beowulf* 1224). SS ii. 18/53 *in tempis in umbraculis quod dicimus louba* ('arbours'), on Aldhelm, *VC* 273 *manet in tempis paradisi hactenus heros,* may derive from the Virgil gloss, since there is nothing in the Aldhelm passage to suggest shade (cf. Meritt, *FL* 4 A 19).

993. ? Vulg. Exod. 29: 23 (*tolles*) *tortamque panis unius, crustulam conspersam oleo*: cf. Karlsruhe MS. Aug. 248 (SS v. 155/50–2) *crustula*

panis est oleo conspersus, in medio concauus, et tortus. coecil 'little cake'
(= ME. kechel) translates crustulam (cf. 288) rather than tortam 'loaf'.

994. troc(h)leis: 'pulleys'; cf. Lib. Gloss. TR 428 trocliae uocatae
quod rotulas habeant per quas funes trahuntur, trochos enim graece rota
dicitur (Isidore, Ety. xix. 2/10+per . . . trahuntur). If stricilum =
Mod.E strickle (so BT 929), it would be a mere guess, like Ld. 4/74
trogleis hlædræ ('ladders'), but there may have been a parallel formation
meaning 'pulley': cf. BT strīcan III 'move, run'.

995. triplia = Gr. τρύβλιον 'cup, bowl' (? on Mt. 26: 23, where the
Greek text reads ἐν τῷ τρυβλίῳ, Vulg. in paropside): cf. Abavus TR 39
trublium parapside and 996 immediately following.

996. ? Vulg. IV Reg. 22: 6 tignariis uidelicet et caementariis (cf. 995 n.)
or Isidore, Ety. xix. 19/2 sarcitector . . . idem et tignarius, quia tectoria
lignis inducit (Jun. 111/41 sarcitector uel tignarius hrofwyrhta): hrofuuyrhta 'roof-maker' (these glosses only) may reflect sarcitector.

997. ? A combination of Virgil glosses, on Aen. i. 505 media testudine
templi, ii. 441 acta testudine, etc., and Geo. ii. 463 uarios . . . pulchra
testudine postis: cf. the preceding items, 26 ef 28–9 triuere tornauere,
timpana tecta uehiculorum (Geo. ii. 444 hinc radios triuere rotis, hinc
tympana plaustris). Brown, T72, points out that bord(t)haca = 'ceiling',
not 'shield-covering, phalanx' (OET 470, TS 101): cf. Cl.I 432/2
latrariis (laqueariis) bordþacan. fænucæ (-ȳce) 'mud-turtle' translates
Aldhelm, Aenig. 100/37 testudo palustris (cf. 611–12 n.) in Riddles 40/
70–1 me is snægl swiftra, snelra regnwyrm | ond fenyce fore hreðre; it may
have been coined to gloss Aldhelm, as Brown suggests, or, conversely,
Aldhelm's phrase may have been coined from it (cf. 881, 947 nn.).

998. ? Philox. TE 133 tessera κύβος σύμβολον σύντονον: cf. 6–7,
178, and Aldhelm, Metr. 164/9 tessera, 21 simbolum; quadrangulum
'square' (Souter, 336) may translate Gr. κύβος. For tasol 'cube, die'
cf. Cp. tasul and Cl.III 526/5 tesellum tæslum (Aldhelm, VC 1337
ruit . . . tessellis fabrica fractis) beside *tesul in Ld. 35/35 tesseras
tesulas (Rufinus v. 18/11 ad tesseras ludit), Maxims I 183 teoselum
weorpeð. *tesul = L. tessella with altered suffix; tasul may be due to
analogy with pairs like hacole/hecile (cf. Pogatscher, § 107), *tæsl to tæfl,
etc. (§ 68 fn. 2, p. lxxix).

999. tertiana (sc. febris) = 'tertian ague'; le(n)ctinadl, lit. 'spring
disease' because it comes from cold, wet weather in the spring
(Geldner, i. 9), is used for fever generally in Jun. 11/31 tipus (typhus)
lengtenadl and Leechdoms, ii. 12/28 wiþ lenctenadle, þæt is fefer.

999a. Sweet, Facs. 26 f 34, prints distulis as OE., presumably for d.p.
ðist(e)lum with L. -is as in ebhatis 854, lopostris 913a, but omits it from
OET. Lindsay, Corpus T86, reads distulisti or distollis, glossing Aen.
iv. 271 qua spe . . . teris otia.

1000. ? Aldhelm, VP 237/10 tubo cataractisque uorantibus: cf. the

Brussels Aldhelm gloss, *ZfdA* ix. 418/61–2 *tubo . . . of þryh uel þeotan* and 232.

1001. *tragelafus* (*-phus*) 'wild goat, antelope' (Vulg. Deut. 14: 5) is confused with *platyceros* 'deer' in Eucherius 157/21–2 *tragelaphus in Deuteronomio platoceros* (v.l. *platoceruus*), *id est cornibus latis*: cf. the Continuation of Philoxenus (*CGL* ii, pp. xi–xii) *tragelafus bestia quam elcum uocamus.* Since Eucherius was a source of Abstrusa (cf. 440 n.), this may be a lost item from the latter.

1003. ? Vulg. I Reg. 13: 21 *acies . . . ligonum et tridentium*: *maettoc* translates *ligonum* (cf. 565, 586), not *tridentium* 'forks'.

1006. *tremulus*: ? 'aspen' (Souter, 428); cf. Plinius Secundus, *De re medica* (*Medici Antiqui*, ed. Aldus (Venice, 1547), 164–211), ii. 12 *corticem de tremulo.*

1008. *toculus* (*ta-*): ? for **taxulus* (Goetz, *CGL* vii. 329), dim. of *taxo* 'meles' (Souter, 413); cf. Herm. 320/11–12 ὕστριξ ('hedgehog') *melis,* ὕστρυξ *taxus,* Jun. 119/2 *taxus uel meles . . . broc.*

1009. *trifulus* (*tru-*) = Ld. *truffulus* 'glib, talkative'(?): cf. It. *truffa* 'deceit', *truffaldino* 'buffoon' (Glogger, ii. 78). For *felospraeci* 'babbling, loquacious' cf. the OE. *Regula Pastoralis* (ed. Sweet, London, 1871–2), 281/14 *se felaspræcea . . . ðe simle on oferspræce syngað.*

1009a. *tabula*: for *tubulus* 'pipe'; cf. Cp., Ld. *tubolo,* Cl.II *tubulo* and Herm. 365/44 *tubus* σωλήν, Cyrillus 338/42 καπνοῦχος ('stove-pipe') *tubulus.* For *fala* 'tube, pipe'(?) cf. ON. *falr* 'tubulus hastilis cui spiculum inseritur' (Lidén, *ESt.* xxxviii. 337–9): Lidén takes *fala* as dat. sg. of **falhuz,* but a wk. n.s.m. **falhōn* would also be possible (ON. *falr* is a masc. *i*-noun).

1010. *terrebellus* (*tere-*): dim. of *terebra* 'auger' (Herm. 23/37, etc.); cf. Cl.II 273/12–13 *terebellus lynibor. nāfogar* is the etymon of ModE. *auger.*

1011. *turdella*: 'mistletoe-thrush'; cf. Isidore, *Ety.* xii. 7/71 *turdela quasi maior turdus cuius stercore uiscum generare putatur.* ModE. *throstle* is the song-thrush, but *throstle-cock* is used dialectally for the male missel-thrush (*OED*).

1012. *tilaris*: ? for **titilaris,* related to *titiare* 'chirp' (L. Diefenbacher, *Glossarium latino-germanicum mediae et infimae aetatis* (Frankfurt, 1857), 583), or **terralis,* from *terra,* like *terraneola* 'lark' (Thompson, in Lindsay, *Corpus* 210), or Ἴτυλος (cf. *Odyssey* xix. 522).

1013. *scric* 'shrike' (here only in OE.) may have been used generically for any bird having a shrill cry (*OED*). Erf. *screc* could be an ablaut variant like ON. *skrækr* sb. 'shriek'.

1014. *wand* 'mole' is otherwise unrecorded, but cf. *uuandaeuuiorpae* 1045.

1015. *tincti* = *tinca* 'tench' (Polemius 544/18): cf. Jun. 180/36 *tinca sliw* and OHG. *slīo*, Ger. *Schleie* 'tench'.

1017. *baest* 'bast' is otherwise unrecorded in Old English.

1018–19. (27 ab 19–20)? Phocas 415/15 *hic tuber*, 425/10 *toreuma toreumatis* (Lindsay, *Gloss.* 120): cf. the next item, 27 ab 21 *tubicen qui cum tuba canit* (? Phocas 415/4 *hic tubicen*). *tumor* also glosses *tuber* in Peterhouse MS. 2.4.6 (§ 9 fn. 3) 596/5–6 *tugor tumor*, *tuber tumor*, where *tugor* = 'swelling' (OE. *āswollaen*): the ultimate source may have been Philoxenus (cf. Lindsay, *Gloss.* 80–1). For *asuollaen* sb. 'swelling' (Gmc. **-ainiz*) cf. Go. *ufswalleins* 'arrogance' (Gmc. **-īniz*) and *spa(e)raen* 460 n. *toreum(a)* = Gr. τόρευμα 'whirling round' (cf. Euripides, *Hercules Furens* 977–8 κίονος κύκλῳ | τόρευμα δεινὸν ποδός, where modern editors read πόρευμα or τόρνευμα), hence OE. *eduella* 'vortex, vertigo' (1068 n.).

1020. Cf. Charisius 61/29 ff. *hoc tapete dicimus...pluraliter haec tapetia, tapetium, tapetibus* (citing *Aen.* ix. 325 *tapetibus altis*), *sed et hoc tapetum ... pluraliter haec tapeta*, etc. and Ld. 42/2 *tapetibus rihum*: ? a grammatical item, attracted to the Hermeneumata batch by *tabetum* 1023, or a Virgil gloss, e.g. on *Aen.* ix. 358 *pulchrosque tapetas*, like 1021 immediately following. *ry(h)ae* (also 1080–1) = later OE. *rēowe*, *rūwe* 'rug' (BT 792, 805), with analogical interchange of *h* and *w* (Campbell, § 412 fn. 3).

1021. ? *Aen.* iii. 289 *considere transtris*: cf. Abstr. TRA 2 *tra(n)stri(s) sedilia nautarum*. For *ses* 'seat' cf. *Beowulf* 2717 *on sesse*, 2756 *bi sesse*.

1022. *trulla*: 'trowel'; cf. Ld. 17/5 *trulla ferrum latum unde parietes liment* (Vulg. Amos 7: 7 *trulla caementarii*) and OE. *scofl*.

1023. *tabetum*: ? for *tapetum* 'carpet, tapestry' (Herm. 473/48 *tapetum* τάπης); if so, *bred* = **bræ(g)d* 'woven fabric' (cf. ON. *bragð* 'embroidered figure'), whence ModE. *braid* (Schlutter, *Angl.* xxvi (1903), 304).

1024. *tin*: ? for **ti(g)n* 'beam, timber', from L. *tignum* (*AEW* 349), or **tin(n)* 'spike', cognate with OHG. *zinna* 'pinna' (BT 988); if the latter, it would be an ablaut variant of *tān* 'twig' (IE. **d(e)in-* Flasdieck, 74).

1025. *tenticum*: ? for *tendicula* 'springe, snare'; cf. Abstr. TE 27 *tendicula quasi retia quae tenditur leporibus aut auibus. sprindil* (**springðila-* ?) is otherwise unrecorded, but cf. ModE. *springe*, *springle* (*OED*) and dial. *sprindle* (*EDD* v. 692).

1026. *telum*: ? for *telam*; cf. Ld. 13/34 *telam orditus inuuerpan uuep* (Vulg. Is. 25: 7 *telam quam orditus est*). If so, the Bible gloss presumably displaced Herm. 20/49 ἱστός *tela*, etc. (cf. 1085).

1027. *felofearth*: 'paunch' (Schlutter, *Angl.* xxx. 254–5); cf. LG 66 *toracem feoluferð* (Lorica 73), Hl. C723 *centumcilio idest pellis* (? = *centumpellio*) *feleferð uel centumpellis*, and SS iii. 321/32 *omasus uilevart*.

1028. *titule* might be a mistake for *tutela* 'protection, fence' (Herm.

474/4 *tutila* ἕρκος), but cf. *titulum* 'protective trench before a camp' (Souter, 422). For *gata loc* 'goat pen' cf. *scipa loc* 'ouile ouium', Li. Jn. 10: 1.

1029. *tudicla*: 'stirrer' (Herm. 20/53 τορινη (-ύνη) *tudicula*, etc.). *thuerae* (? = Cp. *thuaere*) is otherwise unrecorded, but cf. ON. *þvara* 'pot-stick, stirrer'; Schlutter, *Angl.* li (1927), 161–2, takes it as the imperative of *þweran* 'beat', which would be *þwer*, not *þwere*!

1031. *baanrift*: 'legging'; cf. *bān(ge)beorg* 'greave' (TS 62) and OHG./ON. *bein* 'leg'.

1032. *talumbus*: ? for Gr. βούφθαλμον 'ox-eye'; cf. Herm. 536/64 *bubtalmon idest oculo bobis siue maxilla rubeo*. *giscaduuyrt* 'dividing-plant' (here only) would fit a species of clover.

1035. Orosius i. 8/12 *semet . . . accipiendae stipitis taxatione uendiderant*: *raedinnae* therefore = 'valuation, price'; cf. *gafolrǣdenn* 'tax, tribute' (BT 358).

1036. Orosius iii. 1/3 *si non . . . belli tabuisset intentio*: indic. *asuand* would be correct if *si non* were construed as *butan* 'except that' (TS *butan* C II (1)).

1037. ? A gloss on Orosius iii. 15/3 *in tantum abusus est*: cf. Cyrillus 300/46 ἐν τοσούτῳ . . . *in tanto tantisper*.

1038. *scildinnae*: 'protection'; cf. *scildung*, *(ge)scildnes* (BT 437, 831).

1039. *triqua(d)rum* = *triquetrum* 'three-cornered, triangular' (Orosius i. 2/1 *maiores nostri orbem totius terrae . . . triquetrum* (v.l. *triquadrum*) *statuere*); Aldhelm borrows it in *VP* 247/15–16 *triquadra mundi latitudo*, etc. For *ðrifedor* 'three-cornered' cf. *fiðer-* in *fiðerfēte* 'quadrupes', etc. and Go. *fidur-* (*AEW* 103).

1040. *uuinaern*: lit. 'house where wine is drunk' (cf. g.s. *winærnes*, *Beowulf* 654), hence 'tavern'.

1041. *biginan*, *-genan*: 'beyond'; here only, but cf. *begeondan* prep. and adv. (BT 78, TS 72).

1042. Orosius iv. 20/20 *Antiochus, quamuis Thermopylas occupasset quarum munimine tutior . . . fieret, tamen . . . superatus*: *faestin* 'stronghold' may be due to *munimine*, or to a misunderstanding of the passage as a whole. Lindsay, *Corpus* 209, traces Hisperic *termopilas* 'cliffs' in *HF* 408 *fluctiuagaque scropheas uacillant æquora in termopilas*, etc. to this gloss, but the fact that Thermopylae is in the mountains may be sufficient for the name to be used generically for 'cliffs', as *tempe* was for shady places (991 n.).

anstiga(n): 'defiles'; cf. *Beowulf* 1409–10 *stige nearwe,* | *enge anpaðas, uncuð gelad* (= *Exodus* 58). Erf. *anstiga* is presumably the pl. of *stīg* f. 'path' which alternates with *anpaðas* in the *Beowulf* passage; BT 919 takes Ép. *-stigan* as the pl. of a wk. **stiga* or **stige*, but it may be the scribe's misinterpretation of a stroke above *-a* in the exemplar: cf. Erf. *hindbergen* 69 beside Ép. *-beriæ*.

1043a. ? A corruption of *tacta a tangi* (Lindsay, *Gloss.* 31) or of *Geo.* iii. 502 *ad tactum tractanti*: the Erfurt scribe presumably took *tangi* as OE. (Schlutter, *JGP* v. 143), perhaps as some form of *getang, getenge* 'touching', for which he substituted the OHG. equivalent.

1044. Orosius v. 11/3 (*locustarum*) *tabida et putrefacta congeries*: the OE. plurals correspond to the sense of the Latin collective. Ép. *aduinendanan* may represent *aduinendan and* (cf. Erf. *ond*).

1045. *uuandaeuuiorpae*: 'mole'; cf. *wand* 1014 and ModE. *moldwarp*.

1048. *droco* is surely L. *draco* (so Erf.), for which the scribes of Corpus and Werden II substituted their vernacular equivalents *draca* and *dracho*, presumably independently.

1050. ? *Geo.* i. 238–9 *uia secta per ambas* (sc. *zonas*) | *obliquus qua se signorum uerteret ordo*: cf. Ld. 27/28 *in georgicis ubi de cultra agri cecinit uia secta iringaes uuec* (Isidore, *Nat. Rer.* 10/1 has (*zonas*) *Vergilius in Georgicis ostendit dicens* (i. 233) '*quinque tenent caelum zonae*') and 1051. *uia secta* refers to the band of the Zodiac (*ordo signorum*), which intersects the two temperate zones; it was confused by some with the Milky Way according to Isidore, *Ety.* iii. 46 *lacteus circulus uia est quae in sphaera uidetur, a candore dicta quia alba est ; quam aliqui dicunt uiam esse qua circuit sol et ex splendore ipsius transitu ita lucere*.

iringaes uueg: 'the Milky Way' (ON. *Irings vegr*); Widukind, *Res gestae saxonicae* (*MGH Scriptores* iii. 416–67), i. 13, says it was named after Iring, who slew Theoderic the Frank and escaped *uiam ferro faciens*, adding: *si qua fides his dictis adhibeatur penes lectorem est; mirari tamen non possumus in tantum famam praeualuisse ut Iringis nomine quem ita uocitant lacteus coeli circulus usque in praesens sit notatus*. A mythological explanation identifying Iring with the god Heimdallr was proposed by Grimm, i. 358 ff. (also Michiels, 20), but the name may have been a literary epithet, like the *heiti* of ON. poetry which require a Snorri to explain them, possibly derived from the lay on which Widukind's own account was based.

1051. ? *Geo.* iii. 106 *illi instant uerbere torto*: cf. 985–6 and 1050 immediately preceding.

1052. ? *Aen.* iv. 131 *lato uenabula ferro*, etc.: cf. 1050–1 two lines above. For *eborspreot* 'boar-spear' cf. Cl.III 489/24 *uenabulis eoforspreotum* and *Beowulf* 1437–8 *eoferspreotum* | *heorohocyhtum*.

1053. ? Vulg. IV Reg. 18: 16 *confregit Ezechias ualuas templi*, etc.: cf. the preceding item, 28 ab 11 *uascitas interitus* (? Is. 51: 19 *uastitas et contritio*) and § 32 fn. 3.

1054. *auis* may be a mistake for *ouis*, on Vulg. Deut. 18: 3 *siue bouem siue ouem immolauerint, dabunt sacerdoti armum et uentriculum*. For *cesol* 'gullet'(?) cf. 457 n

1055. ? Abol. BA 5 *bascuadas concas aureas*: cf. Cp. 561 *conca mundleu*, Hl. C1888 *conca idest coclea mundleow. mundleu(u)* 'hand-basin' corresponds to ON. *munnlaug* (cf. ON. *laug* 'hot bath'), but it can hardly be borrowed from the Norse word as Holthausen assumes (*AEW* 200), since, chronology apart, the two forms are phonologically distinct, *-laug* being from IE. **lou-kā* (*IEW* 692), while *-leu(u)* represents **-lēaw* (§ 40) from WGmc. **lauwō* or **lauwa-* (cf. L. *lauō*, etc.)

1057. 1099a follows the *ab*-order batch in Erfurt, but the Épinal order is confirmed by Corpus.

1058. ? Abol. VE 25 *uestibulum primum regiae domus aditum*: cf. the preceding item, 28 ab 19 *uligo (h)umor terrae* (? Abstr. UL 11 *uligo humor uel limus). cebærtuun* (? *cæber-* § 38) = 'courtyard' (Cl.I 351/17 *atrium cafertun*, etc.): for the first element cf. L. *capreoli* 'cross-pieces of timber joining and supporting larger beams' and lL. *caprones* 'tigna' (DuCange). Schlutter, *ESt.* xliv (1912), 462, suggests Celtic transmission, comparing Cornish *keber* 'rafter', but the normal OE. form is *cafer-* (TS 115), which would correspond to lL. **cabr-*. Schlutter explains the compound as describing an enclosure (*tūn*) fenced with wattles.

1059. *uoluola*: ? for *conuoluolus* (Pliny xxi. 23 *est flos non dissimilis (lilio) herba quam conuoluolum uocant, nascens per fructeta). wi(d)u-windae* and *uuidouuindae* 348 correspond formally to *wiðewind(e)* 'bindweed', ModE. *with(y)wind*, with *d* for medial *ð* (§ 70), but this spelling is ambiguous, since the first element might also = *widu/wudu* 'wood' (§ 56) as in Cp. *uuduuuinde*, ModE. *woodwind*: cf. Erf. *uuidu-bindae* and *uuidubindlae* 559.

1060–1. (28 ab 22–3) ? *Aen.* vii. 237 *praeferimus manibus uittas, Geo.* iii. 494 *uituli uulgo moriuntur in herbis*: cf. Servius, '*uulgo*' *ubique passim. thuelan* 'fillets' (also Cp. 1991 *taenis ðuaelum*, Napier 53/26 *infula thuælæ*) is presumably identical with OHG. *duahila/duehila* 'towel' from **þwahilō*: cf. *thuachl* 326 n. *o(e)ghuuaer = æghwær*, a weakly stressed form like *oeghuuelci* 709 (n.).

1062. ? Orosius ii. 5/1 *uxoris suae fratres, Vitellios iuuenes*: cf. Ld. 36/22 *uiteleos iuuenes. suehoras* and *sueor* 1099 would then = OHG. *sweher* 'brother-in-law' (so Hessels, *Leiden* 213); but the normal meaning of OE. *sweor* is 'father-in-law' (BT 949), so there may still have been confusion with *uitricus* (cf. 1070) as Goetz suggested (*CGL* vii. 410): it was apparently confused with *geswiria* 'cousin' (214 n.) in Cp. 552 *consobrinus sueor*, etc. (BT *swēor* II).

1063. *uscidae = uiscid(a)e* 'tough(ly)': cf. Ld. 40/1 *uiscide ineluctabile idest maius luctu* (an 'inverted' gloss on Gildas 27/2–3 *indelebile insipientiae pondus et leuitatis ineluctabile* according to Hessels, *Leiden* 240–1) and Æthelwald, *Carm. Rhythm.* ii. 75–6 *erant iuncti bitumine | germanitatis uiscide* (MS. *uscide*). Hessels connects the Épinal–Erfurt gloss with Leiden, but Æthelwald's *uscide* (for g.s. *uiscidae* with *germanitatis*) could have been misinterpreted as an adverb.

tholicae (*tōh-*): 'toughly'; BT 1000 infers an adj. *tōhlic, but the adverb may have been formed directly from adj. *tōh* with the adverbial suffix *-līce*, like *heardlīce* from *heard*, etc. (Campbell, § 664).

1064. *uenetum*: 'blue-green' (Herm. 174/9 *callinos* (καλλάϊνος 'turquoise') *uenetus*); *geolu* may be due to Isidore, *Ety.* xix. 17/13 f., where *uenetum* without an interpretation follows *ochra*.

1065. *uatilla* = *batilla* 'fire-shovels' (Vulg. Num. 4: 14 *urcinos et batilla*): cf. St. Gall MS. Aug. 295 (SS v. 165/1–4) *uatilla idest pala ferrea ad focum similis uasis quibus aquæ de nauibus proiciuntur*. Peterhouse MS. 2.4.6 (§ 9 fn. 3) 596/20 *uatillum arula ferrum est ad focum*. For *gloedscofl* (here only) cf. Cl.I 358/16 *batilla fyrscofl*.

1066. *uulohum*: d.p. of *wlōh* 'hem, fringe' (BT 1261); its association with *uillis* 'fleeces' may come from a misinterpretation of *Aen.* i. 702 *tonsisque ferunt mantelia uillis*.

1067. *unibrellas* = 'umbrellas' (cf. Herm. 326/63 σκιάδ(ε)ιον *umbrella*), but the interpretation suggests confusion with Vulg. Ez. 31: 6 *cumque extendisset* umbram *suam, in ramis eius fecerunt nidos omnia uolatilia caeli . . . et sub* umbraculo *illius habitabat coetus gentium plurimarum*.

stalu: pl. of *stæl* 'place' (BT 907); here only in the literal sense (= BT *steall* III).

1068. *edwalla*: 'turning, whirling' (cf. Cp. 908 *fortex* (*u-*) *edwelle* and 1019), whence 'whirlpool' (TS 179) like L. *uertex, uortex*. The form *edwalla* (*-ae* ?) beside *-welle* (also Napier 53/11 *carybdis eduuallæ*) is presumably a pure *ōn*-stem beside the more common *jōn*-stem type.

1069–70. (28 ab 34–5) ? Orosius i. 8/5 *scabiem et uitiliginem*, i. 12/9 *Oedipum . . . uitricum suum*: cf. Ld. 36/10 *uiti(li)ginem bleci* (= Cp. 2117), 14 *uitricum steuffeder*. *blectha* = 'white leprosy' (cf. Cp., Ld. *bleci* and *blecthrustfel* 139), from *blaiki+*-ipōn* like *clewepa* 'scalpurigo', *spiwepa, gicþa*, etc. (Osthoff, *ESt.* xxxii (1908), 184).

1071–2. (28 ab 38–9) ? Vulg. Sap. 12: 8 *misisti . . . uespas*, Prov. 13: 15 *bona doctrina . . . in itinere contemptorum uorago*, where *uorago* = 'pitfall', an obvious meaning of *hool* not recorded in BT 549, TS 557. OE. *wæps* is recorded only in glosses on *uespa* and *crabro* (255).

1073. *amprae*: 'swelling' (Schlutter, *Angl.* xix. 493); cf. Cp. 595 *cocilus* (*-licus* 303 n.) *ampre* and ModE. *amper* 'tumour, blemish' (*OED*). OET 470 and TS 36 confuse it with the plant-name *ampre* 'dock, sorrel' (Ger. *Ampfer*), as in Br. 300/15 *rodinaps ompre docce*.

1074. *uerberatorium*: 'whisk'; otherwise unrecorded, but cf. *uerberator* 'whipper' (Souter, 439). For *cort(h)r* 'stirrer, whisk' (?) cf. IE. **ger-* 'twist' (*AEW* 58) and Gmc. *-ðra* (Kluge, § 93(b)).

1075. *uerberatrum* (*-tum*): 'curds'; sc. *lac* as in *lac tudiclatum* (605 n.).

1077a. *uerbenaca*: 'vervain', equated with house-leek in Herm. 596/16 *uerminaca erba semperuiridis florem habens albam*, etc., with fennel in

Bd. 72^{vc} *uermenaca idest esprote* (cf. 450 n.). *sura* presumably = *sūre* 'sorrel' (cf. 63, 974).

1078. *ueneria* 'galingale' (Herm. 579/22 *ueneria idest acorum*, etc.) may have been equated with *speruuuyrt* 'elecampane' (Br. 299/7 *innule campane sperewyrt*) because the root of each was used as a confection, like ginger. Erf. *smeruuuyrt* (also Cp., etc.) = 'birthwort' (*Leechdoms* i. 14/8 *herba aristolochia þæt ys smerowyrt*, etc.), presumably an error of the archetype corrected in Épinal.

1080–1. *uill(os)a*: 'rough cloth, rug', the etymon of OF. *velous* (DuCange); cf. Herm. 269/40–1 μαλλωτός *uillosus*, μονόμαλλον *uillosum* (in a list of bed-clothes) and *uellus* 'fleece'.

1082. ? *Ecl.* i. 25 *quantum lenta solent inter uiburna cupressi*: *uuiduuuindae* 'bindweed' (cf. 1059 n.) may be a misinterpretation of *lenta* 'pliant, tough' (581, 614).

1085. *uicium*: ? for *uiciam*; cf. Ld. 13/35 *uiciam pisas agrestes idest fugles beane* (Is. 28: 25 *ponet . . . uiciam in finibus suis*). If so, the Bible gloss presumably displaced Herm. 299/61 βικίον *uicia*, etc. (cf. 1026, 1067 and notes); Ld 47/33 *uicias* could be a conflation of *uiciam* and *pisas*. For *fuglaes bean* 'vetch' cf. OHG. *vogalchrut* (SS i. 606/40) and ModE. *chick-pea*.

1086. *uaricat* means 'transgress' in Philox. VA 56 *uaricat* ὑπερβαίνει and Abstr. VA 19 *uaricat diuertit uel ambulat*, Erf. II 334/43 *ambulat uel deflectitur* (VL Deut. 9: 6 *uaricasti*), but *stridit* 'straddles' (= Middle Dutch *strīden AEW* 326) interprets it literally.

1087. *spadan*: 'spades'; cf. the wk. n.s.m. *spada* in Jun. 106/12 beside the str. fem. *spadu* (Campbell, § 619. 4).

1088. *uirecta*: 'lawns, meadows' (*Aen.* vi. 638 *locos laetos et amoena uirecta*); cf. Servius, '*amoena uirecta*' *uirentia*, Abol. VI 14 *uirecta uiridia*, and Isidore, *Ety.* xvii. 6/2 *uirecta ubi uirgultae nouellae et uirentes*. OET 511, TS 138 take *quicae* as 'couch-grass' (cf. 464 n.), but the adj. pl. *cwice* (sc. *mǣdwa?*), translating *uiridia* or *uirentia*, may have been intended. Napier 2/28 *fructeta i. arbusta cwicas* (Aldhelm, *VP* 245/16 *nequitiae gramina et elationis fructeta*), cited in TS, is misleading since *cwicas* translates *gramina*, not *fructeta*: cf. the Brussels Aldhelm gloss, *ZfdA* ix. 433/30 *gramina cuicas* and 638 n.

1090. ? Herm. 276/54 ἐγγύη *uadimonium fideiussio*, etc.: 'as its fusion with the foregoing in Cp. . . . shows, transposed from the preceding batch' (Brown, U65). The latter ended with *uirecta*, immediately before *uericundiæ concesserim*.

1092. Cf. Erf.II 336/2 *uibrat diregit uel micat* (? applied to Orosius iv. 2/5 *malleolos . . . uibrarent*): *borættit*, presumably a frequentative from *beran* like *brocdaettendi* 735 from *bregdan*, could mean either 'brandish' or 'shimmer' (cf. 434), like *brogdettan* (TS 107).

1093. Orosius iv. 6/38 *inimici ueritatis* . . . *qui uitioso oculo haec uident*: *unþyctgi* is therefore 'jaundiced, evil', not 'weak' (*OET* 571, BT 1133).

1094. *blegnae*: 'blister'; for the wk. form cf. Jun. 152/36 *carbunculus seo blace b(l)egne* beside str. *blegen* (BT 109, TS 97).

1096. *agnettae*: pret. of **āgnettan* 'appropriate, usurp', a frequentative like *boraettit* 1092 n.; cf. *āgnian* in the same sense (TS III).

1097. *uris*: d.p. of *urus* 'aurochs' (? *Geo*. iii. 532–3 *uris | imparibus ductos alta ad donaria currus*); cf. Servius, *Geo*. ii. 374 '*siluestres uri*' *boues agrestes qui in Piranaeo monte nascuntur inter Gallias et Hispanias posito; sunt autem exceptis elephantis maiores animalibus ceteris, dicti* '*uri*' *ἀπὸ τῶν ὀρέων id est a montibus*. For OE. *ūr* cf. the *Rune Poem* 4 ff.:

> (ur) byþ anmod and oferhyrned,
> felafrecne deor, feohteþ mid hornum,
> mære morstapa; þat is modig wuht!

1098. ? Vulg. Lev. 11 : 19 *upupam quoque et uespertilionem*: its position suggests that this is another of the Leviticus glosses which stand at the end of the *a*-order sections under A, B, H, M, and S (see notes to 119, 161, 497, 666, and 978).

1099. *uetellus*: ? a corruption of *Vitellius* (Orosius ii. 5/1 *Vitellios iuuenes*); cf. *uitelli* 1062.

1100. *yripeon* = Gr. αἱρέσεων 'heresies', from Rufinus ii. 13/5 *auctoribus diuersarum haereseon* (Sievers, *ESt*. viii. 157; Lindsay, *Corpus* Y6); *heresearum* is therefore L. *haeresiarum*, and *heresearu* 'war-stratagem' (*OET* 483) is a ghost-word.

INDEX OF LEMMATA

Words found in both texts are given as they appear in Épinal; references to sources not confirmed by Lindsay's batches (§§ 28–33) are indicated by a query.

abies 37. Herm. 26/34, etc.
abilina (auellana) 15. Herm. 185/14, etc.
ablata 104 n.
abortus 80. Orosius iv. 2/2 *extorti abortus.*
absint(h)ium 66. Herm. 317/39, etc.
accearium (aci-) 49. Herm. 325/39 *acciarium.* § 27.
accetum (acci-) 105. Orosius iv. 8/16 *accitum . . . Hamilcarem.*
accitulium 63. *See* acitelum, actula.
ac(c)ega 41 n. § 27.
acerabulus 33 n. § 27.
achalantis (acalanthis) 26 n.
acinum 69. Herm. 27/10, etc.
acitelum 60 n.
aconita 23 n.
acrifolus (-ium) 34 n. § 27.
acris 71 n.
a(u)ctionabatur 86 n.
actuaris 87 n.
actula 59 n.
acu *see* pictus acu.
adclinis 96. Orosius vii. 22/4 *adclinis humi.*
addicauit (abd-) 73 n.
addictus 52 n.
ade(m)pta 102 n.
ade(m)pto 100. Orosius iv. 2/2 *adempto . . . ordine.*
ad expensas 93 n.
adgrediuntur 76. Orosius iii. 1/16.
adlitus (hal-) 89. Orosius iv. 8/11 *halitu . . . pestifero.*
adnitentibus 78. Orosius v. 16/23 *seruis adnitentibus.*
adqueue (atque) 98. Orosius. i 11/3, *etc.*
adridente 85. Orosius v. 18/15 *hac spe adridente.*

adrogantissime 112. Orosius vii. 25/9 *arrogantissime exceptus.*
adsaeculam (-seculam) 101. Orosius i. 12/5 *adseculam deorum.*
adsessore 95 n.
adstipulatus 74. Orosius ii. 11/6 *adstipulatus est.*
aegit (eg-) 90. Orosius: *see* in transmigratione(m).
aere alieno 115 n.
aesculus 22 n.
aestiuo *see* in aestiuo caenaculi.
aestuaria 107. Orosius vi. 8/10 *per . . . aestuaria.*
affectui 109 n.
affricus 118 n.
agrestes 99 n.
alacris 77. Orosius ii. 8/9 *alacri satis . . . expeditione.*
alapiosa 116a n. § 14.
alba spina 19. ? Herm.: *see* spina alba.
albipedius 55 n.
albugo 12. Vulg. Tob. 6: 9 *oculos in quibus fuerit albugo,* etc.
alchior (-cyon) 25 n.
alea 6 n.
aleator 7 n.
alga 47, 58. Herm. 17/30, etc. § 27.
alieno *see* aere alieno.
alites 116b n.
alium 16. Herm. 16/35, etc.
almeta (aln-) 46 n. § 27.
alneum 36 n.
alnus 35. Herm. 264/49. § 27.
alternantium 75. Orosius i. 12/7 *alternantium malorum recursus.*
altrinsecus 51 n. § 35.
alumn(a)e 108. Orosius vii. 27/7 *alumnae putredinis.* § 35.
alum(i)nis 115a n.

alueus 88. Orosius i. 2/33 *in alueum* (*Nili*), etc.
aluiolum (alue-) 57 n.
aluium (-eum) 56. Herm. 20/51, etc.
ambila 64 n.
amentis 106 n.
amiculo 84. Orosius v. 9/2 *detracto amiculo.* § 35.
amites 1 n., 11 n.
anate 116 n.
anconos (-niscos) 50a n.
andeda 4 n.
aneta 17 n.
anet(h)um 21 n.
anguens 68 n.
annua 94 n.
ansa 3a n.
anser 117 n.
antempna (-mna) 111. Orosius vi. 8/14 *antemnarum armamenta.*
antiae 28. ? Abstr. AN 55 *antiae capilli quos mulieres promissos in capite componunt.* § 35.
anticipationem *see* per anticipationem.
anxius 79. Orosius vii. 30/6 *periculo anxius.*
apiastrum 20. Herm. 359/77, etc.
apio 24 n.
aplustra 14 n. § 33.
apparatione (-itione) 97 n. § 14.
appetitus 82. Orosius i. prol. 4 *proprios appetitus.*
aquilae 92. Orosius vii. 6/7 *neque aquilae ornari neque conuelli . . . signa . . . potuerunt.*
aquilium 43 n. § 27.
arbatae (-tabae) 70 n.
arcessitus 103. Orosius iii. 4/5 *arcessitus est,* etc. § 11.
arcibus 110. Orosius vii. 37/6 *hoc . . . Romanis arcibus imminente.*
arcister 114 n.
ardea 42. Herm. 258/3, etc. § 27.
areoli (-ae) 30 n.
argella(-illa) 48. Herm. 564/74 (*g*)*ipsa i. argilla.* § 27.
argillus 3 n.
arguti(a)e 53 n.
ariolatus 10 n.
armilausia 18 n.
armos (-us) 67. Herm. 87/32, etc.

arniglosa (ἀρνόγλωσσον) 65. Herm., e.g. 549/31 *arneglosa.*
arpa 40 n. § 27.
(h)arpago 29 n.
arrius (uarius) 61. Herm. 22/16 *uarium,* etc.
arula 5 n.
ascella (axil-) 38. Herm. 248/6.
ascolonium 62 n.
asfaltum 54 n.
asilo 27 n.
asses scorteas (-os) 31 n.
astu 83. Orosius, e.g. ii. 7/2 *astu . . . instructa.* § 35.
atflarat (adf-) 32. Abstr. AD 58 *adflarat adspirauerat.*
atticus 119 n.
aucapatione (aucu-) 72 n.
aul(a)ea 9 n.
auriculum 39 n., 44 n. § 27.
auriola 45 n.
(h)auserunt 113. Orosius iii. 1/5 *Asiam . . . hauserunt.*
ausus 81. Orosius ii. 6/8 *ausus est,* etc.
auehit 91 n.
auellanus (abellana) 50. Herm. 428/16 *abellanum.* § 27.
axedones 8 n.
axis 13. Vulg. III Reg. 7: 30 *axes aerei,* etc.
axungia 2 n.

bacidones 123 n.
bagula 127 n.
ballena (balaena) 146. Herm. 437/30 *ballenae.*
ballista 136 n.
balus 121 n.
ba(l)sis 128 n.
basterna 137 n.
batat 149 n.
battuitum (-tutum) 140. ? Philox. BA 53 battutum τυπτηθέν ἀναιδέ(s).
beacita 125 n.
beneficium 135. Orosius vii. 6/3 *fidei . . . beneficium.*
berna 156 n.
berruca (ue-) 154. Herm., 312/1, etc.
berrus (uerres) 151. Herm., e.g. 432/51.
beta 132 n.
bicoca 124 n.

bile 141 n.
bis *see* coccum bis tinctum.
bitiligo 139 n.
bitumen 133 n.
blattis 145. ? *Geo.* iv. 243 *lucifugis* . . .
    blattis.
blitum 144 n. Herm. 317/20 βλίτον
    blitum, etc.
bobellum (bou-) 129 n.
bona 157 n.
boreus (-as) 162. ? Herm. 11/19
    βορέας *aquilo*, etc.
bothona 121a n. § 17.
bothonicula 122 n.
bradigabo 131 n.
branciae 158. ? Vulg. Tob. 6: 4
    apprehende branciam eius (Ld.
    20/3.)
bratium (brac-) 130 n.
briensis 126 n.
broel 147 n.
broelarius 148 n.
bruchus 150. ? Vulg.: *see* 119 n.
bruncus 152 n.
bubalis 160 n. ? Vulg. Amos 6: 13
    numquid . . . arari potest in bubalis.
bubu (-o) 142. Herm. 18/2, etc.
buccula 120 n.
bucina 143 n. § 14.
buculus (-ccula) 153. Herm. 368/48
    buccula ὀμφαλός.
bufo (-bo) 161 n.
bulla 134 n.
burrum 159. ? Philox. BU 17 *burrum*
    ξανθόν πυρρόν.
byrseus 155. Herm., e.g. 307/24
    βυρσεύς *corarius.* § 11.
byssum 138. Abol. BI 2 *byssum*
    sericum tortum.

c(r)abro 255. Herm. 90/14 *gabro*, etc.
caccabum 168. ? Vulg. I Reg. 2: 14
    in cacabum.
cacomicamus (-anus) 268 n.
cados 170. Vulg. Lk. 16: 6 *centum*
    cados olei.
caenaculi *see* in aestiuo caenaculi.
caepa 286. ? Herm. 359/52, etc.
calcesta 254 n.
calciculium 263 n.
calculus 165 n., 172 n.
caldica 300 n.

calear (-car) 226 n.
calentes 206 n.
callis *see* deuia callis.
cal(a)metum 302. *See* 289 n.
caloma(u)cus 269 n.
calta 250 n.
camellea 183 n.
camis(i)a 244. Herm. 272/61.
campos (com-) 273 n.
camos (cauma) 274 n.
cancer 258. Herm. 89/31, etc.
canis lingua 184. ? Herm.: *see*
    cynoglossa.
cantarus (-tharis) 310. ? Herm. 441/7.
cant(h)i 292. Vulg. III Reg. 7: 33
    canthi et modioli.
capitium 239 n.
cappa 245 n., 301. ? Isidore, *Ety.*
    xix. 31/3 *cappa . . . ornamentum*
    capitis est.
capsis 231 n.
captu *see* pro captu.
ca(ta)ractis 232 n.
carbo 304. Phocas 413/15 *hic Carbo.*
carbunculus 175. Rufinus ix. 8/1
    his (*ulceribus*) *quae dicuntur car-*
    bunculi.
cardella (-duelis) 266. Herm., e.g.
    319/51 ἀκανθυλλος (-*ís*) *cardelus.*
carduelis 309. ? Herm., e.g. 319/52
    ἀστραγαλῖνος *cardelus.*
carduus 271. Herm. 317/19, etc.
carectum 290. Vulg. Job 8: 11 (*num-*
    quid potest) *crescere carectum sine*
    aqua, etc.
cariscus 238 n.
carix (-ex) 251. ? Phocas 420/31 f. *haec*
    carex caricis (Ld. 46/26).
carpassini (-basini) 298 n. § 32.
carpella 283 n.
cartamo (-damum) 279 n.
cartellus (-tallus) 173. ? Abstr. CA
    118 *cartallum canistrum.*
cartilaga (-o) 174 n.
cartilago grece 312 n.
cassidele (-ile) 297. Vulg. Tob. 8: 2
    de cassidili suo. § 32.
castania (-ea) 249. Herm. 88/13
    castania, etc.
castorius 272 n.
catasta 229 n.
caulem 215 n.

caumeuniae 219 n.
caustella (clu-) 220 n.
cautere 177. Rufinus viii. 12/10
  oculis . . . cautere adustis.
cauterium 227 n.
cefalus (ceph-) 270. Herm. 355/36
  capito κέφαλος, etc.
c(a)elatum 176 n.
celox 230 n.
c(a)ementum 289a. Vulg. Gen. 11: 3
  bitumen pro caemento, etc. § 32.
cemetum 289 n.
censores 197. Orosius iv. 21/4
  *censores theatrum . . . construi
  censuerunt.*
cerasius (-sus) 237. Herm. 26/20
  cerasium, etc.
cercylus 180 n. ? Abstr. CE 52 *cercilus nauicula.*
c(a)erefolium 246 n.
ceruical 296. Vulg., e.g. Mk. 4: 38
  super ceruical dormiens.
c(a)erula 221 n.
cer(u)us 233 n.
chaos 181 n.
cicad(a)e 256 n.
cicer 284. Herm. 26/60, etc.
ciconia 259. Herm. 187/63, etc.
cicuta 185. Herm. 261/40 κώνειον
  cicuta, etc.; 248 n.
circinno (-ino) 293. Vulg. Is. 44: 13
  in circino tornauit illud.
circius 311. ? Herm. 84/59, etc.
ciscillus 262 n. ? Herm. 23/23
  acisclum.
citropodes (chyt-) 171. Vulg. Lev.
  11: 35 *siue clibani siue chytro-
  podes.*
clabatum (clau-) 228 n.
clatrum 224 n.
claua 209. Orosius v. 9/2 *ictu
  clauae.*
clibosum (cliu-) 166 n. ? Abstr.
  CI 69 *cliuosum inequale.* § 11.
clunis 216 n.
coaluissent 198 n.
coccum bis tinctum 169. Vulg. Exod.
  25: 4 *purpuram coccumque bis
  tinctum, etc.*
coc(h)leae 217. ? Isidore, *Ety.* xii.
  6/48 *cochleae uero per diminu-
  tionem quasi conchleae.*

coc(h)leas 267. Herm. 554/22 *bicani
  (βυκάνη) idest cocleas,* etc.
cofinus (coph-) 222 n.
colicum 303 n.
colobium 167 n.
colobostrum (colost-) 261 n. ? Herm.
  288/23 πρωτόγαλα *colostra.*
colonus 163 n.
color 235 n.
colus 306. Phocas 420/8 *haec colus
  coli.*
commeatos (-us) 188. Orosius v.
  15/7 *frumentum et alios commeatus.*
commentariensis 223 n.
commentis 278. ? Rufinus vi. 31/1
  commentis et fraudibus, etc.
commissuras 291. Vulg. I Par. 22: 3
  ferrum . . . ad commissuras, etc. § 32
concedam 200 n.
concesserim 204. Orosius: *see uericundiæ* concesserim.
concidit 195. Orosius iv. 3/3 *uiscerum
  suorum partem Romana seueritas
  concidit.*
condiciones 212. Orosius iv. 9/1 *cum
  . . . condiciones pacis audissent.*
condidit 191. Orosius ii. 3/1 *Baby-
  lonam . . . condidit.*
confugione *see de confugione.*
confussione (confusi-) 203. Orosius
  i. prol. 13 *confusione pressi, etc.*
coniectura 190. Orosius i. 3/4 *ex
  indicio et coniectura lapidum.*
coniurati 210. Orosius vii. 35/21
  coniurati ueniunt ad classica uenti.
conlatio 187 n.
conpar 205 n.
conparantem 196. Orosius iv. 16/13
  *Hasdrubalem . . . exercitum con-
  parantem.*
conpetum (-pitum) 307. ? Orosius i.
  prol. 9 *ex locorum agrestium
  compitis et pagis.*
conquilium (conchyl-) 182. ? Isidore,
  Ety. xii. 6/50 *murex cochlea est
  maris . . . quae alio nomine con-
  chilium nominatur.*
constipuisse (constup-) 207 n.
consubrinus (consob-) 214 n.
contemptum (-im) 186. Orosius v.
  4/6 *ita omnes metu perculit ut . . .
  ipse contemptim et otiosus abscederet.*

contentus 276 n.
contis 211. Orosius vi. 8/13 *falces contis praefixas*, etc.
contribulus 164. ? Abstr. CO 22 *contribuli consanguinei.*
contubernalis 189. Orosius v. 15/22 *uirgines . . . contubernalibus corruptoris sui exposuit.*
contumax 202. Orosius i. 1/9 *hominem autem qui . . . infirmus et contumax est.*
conuenio 210 n.
conuexum 179 n.
conuicta 194. Orosius iv. 2/8 *uirgo . . . conuicta damnataque incesti.*
conuincens 192. Orosius iii. 10/2 *exstitente quadam ancilla indice et conuincente.*
corax (κόραξ) 285. Herm. 89/67 *corax coruus*, etc.
corben (-m) 193. Orosius iv. 15/1 *in corbem.*
corimbus (corym-) 247 n.
cornacula 241 n.
cornicula 240. Herm. 17/41, etc.
cornix 308. ? Herm. 89/68, etc.
co(ho)rs 281 n.
coruis (-bis) 305. Phocas 418/29 *hic corbis.*
corylus 236 n.
cospis (cu-) 225 n.
cotizat 178 n.
cox (-s) 294 n.
coxa 295 n.
crabro 275. Herm., e.g. 319/57.
crebrat (cri-) 213 n.
crepacula 218 n.
crocus 242. Herm. 273/33, etc.
crudesceret *see* in dies crudesceret.
crus 299 n.
crustulla (-ula) 288. Vulg. Exod. 29: 2 *crustulam absque frumento*, etc.
cu(r)culio 257. Herm. 188/54 *gorgulio.*
cuculus 265. Herm. 17/56, etc.
cucumis 253 n.
cucuzata 264 n. § 16.
culcites (-ta) 243. Herm. 22/4, etc.
culinia (-ina) 287 n. § 32.
culix (-ex) 277. Herm. 18/11, etc.
culmus 252. Herm. 261/45, etc.
cummi (gu-) 282 n.

cuniculos 199. Orosius vi. 11/28 *cuniculos perfodiebant.*
cupa 260. Herm. 366/64.
curia *see* in curia.
curiositas 208. Orosius i. 10/17 *curiositate turbantur.*
cyat(h)us 234 n.
cynoglossa (sos) 280. Herm. 620/2 *cino- glosa id est lingua canis.*
cyprinus 178a n.

dalaturae 321 n.
damina (-mma) 346a n. Phocas 412/20 *masculini generis . . . damma.*
debita pensio 336. Orosius v. 1/12 *debita pensio seruitutis.*
decidens (-cedens) 335. Orosius iv. 8/9 *cum uictrici classe decedens.*
de confugione (-endi) 329. Orosius v. 2/1 *de confugiendi statione securo.*
decrepita 322. ? Gregory, *Dial.* iv. 52 *usque ad aetatem decrepitam* (Ld. 39/30).
deditio 337. Orosius v. 7/12 *deditionem sui obtulerunt.*
defecit (-ficit) 344 n.
defectura 334 n.
defructum (-frutum) 314 n.
dehisciat (-it) 343 n.
deliberatio 331. Orosius ii. 17/1 *magna . . . deliberatio fuit.*
delibutus 325 n.
delicatis 332. Orosius iv. prol. 6 *delicatis istis et querulis nostris concedo.*
delumentum 326 n. § 11.
deperuntur (defer-) 342 n. § 11.
depoline 328 n.
desidebat (diss-) 323 n.
detractauit (detrec-) 339 n.
detriturigine 345 n.
deuia callis 340 n.
deuotaturus 318 n.
dies *see* in dies crudesceret.
difficile 338. Orosius iv. 2/5 *non difficile . . . retorserunt.*
digitalium munusculorum 346 n.
disceptant 330. Orosius v. 16/2 *inter se . . . disceptant.*
disparuit 333 n.
distabueret (-unt) 341. Orosius,

e.g. ii. 10/11 *labore, fame, ac metu*
. . . *distabuerunt.*
ditor 327. ? Aldhelm, *Aenig.* 53/5
hac gaza ditor.
dodrans 316 n.
dolatum 315. ? Vulg. III Reg. 6: 7
lapidibus dolatis, etc.
dos 324. ? Phocas 419/4 *haec dos.*
dracontia 345a n.
dromidarius (dromed-) 320 n. § 11.
dromidus 319 n.
dulcis sapa 313 n.
dumus 317 n.

ebor (-ur) 351. Vulg., e.g. II Par. 9:
21 *ebur et simias et pauos.*
ebulum 393 n. Herm. 555/6, etc.
echinus 376 n.
echo 347 n.
(h)edera 348 n., 392 n.
efetidem (ependyten) 390 n. § 11.
effosis 364. Orosius i. 13/2 *effosis
Graeciae luminibus*, etc.
egerere 354 n.
egesta 375 n.
(a)egre 363. Orosius iii. 1/3 *quam
aegre et misere . . . gesserint.*
electirum (-trum) 386 n.
elegio (elo-) 374. Orosius v. 15/5
(*Romam*) *elogio notauit.*
elleborus 388 n.
eluderet 356. Orosius iii. 1/6 *ut
pondus geminae congressionis
eluderet.*
emlemma (emblema) 378 n.
emolomentum (emolu-) 360. Orosius
iii. 13/1 *utili emolumento* (v.l.
emolomento).
empticius (-tius) 349 n.
emunctoria 382 n.
enunum (aenum) 350. ? Vulg. Lev.
6: 28 *uas aeneum*, etc.
ephilenticus (epilept-) 383 n.
epimemia (-enia) 389 n.
eptafolium 387 n.
eptasyllon (ἑπτάφυλλον) 379. ? Herm.
538/47 *eptefilon idest septefolium*,
etc. § 11.
erimio 352 n.
erpica 395 n.
erpicarius 396 n.

(a)erugo 397 n.
(a)esculus 391 n.
est *see* interceptum est.
et *see* pr(a)es et uas, tabida et putrefacta.
etiam *see* quin etiam.
e uertigo (uestigio) 370 n. § 11.
euiscerata 362 n.
exactio 394. ? Gregory, *Dial.* iv. 30
exactionem canonis egerat (Ld. 39/
27).
exagium 380 n.
exaltauit (-halauit) 361. Orosius v.
11/3 *odorem . . . exhalauit.*
exauctorauit 371 n.
excolat 384 n.
exercitus (-iis) 357. Orosius iii. 2/14
pacificisque exercitiis.
ex falange (e pha-) 369 n.
exito (-u) 367. Orosius i. 6/6 *de . . .
exitu Sodomorum et Gomorraeorum.*
exoleuerunt 368. Orosius ii. 18/5
*multo interiectu saeculorum exoleue-
runt.*
expediam 396a n.
expedierunt (-ant) 366. Orosius vii.
35/13 *acies . . . expedierant.*
expeditio 373 n.
expendisse 353 n.; 365. Orosius ii.
4/10 *noxam poena . . . expendisse.*
expensas *see* ad expensas.
expilatam 372. Orosius vi. 3/2
(*Sinopen*) *expilatam atque incensam.*
exposito 359. Orosius i. 4/7 *filio . . .
impie exposito.*
exta 385 n.
extale 381 n.
extentera (exen-) 377 n.
extorti 358. Orosius iv. 2/2 *extorti
abortus.*
exundauit 355. Orosius vii. 35/12
collectis . . . uiribus exundauit.

facitiae (face-) 398. ? Abstr. FA 11
facetias iocos.
facundia 444. ? Abol. FA 5 *facundia
eloquentia.*
fagus 417. Herm. 428/55.
falange *see* ex falange.
falcastrum 449 n.
falces 430 n.
famfaluca 426 n., 447 n.

fa(u)onius 452 n.
fasces 441 n.
fasianus (pha-) 424. Herm 188/19 *fasianus*, etc.
fastidium 406. Abol. FA 31 *fastidium nausia*.
fax 407 n.
fellitat 455 n.
fenicia (phoe-) 411 n.
fenus 435 n.
feriatis 443 n.
ferinum (-a) 415 n.
ferula 450. ? Herm. 192/15, etc.
fiber 399. ? Herm. 248/43.
fibrae 405 n.
fibrans (ui-) 434. Orosius i. 10/10 *toto aere uibrante*.
fibula 408 n., 410 n.
ficetula (ficed-) 422 n.
filix 420. Herm. 301/7.
finiculus (feniculum) 451. ? Herm., e.g. 265/44 *feniculus*.
fiscilla (-ella) 403 n.
fitilium (uitellus) 429 n.
flabanus 431 n.
flabum (flau-) 432 n.
flamma 445 n.
flauum 404 n.
flegmata 412 n.
floccus 448. ? Herm., e.g. 323/61.
flustra 400 n.
focaria *see* petra focaria.
foederatas 436. ? Orosius ii. 4/2 *raptas Sabinas improbis nuptiis confoederatas*.
follis 454 n.
forfices 401 n.
fornicem 442 n.
fornix 453 n.
fouit (-et) 402. Rufinus iii. 23/8 *adulescentem . . . fouet*.
fraga 421 n.
fragor 446. ? Herm. 434/65.
framea 440 n.
fraximus (-nus) 416. Herm. 264/43, etc.
fringella (-illa) 423. Herm. 17/46 *fringuillus*, etc.
frixum 414. Herm. 183/60, etc.
frons 438 n.
frugus 413. ? Abol. FU 36 *frugi parci an auari*.

fucus 430a n.
fulix 419 n.
funestauere 437. Orosius iv. 13/3 *ciuitatem sacrilegis sacrificiis . . . funestauere*.
funestissima 439 n.
fungus 427 n.
furca 409 n.
furfures 428 n.
furunc(ul)us 425 n.
furuum 433 n.
fusarius 418 n.

galbalacrum 476 n.
galla 466 n.
galmaria 471 n.
galmilla 486 n.
galmum 477 n.
garbas 468 n.
gelum 485. Phocas 414/14 *hoc . . . gelu*.
genas 482 n.
genisculas 469a n.
genistae (-a) 465. Herm. 428/70 μυριζ(-ίκη) *genestum*.
genuino 480. Orosius vi. 1/1 *genuino fauore*.
genuinum 487 n.
gibbus 459 n.
giluus 458 n., 483 n.
gipsus (γύψος) 460. ? Herm. 190/23 *gypsos gypsum*, etc.
gladiatores 481. Orosius, e.g. vi. 17/4 *Roma . . . gladiatores suos edidit*.
gladiolum (-us) 463. ? Herm., e.g. 579/43 *xifio(n) gladiolum*.
glarea 461 n.
glaucum 473. Herm. 272/19 χλοερόν *uiride glaucum*.
glis 470 n. ? Phocas 412/2 *glos* (v.l. *glis*) (Ld. 45/6).
globus 478. Orosius, e.g. v. 18/3 *globus ignis . . . emicuit*.
glomer 472. ? Herm. *glomus* 93/3, etc.; *glomera* 369/32.
glumula 462 n.
glus 475 n. ? Herm. 449/79 *glutus*, etc.
gracilis 474. Herm. 13/42, etc.
grallus 469 n. Herm. 435/51 κολεος (κολοιός) *grallus*.
gramen 464 n.
grassator 467. Herm. 372/78 *grassator* λωποδύτης, etc.

grece *see* cartilago grece, olor grece.
gregariorum 479 n.
gurgulio 456. Phocas 413/8 *curculio*
(v.l. *gurgulio*).
gurgulio (curc-) 484. Phocas: *see*
gurgulio 456.
gurgustium 457 n.

habitudines 492 n.
hastilia 489. Orosius v. 15/16 *hastilia*
telorum.
hebesceret 490 n.
hebitauit (hebe-) 491. Orosius, e.g. v.
16/15 *splendor hebetauit* (v.l. *habi-*
tauit).
hebitatus (hebe-) 488. Orosius v. 5/
15 *timoris amentia . . . hebetatus.*
hibiscum 496. ? Abstr. HI 6 *hibisco*
herba mollis.
hirundo 498. Vulg. Jer. 8: 7 *turtur*
et hirundo.
hiulca 495 n.
horno 494. Abol. HO 16 *horno hoc*
anno.
horodius (her-) 497 n.
hyadas 493 n.

ibices 560 n.
ignarium 556 n.
ilium 505. ? Herm. 248/36, etc.
in aestiuo caenaculi (-o) 553. ? Vulg.
Jud. 3: 20 (*rex*) *sedebat . . . in*
aestiuo coenaculo.
incitamenta 516. ? Orosius ii. 11/9
cum . . . incitamenta dixisset.
incom(m)odum 522 n.
increpitans 508 n.
incuba (-o) 558 n.
in curia 549. Orosius iv. 16/19 *senatus*
in curia, etc.
index 544. Orosius iii. 10/2 *ancilla*
indice et conuincente, etc.
in dies crudesceret 529. Orosius iii.
4/5 *cum pestilentia in dies crudesce-*
ret.
indigestae 536 n.
indi(c)tas 542 n.
indruticans 499 n.
industria 527. Orosius iv. 20/17
equitum industria liberatus est.
iners 531 n.
infandum 512 n.

infestus 510 n.
infici 543 n.
infractus 540 n.
infri(gi)dat 561 n. ? Abstr. AL 14
alget infrigidat.
ingratus 514 n.
ingruerit 520. Vulg. Exod. 1: 10 *si*
ingruerit contra nos bellum.
inhians 500. Rufinus ii. 17/17
dapibus inhiantes.
inlecebris 513 n.
inlectus 533. Orosius iii. 8/4 *ad hoc*
. . . inlecti sunt.
inlex 509 n.
inluuies secundarum 501 n.
in mimo 550. Orosius vi. 22/4 *cum . . .*
pronunciatum esset in mimo.
innitentes 537. Orosius v. 18/20
armis suis innitentes. § 11.
inopimum 541 n.
inpactæ 535. Orosius v. 9/2 *ictu*
clauae cerebro inpactae.
inpendebat 528. Orosius iii. 1/13
suscepto negotio duplicem curam in-
pendebat.
inpendebatur 525 n.
inpetigo 502 n.
inpostorem 545. ? Gregory, *Dial.* iii.
14 *uerbo rustico impostorem coepit*
clamare.
inprobus 519. Vulg. Ecclus. 13: 13
ne improbus sis.
inpulsore 539 n.
inritatus 515. ? Vulg. II Mac. 14: 27
criminationibus irritatus.
insimulatione 524 n.
insolens 548. Orosius: *see* insolesceret.
insolesceret 538. Orosius vi. 18/17
in eos insolens per quos ut insole-
sceret agebatur.
instites (-is) 506 n.
interamen 504. ? Herm. 176/53
interanea, etc.
intercaeptum (-ceptum) 511 n.
intercapido (-edo) 547. Orosius iv.
2/1 *consumitur morborum malis*
intercapedo bellorum.
interceptum est 523 n.
interlitam 534. Orosius i. 4/5 *Aethio-*
piam . . . sanguine interlitam.
interpellari 526 n.

inter primores 546. Orosius iv. 10/5
  dum . . . pugnam inter primores ciet,
  etc.
interuentu 532. Orosius iii. 23/66
  interuentu . . . fidei Christianae,
  etc.
intestinum 503. ? Herm. 13/1
  intestina, etc.
intexunt 507. ? Aen. ii. 16 intexunt
  abiete costas.
intractabilis 521 n.
in transmigratione(m) 530. Orosius
  iii. 7/6 in transmigrationem egit.
intula (inu-) 518. ? Herm. 317/13,
  etc.
inuisus 552. Orosius vii. 29/11 inuisus cunctis.
inuoluco 559 n.
inuolucus (-crum) 557 n.
iota 516a n.
isca 562 n.
isic 555 n.
iungetum (iunc-) 517 n.
iurisperiti 551. Orosius vii. 16/5
  Iuliani iuris periti scelere. . . occisus
  est.
iuuar (iub-) 554 n.

labarum 567 n.
lacerna 572. ? Abstr. LA 12 lacerna
  stola uel uestis.
lacessit 580 n.
lacessitus 593. ? Orosius vii. 17/2
  bellis lacessitus.
lactuca 601 n.
lacuna 609 n.
lacunar 597 n. Phocas 415/9 hoc
  lacunar. § 29.
lagoena 584 n.
lagones (li-) 565 n.
lanx 607. Phocas 412/2. § 29.
lapat(h)ium 606. Herm., e.g. 567/11
  lapatium.
lappa 613 n.
laquear 595. Phocas 415/9 hoc laquear.
larbula (laruu-) 569 n.
laris (-us) 610 n.
laxhe 573a n.
lebes 563. ? Vulg. Ezech. 11 : 3 haec
  est lebes.
lectidiclatum 605 n.
legula(li-) 582 n.

lembum (li-) 583 n.
lendina 590 n.
lenoc(in)ium 579. Orosius i. 12/5
  familiarii lenocinio.
lenta 581 n.
lentum uimen 614. ? Abol. LE 33
  lentum uimen molle uirgultum.
lepor 564 n.
lepus leporis 608. Phocas 419/14 hic
  lepus leporis.
leuir 598. Phocas 416/3 hic . . .
  leuir.
lexiua (li-) 591. Herm. 470/49, etc.
liburnices 566 n.
liciatorium 602 n.
licidus 604 n.
lien 594. Phocas 415/1 hic lien lienis.
ligones 586 n. ? Herm. 325/68 ligo,
  etc.
ligustrum 615 n.
lihargum 603 n. ? Isidore: see 39 n.
limax 611 n.
lingua see canis lingua.
liquentes 578. ? Sedulius, Carm.
  Pasch. ii. 159–60 sanctoque liquentes
  | corpore mundauit latices.
litterari see ludi litterari.
lituus 571 n.
liuida toxica 576 n.
lodix 600. Phocas 421/8 haec lodix.
lolium 599 n.
lucanica 588. Herm., e.g. 379/53
  lucanicae.
lucius 587 n.
luculentum (-iam) 574. Orosius v.
  15/2 propter opimam scriptorum
  luculentiam.
ludaris 596 n.
ludi litterari 577 n.
lumbare 573. ? Vulg. Jer. 13 : 1 lumbare lineum.
lumbricus 612 n.
lunules (-as) 570 n.
lupus 592. Herm. 16/55 λάβραξ
  luppus, etc.
lurcones 568 n.
lurdus 589 n.
lutrus 585 n.
lymphatico 575. Orosius iii. 2/9
  lymphatico furore.

mafortae (-te) 627 n.

maialis 652. Herm.: *see* porcellus.

malagna (-ma) 635. Herm. 206/38.

malua 656. Herm. 265/32, etc.

malus 636 n.

mancus 626 n.

manica 631. ? Herm. 272/38 χειρίς *manica*, etc.

manile 633 n. ? Herm. 203/41 *cernibion aquiminale.*

manipulatim 617. Orosius v. 17/7 *manipulatim plebe descripta.*

manitergium (manu-) 634. ? Herm. 269/51.

manticum 645 n.

manubium (-ae) 642. ? Abstr. MA 22–3 *manubiae . . . id est uestes mortuorum.*

margo (man-) 659 n. Phocas 413/23 *hic mango.* § 29.

maritima *see* pro maritima.

marrubium 657. Herm. 194/58, etc.

mars martis 663. ? Phocas 411/33 (*mars* only).

marsopicus (mart-) 648 n. Herm. 319/25 *picus marsicus*, etc.

martis *see* mars.

martus (my-) 637. Herm. 264/3 *myrtus*, etc.

maruca 651 n. ? Herm. 318/29 κήρικες (-υκες) *murices*, etc.

mascus (-a) 646 n.

mastice (μαστίχη) 655. Herm. 537/49 *mastice*, etc.

mastigia 641 n.

matrix 661. Phocas 421/8 *haec matrix.* § 29.

matunos *see* percommoda matu(ti)nos.

maulistis (-tes) 654 n.

megale (my-) 666 n.

melarium 638 n.

melodium (-am) 643 n.

mendacio 618. Orosius iii. 16/12 *mendacio ad tempus composito.*

mergulus 647. Herm. 17/58, etc.

mergus 662 n. Phocas 419/28 *mergus mergi.*

merula 665. Herm. 90/6 *merulus*, etc.

merx 657a. Phocas 412/2.

millefolium 639. Herm., e.g. 569/65 *mirifilon i. millefolium.*

mimo *see* in mimo.

mimoparo (myo-) 630 n.

mirifillon (μυριόφυλλον) 623. ? Herm.: *see* millefolium.

modioli 625 n.

modo *see* quacumque modo.

molestissimum 619. Orosius vii. 29/ 18 *molestissimumque spatium uitae . . . exercuit.*

molibus 640 n.

momentum 632 n.

monarchia 622. Orosius vi. 20/2 *summa rerum ac potestatum penes unum . . . quod Graeci monarchiam uocant.*

mordacius 653 n.

mordicos (-us) 616 n.

morgit 628 n.

mossiclum 629 n.

mugil 660. Phocas 414/20 *hic mugil.*

mulcet 666a n.

mulio 658. Phocas 413/8 *hic mulio.*

municeps 620. Orosius vii. 40/4 *municeps eiusdem insulae.*

munifica 621 n.

munusculorum *see* digitalium munusculorum.

murica 624 n.

muris *see* mus muris.

mus muris 664. ? Phocas 411/33 (*mus* only).

musiranus (mus araneus) 649. Herm. 90/70–1 *mus, araneus*, etc.

mustacia 644 n. § 11.

mustella (-ela) 650. Herm. 18/57, etc.

nanus 686 n.

napi (-y) 687 n.

napt(h)a 677 n., 685 n.

nasturcium 676. Herm., e.g. 593/8 *nasturcius crisson (h)ortensis.*

nauat 685a n.

nauiter 668 n.

naus(e)atio 667 n.

nebulonis 681. Orosius iv. 1/7 *Delphici . . . mendacissimi nebulonis.*

negotio 680. Orosius iii. 1/13 *suscepto negotio*, etc.

nepa 684 n.

nequiquam 683. Orosius, e.g. v. 19/5 *nequiquam repugnare.*

netila (nite-) 675 n.

nigra spina 672 n.

nimbus 682. Orosius v. 15/11
   telorum nimbus ingruerit.
ninguit 669 n.
noctua 673 n.
nodus 688. ? Herm. 26/5 ὄζωι (-οι)
   nodi, etc.
nomisma (nu-) 670 n.
non subs(i)ciuum 679. Orosius iv. 6/
   36 *nihil non subsiciuum.*
nugacitas 678. Orosius iv. praef. 10
   uerbosa nugacitas.
nux 671. Herm. ? 358/50 *nux καρύα,*
   etc.
nycticorax 674 n.

obestrum 703 n.
obligamentum 711. Orosius iv. 13/4
   obligamentum hoc magicum.
obliquum 694 n.
obnixe 708. ? Orosius iv. 1/20 *obnixe*
   . . . *in mutuam caedem ruentibus.*
obnixus 695 n.
obreptione 696. ? Orosius ii. 19/2
   urbem . . . *cuniculis et clandestina*
   obreptione ceperunt.
obtenuit (-tinuit) 706. ? Orosius vii.
   30/1 *imperii summam* . . . *obtinuit.*
obuncans 701 n.
occas 713 n.
occipitium 720.? Abstr.: *see* 715 n.
occiput 715 n.
occupauit 712 n., 717.
oculo *see* uitiato oculo.
ogastrum 704 n.
o(b)ligia 702 n.
olor 700. ? Herm. 17/36, etc.
olor grece 718 n.
omentum 719 n.
omnimoda 709 n.
opere plumari(o) 699. Vulg., e.g.
   Exod. 26: 1 *cortinas* . . . *uariatas*
   opere plumario.
oppillauit (-ilauit) 693 n.
orbita 710 n.
orcus 693 n.
ordinatissimam 707 ? Orosius iii. 1/
   23 *urbem* . . . *ornatissimam* (v.l.
   ordinatissimam).
oresta 705 n.
oridanum 697 n.
origanum 691. ? Herm. 259/65, etc.
ortigome(t)ra 714 n.

oscillae (-a) 689 n.
oscitantes 690. ? Orosius iii. 1/3
   post . . . *vigilias oscitantes.*
osma 692 n.
ostriger 716 n.

palingenesean 783 n.
palla 801 n.
palpitans 735. Orosius ii. 9/10
   campumque crasso et semigelato
   sanguine palpitantem.
paludamentum 740. Orosius vi. 18/
   32 *deposito paludamento.*
palumbes 829 n.
pal(i)urus 819 n.
pampinus 773. ? Herm. 265/3.
pangebant 797 n.
pansa 832 n.
paperum (papy-) 795 n.
papilio 768 n.
papil(i)o 817. ? Herm. 18/8, etc.
papiluus 781 n.
papula 771 n., 791 n.
parabsides (parop-) 764a n.
parcae 764 n.
parcas 761 n.
parrula 806 n.
particulatim 751. Orosius i. 8/7
   particulatim expositione confusa.
partim 731. Orosius iv. 9/13 *partim*
   hostium, partim etiam sociorum
   inhumatas strages.
pastellas (-illus) 830. ? Philox. PA
   151 *pastillus τροχίσκος.*
pastinaca 794. Herm. 266/6, etc.
patena (-ina) 784. Herm. 24/10 λοπάς
   patina, etc.; 786 n.
pauo 826. Phocas 413/16 (*hic*) *pauo*
pecten 825. Phocas 415/3 *hic pecten.*
pedetemptim 834 n.
pedo (-um) 778 n. §29.
peducla (pediculus) 812 n.
p(a)elices 745. Orosius vi. 5/5 *uxores,*
   pelices, ac filias.
pella 818 n.
peltam 838a n.
penduloso (-los) 754 n.
pendulus 816 n.; 838. ? Orosius: *see*
   754 n.
penitus 801a n.
pensio *see* debita pensio.
per anticipationem 757 n.

percitus 742. Orosius v. 19/4 *percitus*
. . . *ante urbem consedit*, etc.
percommoda matu(ti)nos 729 n.
percrebuit 737. Orosius v. 19/14
fama percrebuit.
perduellium (-io) 738. Orosius v.
22/8 *in tali . . . perduellione sociorum.*
perfidia 726. Orosius iii. 12/18
pari perfidia, etc.
permixtum 750 n.
perna 774, 804 n. ? Herm. 14/46
σκελίς *perna*, etc. (Ld. 47/13).
perpendiculum 763 n.
perpendit 836 n.
per seudoterum (pseudothyrum) 741.
Orosius vii. 6/17 *per pseudothyrum
. . . refugiens*, etc.
per(i)stromata 837 n.
pertinaciter 753. Orosius iii. 15/9
pertinaciter moriendo uicerunt, etc.
per uispellones (uespi-) 760 n.
pessul 803 n.
pessum 755 n.
(im)petigo 765. ? Vulg.: *see* 502 n.
petisse 756. Orosius v. 19/14 *fama
percrebuit . . . petisse fratrem . . .
spolia fratris occisi.*
petra focaria (-is) 805. ? Isidore, *Ety.*
xvi. 4/5 (*pyriten*) *uulgus focarem
petram uocant.*
petulans 835 n.
phisillos (psyl-) 746. Orosius vi. 19/
18 *psyllos . . . qui uenena serpentum
e uulneribus hominum hausu reuocare
atque exsugere solent.*
phitecus (pith-) 827. Herm., e.g. 361/
64 *simius* πίθηκος.
pice seuo (-bo) 769 n.
picis *see* pix.
pictus acu 796. ? *Aen.* ix. 582 *pictus
acu chlamydem.*
picus 808 n.
pila 787 n. ? Herm. 79/44, etc.
pingit 785 n.
piraticum (-am) 736. Orosius iii. 12/
21 *piraticam . . . exercere.*
pittacium 789. ? Vulg. Jos. 9: 5 (*cal-
ceamenta*) *pittaciis consuta erant.*
pituita 775. ? Herm., e.g. 246/56
τὸ φλέγμα *pituita phlegma*; 833.
? Philox. PI 55 *pituita* φλέγμα.

pix picis 820. ? Phocas 412/3 (*pix*
only).
plantago 793. Herm. 576/42 *septem-
neruia i. plantago*, etc.
platisa (-essa) 802 n.
pliadas 762 n.
plumari *see* opere plumari(o).
polimita 798. Vulg.: *see* tonica.
pollux (-ex) 821. Phocas 420/29 *hic
pollex pollicis.*
popauer (pa-) 824. Phocas 415/15–16
hoc papauer.
populus 792. Herm. 300/67, etc.
porcaster 810 n.
porcellus 811. Herm., e.g. 258/60
ὁ δέλφαξ *porcellus maialis.*
porcopiscis 809 n.
porfyrio (porph-) 807 n.
praepropera 733 n.
praerupta 747 n.
prætersori(u)m 779 n.
praetextatus 730 n. Orosius iv. 14/6
filium admodum praetextatum.
praxinus (fr-) 772 n. ? Herm.: *see*
fraximus.
pr(a)es et uas 776. Phocas 411/33–4
praes . . . uas uadis.
prifeta 780 n.
primores *see* inter primores.
priuigna 734 n.
probus 748. Orosius vii. 42/3 *uir
nequam magis quam probus.*
pro captu 727 n.
procuratio 721. Orosius vii. 9/3 *ad
procurationem obsidionis.*
prodimur 800 n.
proflicta 814 n.
profligatus (-is) 744. Orosius i. 13/1
*populis utrimque infeliciter pro-
fligatis*, etc.
profusis 723. Orosius ii. 15/7
profusis opibus.
progna (-ne) 828 n.
pro maritima (per m-) 728. Orosius
iii. 6/4 *per maritima loca.*
promulgarunt 724. Orosius v. 17/11
rogationem . . . promulgarunt. § 11.
promulserit (per-) 722. Orosius v.
17/12 *inimicos permulserit.*
pronus 799. Vulg. Gen. 19: 1
pronus in terram, etc.
propensior 743 n.

propropera (prae-) 733 n.
prorigo (pru-) 788. Rufinus i. 8/9
  *prurigo . . . intolerabilis per omnem
  corporis diffusa superficiem.*
proscribit (-scripsit) 739. Orosius
  vii. 4/8 *plurimos senatorum proscripsit.*
proterentem 752. Orosius i. 10/12
  *grandinem . . . homines, armenta,
  atque arbores proterentem.*
proterunt 749. Orosius vii. 40/3
  Francos proterunt.
prouectae 758. Orosius vii. 28/27
  Romae tot saeculis . . . prouectae.
prouehit 725. Orosius ii. 16/8
  *exercitum classemque numero pro-
  uehit.*
prouentus 815 n.
prouetæ (-cta) 759. Orosius vii. 28/27
  *(urbs) a Christiano imperatore
  prouecta.*
prunus 822. Phocas 420/9 *haec
  prunus pruni.*
ptysones (ptisanas) 790 n.
pudor 732. Orosius, e.g. v. 22/5 *pro
  pudor!*
pulenta (po-) 767. Vulg. Lev. 23: 14
  panem et polentam, etc.
pul(e)ium 831. Herm., e.g. 186/20
  puleum.
pulix (-ex) 813 n.
pullentum 780a n.
pullis (pol-) 823. Phocas 418/10 *hic
  pollis pollinis.*
puncto 766 n.
puntus (-ctum) 782. Herm., e.g.
  punctus 427/38.
pus 777. Phocas 412/5.
pustula 770. Vulg. Lev. 13: 2 *diuersus color siue pustula.*
putrefacta *see* tabida et putrefacta.

qua(nti)cumque 843 n.
quacumque (quo-) modo 842. ? Herm.
  151/53.
quadripertitum 841 n.
qualns (-us) 839 n.
quantisper 844 n.
quaternio 847 n. ? Phocas 413/8 *hic
  quarternio.*
quin etiam 846 n.

quinquefolium 848, 1084. Herm.
  572/13 *pentefilon i. quinquefolia,*
  etc.
quinqueneruia 849 n.
quisquiliae 840 n.
quoquomodo 845. ? Rufinus x. 5
  *quoquo modo . . . concilium diremp-
  tum est.*
rabulus 854 n.
radinape (ro-) 861 n. § 11.
radium (-us) 851 n.
ramnus (rh-) 880 n. ? Herm. 359/8
  spina alba ῥάμνος, etc.
rancor 874 n.
rastros 878 n.
ratio(ci)nat(i)o 866 n.
recessus 867. Orosius vi. 8/10
  inaccessos recessus.
reciprocato 864 n.
reclines 865 n.
relatu 869. Orosius, e.g. vii. 36/12
  sub tantorum miraculorum relatu.
re(u)ma 855. Herm. *cursus aquae*
  ῥεῦμα 444/72, etc.; *regima idest
  flussus (-xus)* 575/4.
remex 875 n.
remota 870. Orosius iii. 2/8 *remota
  manu.*
renunculus 850. ? Vulg. Lev. 3: 4
  reticulum iecoris cum renunculis,
  etc.
reserat 872 n.
resina 858. Herm. 194/62, etc.
respuplica (-blica) 859. Herm. 274/
  43 πολιτεία *ciuilitas respu(blica).*
reuma 856. ? Herm. 574/23 *pituita i.
  reumata.*
rictus 852 n.
ridimiculae (redimicula) 877 n.
rien 860. ? Phocas 415/1 *hic rien
  rienis.* § 29.
rigore 871. Orosius i. 2/86 *rigore
  frigoris.*
robor 863 n.
roscinia (rus-) 857 n.
rostratum 868. Orosius, e.g. vi. 19/8
  rostratae . . . naues et . . . sine rostris.
rostris 873 n.
rostrum 862 n.
rumex 876 n.
runcina 853. Herm. 325/63, etc.

ruscus 879. ? Herm. 264/54 βάτος *rubus ruscus.*

sabulcus (su-) 959. Herm. 309/32, etc.
saginabant 930. Orosius i. 13/2 *informe prodigium . . . saginabant.*
sagulum 898. ? Orosius vi. 10/3 *terram . . . sagulis exportando.*
salebrae 881 n.
salix 892 n.
salsa 974 n. ? Herm. 551/8 *agilicos* (ἀλυκός) *salsa.*
salum 966. ? Abstr. SA 10 *salum mare.*
sambucus 893. Herm. 264/63, etc.
sandix 950 n.
sanguinis 903 n.
sapa *see* dulcis sapa.
sarcinatum 886 n.
sarculum 887 n.
sardas 949. ? Herm. 436/59 *sard(a)e.*
sardinas 910. Herm., e.g. 218/50–1 *da . . . sardinas,* etc.
sartago 885. Vulg. Lev. 2: 5 *oblatio . . . de sartagine,* etc.
sartatecta 889 n.
scabris 913a n.
scalbellum (scalp-) 883. Vulg. Jer. 36: 23 *scidit (uolumen) scalpello scribae.*
scalpellum 907 n.
scalprum 891 n.
scapula 963. Herm. 351/1, etc.
scarpinat 906 n.
scasa 927 n.
sceda 964 n.
sc(a)ena 902 n.
sc(a)euus 981 n.
scienicis (scae-) 952 n.
scifus (scyph-) 965. Herm. 22/45 σκύφος *scifus,* etc.
scilla 920 n. Herm., e.g. 553/34 *buluus scil(l)iticus i. squilla.*
scina 904 n., 953 n.
scindulis 943. Orosius: see 769 n.
scira 911 n.
scirpea 894 n.
scnifes (sciniph-) 916 n.
scorelus 909 n.
scorteas *see* asses scorteas.

scrirpea (sci-). 960. ? Vulg.: *see* 894 n.
scrobibus 884 n.; 948. ? Abol. SC 15 *scrobibus fossulis.*
scrofa 912. Herm., e.g. 432/52.
scurra 977a n.
secessum 901 n.
secta *see* uia secta.
secundarum *see* inluuies secundarum.
seditio 900 n.
sella 926 n. Herm. δίφρος *sella* 20/40, etc.; ἐφίππιον *. . . sella* 273/20.
semigelato 931 n.
senecen (-ion) 976. Herm., e.g. 561/ 11 *erigeron idest siniciones.*
senon 968 n.
sentina 890. ? Gregory, *Reg. Past.* iii. 33 *sentina latenter crescens* (Ld. 39/50).
sequester 921. Phocas 415/21.
serio 945. Orosius vi. 22/4 *uel serio uel ioco.*
serpillum 895 n.
seru 979. Phocas 414/14 *hoc seru.*
serum 982 n.
s(a)eta 905 n.
seudoterum *see* per seudoterum.
seuo (-bo) 944. Orosius: *see* 769 n.
sibba 882 n.
sicalia (secale) 918 n.
simbulum (symbol-) 919. ? Isidore, *De ecclesiasticis officiis (PL* lxxxiii. 816c), ii. 23/4 *symbola . . . quae latine uel signa uel indicia nuncupantur.*
sinapio (-i) 917 n.; 922. Phocas 412/15.
sinfoniaca 975 n. Herm., e.g. 567/31 *laterculus i. simphoniaca.*
singultus 958. Herm. 602/29 *ligmos* (λυγμός) *singultus.*
sinuosa 939. Orosius iv. 8/13 *uermis . . . latera sinuosa circumfert.*
sisca 973 n.
situla 923 n.
slens 970 n.
smus (sin-) 969 n.
soccus 951 n.
sollicitat 936 n.
sopitis 942. Orosius vi. 20/1 *sopitis finitisque . . . bellis.*

sorix (-ex) 977 n.
sortem 980 n.
spatiaretur 932. Orosius vi. 5/6 *cum
. . . spatiaretur* §11.
spatula 971 n.
spiculis 937. Orosius iii. 20/7 *saxis
spiculisque adpetentes.*
spina 947 n. *See* alba spina, nigra
spina.
spina alba 956. Herm.: *see* ramnus.
spina nigra 957. ? Herm.: *see* 672 n.
spoma (spu-) 979a. ? Philox. SP 38
spuma ἀλφός.
sponda 955. Herm. 20/37 *sponda
bettibret*, etc.
squalores 933. Orosius i. 10/10 *post
horridos ranarum squalores.*
stabula 896. ? *Aen.* vi. 179 *stabula
alta ferarum.*
stabulum 959. Herm. 260/26 ἔπαυλις
uilla stabulum ouile.
stagnum 962. ? Herm. 246/27 τὸ ἕλος
palus stagnum.
sternutatio 888. Vulg. Job 41: 9
sternutatio eius splendor ignis.
stilio 978 n.
stilium 967 n.
stipatoribus 929. Orosius iii. 23/10
stipatoribus regis . . . praeficitur.
stiria 954. Herm. 245/4 ἡ πάχνη . . .
pruina stiria.
stornus (stu-) 924 n.
strenuæ (-e) 946. Orosius, e.g. vii.
42/10 *Africam . . . strenue tuta-
tus.*
strepitu 928. Orosius iii. 1/22 *strepitu
. . . exterriti*, etc.
strigia (-ga) 913 n.
struere 899 n.
sturnus 908. Herm. 188/19, etc.
sualdam (ualu-) 925. ? Aldhelm, *VP*
245/22 *ualuam recludere*, etc.
sublustris 941 n.
subs(i)ciuum 938. Orosius: *see non
subs(i)ciuum.*
successus 940. Orosius iv. 9/8
*qualescumque successus magnis . . .
malorum molibus obruebantur.*
suesta 972 n.
suffragator 934. Orosius ii. 5/3 *regii
nominis suffragator.*
suffragium 935. Orosius v. 4/10 *in

suffragium praeueniendae cladis*, etc.
sullus 914 n.
surum (-am) 897. ? Vulg. Jud. 15: 8
*ut stupentes suram femori impone-
rent.*
suspensus 915 n.
taberna 1040. Orosius vi. 18/34 *e
taberna meritoria.*
tabetum (tap-) 1023 n.
tabida et putrefacta 1044 n.
tabuisset 1036 n.
tabula 1009a n. § 14
tabunus (taba-) 1016. Herm. 18/10,
etc.
talpa 1014. Herm. 189/35, etc.; 1045.
Phocas 412/20 *hic talpa.*
talumbus 1032 n.
tantisper 1037 n.
tapeta 1020 n.
taxatione 1035 n.
taxus 1005. Herm. 300/43, etc.
telum (-am) 1026 n.
temonibus 1043. Orosius v. 16/18
de . . . plaustrorum temonibus.
tempe 991 n.
tenticum 1025 n.
teres 1047. Phocas 417/23 *hic et haec
teres.*
teris 999a n.
termofilas ('Thermopylas) 1042 n.
terrebellus 1010 n.
tertiana 999. ? Herm. 29/49, etc.
tessera 998 n.
testudo 997 n.
textrina 1030. Herm. 270/25 *textri-
num*, etc.
thymus 1007. Herm. 265/67, etc.
tibialis (-le) 1031. Herm., e.g. 208/50
pericnimia (περικνήμια) *tibiales.*
tignarius 996 n.
tignum 1024. Herm. 268/34, etc.
tilaris 1012 n.
tilia 1004. Herm. 26/16, etc.
tilio (-a) 1017. Herm.: *see* tilia.
tincti 1015 n.
tinctum *see* coccum bis tinctum.
tipo (typho) 1048. Abstr. TI 9 *typho
draco.*
titio 987. Vulg. Is. 7: 4 *titionum
fumigantium.*
titul(a)e 1028 n.

toculus 1008 n.
tonica (tu-) 984. Vulg. Gen. 37: 3
    fecitque ei tunicam polymitam, etc.
tonsa 986 n.
t(h)orax 1027. Herm. 311/24, etc.
toreum(a) 1019 n.
torqu(e)t 1002. ? Aen. i. 108 in saxa
    . . . torquet.
torrentibus 1033. Orosius v. 13/3
    torrentibus igneis superfusis.
torta 985 n. See uerbere torta.
tortum (-am) 993 n.
toxica see liuida toxica.
tractata 1043a n.
traductus 990. Vulg. II Pet. 3: 17
    insipientium errore traducti.
tragelafbus (-phus) 1001 n.
trans 1041. Orosius vi. 18/34 trans
    Tiberim, etc.
transmigratione see in transmigra-
    tione(m).
transtrum 1021 n.
tremulus 1006 n.
tridens 1003 n.
trifulus 1009 n.
triqua(d)rum 1039 n.
triplia 995 n.
troc(h)leis 994 n. Rufinus viii. 10/5
    trochleis distenti.
trop(a)ea 992. Rufinus ii. 25/7
    apostolorum tropea.
trulla 989 n., 1022 n.
trutina 988 n.
trux 983 n.
tuber 1018 n.; 1046. Phocas 415/15
    hoc tuber. § 29.
tubo 1000 n.
tudic(u)la 1029 n.
turdella (-ela) 1011 n.
turdus 1013. Herm. 18/1, etc.
tuta 1034. Orosius, e.g. i. 7/2 tuta
    possessione.
tutellam (-elam) 1038. Orosius iv.
    17/9 diuinam tutelam.

uadimonium 1090 n.
ua(lba) (-ua) 1053 n.
uangas 1087. ? Gregory, Dial. iii. 14
    ferramenta quae usitato nos nomine
    uangas uocamus (Ld. 39/12).
uaricat 1086 n.

uarix 1073 n. ? Phocas 421/6 hic
    uarix uaricis (Ld. 46/27).
uas see pr(a)es et uas.
uatilla (ba-) 1065 n.
uenabula 1052 n.
ueneria 1078 n.
uene(t)um 1064 n.
uentriculus 1054 n.
uerbenaca 1077a n.
uerberatorium 1074 n.
uerberatrum 1075 n.
uerbere torta (-to) 1051 n.
uericundiæ (uere-) concesserim 1089.
    Orosius iii. 3/3 haec ut commemo-
    rata sint magis quam explicata
    uerecundiae concesserim.
uerruca 1049. ? Herm.: see berruca.
uertigo 1068. Herm. 245/64 ἡ εἶλιγξ
    (ἰλ-) uortex uertigo uortigo. See e
    uertigo.
uescada (bascua-) 1055 n.
uesica 1096. Orosius i. 10/11 post
    uesicas efferuescentes, etc.
uespas 1071 n.
uespertilio 1098 n.
uessica (uesi-) 1077. Herm. 13/16
    uessica, etc.
uestibulum 1058 n.
uetellus 1099 n.
uia secta 1050 n.
uiburna 1082 n.
uicatum (fi-) 1057. ? Herm. 218/37
    da ficatum, etc.
uiciligo (uit-) 1069 n.
uicium (-am) 1085 n.
uill(os)a 1081 n.
uillis 1066 n.
uillosa 1080 n.
uimbrat (uib-) 1092 n.
uimen see lentum uimen.
uirecta 1088 n.
uiscus 1083. Herm. 75/60, etc.
uispellones see per uispellones.
uitelli 1062 n.
uitiato (-ioso) oculo 1093 n.
uitiatum 1091. Orosius iv. praef. 10
    delicatis uitiata nutrimentis.
uitricius (-cus) 1070 n.
uittas 1060 n.
ulmus 1079. Herm. 26/24, etc.
undecumq(u)e 1095. Orosius iii. 1/2
    porrectam undecumque occasionem.

unibrellas (umb-) 1067 n.
uoluola 1059 n.
uorago 1072 n.
urciolum (-ceolus) 1056. ? Herm.,
  e.g. 466/68 *urciolum.*
uris 1097 n.
urna 1076. Herm. 270/63 λάρναξ
  ἡμιαμφόριον *urna,* etc.

uscidae 1063 n.
usurpauit 1096. Orosius vii. 8/1
  usurpauit imperium.
ut(ru)muis 1094a. Orosius i. prol. 1
  in utramuis partem, etc.
uulgo 1061 n.

yripeon 1100 n. § 11.

INDEX OF INTERPRETATIONS

Entries common to both texts are given as in Épinal, Latin words in italics.

a 17, 218, 620, 984.
āāc 235, 863.
ab 9, † *ob* 391, † *anb* 509.
āchlōcadum (āh-) 364. §§ 86, 89 fn. 3.
ad 550.
adiuro 210 n.
ādōenrae *see* fram ādōenrae.
āduīnendanan (-dan) 1044 n.
aebordrotae (-ŏrotae) *see* eborthrotae.
āēc þan 846 n. § 57. 1.
aec(h)tath 836. § 57. 1.
aedilra (aeð-) 479 n. §§ 14, 68.
āēgergelu 429 n. § 78.
āēggimang 704 n.
āēgur 316 n. § 57. 1.
aehrian 840 n. §§ 50. 3 and fn. 3, 57.
  1, 66 fn. 1, 72(a), 74 fn. 3.
aelbitu (aelf-) 718. §§ 50. 2, 77.
aeldrum 546. § 50. 2.
aelifnae 115a n. § 50. 2.
æmil 257, aemil 484. § 48.
aend 98, ond 1044 n. §§ 48, 89 fn. 3.
āēngi 845. § 79.
aenid 17. §§ 48, 74.
aeohed (aeth-) 362 n. §§ 54, 90.
aerngeup 40 n. §§ 40, 43. 1.
aesc (-cs) 321.
aesc 180 n., 416, 772. §§ 38 fn. 6, 49.
aescthrotae 450 n. § 49.
(h)aesil *see* haesil.
aespae 1006. § 38.
aestatem 553.
aetgāēru 440 n. §§ 52 and fn. 5, 77.
æthm 89. §§ 4, 39.
āētrinan 576. § 52.
aex 13. § 57. 1.
āferidae 91 n. §§ 4, 49.
āfigaen 414 n. §§ 68, 85.
ā fordh (-th) 529 n.
āfūlodan 1044. §§ 74, 86, 87.
āfȳrid 319.
āgnaettae 1096 n. § 65. 1.
āgnidinne (-ine) 345 n. § 85.
alaer 35. §§ 27, 43. 2, 68, 89 fn. 4.

8111641

aldot(h) 57 n. §§ 43. 2, 70.
ālgiuueorc 556 n. §§ 44. 1, 57. 2.
ali(i) 674, 891.
alterholt (aler-) 46 n. §§ 4, 27, 43. 2,
  67 fn. 3, 68.
ambaer 923, 1076, ambras 170. § 63
  fn. 4, 68 and fn. 1.
ambec(h)t 866 n., ambectae 187 n.
  §§ 65. 1, 79, 89 fn. 3.
ambras *see* ambaer.
amprae 1073 n.
an 51, 91, 370 n. §§ 4, 35, 37.
andlēac 872 n. §§ 57. 1, 87.
anga 43 n. §§ 27, 37.
angseta 770.
anhaebd (-fd) 915 n. § 86.
ānhendi 626 n. § 48.
anhrīosith 520. §§ 42, 70, 83 fn. 2, 87.
anmōd 202.
ans(c)ēot 377 n.
anslegaengrae (-aenrae) 535 n. §§ 68,
  85.
ānstīgan (-a) 1042 n.
ansuebidum (ansuef-) 942. § 74.
ansuēop 32 n. §§ 11, 41.
ānuuald 622.
ānuuillicae 753.
apa 827.
apuldur 636. §§ 46, 64 fn. 3, 67. *See*
  milsc apuldr.
aqu(a)e 890.
āqueorna (ācw-) 911 n. § 44. 1.
āraebndae (araef-) 353 n. §§ 87, 89
  fn. 3.
ārǣddun 366 n.
āraepsid 511 n. §§ 49, 69, 74.
arb(or) 132.
ārectio (-ccio) 396a n., ārec(h)tae 204.
  §§ 57. 1, 58, 71, 83, 84, 87.
āritrid 372 n. § 54.
āscrefan (-pan) 354 n., āscrepaeni
  375 n. §§ 11, 79, 85.
āsiuuid 796 n. § 42.
āslacudae 491. §§ 46, 86.

Q

āsolcaen 531 n. § 85.
āspringendi 334 n. § 87.
āstyntid 488.
āsuand 490, 1036 n., āsundum (āswundun) 341, āsuundnan 1044.
§§ 11 fn. 2 (p. xxvii), 73, 74, 87.
ātae 599 n. § 61.
āthrǣstae 358 n.
ātr 141 n. § 67.
āu(u)ǣgdæ 356. § 84.
aues 218.
augurale 571.
auidi 568.
auis 1054 n.
aula 9.
auram 838a n.
aureum 624.
āuuaerdid 1091. § 50. 1.
auuel 29 n. § 43. 4 and fn. 2.
āu(u)undun 507, āuunden 985, āuund(en)re 1051. § 87.

bā 51. §§ 4, 35.
bāānrift 1031 n. § 62.
bāār 151.
baculum 571.
baecdermi (-ðearm) 385 n.
bāēdendrae 539 n. §§ 52, 65. 2, 79.
baers 592 n. § 43. 1 and fn. 3.
baeso 411. § 46.
baest 1017 n. § 38.
bān see elpendes bān.
bēan 284; see fuglaes bēan.
beanc (-cn) 992. § 76 and fn. 1.
bearug 652. § 56.
bebir (bef-) 272 n., bebr 399. § 67.
bēccae (-ēcae) see bōēcae.
bedd 243, bed 971. § 49.
bēēr 137.
begir 143 n. § 89 fn. 3.
bellici 740.
belonae 975.
bēost 261, 703.
bēouua(e)s 645 n. § 63 fn. 2.
berændae 790 n. § 79.
berc 132. § 57. 2.
berecorn 790.
bestia 346a.
bibitnae 616 n.
bigaet 706. § 47.
biginan 1041 n. § 47 and fn. 4.
bīgongum 357.

binumini 104 n., binumni 102 n. §§ 54, 68, 79, 85.
bīouuyrt 20, 657 n. §§ 4, 54, 59. 3.
birciae 792. §§ 45 and fn. 1, 71.
birēdnae 800 n. §§ 39, 87.
bisceredae 73 n. §§ 50. 1, 73.
biscopuuyrt 496 n.
bisiuuidi 699. §§ 42, 79.
bismiridae 534. §§ 45, 63 fn. 6, 73.
bisuicend 545. §§ 61, 65. 2 fn. 2.
bituīc(h)n 546. §§ 57. 3, 72(b).
bitulin (-um) 145. §§ 56, 66.
blaec 677.
blāēēd (-āēd) 445. § 39.
blēctha 1069 n. § 52.
blēcthrūstfel 139 n. §§ 52, 66, 76.
blēdrae 1077.
blegnae 1094 n. § 66.
blēstbaelg 454 n. § 50. 2.
blīdi (-ði) 77 n.
bodæi 947 n. §§ 59. 6, 71.
bōēcae 22, 417, † bēccae 391. §§ 53, 61.
boga 453, bogan 442.
bol(ster) 296.
bolla 234, 965.
bōōg 67. § 39 fn. 2.
borǣttit 1092 n. §§ 65. 1, 70.
borg 1090.
borohaca (bordth-) 997 n. § 76.
brādaelēac 895 n. §§ 57. 1, 67 fn. 1, 87 fn. 1.
brāēdlāēstu 321 n. § 77.
brand 987.
brandrād 4 n. § 37.
brec(h)tme 928. §§ 57. 1, 58, 63 fn. 5, 79 fn. 1.
brēd 1023 n. §§ 59. 6 fn. 2, 71 fn. 5.
brēdipannae 885 n. §§ 39, 67 fn. 1.
bredīsern 883 n.
brēēr 68. §§ 16, 39.
brīdils 127. §§ 59. 6, 71, 76.
brīig 767. §§ 59. 6, 73.
brīosa 27 n., 1016. § 41.
brocc 1008. § 11.
brocdaettendi (brog-) 735. §§ 65. 1, 74 fn. 2.
brōēc 573.
brōōm 465.
brord 782. § 37 fn. 2.
brūūn 159, 433, brūn 837 n. §§ 4, 11 fn. 2 (p. xxvii).

brūūnbesu 716. § 46.
bucc 120 n. § 11.
burglēod 620. § 42 and fn. 1.
burgrūnae 761 n. § 80.
buturflīogae 817 n. §§ 41, 54, 57. 2, 68.
bydin 260.
byrgea 776, 921. § 71.
byrgeras 760 n. §§ 54, 65. 1.
byris 891 n., 907. §§ 65. 4 fn. 3, 77.
byrst 905.

caelith 561. §§ 51, 83.
caempan 481. § 48.
calc 165 n.
calua 116a n.
caluuaer 471 n., 476.
camb 825. See u(u)ulfes camb.
candelthuist (-tuist) 382 n. § 48.
capiatur 553.
captant 553.
casei 982.
caute 834.
cēapcnext (-ht) 349 n. § 57. 2.
cearruccae 968 n.
cebærtūūn 1058 n. §§ 11 fn. 2 (p. xxvii), 38, 47, 63 fn. 2, 67.
cebisae (cef-) 745. §§ 77 and fn. 2, 80.
cefr 150. §§ 38 fn. 6, 67, 69.
celae 862 n. § 50. 2.
cendlic (cy-) 729 n. §§ 54, 75.
cēol 230 n. § 41.
cesol 457 n., 1054 n. §§ 46, 68.
cest 231. § 47.
cetil 168, 350.
challes 116b n.
chȳae (cȳh-) 240. §§ 59. 5 and fn. 1, 72 fn. 1.
cīan 158. § 59. 3.
cignus (cy-) 718.
cīisnis 406. §§ 39 fn. 2, 47, 55.
cimbing 291 n. § 32.
cīnaendi 495 n.
cīpae 286.
circulorum 984.
circumdari 1059.
cisil 461 n.
cisirbeam 237 n. §§ 40, 62, 76.
cistigian 621. §§ 54, 71, 87.
cistimbēam (cistin-) 249 n. §§ 11 fn. 2 (p. xxvii), 40, 47, 49, 55, 68.
clabre (-fre) 250, 254.

cladærsticca 116 n. §§ 46, 68.
claedur 218 n. § 46.
clātae 144 n.
clauuo 29. §§ 43. 4 and fn. 2, 73.
clēouuae 472 n. § 41.
clibecti (clifihte) 166 n. § 65. 3.
cliderme 928 n. §§ 63 fn. 5, 77 fn. 2, 79 fn. 1.
clidrinnae 928 n. § 77 fn. 2.
clifae 613. § 69.
cliþae 613 n.
clofae 653 n. § 69.
clūstorlocae 220 n. §§ 66 fn. 1, 67 and fn. 3, 79.
clūt 789.
cnēorissa(e) 903 n. §§ 63 fn. 5, 65. 4 fn. 3, 78.
cnīoholaen 879 n. §§ 41, 59. 6, 71.
c(l)oacas 287 n. § 32.
cōcunung 841 n. § 67.
cōēcil 993 n.
coerin 314 n., † coerim 313. §§ 11 fn. 2 (p. xxvii), 53 and fn. 2.
colliguntur 890.
colþrēd 763 n. § 39.
columnis 453.
condicionem 980.
conficitur 894.
conposito 618.
consanguinis (-neus) 164.
cop 390 n.
cort(h)r 1074 n. §§ 67, 70.
cosp 766 n.
cot(t)uc 656.
couel (caw-) 305 n.
crāuuae 241, crāuua(e) 308.
cressae 917 n., 922.
crīopungae 696 n. §§ 41, 79.
crocha 171 n. § 72(a).
crōōg 584.
crop 60.
crōs 773 n. §§ 59. 4, 88 fn. 3.
crūcae 989 n., 1056.
crycc 571.
cubitali 766.
cuicbēam 238 n.
cunillae 246 n. § 54.
curtina 9.
curuum 571.
cūscutan (-otan) 829 n.
cynidōm 859.
cyniuuithan 877 n.

156   INDEX OF INTERPRETATIONS

dāeli 731. § 79.
de 894.
dēatlicostan (dēad-) 439. §§ 40, 73, 87.
del (ð-) 838a n.
dens 487.
dicitur 132, *dicunt* 673. § 11.
dieperdulum 42 n. § 27.
dil 21. § 77.
dilectione 109.
dirigat 1092.
disc 786.
dīslum (ð-) 1043. §§ 57. 3, 72(c).
distulis 999a n.
dobendi (dof-) 322 n. § 86 and fn. 1.
dopaenid 419 n. § 48.
dora 119.
droco (*dra-*) 1048 n. § 14.
dropfāāg 924 n. § 74.
drōs 39 n. § 27.
duerg 686. § 57. 2.
duergaedost(l)ae 831 n. §§ 57. 2, 67.
duolma 181 n. § 62.
durhere 925 n., durheri 1053. § 77.

earbetlicust (earfeð-) *see* erabedlicae.
ēarendil 554 n. § 40.
earngēat (-p) 40 n. §§ 27, 40.
ēaruuigga 44. §§ 4, 27, 40, 56.
ēastnorþwind 162 n. § 40.
ebhatis (efhatum) 854 n. § 72(c).
eborsprēot (ef-) 1052 n.
eborthrotae (ef-) 927 n., † aebordrotae 303 n.
edendo 391.
edisc 147. § 17.
edischaen 714 n.
ediscu(u)eard 148 n. § 43. 1.
edroc 876 n.
edscaept (-ft) 783. §§ 47, 49.
edwalla 1068 n. edu(u)ella 1019 n.
   §§ 50. 2 and fn. 5, 63.
ēgan 1093. § 57. 1.
egdae (egð-) 395. § 66.
egderi (egð-) 396 n. §§ 65. 1, 66.
egisigrīma 569 n. §§ 67 fn. 1, 77.
eglae 470 n. § 66.
elch 233 n., 1001. § 57. 2.
ellaen 893. §§ 50. 2, 66 fn. 5, 68 fn. 2
   (p. lxxx).
elm 1079.
elonae 697 n. § 76.
eloquentia 444.

elothr (-htr) 386 n. §§ 67, 68.
elpendes bān 351.
embrin 121a n. §§ 48, 68 fn. 1.
emer 909 n. § 48.
ēola 346a n. §§ 44. 2, 57. 2, 60, 88 fn. 3.
eordrestae (eorð-) 219 n. §§ 44. 1, 49,
   80.
ēorisc (ēa-) 795 n., 960. §§ 59. 1, 77,
   88 fn. 3.
eornæsti 945. §§ 44. 1, 63 and fn. 1.
   (p. lxxvi), 79 fn. 1.
erabedlicae (earfeð-) 363, earbetlicust 619. §§ 11, 70.
et 42, 332, 1059. § 27.
euocatus 103.

fāāg 61. §§ 39 fn. 2, 74.
fāām 426.
fācni 83. §§ 35, 79.
fæcilae 407. §§ 51, 66, 68.
fāēcni 938.
fāēdun *see* fāēhit.
faegen 273 n.
fāēhit 785 n., fāēdun 797. §§ 11 fn. 2
   (p. xxvii), 59. 1, 70, 72 (a), 88
   fn. 3.
faengae 727. §§ 48, 79.
faerh 811 n. § 57. 1.
faerscribaen (-faen) 52. §§ 63, 69, 85.
faestin 1042 n., faestinnum 110. § 49.
faet(h)maendi 939 n. § 70.
fahamae 780a n.
fala 1009a n. §§ 60, 88 fn. 3.
falaed 129, 959. §§ 43. 2, 68.
falu 483. § 46 fn. 5.
fealga 713 n. §§ 43. 2, 57. 1, 58, 80, 90.
fearn 420. § 43. 1.
felduuop 131 n. §§ 11, 70, 72, 88 fn. 3.
felge 292. §§ 50. 2, 80.
felofearth 1027 n. § 76.
felofor 807 n. § 11.
felosprāēci 1009 n. § 39.
feormat 402. §§ 44. 1, 70.
ferhergænd 467 n. § 63.
ferrēd 739 n. § 63.
ferrum 177, 887.
fertd (-rd) 373 n. §§ 50. 1, 74 and fn. 3.
ferth (-ht) 748 n. § 57. 2.
feruuaenid 548 n. § 63.
feruuitgeornnis 208. § 44. 1.
fetod 103. § 86.
fetor 121, 778. §§ 29, 56.

fēx 430a n. §§ 52, 72.
fibulae (fif-) 3a n. §§ 66, 69.
fierst 595. §§ 45, 55, 90.
fīfaldae 768 n. §§ 61 fn. 1, 63 fn. 6, 69 fn. 5.
filia 734.
fīna 648, 808 n. §§ 11, 88 fn. 3.
finc 423.
fingirdoccuna 346 n. §§ 67, 81.
finugl 451.
firgingāett (-āet) 560 n. §§ 45 and fn. 1, 52, 65. 4.
fit 501.
flāch 510 n.
flānum 937.
flēah 813 n. § 57. 1.
flēotas 107. § 41.
flēti 605 n., 1075. §§ 55, 80.
flicci 774, † flicii 804 n.
flint 805.
flīo 12. §§ 42, 57. 3, 59. 3, 88 fn. 3.
flītad (-ŏ) 330.
flītere 854. § 65. 1.
flōdae 597. § 29.
flōōc 802 n.
fnora 888.
fōērnissae 530. § 89 fn. 3.
fōē(s)tribarn 108 n. § 43. 1.
folia see *vii folia*.
fomenti 685.
fōōr 810 n.
forae 873 n.
foramine 766.
fordh (-rŏ) *see* ā fordh.
fornaeticli 178a n. § 65. 1.
forslaegæn 814, forsleginum 744. §§ 51, 63, 68, 85.
forsōc 339.
fōsturbearn 108 n. §§ 35, 67.
fō(o)t *see* hraefnaes fōt.
fōthr 378 n. § 67
fōtmēlum 834 n.
fraam 71. §§ 37, 89 fn. 3.
fraehraedae (-ŏae) 733 n. § 87.
fram ādōenrae 870 n. §§ 59. 4, 75.
framlicae 946.
frangat 685a n. § 70 fn. 1.
frecnis 475 n.
fremu 135. §§ 48, 77.
friat 666a n. §§ 59. 3, 70.
fric(h)trung 10 n. § 57. 3.
frigus 553.

fristmearc 547. §§ 43. 1, 57. 1.
frōdrae 758.
frost 485. § 76.
frugibus 1059.
fuglaes bēan 1085 n.
fuglum 1067.
fūlaetrēa 36 n. §§ 4, 41, 63 fn. 6, 67 fn. 1, 73, 87 fn. 1.
fulfum (-uum) 404.
fultēam 360.
fultemendi 74, fultemendum 95. §§ 65. 2, 68, 86.
furhum 884 n. § 72(c).
fusa (-us) 967.
fyrpannae 5 n. §§ 37, 54.

gabelrend (gaf-) 293. §§ 46, 68.
gabutan (gaf-) 764a n.
gaebuli (gaef-) 115 n. §§ 46, 66, 69, 79.
gǣc 265. § 57. 1. *See* gēacaes sūrae.
galluc 466 n.
gānaendae 690. § 86.
ganot 419 n.
gārlǣc 16. § 57. 1.
gāta loc 1028 n.
gēacaes sūrae 63 n., iāces sūra(e) 263. §§ 40, 57. 1, 71.
gearuuae 639, ge(a)ruuae 623. § 47 and fn. 1.
gebēru 492 n.
gebil (gef-) 336. § 51.
gebles (gef-) monung 394 n. §§ 51, 66.
geboronae 359. §§ 64 and fn. 6, 79, 85.
gecilae 954. § 66.
gecyndilican 480.
gedæbin (-fin) 336. §§ 51, 68, 85.
geddi 374. § 79.
geeornnissae (geo-) 527. §§ 44. 1, 79.
gefetodnae 105. § 86.
gegeruue(n)dnae 196, gigeruuid 730 n. §§ 50. 1 and fn. 3, 74 and fn. 1.
gelēod 229 n. § 42 fn. 1.
gelplih 112 n.
gelu 242, 432, 458, geolu 1064 n. § 56.
genicldae 701 n. §§ 54, 67, 87.
genus 685, 740.
genyc(h)tfullum 723 n.
geolu *see* gelu.
geōmette (-nette) 717. § 88 fn. 3.
geormantlab (-lēaf) 656 n. §§ 44. 1, 75.

geornlice 708. § 44. 1.
georuuierdid (-ŏid) 990 n. §§ 42, 45, 55, 90.
gerādnodae 618 n. §§ 79, 86.
gerd 614. § 50. 1.
gerec 566 n.
geregnodae 618. §§ 79, 86.
gēri 494. § 79.
gērlicae 94 n. §§ 39, 87.
ge(a)ruuae see gearuuae.
gesnida(e)n 315. §§ 63 fn. 4, 85.
gespan 624 n.
gesuedradum (-ŏradun) 368, gesui-dradrae (-dae) 207 n. §§ 11 fn. 2 (p. xxvii), 86, 87.
gesuirgion (-an) 214 n. §§ 64, 80.
geuuitendi 335.
gibaen (gif-) 525. §§ 47 and fn. 3, 85, 87.
gibēataen 140. §§ 40, 61, 85.
gibrēc 775, 856.
gibūūr 163.
gidopta (-ŏofta) 189.
gidyrstig 81. § 54.
gifōēgnissae 889 n. §§ 53, 63 fn. 3, 6, 80.
gifraemith 725, gifraemid 759. § 70.
gifyrdro (-ŏro) 327 n. § 83.
gigeruuid see gegeruue(n)dnae.
gigiscdae 693 n. §§ 11, 74 and fn. 4.
gigræmid 515, gigraemid 593. § 74.
gihaeplicae 205 n. § 87.
giheldae 371 n. § 50. 2.
gihiodum (geēodun) 76. §§ 4 fn. 1, 41, 63 fn. 1, 72 fn. 6, 87.
gihuuuelci (gihw-) 842. §§ 50. 2, 66, 79.
gilēbdae (-fdae) 1089. §§ 55, 84.
gillistrae 833 n. § 61 fn. 2.
gilodusrt (-wyrt) 379 n. § 11.
gimāch 519.
gimaengdae 543 n. § 87.
gimaengiungiae (-gae) 203 n. §§ 48, 71, 79.
gimengidlicæ 750 n. § 48.
gimōdae 201.
ginath 149. § 56.
ginehord 276 n. §§ 44. 1, 72 fn. 6.
ginumni 100. §§ 54, 68, 79, 85.
girōēdro (-ŏro) 14 n. §§ 33, 53, 70.
girōēfa 223 n., girōēfan 197. §§ 53, 69.

gisalbot (-d) 325 n. §§ 74 and fn. 1, 86.
giscāduuyrt 1032 n.
gisettae 191, þa gisettan 542, ŏ(a) gisettan 707. § 87.
gisiuuid 886. § 42.
gislōg 195.
gistaebnændrae (gistaef-) 864 n. § 79.
githuornae 605. § 80.
gitīungi 97 n. §§ 42, 57. 3, 59. 3, 79, 88 fn. 3.
gitrēēudae (gitrēu-) 436. §§ 42, 80.
gitsung 82.
gitychtid 533.
giuuaemmid 540 n.
gla(e)dinae 920 n. § 49.
glīu 398, glīuuae 550. §§ 42 and fn. 2, 79.
glōēd 229 n., 304.
glōēdscofl 1065 n. §§ 67, 69 and fn. 4.
glōōb (-f) 631. § 69 and fn. 2.
goduueb 441 n. § 49.
gōōs 117.
graemid (-iŏ) 580.
graennung 852 n. § 48.
græsgrōēni 298 n. § 32.
granae 644 n.
grēdig 500.
grēi 473. §§ 59. 6, 71.
grīma 646 n., 904, 953 n.
grimrodr (gim-) 345a n. §§ 44. 1 fn. 4, 66.
grōēpum 948 n.
grōētu 210. §§ 53, 83.
grundsuopa 312 n.
grytt 823.
gundaesuelgiae 976 n. §§ 50. 2, 67, 71.
gybyrdid (gi-) 228 n.
gycinis 788 n.
gyrdils 573. § 76.
gyrdislrhingae (-hringae) 582 n. § 76.

haam see ham.
hāām 177 n. § 72 fn. 6.
habens 277.
habern see ha(e)fern.
haca 803 n.
hādga (-da) 709 n.
haecid 587, 660. §§ 51, 68, 72 fn. 6.
haecilae 572, 740. §§ 51, 63 fn. 3, 6, 66, 68.
haegtis 913. §§ 38, 65. 4.

haeguthorn 19, 956. §§ 4, 46.
haen 906 n. § 48.
haesil 236, (h)aesil 50. §§ 38, 67, 72.
hāētendae 206 n. §§ 61, 80, 86.
haeth (-t) 269 n.
hāēth 1007.
hāēuui 221 n., hǣuui 473. § 52.
ha(e)fern 258 n., ha(e)bern 684. §§ 37
  and fn. 5, 38, 43. 1 fn. 3, 69, 76.
halbae (-fae) 51. §§ 4, 35, 43. 2, 69, 80.
halbclungni (half-) 931 n. § 79.
haldae 865.
halstān 288 n.
halŏi see ohaelŏi.
ham 167, haam 244. § 37 fn. 2.
hama 501.
hāman 256 n.
handful 645 n.
handmitta (and-) 380 n.
handu(u)yrp 126 n. § 17.
hara 608. § 46.
hēamol 413.
heardhara 270 n.
heardhēui 262 n. § 55.
heardnissae 871. § 79.
hearma 666 n., 675.
hebild (hef-) 602 n.
hederae 1059.
helor 607 n., 988, (he)olor 573a n.
  §§ 29, 56.
helostr 901, helustras 867. § 66.
herba 1059.
herebāēcon 919. §§ 57. 1, 67.
heresearum 1100 n.
hēringas 910 n.
he(o)rth 5. § 44. 1.
heruuendlicae 186. § 65. 2.
higrae 156 n., 808 n. § 66.
hindberiæ 69 n. § 49.
hindbrere 352 n.
hirnitu (hy-) 275. §§ 54, 65. 4, 77.
hlāēodrindi (hlēoŏ-) 508. §§ 41 fn. 5,
  86.
hlēor 438, 482. §§ 41, 72 fn. 6.
hlūtrae 578.
hnitu 590. § 77.
hnutbēam 671. § 77.
hofr 459, (h)ofr 1046. §§ 11, 29, 67,
  69, 72.
hold 415 n.
holegn 34 n. § 27.
holopannae 784 n.

holthana 41 n. §§ 27, 37, 72.
hōlunga 683.
hondgong 337 n.
hōōd 239.
hool 1072 n. § 37 fn. 2.
horh 412.
horsclicae 668.
horsthegn 658.
horuaeg (orweg) 340 §§ 62, 72 fn. 6.
hraebn (-fn) 285. § 67. See hraefnaes
  fōt.
hraebreblētae(hae-)124 n. §§ 38,67,69.
hraefnaes fōt 1084, hraebnǣs fōōt
  848. §§ 49, 69.
hraecli (-gli) 84. §§ 35, 38, 67, 74 fn.
  2, 79.
hraed 742. § 72 fn. 6.
hraen 400. §§ 37, 43. 1 fn. 3, 72, 76.
hrāgra 42. § 27.
hramsa 59 n., hramsa(n) 60. §§ 37,
  89 fn. 4.
hran 146.
hreacca (hn-) 715 n. §§ 46, 56.
hrēadaemūs see hrēatha(e)mūs.
hrēatha(e)mūs 978 n., hrēadaemūs
  1098. § 67 and fn. 1.
hrēod 290.
hringiae 410 n. § 71.
hringfāāg 798 n., 984. § 74.
hrīsil 851. § 67.
hrōf 609. § 72 fn. 6.
hrōfuuyrc(h)ta 996 n.
hrōōc 469. § 72 fn. 6.
hrutu (hn-) 15. § 77.
hsniuuith (sn-) 669. § 72 fn. 6.
huāēg 978, 982.
hualb (-f) 179 n.
hu(a)et 604 n. §§ 38, 72 fn. 6.
huetistān 294.
huītfōt 55 n. § 4.
huītti (-īte) 254. §§ 61, 63, 87 fn. 1.
hūnae 657.
hunaegaepl 830 n. § 67.
hunaegsūgae 615 n.
hunhīeri (un-) 983. §§ 42, 55, 72 fn.
  6, 90.
huuananhuuoega 1095. § 62.
huuēolrād 710 n. §§ 59. 2, 74, 88
  fn. 3.
huuer 563.
huuītquidu 655. § 56.
hȳdde (-ȳŏe) 329. § 61.

160 INDEX OF INTERPRETATIONS

hymblicae 185. §§ 54, 75.
hynnilāēc (ynni-) 62 n. §§ 4, 54, 57. 1,
 61 fn. 1, 72 fn. 6.

iāces sūra(e) see gēacaes surae.
idest 177, 218, 346a, 379, 487, etc.,
 id(est) 820, 878, 887, 980, 982.
iesca 958. § 71.
ifaenucæ (faenȳcæ) 997 n. §§ 48, 54.
īfeg 392. §§ 55 and fn. 5, 60, 69, 72.
iiii. 172.
ilugsegg 781 n. § 49.
in 501, 515, 571, 624, 766, 890.
in 530, 549, 550, 854.
inliciendi (-o) 509.
innifli 504. §§ 65. 4, 69, 76.
interiecto 766.
intimum 487.
inuidia 874.
īringaes 1050 n.
īsærn (-earn) 25 n. §§ 43. 1 and fn. 3,
 44. 1.
īsærn 121. § 43. 1 fn. 3.
īuu 1005. §§ 59. 6 fn. 2, 73.

lāām 48. § 27.
lāāth see lāth.
lāec 64. § 57. 1.
laempihalt 589 n.
lændino 860, lændnum 216. §§ 29, 48.
laepaeuincæ (hlēa-) 264 n. §§ 40, 67.
landae 370 n.
lapillus 172.
lāth 514, lāāth 552.
latin(e) 718.
lāuuercae 1012. §§ 66 fn. 1, 67 fn. 3.
lēactrogas 247 n. §§ 40, 57. 1, 74 fn. 2.
lēag 591. § 57. 1.
lēasung 426 n. § 40.
leax 555. §§ 43. 3, 57. 1, 58, 72.
lebil (-fil) 633 n., 995.
lēccressae 676 n., § 57. 1.
lēceas 746. § 71.
lēciuuyrt 849 n.
lectha 890 n. § 66.
le(n)ctinādl 999 n. §§ 48, 67, 70.
lediruuyrcta (leðiruuyrchta) 155 n.
 §§ 17, 67.
lēlothrae 861, lēlodrae 606 n. §§ 57. 1,
 88 fn. 3.
lēoma 478, 554. § 41.
lerb (-fr) 894 n. §§ 66, 76, 80.

lē(a)uuīs 977a n.
libr (-fr) 1057. § 67.
librlaeppan (lif-) 405 n. §§ 46, 67.
lidrinae (lið-) 31. § 63 fn. 6.
ligno 766.
ligones 878.
līīn 634. § 15.
līm 133 n., 289a, līīm 486. § 32.
linaethuigae (-tuigae) 309 n.
lind 1004, 1017.
linnin 1081. § 61.
lipidum (la-) 289a n. § 32.
liquor 982.
listan 583.
līthircadae 722 n. §§ 84, 86.
loc see gāta loc.
loca 448 n.
locaer 853 n.
loccas 28. § 35.
loda (-ða) see lotha.
loerg(a)e 1 n. §§ 53, 80.
logdor (-ðor) 268 n. § 67.
longas 277.
longe 801a n.
lopostris (-rum) 913a n.
lotha 572, 600, loda 898.
ludgaet 741 n. § 47.
lundlaga 850.
luscin(i)a 26 n.
lūūs 812.
lybb 711. § 54.
lynisas 8 n. § 66.
lypbcorn (lyb-) 279 n. § 74 and fn. 3.
lȳtisnā 200 n. §§ 54, 78, 89 fn. 3.
lȳtlae 217. § 54.

māānful 512.
maerh 588 n. § 57. 1.
maesttun 930. § 49.
maethlae 549. §§ 38, 70 and fn. 5, 79.
maettoc 1003 n., mettocas 565, 586,
 878. §§ 46, 68 fn. 2 (p. lxxx).
maffa 719 n. § 46.
magna 1077a.
malt 130.
mand 193, 222, 839 n.
mapuldur 323. §§ 11, 27, 46, 67.
māsae 806 n.
mat(t)a 894.
mear(c)īsern 227 n. §§ 43. 1, 57. 1.
mearth 425 n, § 43. 1.
mēēg 164.

mēēli 56. § 39 and fn. 2.
mēgsibbi 109. §§ 39, 79.
meinfol 512. § 39 fn. 1 (p. lxi).
meldadum (-n) 342 n. §§ 11 fn. 2 (p. xxvii), 70 fn. 5, 86.
mēn (-ēu) 610. §§ 52 fn. 4, 59. 6, 73.
menescillingas 570 n. § 48.
mengio 659 n. §§ 29, 48, 71 and fn. 4, 83.
mera(e) 558 n. §§ 38, 63 fn. 5.
mēre 737.
meri 962.
merici 24 n. §§ 49, 77.
merisc 289, merix 302. § 76.
merze 657a n. §§ 44. 1, 71.
mettocas see maettoc.
mich see mygg.
milciþ 628. § 83.
millefolium 623.
milsc apuldr 638 n. §§ 46, 67.
milti 970, † multi 594. § 62.
mimarios 550.
mimografos (-phos) 550.
misbyrd 80 n. § 54.
mistil 1083.
miδ 796. § 89 fn. 3.
modicis 994.
molegn 477 n., 486. § 76 and fn. 1.
monung see gebles monung.
morgenlic 729. § 75.
mu(ni)cipio 620.
multae 890.
multi see milti.
mundbora 934.
mundbyrd 935.
mundlēu(u)1055 n. §§ 40, 52 fn. 4, 73.
mūs 664, 977.
muscellas 469a n.
mygg 916, mich 277. §§ 54, 74.
mynit 670. § 54.

nāāmun 113. § 39 fn. 2.
nabae(-fae) 625. §§ 38, 46 and fn. 6, 80.
naechthraebn (-fn) 673 n., 674. §§ 49, 57. 1.
nāēp 687 n. § 39.
naesgristlae 174.
nāētendnae 752.
nāēδlae 796. §§ 39, 70, 79.
nafogār 1010 n. §§ 69, 74 fn. 3.
natando 17.
nauis 180, nauem (-e) 890.

neb 862.
nec(h)taegalae 857, nectigalae 673 n., n(e)ctigalae 26. §§ 38 fn. 6, 43. 2, 3 fn. 1, 46 fn. 6, 50. 3, 57. 1, 58, 63 fn. 6, 67 fn. 1, 78, 80.
nest 389.
nettae 702 n. § 49.
neuunsēada (-δa) 505 n. §§ 4, 41, 45 and fn. 4.
nift 734 n.
nihol 799. §§ 57. 3, 72(a).
nitatio (imi-) 953.
nyttum 93. §§ 4, 54.

ob see ab.
ob (-f) 369 n.
obaerstāēlendi (of-) 192, obaerstāēlid 194. §§ 39, 63, 70.
obbenda (olf-) 319 n.
oberuuaenidae (of-) 538 n. §§ 63, 84.
obtt (ofet) 421 n.
obust (of-) 757. § 66.
ōcusta 38 n.
odium 874.
ōēghuuelci 709 n. §§ 50. 2, 52, 66, 79.
(h)ofr see hofr.
ō(e)ghuuāēr 1061 n. §§ 39, 52.
ōhaelδi 838, (ō)ha(e)lδi 754 n. §§ 50. 2, 70.
(he)olor see helor.
ond see aend.
ōnettae 712 n. §§ 37, 60, 65. 1 and fn. 1, 88 fn. 3.
orc 698 n.
ordoncum (orδ-) 278.
orfiermae 933 n. §§ 45 and fn. 2, 55, 80, 90.
oritmon (ēored-) 320 n. §§ 44. 2 fn. 5, 57. 2, 60, 63 fn. 3, 74, 88 fn. 3.
ormētum 640 n.
ornamenta 837.
orsorg 1034.
ōslae 665 n.
ōst 688.
otr 585, otor 914. § 67.

paad 779 n.
palester 225 n. §§ 43. 2, 66 fn. 2, 67.
palpitat (-ans) 983 n.
parte 571.
paruulus 501.
passim 1061.

paturum 778 n. § 29.
pauua 826. § 43. 4 fn. 2.
pearroc 224. § 43. 1.
pede 834, *pedes* 171, 766.
per 553.
perditio 367.
pertinet 550.
pīc 820.
piscis 376, *pisces* 913a n.
platocer(u)us 1001 n.
plūmae 822 n.
pōēdibergæ (wōē-) 388 n. § 11.
polimita (poly-) 984.
pomo 979a n.
popaeg 824, popeg 253 n. §§ 53 fn. 2,
    63 fn. 4.
prima 571.
pumilio 686.
pung 297 n. § 32.
pustula 791.

qua 218, 894, *quae* 1059.
quadrangulum 998 n.
quaerulosis 332.
quasi 834.
quatern 847 n. § 38.
quicae 1088 n., † quiquae 464 n.
quietis 443.
quiða 661. § 29.
quo 501, 766, *quod* 550.

raebsid (raef-) *see* raefsed.
raedgaesran 493 n. §§ 4, 11 fn. 2
    (p. xxvii), 39, 52.
rāēdinnae 212, 1035 n. §§ 39, 79, 80.
raefsed 526, raebsid 523 n. §§ 49, 69,
    74, 87.
ragu 629. § 46.
randbēag 153. § 57. 1.
ratio 172.
rēad 404, rē(a)de 250. §§ 40, 87.
recessus 199 n.
rēdboran 551.
rē(a)de *see* rēad.
r(a)edisnae 123 n. §§ 38, 71.
reftras 11 n. § 49.
regenuuyrm 612 n. § 66.
restaendum 443. §§ 49, 65. 2.
rēs(w)ung 190. §§ 73, 89 fn. 3.
ribbae 184, 280.
ridusaendi 816 n. § 86.
rift 801.

riftr 430. § 67.
(h)risaendi 434. §§ 11, 65. 2, 72, 86
    and fn. 1.
riscthȳfil 517 n. §§ 62, 69.
rixam 515.
roactun 342 n. § 35 and fn. 2 (p. lvii).
rōēdra (-ŏra) 875.
roscin(i)a 26 n.
rost (rū-) 397.
rōthor 986. § 67.
rotis 994.
rotunditate 984.
rȳae 1020 n., rȳhae 1080, 1081. §§ 59.
    5, 72(a).
rygi 918. § 77.
rȳhae *see* rȳae.
rysil 2. § 54.

sadol 926.
sadulbogo (-a) 283. § 64 and fn. 6.
sadulfelgae 818 n. §§ 50. 2, 90.
sāēgesetu 728 n. §§ 52, 63, 73.
saeppae 37 n. § 49 and fn. 4.
salb (-f) 635.
salch 892.
saldae 528.
sandae 188. § 80.
satul 926 n.
satyrus 558.
scābfōōt (scāf-) 832 n.
scaedugeardas 991 n. §§ 46, 47, 56.
scaeptlōan (scaeft-) 489 n., sceptlōum
    106 n. §§ 38, 47, 59. 4, 88 fn. 3.
scaet 157. §§ 38, 47.
scaldthȳflas 58 n. §§ 43. 2, 54, 69.
scalfr 647 n., 662. §§ 67, 69 fn. 1.
scalu 462. § 46 fn. 5.
scamu 732. §§ 37 fn. 1, 64 fn. 4.
sceaba (-fa) 853. §§ 47, 56.
scēabas (-fas) 30 n., 468. §§ 40, 47, 69.
sceadu 902. §§ 47, 56.
scel 376 n.
sceldreda (-hrēoða) 997. §§ 41, 47, 72.
sceolhēgi 981 n. §§ 44. 2, 55, 60, 72(c).
sceptlōum *see* scaeptlōan.
scēroro 401 n. § 66.
scīa 299 n. § 59. 3.
scic(c)ing 245 n.
scīdum 943.
scīir *adj.* 941. § 39 fn. 2.
scinlāēcean 681. §§ 52, 71.
scinneras 952 n. §§ 61, 65. 1.

scipes 862.
scīrde 86 n.
sclindinnae (scild-) 1038 n.
scocha 579 n. § 72(a).
scofl 1022 n. §§ 67, 69 and fn. 4.
scrēc 1013 n. § 52.
scrēuua 649 n. §§ 40, 52 fn. 4.
scribun (-fun) 724.
scrīc 1013 n.
scripit 906 n. §§ 70, 83.
sculdur 963. § 67.
scur (-īir) sb. 721.
scybla (-fla) 627 n. § 66.
scȳhend 654 n. §§ 72(a), 89 fn. 3.
scytihalt(h) 694. §§ 11, 70.
scytil 632 n.
sě 320 n.
searuum 278. § 73.
sech see segg (1).
secundarum 501 n.
securis 443.
segg 'sedge' 463, sech 251. § 49.
segg 'sea' 966 n. § 49.
segilgaerd 111. §§ 50. 1, 67.
segitibus (sege-) 218.
segnas see seng.
selma 955 n.
seng (-gn) 567, segnas 92. §§ 67, 76 and fn. 1.
sententia 172 n.
septenerbia (-uia) 793.
sercae 18. § 50. 1.
ses 1021 n.
seto 896.
sētungae 72 n. §§ 39, 79.
sibaed (-faeð) 70 n., siuida 428. §§ 63, 69 and fn. 5, 70, 80 and fn. 3.
siftit 213. § 70.
sifunsterri 762 n. §§ 45 and fn. 2, 69.
sigbēacn 992. §§ 57. 1, 66.
sigdi (-ði) 430. §§ 66, 77.
sigil 134 n., 408, 882 n.
sigiras 568 n. § 66.
signa 992.
sīid (-ð) 384. §§ 57. 3, 59. 3, 88 fn. 3.
similis 1059, similes 913a.
sinfullae 387 n., 819 n.
sinuurbul (-hwurful) 1047. §§ 45 and fn. 3, 68, 69, 72, 76.
siuida (-fiða) see sibaed.
slāchthorn 672 n., slāghthorn 957. § 74 and fn. 3.

slægu 603 n. § 46.
slī 1015 n. § 73.
smael 474.
smeltas 949 n.
smeruui 944, † sperwi 769. §§ 44. 1, 79.
smeruuuyrt 1078 n.
smigilas (smy-) 199 n. §§ 54, 66.
smitor (-n) 437.
snāēdil uel thearm (snāēdilthearm) 381 n. § 39.
snecca (hn-) 720.
snegl 651, snēl 611, sneglas 217. §§ 59. 6, 71.
snel 77.
snīdstrēo (snīð-) 973 n. § 40 and fn. 2.
snōd 301.
soærgændi (soer-) 79. §§ 53, 65. 2, 86 and fn. 3.
sōchtae 756. § 87.
soctha 516a n.
solet 1059. § 4.
sooc (-occ) 951. § 37 fn. 2.
sororis 734.
spadan 1087 n.
spald(u)r 54 n. §§ 43. 2, 66, 67, 70 fn. 5.
spa(e)raen 460 n. § 65. 2.
sparuua 897 n. § 43. 1.
spatio 766.
spearuua 435 n. § 43. 1.
spelli 869.
sperwi (sm-) see smeruui.
speruuuyrt 1078 n.
spilth 755. § 70.
spinil 967.
spōēd 815, 940.
spora 226.
sprēotum 211. § 41.
sprindil 1025 n.
spryng 791, spyrng 175. § 76.
spurcus 835.
spyrng see spryng.
staeb 367 n.
staeblidrae (staeflið-) 136 n. §§ 38, 69, 70.
staebplegan (staef-) 577 n. §§ 56, 69.
staefnændra 75 n. §§ 49, 65. 2, 69.
staeg 962 n.
stāēgilrae 747 n. § 52.
staer 908 n.
stærn 125 n., † sterm 908 n. § 43. 1.

stalu 1067 n. § 46 fn. 5.
stanc 361.
stappa (sto-) 122.
statera 988.
statim 370.
statione 329.
stearno (-a) 125 n.
stēēli 49. §§ 27, 39 fn. 2, 50. 3, 60, 88 fn. 3.
stefad 837 n. §§ 69, 86.
stegn (-ng) 209. §§ 48, 76 and fn. 1.
stela 215. § 56.
stēor 596, 780. § 41.
sterm (-earn) *see* stærn.
stēupfaedaer 1070. §§ 41, 63.
stigu 45 n. § 56.
stomachus 1054.
storc 259.
storm 682.
strabus 981.
strēam 855, strē(am)um 1033.
strēamrād 88. § 40.
strēl 9 n. §§ 59. 6, 71.
strēlbora 114 n.
stricilum 994 n. § 66.
str(ē)idae 899 n. §§ 55 and fn. 6, 59.
2 and fn. 1, 59. 6 fn. 2, 71 fn. 3, 73, 84.
strīdit 1086 n. § 70.
strīmaendi 695 n.
stug (-īig) 340.
styccimēlum 751.
styria 809.
suā 729 n., suāē 843–4 n., 865 n. § 39.
suadu (-ðu) 972 n.
sualuuae 498, suualua 828. § 63 fn. 5.
suamm 427.
suan 700.
suān 431, 961.
subtilitas 564.
suedilas (sueð-) 506. § 66.
suēor 1099, suehoras 1062 n. §§ 57.
2 and fn. 1, 59. 2, 66, 72(a), 88 fn. 3.
sugga 422 n.
suggit 455 n. §§ 61, 70, 83.
sugu 912.
suicae 692 n. § 79.
suicudae 932. §§ 56, 86.
suilcae 98. § 66.
suīna 972.
suinsung 643. § 11.
suipan 641, 1051.

suīthae 843–4 n., suīþae 1037.
sum(a)e 731. § 79.
suōēg 446.
suol 274.
(ā)suollaen 1018 n. § 65. 2.
suornodun 198 n. §§ 62, 84, 86, 87.
super 171, 453.
sūrae 974 n., sūra(e) 1077a n. § 63 fn. 5. *See* gēacaes sūrae.
sylenorum 895 n.

tabula 218.
tācor 598.
tāēcnaendi 544. § 52.
tāēnil 403. § 52.
tamen 550.
tangi 1043a n.
tarda 581. § 35 fn. 7.
tasol 998 n. § 68.
tēac (-g) 964 n. §§ 57. 1, 74.
tebelstān (tef-) 172 n. § 68 and fn. 2.
teblae (tef-) 6 n. §§ 38 fn. 6, 49, 66, 68 and fn. 2.
teblere (tef-) 7. §§ 38 fn. 6, 49, 65. 1, 66, 68 fn. 2, 69.
teblith (tef-) 178 n. §§ 66, 68 fn. 2.
tecīnid (-ð) 343 n. § 63.
tedridtid 344 n. § 63.
tefil 6 n. §§ 66, 68 and fn. 2, 69.
telorum 489.
temptans 834.
tenentur 766.
territantur 218. § 11 fn. 1 (p. xxvii).
teru 282, 677, 858.
tetr 502, 765, 791, teter 128. § 67.
thā 439, 576, þā 542, ð(ā) 707. § 87.
þan *see* āēc þan.
ōgisettan *see* thā, gisettae.
thearm 503. § 43. 1. *See* snaedil uel thearm.
thebanthorn (thef-) 880 n. § 76.
thebscib (thēofscip) 630 n.
thegn 101. § 67.
thēoh 295. § 57. 2.
thinga 709 n., þinga 845.
thingungae 532. § 79.
thīstil 271. § 67.
thīstil(tuigae) 266 n. § 67.
thōhae 3 n. §§ 59. 4, 72(a).
thōlicae (tōh-) 1063 n. § 75.
þōōt (wōōth) *see* uuōþ.
þor(h)gifec(h)t 738 n. §§ 57. 2, 89 fn. 3.

þorh 741, 760, þorch 757. § 89 fn. 3.
thothor 787 n. § 67.
thrauu 53. §§ 11, 43. 4 and fn. 2, 73.
ðrifedor (-ðor) 1039 n. § 56.
thriuuuintri (thriw-) 780 n.
thrēatae 369. § 79.
thrēatmēlum 617 n.
thrēs 583 n., 705.
thrōh 874 n.
ðrop 307. § 76.
throstlae 1011 n.
throtbolla 456.
throuadae 365. §§ 86, 87.
thrūūch 1000.
thuachl 326 n. §§ 43. 3 and fn. 1, 50.
    3 fn. 1, 67, 72(b) and fn. 2.
thuearm 891 n. §§ 4 fn. 1, 43. 1.
thuēlan 1060 n. §§ 50. 3 and fn. 1,
    59. 2, 88 fn. 3.
thuerae 1029 n. § 38 fn. 6.
thuerhfyri 881 n. §§ 57. 2, 60 and
    fn. 3, 67, 80, 88 fn. 3.
thūma 821.
thungas 23 n.
þūs 1037.
þūþīstil 601 n. §§ 11, 67.
thyctin (tych-) 579, tyctinnae 516,
    tyctinnum 513. § 80.
thyrnae 317 n.
thȳs 494. § 54.
tibias 277.
tīg 663 n. §§ 59. 6, 73.
tilgendum 78. §§ 56, 65. 2, 86.
tin 1024 n.
tindicti 868 n.
tindum 873.
tislōg 195. § 63.
tō 93, 1067. § 4.
tōch 581 n., 614 n. § 35 fn. 7.
tōhald 96. §§ 43. 2, 70.
torbus (-tus) 981 n.
torchtnis 574.
torc(h)tendi 544 n. § 86.
totridan 689 n.
treddun 749 n. § 87.
trēulēsnis 726. §§ 41, 55, 73.
trimsas 31 n. §§ 62, 66.
tumor 1018 n.
tunica 624.
tusc 487.
tūūn 307, † tūūni 281 n.
tuum (tuuīn) 138. §§ 59. 6, 63 fn. 3.

tūūncressa 676 n.
tychtit 936, tyctendi 85. §§ 54, 65. 2,
    70, 79.
tyc(h)taend 509.
tyc(h)tendi see tychtit.
tyc(h)tinnae, -um see thyctin.
tylg 743 n. § 87.
tyndir 685.
tyndirm 562 n.
tyndrin 562 n.

u(u)āar 47. § 27.
u(u)aeps 255, waeffsas 1071 n. § 69.
u(u)ard see uueard vb.
ubi 553, 890.
uel 5, 9, 26, 29, 103, etc.
u(u)e(a)rnu(u)īslicæ 338 n.
uespertilio 978 n.
uestimenti 740.
uicinus 163 n.
vii folia 379.
uinctorum 766.
unam 890.
unāmaelti 769 n. §§ 50. 2, 79.
unāseddae 541 n.
unbrȳci 522. § 61.
uncenos (-inos) 50a n.
uncystig 413.
undae 400.
unēmotan 680 n.
unfāecni 679. § 52.
ungisēēm (-ni) 333 n. §§ 39 fn. 2, 50.
    3 and fn. 2, 60, 88 fn. 3.
unlidouuāc (unliðo-) 521. § 56.
unnytnis 678.
unofaercumenrae 536 n. §§ 63, 69.
unsibb 900.
unsibbadae 323 n. § 86.
unþyc(h)tgi 1093 n. § 79.
uomitus 667.
uppae (yp-) 553. § 54.
u(u)rāstum 332. §§ 52, 82 and fn. 1.
ūrum 1097 n.
ut 891.
ūtāthrungaen 176 n. § 85.
uterque 1094a.
u(i)tibus 1059.
waeffsas (waefs-) see u(u)aeps.
uuaega (uue-) see uueg.
uuaegbrādae see uuegbrādae.
uuaelrēæb (-f) 642. § 38.
uuaes 523, 525. § 87.

uuaeterthrūch 232 n. § 63.
uualhh(a)ebuc 497 n. § 46.
uualhmorae 794. §§ 60, 88 fn. 3.
uualhuuyrt 518 n., uualhuyrt 393 n.
uuallum 873 n.
uuananbēam 418 n.
wand 1014 n.
uuandaeuuiorpae 1045 n. §§ 44. 1, 67.
uuannan 576. § 87.
uuapul 447 n. § 46.
u(u)udubil see uuidubil.
uuēadhōc (uuēo-) 887 n. § 41.
uueard (-rð) 737, u(u)ard 333. § 43. 1.
uueard 950 n.
uueargrōd 409. §§ 43. 1, 57. 1.
uueartae 154, 771 n., 1049. § 43. 1.
uueb 1026, 1030. §§ 49, 62.
uuefl 300. §§ 67, 69 and fn. 4.
uueftan 328 n.
uueg 91, 1050 n., uuaega 842. § 62.
uuegbrādae 65, uuaegbrādae 793. § 62.
uuellyrgae 969 n. §§ 50. 2, 65. 4 and
    fn. 4.
(ā)uuēol 355.
uuerci 699. §§ 57. 2, 79.
uuergendi 318. §§ 50. 1, 87.
uuermōd(ae) 66 n.
uuestnorduuid (-norðuuind) 311 n.
westsūþwind 118 n., uuestsuduuind
    452 n.
uuesulae 650. § 66.
ūūf 142, 161. §§ 39 fn. 2, 69.
uuibil (-fil) 310.
uuicingsceadan (-ðan) 736 n. §§ 47,
    56.
uuidirhliniendae (uuið-) 537. §§ 63,
    67, 86.
uuidubil 449, u(u)udubil 430 n.
    § 56 and fn. 2.
uuidubindae 1059 n., 1082. § 56 and
    fn. 2.
uuidubindlae 559 n. §§ 56 and fn. 2,
    62.
uuidouuindae (uuið-) 348 n., uuidu-

uuindae 1082 n., wi(ð)uwindae
    1059. § 56 and fn. 2.
uuildae 99.
uuilmōd (wu-) 306 n.
uuilocrēad 169. §§ 11, 40, 56 and
    fn. 2, 62 fn. 3.
uuilucscel 182 n. §§ 56 and fn. 2, 62.
uuīnaern 1040 n. §§ 37, 43. 1 fn. 3,
    76.
windil 173. § 11.
uuituma 324 n. § 56 and fn. 2.
uulanclicae 112 n.
uulātung 667. §§ 46, 68.
u(u)ulfes camb 183 n. § 69.
u(u)ulluc 557 n.
uulōhum 1066 n. §§ 72(a), 56, 62. 89
    fn. 3.
uuōda 383 n.
uuōdaeu(u)istlae 248 n. §§ 67 fn. 1,
    72, 75, 87 fn. 1, 88 fn. 3.
uuōēndendi (uuōēd-) 575. § 79.
uuōrhana 424 n.
uuorsm 777. § 76.
uuōþ 564, † þōōt 444. §§ 11, 70.
uuraec vb. 90, 1002. § 38.
uuraec sb. 87 n. § 38.
uurāēni 835 n. § 52.
uurāēstendi 499 n. § 52.
u(u)urmillae 691 n. § 54.
uurōc(h)tae 524. § 79.
uurōt 152 n.
uuryd (-īð) 252 n. § 62.
uu(e)send 160 n. §§ 65. 2 fn. 2, 68.
uuy(r)d 980, uuyrdae 764. § 80.
uuydumer (wu-) 347 n. §§ 38, 62.
uuylocas 267. § 62.
uuȳr 637. § 62.
uuyrdae see uuy(r)d.

ymbdringendum (ymbð-) 929 n.
ymbdritung (-ðridung) 331 n.
ymbhringendum 929.

zangi 1043a n.